MARK C. TAYLOR is professor of religion and chair of the Department of Religion at Columbia University. He is the author of nineteen books, including, most recently, *Mystic Bones* and *Confidence Games*, both published by the University of Chicago Press.

After God

ALSO BY MARK C. TAYLOR

Mystic Bones
Confidence Games: Money and Markets in a World without Redemption
The Moment of Complexity: Emerging Network Culture
Grave Matters (with Christian Lammerts)
About Religion: Economies of Faith in Virtual Culture
The Picture in Question: Mark Tansey and the Ends of Representation
Hiding
The Réal: Las Vegas, Nevada (CD-ROM, with José Marquez)
Imagologies: Media Philosophy (with Esa Saarinen)
Nots
Disfiguring: Art, Architecture, Religion
Double Negative
Tears
Altarity
Erring: A Postmodern A/theology
Deconstructing Theology
Journeys to Selfhood: Hegel and Kierkegaard
Religion and the Human Image (with Carl Raschke and James Kirk)
Kierkegaard's Pseudonymous Authorship: A Study of Time and the Self

BOOKS EDITED BY MARK C. TAYLOR

Critical Terms for Religious Studies
Deconstruction in Context: Literature and Philosophy
Unfinished Essays in Honor of Ray L. Hart

After
God

Mark C. Taylor

THE UNIVERSITY OF CHICAGO PRESS
CHICAGO AND LONDON

RELIGION AND POSTMODERNISM
A series edited by Mark C. Taylor and Thomas A. Carlson

Mark C. Taylor is professor of religion and chair of the Department
of Religion at Columbia University. He is the author of nineteen books,
including, most recently, *Confidence Games* and *Mystic Bones*,
both published by the University of Chicago Press.

The University of Chicago Press, Chicago 60637
The University of Chicago Press, Ltd., London
© 2007 by The University of Chicago
All rights reserved. Published 2007
Printed in the United States of America

16 15 14 13 12 11 10 09 08 07   1 2 3 4 5
ISBN-13: 978-0-226-79169-2 (cloth)
ISBN-10: 0-226-79169-6 (cloth)

Library of Congress Cataloging-in-Publication Data

Taylor, Mark C., 1945–
   After God /Mark C. Taylor.
      p.   cm.
   Includes bibliographical references and index.
   ISBN-13: 978-0-226-79169-2 (cloth : alk. paper)
   ISBN-10: 0-226-79169-6 (cloth : alk. paper)
1. Religion—Philosophy. 2. Religion—Philosophy—History. 3. Church
history. 4. Postmodernism—Religious aspects. 5. Civilization—20th
century. 6. Religion and civilization. I. Title.
   BL51.T3944 2007
   200.9'03—dc22

                                                    2007005015

♾ The paper used in this publication meets the minimum requirements
of the American National Standard for Information Sciences—
Permanence of Paper for Printed Library Materials, ANSI Z39.48-1992.

FOR SELMA LINNEA TAYLOR

CONTENTS

FIGURES

TABLES

ACKNOWLEDGMENTS

I no longer believe in circles as I once did. With time, they lengthen and become ellipses, which, more often than not, form an ellipsis. I will not, therefore, say that with this book I have come full circle by returning to the subject with which I began—religion. Though often not oblivious to commentators and critics, I have always been thinking and rethinking the intriguing ways in which religion shows itself by hiding in unexpected places. Over the years, I have acknowledged the support of family, friends, and colleagues many times and, thus, will not repeat those names again. They know who they are and they know that I know that they have, in large measure, made me what I am. I do, however, want to express special thanks to Morton O. Schapiro, president of Williams College, and William G. Wagner, dean of the faculty, for their unusually generous support of my work. I also want to single out once more two friends who have always been there but never more so than during the past year—Jack Miles and Alan Thomas. When I was not sure whether I would be able to finish this book, they promised they would see it through to completion. Leaving an unfinished manuscript in the hands of others is like asking a friend to raise your child. It takes complete confidence, and such confidence is no game.

Much of this book is devoted to the past that has brought us to the critical point where we now find ourselves. In looking back, my concern is with the present and the future, which I believe are far more perilous than we are willing to admit. *If* our children and their children are to have a future, we must honestly acknowledge and responsibly address the massive problems we have created for them. Time is short; indeed, midnight might be approaching. I was no more certain that I would meet my first granddaughter—Selma Linnea Taylor—than that I would finish this book. Her parents, Aaron and Frida, had the faith to bring her into a world that seems to be inching toward chaos. It is my responsibility to do what little I can to be sure she has a future. I dedicate this book to Selma in the hope that she and her generation will always be able to hope.

INTRODUCTION

You cannot understand the world today if you do not understand religion. Never before has religion been so powerful and so dangerous. No longer confined to church, synagogue, and mosque, religion has taken to the streets by filling airways and networks with images and messages that create fatal conflicts, which threaten to rage out of control. When I began pondering these issues in the 1960s, few analysts or critics would have predicted this unexpected turn of events. The governing wisdom at that time was that modernization and secularization go hand in hand: as societies modernize, they secularize through a process that is inevitable and irreversible. I was never convinced by these arguments, for two reasons. First, all too often critics did not appreciate the intricate relation between secularity and the Western religious and theological tradition. As we will see, religion and secularity are not opposites; to the contrary, Western secularity is a *religious* phenomenon. Second, and closely related to this point, the critics who advanced the secularization theory usually had a simplistic understanding of religion, which tended to restrict its scope in a way that limited its importance. Secularists misinterpret religion as much as believers misunderstand secularism. Religion is not a separate domain but pervades all culture and has an important impact on every aspect of society.

To appreciate religion's abiding significance, it is necessary to consider not only its explicit manifestations but also its latent influence on philosophy, literature, art, architecture, politics, economics, and even science and technology. To the tutored eye, religion is often most influential where it is least obvious. Over the years, I have tracked the traces of the elusive subject that has long obsessed me into places where it frequently remains hidden. I could not have anticipated the surprising twists and turns this journey has taken. To many friends and critics it has seemed that I stopped studying religion a long time ago. But this is not true—indeed, I have never left the study of religion behind but have always attempted to expand its scope and significance. The following pages are devoted to analyzing how we have arrived at this unanticipated juncture at the beginning of the twenty-first century and to elaborating an alternative vision better suited to addressing the urgent challenges that must be met if the future is not to turn deadly.

In the course of this endeavor, I have been consistently guided by leading eighteenth- and nineteenth-century European thinkers and writers. Though it has become fashionable to deny it, the fact is that our world has been decisively shaped by these seminal figures. Moreover, these men—and they were men—were Christian and, more specifically, Protestant. Modernity as well as postmodernity is inseparably bound up with Protestantism. Needless to say, other societies and cultures have followed different courses of development; but with the rise of globalization, it is no exaggeration to say that no society or culture has been untouched by this originally Western movement. It is undeniable that, for better and for worse, the world as we know it would not have come about without Protestantism. Max Weber did not know the extent to which he was right; were he writing today, the title of his book would have to be *The Protestant Ethic and the Spirit of Globalization*.

It is important to note, however, that there is a significant difference between Weber's analysis and the argument I develop in this book. Whereas Weber places Calvinism at the center of his analysis, I focus more on the contribution of Luther and those who work in the tradition he began. This is not, of course, to deny that there is a very close relation between Lutheranism and Calvinism or that Calvinism has played a major role in forming modern institutions and ideas. The continuing influence of Calvinism is nowhere more evident than in the United States. The history of the Protestants who came to this country from England, Scotland, and the Netherlands is already well known. But the story of Protestantism's ongoing influence is richer than this familiar narrative suggests. By returning to Luther and the revolution he launched, it is possible to detect an additional trajectory that complicates the emergence of modernity and by extension our own postmodern condition. In this complementary line of analysis, Germany plays a pivotal role. Without in any way minimizing the contributions of figures like Locke, Hume,

Smith, and Darwin, it is no less important to acknowledge the significance of Kant, Hegel, Schleiermacher, Friedrich and Wilhelm Schlegel, and Nietzsche, all of whom were implicitly or explicitly Lutheran. Other writers who were Lutheran but not German, like Kierkegaard, or German but not Lutheran, like Marx, were nonetheless decisively influenced by the German Lutheranism that surrounded them. To reread the past three centuries through their eyes is to see our own time anew.

I do, of course, realize that the argument developed in the following pages seems to run counter to many of the critical perspectives that have been most influential for the past several decades. For intellectual as well as political reasons, so-called metanarratives have been declared a thing of the past and have been replaced with micronarratives focused on the local rather than the global. Though rarely acknowledged, the interpretive perspectives of many self-professed avant-garde critics actually reflect and reinforce many of the most conservative aspects of the contemporary research university, where hyperspecialization produces scholars whose critical vision remains limited. When microanalysis produces nothing but micronarratives, it becomes impossible to know where one is because one does not know where one has come from. The inadequate appreciation of the Western religious tradition has led to the failure to understand how critical perspectives, which have been so influential in recent decades, are thoroughly imbricated in the Jewish and Christian traditions. As critics change with the times, they, like those they attack, "get religion." But the more they write, the more embarrassingly evident it becomes that they do not get religion at all. The problem is that neither those who defend nor those who attack religion today have an adequate understanding of it.

Any investigation of the role religion plays in society and culture today must, therefore, begin by asking a question these very critical theorists have forbidden for several decades: What is religion? In formulating my response, I draw on the insights of social and natural scientists as well as theologians, philosophers, and literary critics. By elaborating an expanded notion of religion, it becomes both possible and necessary to explore aspects of culture usually overlooked in such investigations. The definition of the origin and function of religion that I develop in the first chapter frames the substance and structure of the entire analysis that follows.

In chapters 2 and 3, I examine the role that Luther's turn to the subject played in the emergence of modernity and postmodernity. By privatizing, deregulating, and decentering the relation between the believer and

God, Luther initiated a revolution that was not confined to religion but extended to politics and economics. The Reformation was an information and communications revolution that effectively prepared the way for the information, communications, and media revolution at the end of the twentieth century. The far-reaching implications of Luther's self-contradictory subject are not fully articulated until the end of the turn of the nineteenth century, when religion, art, and politics intersect in the vexed notions of autonomy and representation. The understanding of the autonomous subject, which is inseparable from modern democracy and markets, and the conception of self-referentiality, which is definitive of the modern work of art, emerge at the same time and derive directly from the Christian understanding of God. Changes in religion, art, and philosophy influence political, economic, and technological developments, which, in turn, condition cultural evolution. In this way, nature, society, culture, and technology are joined in mutually conditioning and reciprocally transformative feedback loops. When art displaces religion as the focus of spiritual striving, religious prophets become avant-garde artists whose mission is to realize the kingdom of God on earth by transforming the world into a work of art.

Secularity, I have suggested, is a religious phenomenon. In chapter 4, I explore the way in which secularity emerges within the Judeo-Christian tradition. Throughout the history of the West, God has repeatedly disappeared by becoming either so transcendent that he is irrelevant or so immanent that there is no difference between the sacred and the secular. During the opening decades of the nineteenth century, the immanence of idealism and romanticism displaced the transcendence of deism. Theologians, philosophers, and artists, who were among the most influential founders of modernism, understood nature and history to be the self-embodiment of God. Their belief grew out of creative reinterpretations of the classical Christian doctrines of the Incarnation and the Trinity. The implications of this unexpected turn do not become evident until the advent of twentieth-century death of God theology and the social and cultural changes it both reflects and indirectly promotes. This insight leads to the unexpected but nonetheless inescapable conclusion that contemporary secularity is actually implicit in classical Christology as it was defined in the great church councils of the fourth and fifth centuries.

In chapters 5 and 6, the focus shifts to developments during the last half of the twentieth century and first years of the new millennium. What the nineteenth century conceptualized the twentieth century actualized.

As transcendence gives way to immanence, the avant-garde agenda of transforming the world into a work of art is realized through new technologies that increasingly obscure the line supposedly separating image and reality. When images become real and reality appears to be nothing more than shifting images, more and more people become obsessed with finding a firm foundation they believe can provide certainty and security in a world that often seems to be drifting toward mere chaos. But the quest for self-certainty and security quickly turns destructive. In the complex systems and networks that make up today's world, uncertainty and instability can be creative. The new emerges far from equilibrium at the *edge* of chaos in a surprising moment of creative disruption that can be endlessly productive.

The religious wars threatening to rend the world in the opening decade of the twenty-first century have their roots in the culture wars whose most recent peak came during the 1960s. Here once again opposites share more than initially is evident. Hippies, radicals, Evangelicals, and Pentecostals were all searching for authentic personal experience in the name of which they could resist centralized systems and hierarchical power. By the end of the millennium these shared values had prepared the way for a political and economic agenda based on the principles of privatization, decentralization, and deregulation. The neofoundationalism of the New Religious Right underwrites the neoconservatism and neoliberalism that reign as the governing ideology today. With these developments, it becomes clear that unquestioned religiosity and moralism are actually much more dangerous than the beliefs and practices they are designed to resist. Through another unexpected reversal, ostensible opposites reveal a hidden identity. The very counterculture charged with leading society down the slippery slope of relativism and nihilism is actually a spiritual or even religious phenomenon, and the moral zealots who attack relativism in the name of absolutism are nihilists who reject the present world for the sake of a future kingdom they believe is coming.

The most pressing dangers we currently face result from the conflict of competing absolutisms that divide the world between oppositions that can never be mediated. In the final two chapters, I develop an alternative interpretive framework (or, more precisely, schema) that entails different values, ones that promote policies and programs better adapted to the complexities of contemporary life. In a world where to be is to be connected, absolutism must give way to relationalism, in which everything is codependent and coevolves. After God, the divine is not elsewhere but is the emergent creativity that figures, disfigures, and re-figures the infinite fabric of life. A religion without God issues in ethics without absolutes to promote and preserve the creative emergence of life across the globe.

As one begins to comprehend the scope of the problems we face, it is difficult not to despair—the obstacles do seem insuperable. Processes have been set in motion that cannot be reversed, and it is unclear whether people will be willing or able to make the changes required to delay, if not avoid, looming disaster. The acknowledgment of peril can, however, provoke committed struggle rather than resignation to inevitable defeat. Even if the cause is lost, its pursuit is just. To affirm possibility while confessing impossibility requires risking a faith that embraces uncertainty and insecurity as conditions of creative emergence. This absolutely paradoxical faith is the consummation of the revolution Luther began.

CHAPTER ONE

Theorizing Religion

RELIGION VISIBLE AND INVISIBLE

The 1966 Easter edition of *Time* bore a black cover with the question "Is God Dead?" emblazoned in large red letters. Well versed in the history of philosophy and theology, the authors of this much-debated article explain:

> Some Christians, of course, have long held that Nietzsche was not just a voice crying in the wilderness. Even before Nietzsche, Søren Kierkegaard warned that "the day when Christianity and the world become friends Christianity is done away with." During World War II, the anti-Nazi Lutheran martyr Dietrich Bonhoeffer wrote prophetically to a friend from his Berlin prison cell: "We are proceeding toward a time of no religion at all."
>
> For many, that time has arrived. Nearly one of every two men on earth lives in thralldom to a brand of totalitarianism that condemns religion as the opiate of the masses—which has stirred some to heroic defense of their faith but has also driven millions from any sense of God's existence. Millions more, in Africa, Asia and South America, seem destined to be born without any expectation of being summoned to the knowledge of the one God.[1]

Ten years later *Newsweek* declared that "the most significant—and overlooked—religious phenomenon of the 70s" was "the emergence of evangelical Christianity into a position of respect and power."[2] Today Evangelicalism is alive and well in this country, and Pentecostal Protestantism is the fastest-growing religion in Africa, Asia, and South America. Why did this apparent reversal occur in such a short span of time? How could so many intelligent people have been so wrong about religion and the modern world?

The short answer to these complicated questions is that influential commentators, critics, and theorists simply misunderstood the relationship of religion to modernization and secularity. Religion and secularity, they assumed, are opposites and, thus, when one waxes, the other inevitably wanes. As societies modernize, the argument went, they become more secular. This process was supposed to be inevitable and irreversible. For some, secularization represented the demise of religion and, for others, its most complete realization. Few seemed to doubt that in the future religion would be less, rather than more, important in the lives of individuals and societies.

What went largely unnoticed at the time was the fact that the 1960s was not only the era of the death of God and the birth of the counterculture but also the period during which what eventually became the New Religious Right began to appear. As we will see in chapter 6, conservative Protestants and Catholics decided to set aside doctrinal differences to combat what they regarded as the pernicious effects of the social and cultural revolution that was occurring. Far from a return to premodern forms of belief and practice, the emergence of what might best be described as neofoundational religion during the latter half of the twentieth century is best understood as a distinctively postmodern phenomenon that is inseparably related to processes of globalization. Over the years, the consistent goal of the New Religious Right has been to reverse what they consider to be the religious, moral, and social decline that began in the sixties by returning to basic values and foundational beliefs. Increasingly alarmed by the growing social, political, cultural, and economic power of religion, recent critics of the New Religious Right, who call themselves secularists, maintain that the persistence of "naïve" religious belief and the political agenda it promotes is a threat not only to the nation and the international order but also to the future of civilization. As the debate becomes more heated, misunderstandings become more profound. Many of the most prominent supporters and critics of religion tend to be historically uninformed and critically ignorant. A more sophisticated understanding of the history of the interplay of religion, society, and culture in the West shows that the conflict between the faithful and the secularists is not new but can be traced back to the founding of this country. What makes so much contemporary debate pointless is that neither side realizes that secularity is a *religious* phenomenon, which grows directly out of the Judeo-Christian tradition as it develops in Protestantism. Indeed, it is no exaggeration to insist that not only the modern but also the postmodern world effectively began with the Protestant revolution of the sixteenth century. This admittedly controversial claim runs counter to trajectories charted by recent critics. In the following chapters, I argue that there is an unrecognized religious dimension to globalization that does not reflect a generic spirituality but is Protestant through and through.

To begin to appreciate the complex interrelation between religion and secularity, it is necessary to develop an expanded notion of religion. Religion is not limited to what occurs in churches, synagogues, mosques, and temples; rather, there is a religious dimension to all culture. Religion, moreover, is often most influential where it is least obvious. Supporters as well as critics fail to discern the pervasive influence of religion because their understanding of it is too limited. When the invisible as well as the visible aspects of religion are recognized, the simplistic opposition between secularity and religion collapses and the terms of analysis are effectively recast.

With the expanded interpretation of religion that I will develop in the following section, it becomes possible to approach the question of why there has been such a resurgence of conservative religion in recent decades. The worldwide rise of neofoundationalism is a symptom of and response to the process of globalization. While modernism is coterminous with industrialization, postmodernism is inseparable from the emergence of postindustrial network culture.[3] With the development and distribution of information, telematic, and communications technologies, the infrastructure of social, economic, political, and psychological processes has been radically transformed. Once again, religion exercises a hidden influence: what began with the sixteenth-century information and communications revolution brought about by the coemergence of print and the Reformation is coming to completion in the information and network revolution of the latter half of the twentieth and early twenty-first centuries. Deregulated, decentralized, and distributed networks effectively collapse distance and compress time to create a world in which to be is to be connected. As connectivity spreads, complexity increases and, correlatively, instability and uncertainty grow. These developments, in turn, lead to a longing for simplicity, certainty, and security. Neofoundationalism in all of its guises across the globe represents, among other things, an effort to satisfy this desire. Contemporary foundationalism takes a surprising variety of forms, ranging from the scriptural literalism of Christian Evangelicals and Islamists to the genomic logocentrism and neurophysiological reductionism of some of today's most sophisticated scientists. These seemingly disparate forms of belief are alternative versions of a religiosity that privileges simplicity, security, and certainty over complexity, insecurity, and uncertainty. Such religiosity attempts to banish doubt by absolutizing relative norms and dividing the world between exclusive opposites (good/evil, sacred/profane, religion/secularity, West/East, white/black, Christianity/Islam, etc.). Its premise is that reality is solid—everything is clear, neat, pure, precise, and, thus, nothing remains subtle, ambiguous, uncertain.

Religiosity, however, is not the same as religion. When understood in all its rich complexity, religion does not simply provide secure foundations but destabilizes every type of religiosity by subverting the oppositional logic of either/or.

> It is not the premise that reality
> Is a solid. It may be a shade that traverses
> A dust, a force that traverses a shade.[4]

This shade (of difference) can be thought only through an elusive neither/nor, which makes it possible to imagine religion in a way that embraces the complexity, uncertainty, and insecurity that are the marks of life in a world where the future remains open.

AGAINST THEORY

It has never been more important to study religion critically than today, but it has never been more difficult to do so. By now it should be clear that far from disappearing, the influence of religion continues to grow. It is, therefore, imperative to develop a better understanding of what religion is and how it functions. There are, however, forces beyond as well as within the university that make responsible reflection on this important problem difficult, if not impossible. As the stakes of devotion to competing religious beliefs increase, political correctness on the left becomes religious correctness on the right. The deepening entrenchment of opposing views creates a growing resistance to every form of criticism and makes constructive dialogue virtually impossible. It is precisely this resistance that underscores the urgent need for renewed critical analysis.

Given these circumstances, it is necessary to return once again to the recurrent, though recently neglected, question "What *is* religion?" For the past several decades, this question has been widely regarded as illegitimate for political as well as philosophical reasons. The reluctance to engage in critical reflection on the nature of religion has led to an interpretive vacuum that has been filled by a variety of reductive analyses in which religion is understood as a mere epiphenomenon of more basic or fundamental processes. Some analysts even go so far as to insist that there is no such thing as religion. Jonathan Z. Smith has influenced many scholars with what might be described as an archaeology or genealogy of the concept "religion." "Religion," he argues, "is not a native category." Indeed, the very notion of religion, it seems, emerges as a result of nascent globalization. In the sixteenth century, Europeans exploring the so-called New World encountered a startling array of strange beliefs and practices, which they eventually described as religious. Smith explains that religion "is not a first person term of self-characterization. It is a category imposed from the outside on some aspect of native culture. It is the other, in these instances colonialists, who are solely responsible for the content of the term. . . . Even in these early formulations, there is an implicit universality. 'Religion' is thought to be a ubiquitous human phenomenon." Smith insists that "no specific historical or cultural phenomena correspond to the general term 'religion.'"[5]

The etymology of *religion* compounds rather than clarifies the difficulties. According to the *Oxford English Dictionary*, *religion* is "of doubtful etymology." It appears to derive from at least two Latin terms. The first and more widely acknowledged is *religare*, which means "to bind back" (*re-*, "back," plus *ligare*, "to bind"). *Leig* is also the stem of "ligament," "ligature," and "obligation." Cicero, by contrast, maintains that "religion" derives from *relegere* (to read over again), whose stem, *leg*, means "thought through again." Throughout the Western tradition, these alternative etymologies have led to contrasting interpretations of religion. The definitions of religion that eventually emerge from this divided origin appear to lend support to Smith's claim that the category is culturally biased. The first three definitions listed in the *Oxford English Dictionary* are remarkably limited.

1. A state of life bound by monastic vows; the condition of one who is a member of a religious order, especially in the Roman Catholic church.
2. A particular monastic or religious order or rule.
3. Action or conduct indicating a belief in, reverence for, and desire to please, a divine ruling power; the exercise or practice of rites or observances implying this.

The American Heritage Dictionary only deepens the confusion by defining religion as

1. The expression of man's belief in and reverence for a superhuman power recognized as the creator and governor of the universe.
2. Any particular integrated system of this expression.
3. The spiritual or emotional attitude of one who recognizes the existence of a superhuman power or powers.

These definitions obviously exclude many beliefs and practices, ranging from Buddhism and pantheism to myriad new religions and alternative spiritualities, that many practitioners and analysts accept as religious.

During the nineteenth century, increasing travel and communications combined with the growth of scholarship to expand the knowledge of other cultures exponentially. The encounter with so many new beliefs and practices created a taxonomic imperative that required an acceptable definition of religion. Smith points out that, from the time of the early Christian apologists, "the most common form of classifying religions . . . is dualistic and can be reduced, regardless of what differentium is employed, to 'theirs' and 'ours.'"

> By the time of the fourth-century Christian Latin apologists, a strong dual vocabulary was well in place and could be deployed interchangeably regardless of the individual histories of the terms: "our religion"/"their religion," with the latter often expressed through generic terms such as "heathenism," "paganism," or "idolatry"; "true religion"/"false religion"; "spiritual (or "internal") religion"/"material (or "external") religion"; "monotheism" (although this term, itself, is a relatively late construction)/"polytheism"; "religion"/"superstition"; "religion"/"magic."[6]

These normative distinctions continue to shape classificatory systems. Throughout the nineteenth century, there were only four acknowledged categories of religion: Christianity, Judaism, Mohammedism (any one of which might be regarded as true), and the rest, that is, paganism, heathenism, idolatry, and polytheism (all of which were declared false). The notion of world religions, which remains influential today, was not developed until the 1920s. It includes twelve "living traditions": Judaism, Christianity, Islam, Zoroastrianism, Hinduism, Jainism, Sikhism, Buddhism, Taoism, Confucianism, Shinto, and Primitivism.[7] As knowledge of different traditions became broader and deeper, the challenge of finding a definition that identified similarities while preserving differences became considerably more formidable. The very proliferation of information that created the need for an accepted definition of religion made its formulation all the more difficult.

The resistance to developing a definition of religion that could be used within as well as across traditions is not, however, simply a result of the recognition of historical differences and cultural relativity but also reflects profound philosophical reservations about any such undertaking. For the past four decades, the study of religion has been caught in theoretical currents circulating throughout the arts, humanities, and social sciences. For our purposes, the two most relevant trajectories are structuralism and poststructuralism. In this context, these interpretive alternatives must be understood more broadly than is customary. While structuralists maintain that it is possible to identify common or even universal forms and patterns in different psychological, social, and cultural phenomena, poststructuralists insist that purportedly universal forms are actually artifacts designed to fulfill certain desires and advance specific ideological agendas.

When understood expansively, structuralism encompasses the version of phenomenology that has been most influential in the study of religion. No work has been more important in debates about the definition of religion than Mircea Eliade's *The Sacred and the Profane* (1957). Bringing together aspects of Husserl's phenomenology with the history of religions, Eliade developed a hermeneutical position that effectively recasts Platonism as methodological idealism. That is to say, he derives a strategy for uncovering the one essential form or implicit idea of religion amid its multiple appearances. In the opening pages of the analysis, he explains: "the important thing for our purpose is to bring out the specific characteristics of *the* religious experience [emphasis added], rather than to show its numerous variations and the differences caused by history."[8] Several points in this telling comment deserve emphasis. First, in accord with the turn to the subject that marks the beginning of modern theology in Friedrich Schleiermacher's *Speeches on Religion to Its Cultured Despisers* (1799), Eliade privileges experience rather than thought or action in his account on religion. Second, like Schleiermacher, he is convinced that experience can be distinctively religious. Third, Eliade assumes that amid the vast variety of religions, it is possible to identify *the* religious experience. There is, in other words, one true religious experience of which all purportedly religious experiences are variations. Finally, this experience is *sui generis* and, thus, cannot be reduced to anything other than itself. Eliade defines this invariant feature of religion by reinterpreting Émile Durkheim's distinction between the sacred and the profane through Rudolph Otto's category of "the holy." "Our primary concern," he explains, "is to present the specific dimensions of religious experience, to bring out the differences between it and profane experience of the world."[9] In anticipation of issues to be probed in the next chapter, it is important to note that Eliade points out that Otto's notion of the holy derives from Luther's account of the "terrible power, manifested in the divine wrath."

> In *Das Heilige* [which was published in English with the misleading title *The Idea of the Holy*], Otto sets himself to discover the characteristics of this frightening and irrational experience. He finds *the feeling of terror* before the sacred, before the awe-inspiring mystery (*mysterium tremendum*), the majesty (*majestas*) that emanates an overwhelming superiority of power. . . . Otto characterizes all these experiences as numinous (from Latin *numen*, god), for they are induced by the revelation of an aspect of divine power. The numinous presents itself as something "wholly other" (*ganz andere*), something basically and totally different.[10]

The further details of Eliade's analysis need not concern us in this context. The important point here is his claim that it is possible to identify the essence of religion and that this "elementary form" can be defined in terms of the binary opposition between the sacred and the profane.

At the same time that Eliade was building his hermeneutical method on Husserl's phenomenology, Claude Lévi-Strauss was appropriating Ferdinand Saussure's linguistic theory to develop his version of structuralism. Just as Husserl insisted that all phenomena—cultural and otherwise—harbor a hidden essence, so Saussure argued that all linguistic practices (*la parole*, "speech") presuppose foundational principles, rules, or structures (*la langue*, "language"). Lévi-Strauss first extends Saussure's notion of speech to include all cultural phenomena and then argues that the structures, which are the transcendental conditions of the possibility of speech, are universal. These foundational structures themselves presuppose the metastructure of binary opposition. In structural analysis, all cultural phenomena are grounded in infrastructures, which secure their determinate meaning. For those who know the code, everything is decipherable.

As phenomenology and structuralism spread during the middle decades of the last century, philosophical and political misgiving about these hermeneutical strategies gained momentum. For critics, the "essentialism" of phenomenology and what came to be described as the "logocentrism" of structuralism reinscribe what Heidegger identified as the Western ontotheological tradition, which privileges the presence of identity and represses or excludes otherness and difference(s). Three influential criticisms of essentialism and logocentrism emerged: history of religions, social constructivism, and deconstruction. While there was, of course, a long tradition of the history of religions before the twentieth century, the growing sophistication of the social sciences and the increasing differentiation between theology and the practice of religion changed the interpretive landscape. In addition to this, the emergence of the academic study of religion led to the creation of subfields like the history of religions, the sociology of religion, the anthropology of religion, and the psychology of religion and opened new avenues of research that posed further additional questions. The unrelenting gaze of the social sciences threatened to dissolve their very object of investigation. If there are only different religions, which are symptomatic of unique historical and cultural contexts, then there appears to be no such thing as religion as such. This line of analysis implies a methodological nominalism in which the term *religion* can refer only to a specific set of beliefs and practices. In the absence of a general concept of religion, however, problems of definition are insurmountable and comparative analysis is impossible. While knowledge does not necessarily require universality, it does presuppose that a certain level of ascertainable generality characterizes patterns constitutive of phenomena in the real world. As we will see below, it is possible to understand these formative patterns as neither essentialist nor logocentric.

In addition to these epistemological difficulties, the interpretive dilemma is further compounded by what Paul Ricoeur labeled "the hermeneutics of suspicion." From this point of view, different religions are not, as Eliade insists, sui generis but are actually effects of supposedly more basic social, economic, political, and psychological processes. Since religious beliefs and practices are epiphenomenal, they must be understood by reducing them to something other than themselves. Though rarely acknowledged by professional students of religion, these methodological approaches call into question the study of religion as such and undercut the rationale for independent departments and programs in religious studies. If there is no such thing as religion, then why do we need departments to study it?

The emergence of social constructivism during the past several decades has politicized this debate. For many concerned people beyond ivied walls, these heated debates often are not only baffling but also deeply disturbing. If one is patient enough to listen, however, it gradually becomes clear that, far from merely academic, these controversies reflect pressing conflicts resulting from uncertainties and instabilities created by globalization. As students and faculty members have become more diverse, long-accepted traditions and categories of classification and interpretation have been subjected to thoroughgoing criticism. For many, foundational essences and structures are not merely theological vestiges that represent philosophical mistakes but social constructs devised to serve political ends. Cultural artifacts, critics argue, are recast as natural phenomena to reinforce dominant power structures. This line of argument represents a noteworthy reversal of some of the most important ideas that lie at the heart of modernity and its institutions. During the Enlightenment, the notion of human nature and, correlatively, natural rights formed the foundation of both the American and the French Revolutions. Over two centuries later, human nature has become for many a reactionary, rather than a revolutionary, principle. If human nature is real, the argument goes, natural determination is inevitable and radical change is impossible. For social constructivists, what others claim to be natural is actually cultural. Naturalism and essentialism, they argue, create cultural hegemony, which reinforces political hegemony by creating ideological justifications to support those in power. Rephrasing Marx's opening comments in his well-known response to Hegel's *Philosophy of Right,* social constructivists argue that the criticism of naturalism and essentialism is the premise of all criticism. By exposing ideological superstructures as epiphenomenal, critics claim to clear the way for thoroughgoing social, political, and economic transformation.

While sensitive to the political significance of different interpretive strategies, deconstruction is more concerned with how implicit theological and philosophical assumptions continue to shape the Western cultural tradition. As we will see in detail below, the gods or their functional equivalents do not simply disappear but go underground, where they continue to support human life. This transformation of religious dogma leads to unrecognized theological and philosophical assumptions that inform many of the most sophisticated theories in the natural and social sciences. For poststructuralists, the task of criticism at the end of modernity is (paraphrasing Heidegger's interrogation of thinking at the end of philosophy) to expose the instability of all foundational structures and incompletion of all purportedly comprehensive systems.

In this way, deconstruction effectively calls into question every system constructed to provide security, certainty, and stability.[11] With the rise of religious and political absolutisms, this critical gesture has never been more important than it is today. But deconstructive criticism is not enough—it is also necessary to articulate alternative structures that can inform creative cultural production and effective sociopolitical transformation.

The resistance to any theory designed to answer the question "What is religion?" has led to unexpected results. Critics who insist that it is impossible as well as illegitimate to ask questions about the origin, nature, and function of cultural phenomena create an opening for more extreme forms of reductive analysis. The remarkable advances in the biological and neurological sciences in recent years have led to different forms of biologism, according to which mental, social, and cultural processes can be reduced to natural laws and genetic determinants. The three most important versions of biologism are sociobiology, genetic logocentrism, and neurological determinism. Though differing in important ways, all of these lines of analysis assume some kind of code, which, when cracked, *exhaustively* explains the phenomenon under investigation. Molecular biologist Dean Hammer carries the argument to its logical (or illogical) conclusion in his controversial book *The God Gene: How Faith Is Hardwired into Our Genes*. The genetic modifications that have led to religion are supposed to lend individuals and groups adaptive advantages that increase the chance of their survival. Such an approach is obviously one-sided and cannot do justice to the multiple dimensions of religion and its complex relation to physical and biological systems. Though parading as cutting-edge science, biologism is actually a different version of essentialism, which is consistent with the neofoundationalism threatening the world today.

These remarks suggest that for the most influential critics of the latter half of the twentieth century and their epigones, the three greatest philosophical and political errors of the era are totalization, hegemony, and foundationalism. During the middle decades of the last century, social and cultural critics faced with terrorism on the left (i.e., communism) and the right (i.e., fascism) took as their primary task the subversion of structures of repression by turning their logic against themselves to expose an inherent aporia. Their critical success, however, turned into political failure: the repressed returned to unleash neofoundationalisms harboring terror that is more dangerous because it is more diffuse.

NETWORKING SYMBOLS

If we are to develop an adequate theory of religion that creates the possibility of criticizing flawed orthodoxies and developing alternative visions for the future, it is necessary to learn from but move beyond these influential theories of the recent past. Though structuralism and poststructuralism provide valuable insights, they remain incomplete. Structuralists understand the necessity of forms and patterns for creating the order without which life is impossible, but they cannot explain how these structures emerge and change over time. Having recognized the fatal consequences of fixed forms, poststructuralists insist that vitality is impossible without the repeated disruption and dislocation of static structures. But they have a monolithic view of systems and structures and cannot conceive of structures that act as a whole without necessarily totalizing. It is, therefore, impossible for poststructuralists to move beyond the moment of criticism to fashion new structures that promote creativity. In an effort to overcome these shortcomings and develop a critical perspective adapted to contemporary network culture, I will bring together structuralism and poststructuralism through an appropriation of the theory of complex adaptive systems to interpret the emergence, development, and operational logic of religion. The threads holding the argument together will be drawn from information and network theory.

At a minimum, any adequate theory of religion must

1. describe and/or explain the complex origin, operational logic, and multiple functions of religion;
2. clarify the dynamics of the emergence, development, and transformation of different religious networks;
3. show how religions relate to and interact with each other as well as the physical, biological, social, political, and economic aspects of life; and
4. include a "principle" of "internal" criticism that leaves the theory open to endless revision.

The following definition is designed to meet these requirements:

> Religion is an emergent, complex, adaptive network of symbols, myths, and rituals that, on the one hand, figure schemata of feeling, thinking, and acting in ways that lend life meaning and purpose and, on the other, disrupt, dislocate, and disfigure every stabilizing structure.

It is important to emphasize at the outset that this definition of religion identifies two interrelated moments: one that structures and stabilizes and one that destructures and destabilizes. These two moments are inseparable and alternate in a kind of quasi-dialectical rhythm. As the threat of disruption increases, devotees tend to absolutize, reify, or fetishize their beliefs and practices. When this occurs, religion devolves into a religiosity that resists the new by clinging to the old. But such efforts inevitably fail; the deeper the entrenchment, the more likely becomes the very disruption religiosity is designed to avoid. Any theory of religion that concentrates on one of these moments to the exclusion of the other is unsatisfactory.

To begin to unravel the strands in this definition of religion, it is necessary to consider the meaning and operation of *schemata*. I have borrowed this notion from Murray Gell-Mann, who is a Nobel laureate in physics. "In complex adaptive systems," he argues, "information about the environment . . . is not merely listed in what computer scientists would call a look-up table. Instead, the regularities of the experience are encapsulated in highly compressed form as a *model* or *theory* or *schema*. Such a schema is usually approximate, sometimes wrong, but it may be adaptive if it can make useful predictions including interpretation and extrapolation and sometimes generalization to situations very different from those previously encountered."[12] Schemata enable complex adaptive systems to fulfill five critical functions. First, the system must be able to identify regularities in its environment. Every system is embedded in multiple networks that provide streams of data that must be processed. For a system to function effectively, it must be able to identify regularities, patterns, and redundancies in surrounding flows. Second, once a regularity has been identified, the system must generate schemata that enable it to recognize the pattern if it occurs again. For a schema to work well, it must compress as much data as possible. Third, schemata in complex adaptive systems must be able to modify themselves in relation to changing circumstances. Fourth, schemata cannot be merely reactive but must be capable of being deployed to anticipate surrounding activities in a way that guides responsive action. The effectiveness of a schema is a function of the accuracy of its descriptions, the reliability of its predictions of relevant events in the environment, and the effectiveness of the actions it prescribes. Finally, different schemata within a system and schemata in different systems must be able to compete effectively with other schemata. Those that prove to be best adapted to the environment survive and the others eventually disappear. Gell-Mann offers a concise summary of these points:

> In studying any complex adaptive system, we follow what happens to the information. We examine how it reaches the system in the form of a stream of data. . . . We notice how the complex adaptive system perceives regularities in the data stream, sorting them out from features treated as incidental or arbitrary and condensing them into a schema, which is subject to variation. . . . We observe how each of the resulting schemata is then combined with additional information, of the same kind as the incidental information that was put aside in abstracting regularities from the data stream, to generate a result with applications to the real world: a description of an observed system, a prediction of events, or a prescription for behavior for the complex adaptive system itself. . . . Finally, we see how the description, prediction, or behavior has consequences in the real world that feed back to exert 'selection pressures' on the competition among various schemata.[13]

Two seemingly disparate analogies help to clarify the operation of schemata: ancient cosmogonic myths and modern information theory.[14] Creation narratives in many religious traditions recount variations of a common myth of origin: the cosmos emerges from the interplay between the principles of order and chaos. This struggle is represented in the conflict between benevolent and malevolent deities whose specific characteristics vary from tradition to tradition. In the West, the ancient Babylonian epic recounting the battle between Marduk and the marine monster Tiamat reappears in the opening lines of Genesis:

> In the beginning of creation, when God made heaven and earth, the earth was without form and void, with darkness over the face of the abyss, and a mighty wind that swept over the surface of the waters. God said, "Let there be light," and there was light; and God saw that the light was good, and he separated light from darkness. (1:1–4)[15]

Water and word correspond respectively to chaos (formless) and order (form). The cosmos appears when order emerges from chaos through formation brought about by the word. Plato presents one of the most influential versions of this narrative in *The Republic*. According to his myth of origin, a Demiurge brings together eternal forms with formless matter, which is always in flux, to create the world as we know it. The world, therefore, is matter in form, or in-formed matter. Every variation of this narrative presupposes one or another set of binary oppositions that somehow must be mediated or negotiated. Schemata are similar to the forms, and data streams are roughly equivalent to what Plato labels matter. We will see in what follows that schemata, like Platonic forms, are both epistemological and ontological. There are, however, four important differences between the structure and operational logic of schemata and the data stream in complex adaptive systems, on the one hand, and the forms and matter in ontotheological myths of origin, on the other. Schemata are not independent of each other but are interrelated and mutually constitutive. Hence, schemata are neither eternal nor unchanging like the forms but are emergent and evolve over time. Moreover, unlike chaos or matter in cosmogonic myths, the data stream is not completely undifferentiated but harbors implicit relations and patterns. In other words, there is an order to things that is not imposed from without but emerges within the world's fluxes and flows. Finally, order and disorder are not simply opposite but are codependent in such a way that neither can be what it is apart from the other.

The relation between order and chaos in cosmogonic myths can be understood in terms of the interplay between information and noise in information theory. In their groundbreaking book *The Mathematical Theory of Information* (1949), Claude Shannon and Warren Weaver developed a notion of information that differs significantly from the common sense of the term. "The word *information*, in this theory," Weaver explains, "must not be confused with its ordinary usage. In particular, *information* must not be confused with meaning."[16] Meaning, as we will see, arises at a different level from information. According to Shannon and Weaver, information, in the strict sense of the term, is inversely proportional to probability: the more probable something is, the less information it conveys; the less probable it is, the more information it conveys. Gregory Bateson clarifies this notion of information when he explains that "information is a difference that makes a difference."[17] Information must be sufficiently different to convey something new but not so different that it is completely unrecognizable or undetectable. The domain of information, then, lies *between* too little and too much difference. On the one hand, information *is* a difference and, therefore, in the absence of difference there is no information. On the other hand, information is a difference that *makes a difference.* Not all differences make a difference: if they are redundant, they are inconsequential. Since both too little and too much difference issue in noise, information always emerges at the two-sided edge of chaos. Pattern emerges from noise through the articulation of difference (fig. 1). Information and noise are not merely

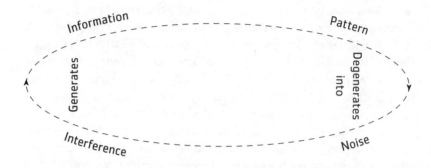

Figure 1. Information and Noise

opposites but coemerge and remain codependent: *information is noise in formation*. Noise, in turn, interrupts by interfering with informative patterns. When understood in this way, information stabilizes noise and noise destabilizes information. Inasmuch as the process of destabilization provides the occasion for the emergence of new informative patterns, it is not merely negative.

With this understanding of information and noise, it is possible to diagram the operation of schemata in complex adaptive systems (fig. 2). Schemata function both theoretically and practically first to screen data in order to detect, form, and reform patterns that simultaneously describe, prefigure, and predict entities and events and second to model adaptive actions in the real world. The viability of schemata depends upon their theoretical accuracy and practical efficacy. New data can lead to the modification or even the destruction of schemata. Neither a priori nor a posteriori, schemata arise within a specific context, which establishes the parameters of constraint that are the conditions of new entities and events. Once having emerged, they continue to develop through a competitive coevolutionary process with other schemata. As we will see in detail below, religious myths and symbols function as schemata in complex adaptive systems. It is important to recognize, however, that schemata are neither necessarily conscious nor deliberately constructed and, thus, are not limited to conscious or self-conscious systems. When fully deployed, schemata self-organize and operate in physical, chemical, and biological as well as social, political, and economic systems. For example, the immune system, the market, and even the process of evolution itself would be impossible without schemata to process information.

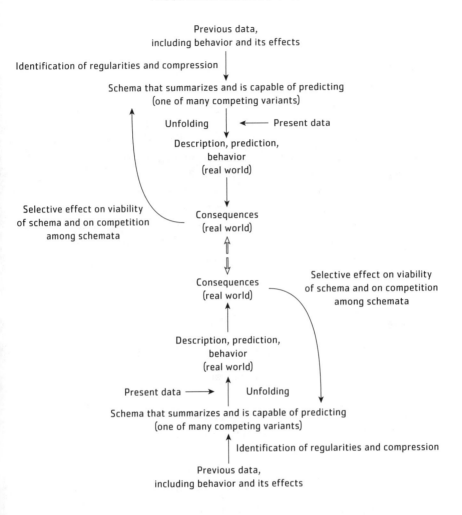

Figure 2. Schemata in Coadaptive Complex Systems (adapted from Murray Gell-Mann, *The Quark and the Jaguar: Adventures in the Simple and the Complex* [New York: W. H. Freeman, 1994], 25)

To understand how religious symbols and myths function as schemata that lend life meaning and purpose, it is helpful to begin with a consideration of their role in cognitive activity. Theory and praxis, I have noted, are not separate in schemata: descriptive representations provide models *of* the world that serve as models *for* activity in the world.[18] Schemata process data in such a way that information, knowledge, and meaning are woven together to create patterns for thought and action, and these, in turn, bring about revisions and adaptations in the schemata. The patterning of data creates information, which, then, is fashioned into knowledge that can be rendered meaningful. This complex process entails the coordination of different cognitive activities: intuition, perception, consciousness, self-consciousness, and reason.

The relationship among these activities as well as their products is hierarchical yet nonlinear. Each higher level simultaneously emerges from and acts back upon lower levels (fig. 3). Through the process of schematization, subject/object (and self/world) mutually emerge and, therefore, are codependent. It is a mistake to privilege object over subject (empiricism or realism) or subject over object (idealism or social constructivism). Intuitions of the data stream are intuited as sense perceptions and then fashioned into the objects of consciousness. Taken together, these objects form the physical world. With the emergence of the world, it becomes possible for the subject first to become conscious and eventually to turn back on itself to become self-conscious

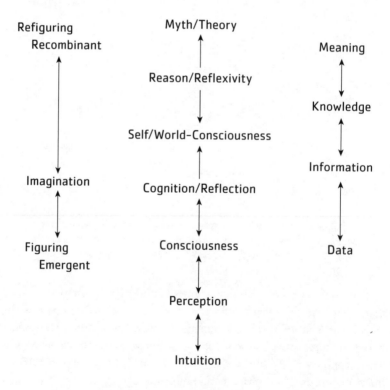

Figure 3. Process of Schematization

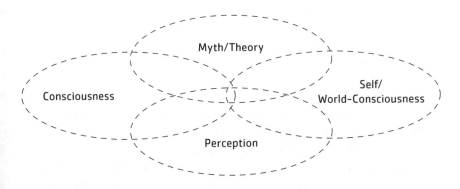

Figure 4. Symbolic / Cognitive Network (I)

(fig. 4). Self-consciousness, however, presupposes not only differentiation from the world but also the relation to the world as well as other self-conscious agents. Subjectivity, in other words, is necessarily inter-subjective. Reason doubles self-reflection by joining consciousness and self-consciousness in strange loops that never completely close. The gap in the structure of self-reflexivity creates the opening for the indeterminacy without which creativity is impossible and the future is closed. At the highest level of schematization, symbols and myths integrate sense experience, information, and knowledge into patterns that provide meaning and purpose. Since the relation among these different levels and operations is simultaneous rather than sequential, different cognitive operations mutually condition each other. The images, concepts, and symbols through which the world is organized emerge from and change with the data of experience, which they simultaneously shape. The nonlinearity of these operations creates an *interactive* cognitive network.[19] Even at this microlevel, the structure and operational logic of the cognitive network conform to the complex adaptive systems. Proliferating connections lead to adaptations, which lead to new connections, which lead to further adaptations. . . .

Different schemata function in a similar way at every level of the cognitive network. One of the functions of the imagination is to coordinate other cognitive activities. Just as it is necessary to have an expanded notion of information to understand how physical, chemical, biological, social, political, and economic systems function as information processes, so it is necessary to develop an expanded understanding of the imagination to appreciate how it works throughout the cognitive network. The imagination *informs* cognitive, which is not necessarily to say conscious, processes through the activity of *figuring*. Since figuring (or figuration) is a pivotal notion that will return repeatedly throughout the following chapters, it is important to understand it precisely. Both a noun and a verb, *figure* is an unusually rich word, which can mean inter alia: "form, shape; an embodied (human) form; a person considered with regard to visible form or appearance; the image, likeness, or representation of something material or immaterial; an arrangement of lines or other markings forming an ornamental device; to form, shape; to trace, mark; to be an image, symbol, or type; to adorn or mark with figures; to embellish with a design or pattern; to calculate; to take into consideration; to solve, decipher, or comprehend."[20] Drawing on the multiple meanings and nuances of *figure*, the imagination can be understood as the activity of figuring through which figures emerge. These figures are the schemata that enable the data of experience to be figured, that is, formed as well as calculated. Schemata and the imagination work together to create complex information-processing networks. As data shift and patterns interact competitively, schemata repeatedly adjust by refiguring themselves. The activity of the imagination, therefore, has two sides: figuring, which is emergent (i.e., productive and creative), and refiguring, which is recombinant (i.e., reproductive and re-creative).

Insofar as every figure presupposes the process of figuring, it includes as a condition of its own possibility something that cannot be figured. That is to say, figures "include" but do not incorporate something that can be neither represented nor comprehended. Figures, therefore, are always disfigured *as if* from within. Far from a flaw, this disfiguring keeps figures open and as such is the necessary condition of emergent creativity. These two sides of the imagination correspond to the two moments of religion. While figures structure and stabilize, figuring disrupts, dislocates, and destabilizes every ostensibly stabilizing schema, even as it invites a new schematization.

Before proceeding to a more detailed consideration of symbolic networks, it is important to note that the complex nonlinearity of cognitive networks calls into question any theory that associates religion exclusively with thinking (cognition), acting (volition), or feeling (affection) (fig. 5). From the eighteenth century to the present, many of the most influential interpreters of religion have tended to concentrate on one of these faculties at the expense of the other two.[21] If, however, cognitive networks are wired as I have described them, different faculties cannot be separated, because they are interactive. Feeling, thinking, and acting

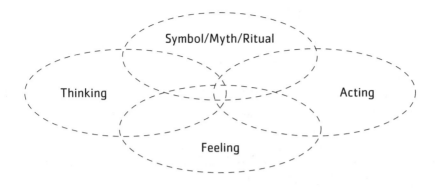

Figure 5. Symbolic / Cognitive Network (II)

mutually influence each other; as one changes, the others inevitably are modified. Symbols, myths, and rituals both condition and are conditioned by these interactions.

Symbols, myths, and rituals form and are formed by networks, which, in turn, form and are formed by more expansive webs. Just as different schemata arise through competitive interaction, so symbolic networks coemerge and coevolve in relational webs that function according to the principles of complex adaptive systems. Regardless of context, all complex adaptive systems have the following characteristics:

1. They are composed of many codependent parts connected in multiple and changing ways.
2. They display spontaneous self-organization, which occurs within parameters of constraint that leave space for the aleatory.
3. The structures resulting from spontaneous self-organization emerge from but are not necessarily reducible to the components in the system.
4. Self-organizing structures are open and, therefore, are able to adapt and coevolve with other structures.
5. As connectivity increases, networks become more complex and drift toward disequilibrium until they reach a tipping point, when a discontinuous phase shift occurs.

Since the structure and functional logic of complex adaptive systems are isomorphic across media ranging from the so-called material to the so-called immaterial, networks are always networks of other networks. In different terms, complex adaptive networks are fractal—they display the same structure at every organizational level and in every operational phase.

To function religiously, symbolic networks must address theological, anthropological, and cosmological issues. These three dimensions of experience are articulated in the interrelated figures of God, self, and world or their functional equivalents (fig. 6). Theology, anthropology, and cosmology mutually condition each other: the way in which God is imagined determines the way in which the self and the world are conceived and vice versa. In theistic traditions, for example, God is believed to be a quasi-personal being who creates and governs the world. As we will see in detail below, traditionally there have been two alternatives within the parameters of this vision: either God's will follows God's reason, in which case the world is ultimately comprehensible, or God's will is antecedent to reason, in which case the world is radically contingent and irreducibly mysterious. Human being, correspondingly, is understood either as essentially rational or as governed by the irrational or, more accurately, arational will, drives, and desires. Other ideas and doctrines characteristic of a particular symbolic network—notions of good and evil, time and space, history and nature, fall and redemption, etc.—can be interpolated from these three nodal concepts. When religion is understood as a complex adaptive network, it becomes clear that these contrasting theological alternatives are coimplicated in such a way that neither can be itself apart from the other and each becomes itself in and through the other.

Like everything else, symbolic networks are never formed in isolation but emerge in complex relational webs within and among tradi-

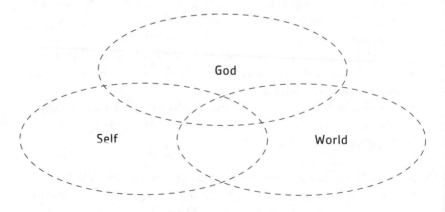

Figure 6. Religious Network

tions. These webs have synchronic and diachronic axes, which issue in the codependence and coevolution of particular symbolic networks (fig. 7). The specificity of any symbolic network within a tradition is a function of its similarities to and differences from other religious alternatives available at a given moment in time (synchronic axis). Today's Evangelical Protestants, for example, define themselves by their relation to other Christian sects and denominations as well as their opposition to so-called secular humanists. In addition to this, every religious position is also temporally and historically situated—it grows out of a past that shapes it and anticipates a future that can transform it (diachronic axis).[22] The endless interplay among competing versions of the "same" tradition results in constant revisions and repeated reformations. So understood, history is neither linear nor circular.

Just as no version of a particular tradition can emerge apart from other versions of that tradition, so every religious tradition is constituted by its interactions with other religious traditions. Different traditions provide contrasting symbolic networks, which offer alternative schemata for figuring meaning and purpose. The multiple vectors in these diagrams suggest the webs in which competing symbolic networks are articulated (fig. 8). The dynamics between and among traditions are the same as the dynamics within a single tradition. As the interrelation of competing schemata increases, the stability of particular traditions and of the webs connecting them decreases. There are three characteristic responses to the growing volatility and insecurity that result from these developments: conservative, progressive, and transformative.

Religious traditions and cultural institutions tend to be deeply resistant to change. Conservatives cling to the old and resist the new. There are, of course, different degrees of resistance, ranging from traditionalists to reactionaries. When societies change, many seek security and stability through traditional beliefs and practices. As the rate of change increases, a more radical reaction tends to set in. True believers set themselves apart from infidels by constructing an ideal past, which, they believe, has been corrupted in the present. The goal becomes to "recover" this past by purifying the present through the conversion or elimination of nonbelievers. Devotion to this reactionary agenda tends to absolutize faith in unquestionable foundational principles and, in many cases, is accompanied by total obedience to authoritative figures. Reactionaries can be found today, for example, in all three religions of the book: ultranationalistic, hyperorthodox Jews; militarist, internationally revanchist Muslims; and morally absolutist, internationally expansionist, of-

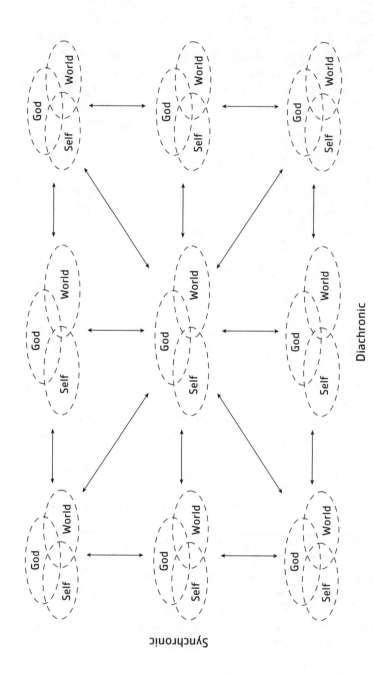

Figure 7. Web of Symbolic Networks in a Single Religious Tradition

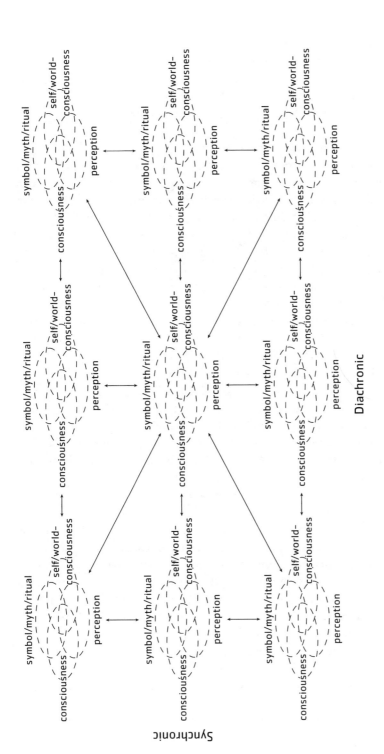

Figure 8. Webs of Symbolic Networks in Multiple Religious Traditions

ten millennialist Christians. Though obviously different in many ways, these forms of belief share more with each other than they do with many strands in their respective traditions. Religious reactionaries provide the clearest example of the religiosity that absolutizes the relative by reifying or fetishizing a particular version of an emergent complex symbolic network.

In the opinion of many believers, however, reactionary responses are not only counterproductive but actually dangerous. Simplistic and unbending faith in a complex and changing world carries the threat of violence and destruction. To avoid disaster, progressive critics of reactionary foundationalism counsel the selective adaptation of beliefs and practices to changing circumstances. The nature, scope, and rate of change promoted by different groups lend them their specific identity. Regardless of period or context, such believers are liberals or modernists who understand that religious traditions and systems must change if they are to remain viable. As the voices of conflicting religious orthodoxies have risen to fever pitch in recent years, however, the voices of religious liberals in different traditions have fallen silent. Indeed, in today's world the ascendancy of neofoundationalism has made the notion of religious liberalism virtually oxymoronic. For conservatives, traditionalists, and reactionaries, the willingness of self-confessed believers to modify faith to accommodate contemporary circumstances provides further evidence of the moral decline that fuels outrage.

During periods of great instability like our own, incremental change cannot continue forever. As worldwide webs expand, competing visions clash and create noise that amplifies until the networks in which schemata are formed reach what complexity theorists describe as a condition of "self-organized criticality" or, in a more popular idiom, the tipping point. Physicist Per Bak has analyzed such events in great detail and has developed a theoretical explanation of them. He goes so far as to propose a new "science of self-organized criticality," which will disclose previously undetected laws that illuminate the nonlinear dynamics of complex systems. "Complex behavior in nature," Bak argues, "reflects the tendency of large systems with many components to evolve into a poised 'critical' state, way out of balance, where minor disturbances may lead to events called avalanches, of all sizes. Most of the changes take place through catastrophic events rather than by following a smooth gradual path. The evolution of this very delicate state occurs without design from any outside agent. The state is established solely because of the dynamical interactions among individual elements of the system:

the critical state is *self-organized*."[23] Self-organized criticality occurs in complex systems governed by nonlinear dynamics. As a result of this nonlinearity, events are amplified through positive feedback loops and can have effects disproportionate to their causes. Dynamic interactions among individual elements in the system generate global events that require a holistic description that cannot be reduced to an account of individual elements. When a system reaches the tipping point, the effect of individual events becomes unpredictable. While it is possible to know that at some point a significant change or avalanche will occur, it is never possible to predict which event will tip the balance and upset the equilibrium.

Bak's analysis of natural systems can be extended to symbolic networks. As conditions in the world change more quickly than the schemata that figure them, the map no longer fits the territory and orientation becomes more and more difficult. In the absence of familiar signposts and reliable guides, meaning and purpose become obscure. Incremental change eventually gives way to systemic transformation in which new schemata emerge from the competition and combinatorial play of old figures and forms. By unsettling organizing structures that do not adapt well to changing circumstances, the activity of figuring creates the conditions for the evolution or, more precisely, the coevolution of more effective schemata and symbolic networks. The evolutionary success of schemata and networks in rapidly changing environments presupposes the capacity

1. to accommodate increasing interconnection and, therefore, growing complexity,
2. to manage increasing volatility and instability effectively,
3. to remain open and adaptive, and
4. to change quickly and efficiently.

Evolution—be it biological or religious—is not a continuous process but is characterized by what biologists describe as *punctuated equilibrium*. Periods of relative stability and gradual change are interrupted by phase shifts that lead to structural and morphological transformations. Since development is punctuated rather than continuous, change is episodic and unpredictable. Within the coevolutionary framework of connected networks, disruptions are simultaneously destructive and creative. In whatever medium evolution occurs, there can no more be construction without deconstruction than there can be deconstruction without construction. Once articulated, new configurations inevitably

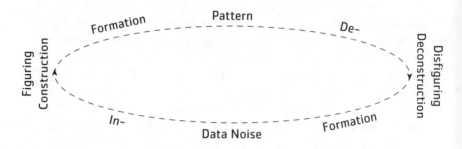

Figure 9. Imagination

drift toward the edge of chaos, where the process repeats itself. If understood in this way, the operation of emergent complex adaptive networks of symbols, myths, and rituals involves information processes that figure changing organizational patterns. Such figuring extends the activity of the imagination beyond the limits of the human mind to processes embodied in nature and history[24] (fig. 9). Just as information emerges from noise in formation, so figuring and disfiguring issue in and constantly transform the figures and patterns that lend life ever-changing meaning and purpose in the absence of secure foundations. To appreciate the far-reaching implications of this insight, a further extension of the relational webs in which religious symbols, myths, and rituals are embedded is necessary. Having traced the emergence of schemata and symbolic networks within single and among multiple religious traditions, it is now necessary to consider their relation to broader natural, social, and cultural patterns.

As I have indicated, emergent complex adaptive networks are not limited to culture but can be found throughout the natural and social systems that compose the everyday world. They are not, in other words, merely subjective and epistemological but are also objective and ontological. In the final two chapters I will attempt to show how life itself is an emergent complex adaptive network that harbors important religious dimensions, ethical norms, and political imperatives. In the present context, it is important to stress that networks and webs have the same structure and operational logic in natural, social, and cultural systems. Moreover, the interrelation and coevolution of nature, society, and culture are also governed by the dynamics of emergent complex adaptive networks (fig. 10). Whole and part are isomorphic; once again, interrelated networks display a fractal design. Networks are networks of net-

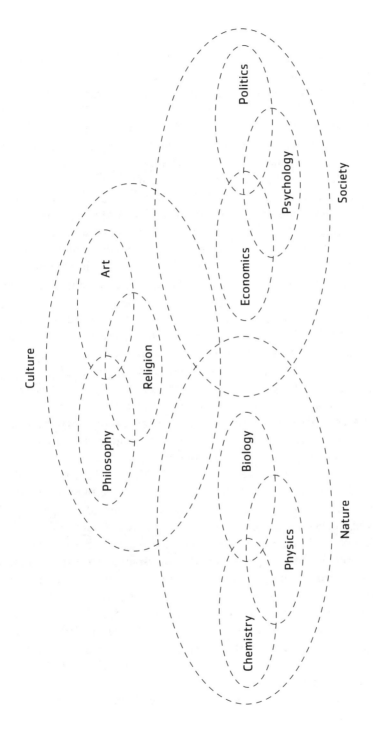

Figure 10. Codependence of Nature, Society, and Culture

works that emerge through iteration and interrelation. Nature, society, and culture mutually condition and codetermine each other as a result of the nonlinear dynamics of networks. Culture, for example, conditions nature as much as nature conditions culture.

To complete this already-complex picture, a final factor must be added: technology. Technological developments simultaneously grow out of and act back upon natural, social, and cultural systems. Technology, of course, is not limited to the human world but extends to the realm of animals and even beyond to simpler so-called lower forms of life. Within the human domain, the shift from mechanical to electronic forms of production and reproduction marks a tipping point that profoundly transforms the relation of technology to nature, society, and culture (fig. 11). If natural, social, and cultural processes are, in effect, distributed information processes, then the digital revolution is creating technologies whose structure and function not only reflect but more importantly amplify and transform what is already occurring in the world. When information machines are connected in webs that have the same structure as natural, social, and cultural systems, coevolution becomes inevitable even if its direction is impossible to predict. This development leads to a further obscuring of the line between nature and culture or natural and artificial systems. With the deepening understanding of the genome and the growing sophistication of digital and nanotechnologies, bioinformatics will be to the near future what computers have been to the recent past. As information and biological processes increasingly interface, life itself will change, and the interrelation of nature, society, and culture will be radically reconfigured.

These insights and developments obviously have important implications for the study of religion as well as all other cultural phenomena. If the real world is a relational network, it cannot be comprehended through conceptual grids that create divisions and oppositions rather than links and connections. For knowledge to be possible, the structure and development of cognition must be consistent with the structure and development of investigated phenomena. If the mind is wired one way and the world another way, the world as such remains unknowable. As we have seen, however, subject/object, self/world, and mind/phenomena are not opposites but coemerge and coevolve in shared networks and webs. Cognitive processes, therefore, are implicated in objects and events through recursive feedback loops that constantly reconfigure them. The constantly changing interrelations that create greater complexity also constitute the conditions for the reliability of whatever knowledge we have.

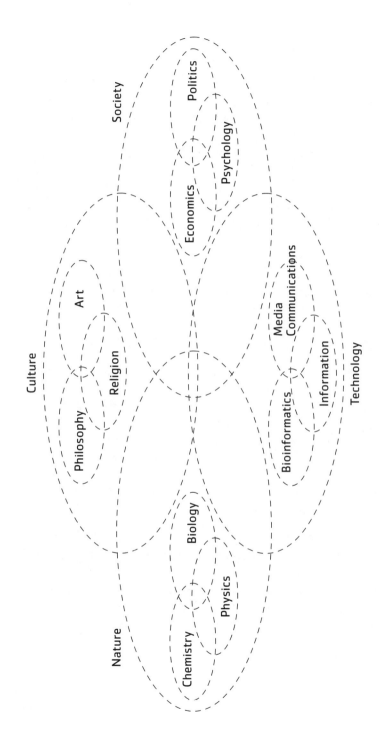

Figure 11. Codependence of Nature, Society, Culture, and Technology

As knowledge evolves, the organization of curricula, universities, and academic professions must be transformed. Concentration and specialization are necessary but not sufficient to understand the complexities of the contemporary world. Creative insights emerge at the margins—in the gaps between and among established disciplines. Academic disciplines, like religious systems, resist change as long as possible. As maps drift apart from territories, disciplines eventually reach the tipping point and lines of inquiry must be redrawn. With the limits of hyperspecialization becoming undeniable, a phase shift is beginning to occur along "the edges and inchings" of inquiry. To pursue this emerging trajectory, it is necessary to approach religion from multiple perspectives and to place it in the context not only of different religious traditions but also of other cultural systems (i.e., philosophy, art, music, theater, dance, etc.), as well as social (economics, politics, psychology, etc.)[25] and natural systems (i.e., physical, chemical, and biological). Since these systems are interdependent, one cannot be reduced to the other and, therefore, every form of reductive foundationalism is illegitimate.

At the outset of this analysis, I claimed that at a minimum any adequate theory of religion must

1. describe and/or explain the complex origin, operational logic, and multiple functions of religion;
2. clarify the dynamics of the emergence, development, and transformation of different religious networks;
3. show how religions relate to and interact with each other as well as the physical, biological, social, political, and economic aspects of life; and
4. include a "principle" of "internal" criticism that leaves the theory open to endless revision.

I then proceeded to define religion as an emergent complex adaptive network of symbols, myths, and rituals that, on the one hand, figure schemata of feeling, thinking, and acting in ways that lend life meaning and purpose and, on the other, disrupt, dislocate, and disfigure every stabilizing structure. The explanation and elaboration of this definition have been designed to meet the established criteria. In the following chapters, I will attempt to show how this theory, which grows out of the Western philosophical and theological tradition, can help us to understand and criticize the role of religion in contemporary society and how this perspective can be elaborated to fashion an alternative religious vision that promotes a global ethic of life. Before proceeding with this admit-

tedly ambitious program, it is necessary to examine the general characteristics of the alternative ways of being religious, which can be found
throughout history and continue to define the poles of current religious
conflict.

THREE WAYS OF BEING RELIGIOUS

In his classic study *The Varieties of Religious Experience: A Study in Human
Nature*, William James defines religion as "*the feelings, acts and experiences
of individual men* [sic] *in their solitude, so far as they apprehend themselves
to stand in relation to whatever they may consider divine.*"[26] While James
designed this definition to be as inclusive as possible by insisting that
religion does not necessarily presuppose belief in God, his perspective
remains limited in at least two important ways. First, and most obviously, by focusing on the solitary individual, James reduces the social
dimensions of selfhood and aspects of religion to a secondary status.
Any approach to the study of religion that privileges the individual at
the expense of the social or vice versa is inadequate. Second, James ac-
knowledges that religion involves different ways of thinking and acting
but concentrates on *experience*, which he regards as primarily affective.
This unnecessarily limits his analysis in ways that tend to obscure the
interplay of cognition, volition, and affection. Though his method is
empirical and is largely limited to description, his approach is surprisingly similar to the phenomenological analysis that Eliade eventually
developed. Like Eliade, James assumes that there is such a thing as human nature and that religion or its functional equivalent is inseparable
from it. Unlike Eliade, however, James does not think there is only one
type of religious experience. He identifies two basic varieties of religious
experience—healthy-mindedness and the sick soul—which he analyzes
through a richly documented comparison. "In many persons," James
points out,

> happiness is congenital and irreclaimable. "Cosmic emotions" in-
> evitably takes in them the form of enthusiasm and freedom. I speak
> not only to those who are animally happy, I mean those who, when
> unhappiness is offered or proposed to them, positively refuse to feel
> it, as if it were something mean and wrong. We find such persons in
> every age, passionately flinging themselves upon their sense of the
> goodness of life, in spite of the hardships of their own condition, and
> in spite of the sinister theologies into which they may be born. From
> the outset their religion is one of union with the divine.

The healthy-minded person enjoys a sense of "religious gladness," which makes "deliverance from any antecedent burden" seem unnecessary. The most important aspect of this type of religion is the conviction that there is an original union or identity between self and God, which persists throughout life and renders all evil and corruption epiphenomenal. While James places two movements, which were influential in New England at the time, in this category—Unitarianism and Protestant liberalism—he insists that the clearest examples are romantic poets and philosophical idealists like Walt Whitman and Ralph Waldo Emerson.[27]

The sick soul is the polar opposite of the healthy-minded type. "In contrast with such healthy-minded views," James explains, "if we treat them as a way of deliberately minimizing evil, stands a radically opposite view, a way of maximizing evil, if you please so to call it, based on the persuasion that the evil aspects of our life are of its very essence, and that the world's meaning most comes home to us when we lay them most to heart." What meaning life has for the sick soul, however, is severely limited because there are unavoidable elements "of the universe which may make no rational whole in conjunction with the other elements, and which, from the point of view of any system which those other elements make up, can only be considered so much irrelevance and accident—so much 'dirt,' as it were, and matter out of place." The pervasiveness of evil and absence of meaning lead to a sense of melancholy, which tends to degenerate into "self-mistrust and self-despair; or . . . suspicion, anxiety, trepidation, fear." When despair becomes overwhelming, there are only three ways to overcome it: death or suicide, flight from the corrupt world, or radical self-transformation. While healthy-minded individuals are once-born, sick souls are twice-born—they must pass through a dark night of the soul to find redemption. One of the most striking examples of a sick soul is someone James strangely never mentions in *Varieties:* Søren Kierkegaard. The titles of Kierkegaard's best-known works disclose the temper of his soul: *Fear and Trembling, The Concept of Dread, The Sickness unto Death.* Since James is convinced that human experience inevitably includes good and evil as well as light and darkness, he argues that "morbid-mindedness ranges over a wider scale of experience." The self, he argues, is always divided and man, therefore, is *Homo Duplex.* The therapeutic function of religion is to unify the divided subject. Though James never admits it, his typology repeats the familiar religious narrative that recounts the movement from original unity (the healthy-minded) through division and opposition (the sick soul) to unity and reconciliation (the twice-born).

As I have noted, James's concentration on experience and preoccupation with description prevented him from working out the far-reaching implications of the varieties of religious experience he identifies. Nearly half a century later, Paul Tillich published a provocative essay entitled "Two Types of Philosophy of Religion," in which he effectively extends James's analysis by explaining its philosophical presuppositions and theological implications. Though he was working in a completely different intellectual tradition with very different interests, the two types of philosophy of religion Tillich defines are strictly parallel to James's two varieties of religious experience. Tillich organizes his analysis around the traditional arguments for the existence of God: the ontological argument and the cosmological argument, which, he maintains, includes the teleological argument. While the ontological argument proceeds from the thought to the being of God, the cosmological approach argues from effect (the existence or design of the world) to God as necessary and sufficient cause. Tillich associates the former type with Augustinianism and the latter with Thomism. "One can distinguish two ways of approaching God: the way of overcoming estrangement and the way of meeting a stranger. In the first way man discovers *himself* when he discovers God; he discovers something from which he is estranged, but from which he never has been and never can be separated. In the second way, man meets a *stranger* when he meets God. The meeting is accidental. Essentially they do not belong to each other."[28] While James focuses on experience, Tillich is preoccupied with knowledge. According to Tillich, the ontological type of philosophy of religion entails the following claims:

1. The knowledge of God is knowledge of truth.
2. The question of God (i.e., truth) presupposes an implicit knowledge of God (i.e., truth).
3. God is Being or the power of Being.
4. Epistemology and ontology are inseparable.
5. Self and God are ultimately identical.

"The Augustinian tradition," Tillich concludes, "can rightly be called mystical, if mysticism is defined as the experience of the identity of subject and object in relation to being itself." If God is Being or, in Tillich's terms, "the power of Being," then everything that exists is, in some way, united with the divine and evil is ultimately unreal. God, in other words, is immanent in self and world.

In the cosmological type, by contrast, God is not Being itself but is *a* being, who is transcendent to, rather than immanent in, the world. The relation between the human and divine, therefore, is mediated or indirect. "For Thomas," Tillich argues, "all this follows from his sense-bound epistemology: 'The human intellect cannot reach by natural virtue the divine substance, because, according to the way of the present life, the cognition of our intellect starts with the senses.' From there we must ascend to God with the help of the category of causality." In the cosmological type, knowledge of God is a posteriori rather than a priori as it is in the ontological type. God or truth, therefore, is the conclusion and not the presupposition of argumentation. Because God is transcendent, human reason alone cannot reach the final truth of the divine. At the limit of human understanding, faith must supplement reason.

While James gives priority to the sick soul over the healthy-minded, Tillich privileges the ontological over the cosmological type. He actually goes so far as to maintain that the cosmological type represents "a destructive cleavage" that establishes oppositions that inevitably lead to human estrangement. Such estrangement or alienation can be overcome only through the recognition of a more primal unity that is always *present* beneath or behind every form of separation. Summarizing this important point, Tillich writes: "The ontological principle in the philosophy of religion may be stated in the following way: *Man is immediately aware of something unconditional which is the prius of the separation and interaction of subject and object, theoretically and practically.*" To overcome the cleavage between the finite and the infinite, it is necessary to return to unity with the divine, which is never really absent. Tillich, like James, revises the biblical narrative by erasing its primal distinction between creator and creature and rewriting Creation, Fall, and Redemption as the movement from unity through opposition to reunion.

When taken together, James's two varieties of religious experience and Tillich's two types of philosophy of religion provide helpful insights for analyzing and organizing particular symbolic networks within, between, and among religious traditions. Though useful for historical purposes, any such twofold typology is, however, finally inadequate for understanding the interrelation of nature, society, and culture in today's culturally pluralistic world. The analyses of James and Tillich must, therefore, be refined and extended in two ways. First, it is necessary to identify and explore a third alternative that has emerged explicitly only recently but that the other two religious frameworks actually presuppose; and second, typological analysis must be recast in terms of schemata as they have been described in our consideration of symbolic networks. James's varieties and Tillich's types tend to be static and, therefore, do not enable us to understand how religious networks adapt and evolve. Furthermore, their influential accounts do not offer a way to articulate the interrelation of elements within a particular symbolic network or the relations between and among different traditions. Schemata, as we have seen, emerge from and adapt to patterns in the stream of experience and coevolve with other schemata. In addition to the monistic and dualistic schemata, it is necessary to include a complex schema. While the monistic type roughly corresponds to James's healthy-mindedness and Tillich's ontological type, the dualistic type is generally equivalent to the sick soul and the cosmological type. Neither monistic nor dualistic schemata, however, illuminate the operational logic of religion in contemporary emerging network culture. In order to define the distinctive contours of these three schemata, I will consider the position of each alternative on six critical issues that grow out of the interplay of God, self, and world in different symbolic networks: the locus of the real, the relation of identity and difference, the source of order, the status of time and history, the relation of self to world, and the prospect of redemption (table 1).

Every religious schema must provide a way to figure the real. It is, therefore, necessary to begin by asking how the real is conceived and where it is located. Is it here or elsewhere? Above or below? Inside or outside? In the past, the present, or the future? In the first religious schema, the real one is always in some way *present* here and now. Since it is not elsewhere, the relation to the real is immediate, implicit, or direct and, thus, requires neither intermediaries nor mediation. Though not always obvious, the real is immanent in natural and historical processes as their generative ground and unifying principle. Appearances to the contrary notwithstanding, difference, diversity, and multiplicity are unreal; an original unity is always antecedent to and a condition of the possibility of all separation and division. Differences once articulated can become oppositions, but the unity grounding them is never lost. In many variations of this schema, primal unity is initially implicit and unfolds gradually. To invoke a familiar metaphor, the oak is in the acorn, or in a more contemporary idiom, temporal development is programmed before it begins. History, then, is an archaeoteleological process in which the beginning comes to full realization at the end. This circularity is captured in the alternating rhythms of the loss and recovery of unity. Though the future often seems uncertain, retrospectively it becomes clear that things could not have been otherwise. Since the real is immanent in nature and history, the self is at home in the universe. The challenge facing individual subjects is not to change themselves or the world but to learn

Table 1. Religious Schemata

	MONISTIC (BOTH/AND)	DUALISTIC (EITHER/OR)	COMPLEX (NEITHER/NOR)
Locus of the real	Present Immanent	Absent Transcendent	Neither absent nor present Neither transcendent nor immanent
Relation of identity and difference	Identity-without-difference Negation epiphenomenal	Identity-in-opposition-to-difference Affirmation-by-negation	Identity-in-difference / difference-in-identity Affirmation of affirmation and negation
Source of order	Implicit Unfolds gradually	External Imposed from without	Emergent Spontaneous self-organization
Status of time and history	Archaeoteleological process	Struggle between closed systems	Interplay of open systems
Relation of self to world	Primordially unified At home in the universe	Primordially divided Estranged from the world as it is	Nodular Infinite restlessness
Possibility of redemption	Realized eschatology Always already redeemed (actual)	Apocalyptic eschatology Redemption certain but in the future (possible)	Emergent creativity (virtual)

to accept what is as what ought to be. This framework implies an ethics of compliance rather than resistance. Forever at one with the real, the self is always already redeemed. This is a realized eschatology in which salvation is at hand here and now.

The second schema is dualistic: the real is not present here and now but is absent or, more precisely, is elsewhere. In theological terms, the real is transcendent. Such transcendence can be expressed spatially or temporally; accordingly, the real can be conceived, on the one hand, as above or below and, on the other hand, as in the past or the future. Such transcendence establishes a foundational opposition between the real and the not-real, which, in turn, grounds a series of related structural oppositions that simultaneously provide order and carry the threat of disorder. At the most rudimentary level, the relation—or nonrelation— between the real and the not-real entails the exclusive logic of either/or in which identity is established by opposition to difference. In contrast to the monistic schema, here differences are not finally identical but are constituted oppositionally and, thus, remain irreducible. The logic of either/or always appears to be precise, and therefore, it seems to be possible to make theoretical and practical distinctions with precision, clarity, and certainty.

Since there is no direct, essential, or implicit association with the real, the relation to and awareness of it are not immediate but must be mediated. Insofar as the religious imagination conceives the real in terms of God, awareness of and relation to it must be given or revealed through intermediaries like prophets, saints, and messiahs or in rituals and oral and written sacred texts. Within this schema, the history of religions is, in large measure, the story of competing narratives about various intermediaries, which are constructed to establish and maintain the relation between the real and the not-real. Though details obviously vary, the binary structure of all such schemes remains the same. Since the real is transcendent rather than immanent, the relation to it is contingent instead of necessary. The difference between the real and everything else tends to lead to the contrast between those who are chosen and those who are not. In other words, the opposition between the transcendent and the immanent translates into intraworldly oppositions between good and evil, believers and nonbelievers, redeemed and condemned, etc.[29] If meaning and order are not intrinsic but are extrinsic, the significance and purpose of things and events can be established only by pointing beyond them. For those with eyes to see, everything becomes a sign referring to a transcendent referent, which secures the foundation of knowledge and basis of action. In an alternative idiom, if one knows the algorithms God prescribes, it is possible to decode the program of both personal and cosmic history.

The logic of either/or leads to closed systems that make negotiation difficult and compromise often impossible. The situation can become perilous when equally self-certain and uncompromising closed systems encounter each other. Though appearing to be radically different, these polar or binary opposites are actually mirror images of each other. The structure of both systems is the same but the signs are reversed: what is positive in one is negative in the other and vice versa. Both sides subscribe to a vision of history as the tale of struggle with the evil Other. As long as the forces of evil—however they are conceived—are not vanquished, things are not as they ought to be. If the real is not fully present here and now, it must be affirmed by negating what currently exists. Individuals and communities find meaning and purpose by participating in the struggle to destroy the darkness of the present age so that the light of a new world order can dawn. The eschaton might be delayed but for true believers there is no doubt it will arrive.

The complex type is the third religious schema. In contrast to the monistic and dualistic types, the real in this case is neither present nor absent; rather, it is irreducibly interstitial or liminal and as such is *virtual*. It is important to understand the precise meaning of *virtual* in this context. The virtual is not simply the possible but is the *matrix* in which possibility and actuality emerge. While the logic of monism is both/and and the logic of dualism is either/or, the logic of complexity is neither/nor. Rather than the synthesis or union of the first and the second, the third schema is the condition of their possibility, which they presuppose but cannot include or comprehend. In this way, the complex schema exposes the inadequacy of every version of monism and dualism. Nothing is either simple or self-identical because everything is codependent and coevolves. Identity and difference, for example, are not oppositional but are thoroughly relational: each is relative to the other, and thus each inhabits and is inhabited by the other. Instead of wrapping identities in a solipsistic shroud, such relativity or, more precisely, *relationalism* draws them out of themselves in a creative play of differences.[30] In this schema, to be is to be related, or in current terms, *to be is to be connected*. Neither self-identical nor oppositional subjectivity is nodular.[31] As the shifting site of multiple interfaces, nodular subjectivity not only screens the sea of information in which it is immersed but is itself a screen displaying what it is and what it is not.

Far from merely possible, imaginary, or unreal, the virtual is the elusive real in and through which everything that exists comes into being and passes away. Always betwixt and between, it is neither immanent nor transcendent—neither here and now nor elsewhere and beyond. To the contrary, the virtual is something like an immanent transcendence, which is inside as an outside that cannot be incorporated. This interior exterior or exterior interior is the source of the endless disruption that keeps complex systems open and makes them subject to constant transformation yet also preserves them from disintegration and simple extinction. Nothing remains stable, secure, or certain; rather than forces to be repressed, instability, insecurity, and uncertainty are the conditions of creativity. Disorder is not the opposite of order but, if it does not lead to systemic collapse, can make new forms of order possible. Such order, therefore, is neither inherent (as in monism) nor imposed from without (as in dualism) but emerges from the ceaseless interplay of interacting elements and agents. Infinite restlessness issues in emergent creativity. Within this schema, the goal is neither to accept what is as what ought to be nor to negate what is in an effort to affirm what ought to be; rather, the aim of life is to embrace the infinitely creative process whose purpose is nothing other than itself. Instead of present or deferred, the end is always emerging by forever withdrawing.

These three schemata bear a complicated relation to time. Though monism, dualism, and complexity develop successively, their relation is not strictly linear. An earlier schema obviously can persist after a later schema emerges. It is, after all, possible to be a committed monist or dualist in an era of complexity. The schemata can, therefore, overlap. More importantly, the third schema is not the culminating synthesis of the other two. The complex schema is the nonsynthetic third, which bends back, though not precisely on itself, to inscribe the margin of difference between monism and dualism. As such, complexity is the matrix in which monism and dualism are figured. In other words, the virtual reality articulated in the third schema is both the result and presupposition, which is not to say foundation, of the first and second stages in a coevolutionary process. As a result of the nonlinearity of this complex structure, the first two schemata are already inscribed through the third before it explicitly emerges. While surely impossible within the framework of linear time, the third schema is nonetheless the after that is before the first and second types. To think after God is to think the after that is forever before us.

These schemata can be used for both synchronic and diachronic analysis. Synchronically, they can provide a taxonomic structure that makes it possible to compare and contrast different symbolic networks within and among religious traditions. Though the variations are multiple, the patterns are similar. In many cases, beliefs and practices in different traditions turn out to be more similar to each other than they are to contrasting versions of their respective traditions. As I have suggested, Evangelical Protestantism and radical Islamism are closer to each other than either is to liberal forms of Christianity or Islam. The schemata can also be deployed diachronically to interpret the historical development of different traditions. By understanding how competing schemata function, it becomes possible to identify the most important factors contributing to cultural evolution and sociopolitical change.

The definition of religion and account of schemata developed in this chapter provide the interpretive framework for the argument developed in the following pages. My aim is both analytic and constructive: first, I seek to show how and why religion continues to play such an important role in the modern and postmodern world, and second, I attempt to provide a more adequate religious vision and ethical framework for negotiating the complexities and contradictions of life at the beginning of the twenty-first century.

CHAPTER TWO

The Protestant Revolution

THE DIVIDED SUBJECT

Modernity is a *theological* invention. In his recent book on the Reformation, Patrick Collinson notes that Thomas Carlyle claimed: "if Luther had not stuck to his guns at the Diet of Worms, where he stood before the Holy Roman emperor and refused to recant ('Here I stand'), there would have been no French Revolution and no America: the principle that inspired those cataclysmic events would have been killed in the womb."[1] Though the notion of history that Carlyle's point represents has lately become suspect, there is no doubt that modernity as it has emerged in the West and spread throughout the world would not be what it is without the Reformation. Indeed, it is not an exaggeration to insist that Luther and the theologians and philosophers who inspired his work (i.e., the Rhineland mystics and medieval nominalists) were actually the first modernists. What began as a theological revolution became a social, political, and economic revolution that continues to transform the world today. The distinctive institutions of the modern world—democracy, the nation-state, and the free market—are inseparable from Protestantism and its history. This is not to imply, of course, that different sociocultural traditions can never become modern; it is, however, to insist that the ongoing interplay between modernity and Westernization would have been impossible apart from the changes the Reformation set in motion. The religious and political conflicts that continue to rend the world today are unintelligible apart from the theological genealogy of modernity. It is, therefore, necessary to extend Max Weber's famous analysis of "the Protestant ethic and the spirit of capitalism" to a consideration of Protestantism and the spirit of globalization.

At the heart of the revolution Luther unleashed lies his radical notion of the self or human subjectivity. His vision grows out of a reinterpretation of the letters of Saint Paul and the theology of Saint Augustine. As we have seen, in any symbolic network, notions of God, self, and world are codependent. In this chapter, I will consider how Luther's refiguring of theology, anthropology, and cosmology prepared the way for what eventually became the modern world. In the next chapter, I will analyze how late-eighteenth- and nineteenth-century theologians, philosophers, poets, and artists directly and indirectly refined and extended the Reformation account of subjectivity in ways that created the conditions for the rise of postmodernism at the end of the twentieth century. In the course of this analysis, it will become clear that the Reformation was, in effect, an information and communications revolution that not only anticipated but actually set in motion developments without which the information and communications revolution sweeping across the globe today would have been impossible.

Beginnings are never precise and inevitably vary with the interpretive schemata with which they are framed. Does modernity begin with the scientific revolution: Copernicus's heliocentrism (1543), Galileo's discovery of sunspots (1612), Newton's law of universal gravitation (1687), or Renaissance humanism (1400–1650)? Or with political revolutions: the American Revolution (1776), the French Revolution (1789), or the Russian Revolution (1917)? Or, perhaps, an artistic revolution: Manet's *Olympia* (1863) or Gropius's Bauhaus (1919)?[2] During the last several decades, cultural critics working in a wide variety of disciplines have repeatedly turned to Heidegger's philosophical account of the rise of modernity for guidance. Like many others, Heidegger associates the advent of modernity with the emergence of modern science and its application in new technologies. What distinguishes his analysis is the claim that science and technology mark the culmination of what he describes as "the western ontotheological tradition." In the course of Western history, Heidegger argues, human beings replace God as the source of creative and destructive power. The work of Descartes marks a decisive turning point in this narrative of human development. Cartesian philosophy effectively reverses the Copernican revolution: whereas Copernicus had displaced man from the center of the universe by discovering that the earth circles the sun, Descartes insisted that everything revolves around man. From this point of view, Heidegger explains, "That which is objective is swallowed up into the immanence of subjectivity."[3] Descartes overcame the doubt created by the advent of the modern world by collapsing truth into the self-certainty of the *ego cogito*. With this inward turn of consciousness, objectivity appears to be constituted by and to exist *for the sake of* subjectivity. Reason, in turn, becomes calculative in science and instrumental in technology. Heidegger identifies the telos of this trajectory as Nietzsche's metaphorical proclamation of the death of God. No longer determined by an Other, man becomes self-determining:

> What is decisive is that man himself expressly takes up this position as one constituted by himself, as he intentionally maintains that it is that taken up by himself, and that he makes it secure as the solid footing for a possible development of humanity. Now for the first time is there any such thing as a "position" of man. Man must depend upon himself the way in which he must take his stand in relation to whatever is objective. There begins that way of being human which means the realm of human capability as a domain given over to measuring and executing, for the purpose of gaining mastery over that which is as a whole.

This will to mastery is most forcefully expressed in Nietzsche's will to power, in which "the will wills itself."[4] In this absolute voluntarism, divine creativity becomes human destructiveness, which, according to Heidegger, ultimately portends nuclear holocaust. Through a paradoxical reversal, the search for security that launched the turn to the subject results in radical insecurity created by what Hegel describes as "the fury of destruction."[5] While Heidegger's analysis is helpful, it is inadequate; though he appreciates the theological stakes of the developments he charts, he does not realize that it was Luther in one of his hymns, rather than Nietzsche, who first declared the death of God. Nietzsche's will to power grows out of the theological voluntarism Luther borrowed from the medieval nominalist William of Ockham and his theological followers at the University of Erfurt. It is, therefore, necessary to extend Heidegger's analysis of the relation between philosophy and the rise of the modern world by tracing its theological roots back to the late Middle Ages and the Reformation.

Whether considered philosophically, theologically, or historically, modernity presupposes self-reflexivity—to be modern, it is necessary to regard oneself as *different* from others who have gone before. The word *modern* derives from the Latin *modo*, which means "just now." As the notion of modernity has developed in the West, it has been constituted not simply by the binary opposition between the modern (present) and the

nonmodern (past) but by a more intricate triadic, or more precisely trinitarian, structure: ancient, medieval, modern. The Middle Ages were not,
of course, the middle for the people who lived through them; rather, they
came to be defined as the middle by those who regarded themselves as
modern. Medieval historian Francis Oakley maintains: "The very idea of
a middle age interposed between the world of classical antiquity and the
dawn of the modern world was ultimately of humanist vintage. What is
lost in simplicity is gained in firmness during the Reformation era, drawing added strength from the Protestant depiction of the thousand years
preceding the advent of Martin Luther as an age of moral turpitude, religious superstition, and untrammeled credulity. Even more clearly than
their humanist predecessors, the reformers saw their own era as one of
revival and restoration, though the restoration this time was not simply
of the arts of learning, and of 'good letters,' but also of the Christian faith
to its original purity."[6] The theological roots of modernity are, however,
even deeper than Oakley realizes. In his *History of Christian Thought*, Paul
Tillich argues that the twelfth-century Italian mystic Joachim of Floris
developed the interpretation of history that formed the background
for most revolutionary movements throughout the Middle Ages as well
as the modern era. Expanding what had come to be known as the "economic" doctrine of the Trinity to form an account of history as a whole,
Joachim identified three overlapping ages or dispensations: the age of
the Father, which runs from Adam to John the Baptist and the birth of
Christ; the age of the Son, which extends from King Uzziah (Isaiah 6)
to 1260 CE; and the age of Spirit, which begins with Benedict and the
founding of monasticism in the sixth century and also ends in 1260 CE.[7]
Though the dates now seem arbitrary and the overlapping of the periods
is confusing, what proved decisive for later developments was the tripartite structure and the overall trajectory of Joachim's schema. Within
this narrative, the long march of history is characterized by the spread
of freedom across the world. While the age of the Father is governed by
the law, in the age of the Son "sacramental reality makes the law unnecessary." The abiding authority of the clergy, however, limits the freedom
of everyone else. The third era—the age of Spirit—marks the culmination of this developmental process: freedom no longer is limited to a few
but now is enjoyed by everyone. As Tillich explains: "The inner part of
this period is freedom, that is, autonomy, not being subject to any more
state or church authorities. For Joachim there is a higher truth than that
of the church, namely, the truth of the Spirit. From this it follows that
the church is relative. It is *inter utrumque*, between both the period of

the Father and the period of Spirit. Its shortcomings are due not only to distortions, but also to its relative validity. In this scheme the church is relativized. Only the third period is absolute; it is not authoritarian any more, but autonomous. Every individual has the divine Spirit within himself."[8] If, as Joachim insists, "every individual has the divine Spirit within himself," then the authority and hence the power of the church is undermined. What Joachim theorized, Luther actualized.

In *The Varieties of Religious Experience*, William James cites Luther and the Protestantism he inspired as paradigms of the sick soul: "In the extreme of melancholy the self that consciously *is* can do absolutely nothing. It is completely bankrupt and without resources, and no works it can accomplish will avail. Redemption from such subjective conditions must be a free gift or nothing, and grace through Christ's accomplished sacrifice is such a gift."

> God, says Luther, is the God of the humble, the miserable, the oppressed, and the desperate, and of those that are brought even to nothing; and his nature is to give sight to the blind, to comfort the brokenhearted, to justify sinners, to save the very desperate and damned. . . . But here lieth the difficulty, that when a man is terrified and cast down, he is so little able to raise himself up again and say, "Now I am bruised and afflicted enough; now it is the time of grace; now it is time to hear Christ."

"Nothing in Catholic theology," James concludes, "has ever spoken to sick souls as straight as this message from Luther's personal experience."[9] As these remarks suggest, Luther's theology is radically existential—it grows out of his tortured personal experience. He did not initially set out to break with the Catholic Church; to the contrary, Luther was a devout monk and a faithful member of the Augustinian order, who thought changes were necessary to strengthen the church. He was, however, torn by psychological conflicts brought about by a profound sense of guilt that grew out of a very complicated relationship with his father.[10] The more tormented Luther's inner turmoil, the more urgent his religious quest became; and yet, the more he tried to fulfill his religious obligations, the less he was able to do so. His sense of personal corruption and impotence increased until he reached what can best be described as the tipping point. Like Paul on the road to Damascus and Augustine in the garden, Luther underwent a transformative experience in the Tower. He was in his early thirties and lecturing on the Psalms at the University of Wittenberg when his life changed radically. In his lectures as well as life,

Luther was preoccupied with the interrelated problems of righteousness and justification and was struggling to come to terms with the opening verses of Psalm 71:

> In thee, O Lord, I have taken refuge;
> never let me be put to shame.
> As thou art righteousness rescue me and save my life;
> hear me and set me free, be a rock for me,
> where I may ever find safety at thy call.

The difficulty Luther faced was that his sense of sin was so deep that he felt there was nothing he could do to fulfill the law, and therefore, salvation seemed impossible. The turning point in his life came when he understood a crucial passage in Paul's Epistle to the Romans in a new way:

> For I am not ashamed of the Gospel. It is the saving power for everyone who has faith—the Jew first, but the Greek also—because here is revealed God's way of righting wrong, a way that starts from faith and ends in faith; as Scripture says, "he shall gain life who is justified through faith." (1:16–17)

Luther's reinterpretation of these verses forms the cornerstone of Reformation theology. Justification, he concludes, comes through faith alone and not, as medieval Catholic theology held, by accumulating merit or by doing good works. Redemption, in other words, is a free *gift* and as such can never be earned. The agent of justification is God, not man, and therefore, human righteousness is passive rather than active. To appreciate the revolutionary implications of Luther's insight, it is necessary to understand the social, political, and cultural context in which it arose.

The dynamics of personal and sociocultural transformation follow the same pattern. As we have discovered, the systems and networks that provide meaning and purpose tend to drift toward disequilibrium as circumstances change. When gradual modifications of organizational structures are no longer adequate for effective adaptation, a phase shift occurs and new organizing schemata emerge. As a result of the complexity and nonlinearity of emergent systems, once networks reach the condition of self-organized criticality, an event can have effects disproportionate to its ostensible cause. Just as a seemingly minor event can have major consequences in an individual's life, so the experience of a single person can be amplified through positive feedback loops until it leads to global transformations. What made Luther's ideas resonate at the time was the fact that his experience embodied the uncertainties and anxieties of his era. As Tillich observes, "toward the end of the Middle Ages the anxiety of guilt and condemnation was decisive. If one period deserves the name of the 'age of anxiety' it is the pre-Reformation and Reformation. The anxiety of condemnation symbolized as the 'wrath of God' and intensified by the imagery of hell and purgatory drove people of the late Middle Ages to try various means of assuaging their anxiety. . . . In short they asked themselves ceaselessly: How can I appease the wrath of God, how can I attain divine mercy, the forgiveness of sin?"[11] This anxiety grew out of the insecurity and uncertainty that resulted from the dissolution of the social structure, ecclesiastical order, and theological synthesis that had developed in the High Middle Ages. With the fall of Rome in 410 and end of the empire at the hands of Odoacer and his barbarian confederacy in 476, Europe was thrust into turmoil for several centuries. The void created by this political defeat created the opportunity for the church to expand and consolidate its power.

> As a result, by the time of the emperor Charlemagne in the early ninth century, there had emerged in the West a single public society— church, empire, Christian commonwealth, call it what you will—a universal commonwealth that was neither voluntary nor private. To that commonwealth all Europeans, even after the collapse of the Carolingian Empire, felt they belonged. And the idea of a universal Christian commonwealth coterminous with Christendom, sustained in theory by the memories of ancient Rome and guaranteed in practice by the universal and international character of the ecclesiastical structure itself, lingered long after the appearance of the national monarchies, until, with the advent of the Protestant Reformation, the unity of that ecclesiastical structure was itself finally destroyed.[12]

At the height of the church's power in the eleventh century, the pope declared himself the true emperor whose power did not depend on secular authorities. By claiming the title *pontifex maximus*, the bishop of Rome assumed the imperial mantle that can be traced back to Caesar Augustus. In the centuries preceding the Reformation, "the papacy could make a credible claim to have reconstituted and prolonged, in its own attenuated, religiopolitical version, the universal empire that it was the glory of Rome to have created."[13]

While the reach of the church was expanding, the face of Europe was changing. As advances in agricultural technology increased the productivity of medieval farming significantly, manors were able to move from operating at a subsistence level to producing a surplus that could be marketed. With more food of better quality available, the population began to increase; between 1000 and 1250 the number of people living in Europe doubled. Urban populations grew and there was a revitalization of industry and commerce. When trade routes again opened, rural life and parochialism started to give way to city dwelling and cosmopolitanism. These developments triggered a remarkable intellectual revival, which began around 1000. Learning migrated from schools associated with local cathedrals to new universities established in major urban centers. Changing circumstances brought new challenges as well as opportunities. Nowhere was this more apparent than in theology.

These events did not, of course, take place in a vacuum. Ecclesiastical and theological developments were closely related to the emergence of European identity, which, in turn, was bound up with the encounter with Islam. Having reached Gibraltar by the early eighth century, Islam continued to expand northward throughout the Iberian Peninsula until it reached as far as Toledo and beyond. At the same time, Mohammedan tribes tightened their grip on portions of what had been the Eastern Empire. Throughout the early Middle Ages, Christians from the West regularly made pilgrimages to the Holy Land to pray at the Holy Sepulcher. In 1009 Hakem, the Fatimid caliph of Egypt, without warning ordered the destruction of the Holy Sepulcher and all Christian buildings in Jerusalem. This religious conflict and social unrest only increased the desire of Western Christians to travel to Jerusalem, which had been under Muslim control since the eighth century. Bishops, princes, and knights as well as thousands of people from lower social classes undertook the arduous journey to the Holy Land. When the Seljuk Turks took over Jerusalem in 1070, it became apparent that the entire Eastern Empire faced the possibility of falling under Muslim control. While tensions and intermittent conflicts between Eastern and Western Christendom delayed efforts to counter this expansion, the West eventually responded to the eastern emperor's request for aid from the pope. The Reconquista began in Iberia well before the retaking of Toledo in 1085 but did not end until Granada was returned to Christian rule in 1492. The early success in Toledo encouraged efforts to recapture major Christian centers in the East. While it is generally acknowledged that the First Crusade was undertaken in 1095 to regain control of the Holy Sepulcher and the last of eight Crusades began in 1270 under the direction of Saint Louis, the Crusades actually continued until the end of the seventeenth century. Though the motives of crusaders were not merely religious, there is no doubt that these conflicts played a major role in shaping Europe's sense of itself as Christian. The ramifications of these developments are still being felt today.

The encounter between Christendom and Islam had a significant impact on Western philosophy and Christian theology. When Muslims migrated to Spain, they brought with them a wealth of philosophical, theological, and literary materials. Many of these texts were Arabic translations of Greek philosophy and early Christian writings, which were often accompanied by extensive commentaries in Arabic. After being rendered into Latin, these works were distributed throughout the West. The most important writer to be rediscovered during this period was Aristotle. As a result of Augustine's enormous influence, early Christian theology had drawn its philosophical inspiration almost entirely from Plato and Neoplatonism. In the East, by contrast, Arabic philosophers took Aristotle as their guide. The recovery of Aristotle sent shockwaves through European intellectual communities. Aristotle's writings provided a sophisticated and highly coherent vision of God, self, and world that differed significantly from what had become traditional Christian wisdom. While many rejected Aristotle and forcefully reasserted different versions of Christian Platonism, others sought to refigure Christian doctrines in Aristotelian terms. Thomas Aquinas was the most influential person to accept the challenge of rethinking traditional theology in relation to Aristotle's works.

By bringing together Christian doctrine and Aristotelian philosophy, Aquinas created an intellectual synthesis that has often been described as the theological counterpart of the Gothic cathedral. Reason was his guide, Aristotelian logic his method. Thomas's theological edifice rests upon the fundamental distinction between the natural and the supernatural, which he elaborates through a series of complementary binaries: nature/grace, reason/faith, philosophy/theology, natural virtues/theological virtues, and state/church. For Thomas, these distinctions never become oppositions; in every case, the latter completes and fulfills, without destroying, the former. The Thomistic synthesis, however, points in two opposite directions: on the one hand, the natural domain is understood as distinct from but subordinate to the supernatural, and on the other hand, the natural realm in all of its manifestations is characterized by an autonomy that eventually leads to its independence from the supernatural. In this way, the formation of the medieval synthesis already marks the beginning of its dissolution, which, in turn, prepares the way for modernity and eventually postmodernity.

In my analysis of religious networks, I argued that images of God, self, and world are codependent. I also noted that there are two primary theistic models of God—one in which God's reason governs God's will and the other in which divine will is antecedent to and has priority over divine reason. Aquinas provides the clearest example of the former alternative in the history of Western theology. His God is always reasonable and never arbitrary; indeed, for Aquinas, it is unthinkable for God to act in an irrational way. He makes this all-important point concisely in his *Summa Theologica*: "There is will in God, just as there is intellect: since will follows upon the intellect." Because God's will is informed by his reason (or intellect), the world is always rational. "Now God is the cause of all things by His intellect," Aquinas explains, "and therefore it is necessary that the exemplar of every effect should pre-exist in Him, as is clear from what has gone before. Hence, the exemplar of the order of things ordered towards an end is, properly speaking, providence." In brief, Aquinas concludes: "*Providence is the divine reason itself, which seated in the Supreme Ruler, disposes all things.*"[14]

The world, which is rationally created and governed, is organized hierarchically. Human being is located between spiritual beings known as angels and the natural domain, which includes animals, plants, and inorganic matter. Though comprised of body (matter) and soul (spirit), man, like God, is essentially rational: "The difference that constitutes man is rational, which is said of man because of his rational intellectual principle. Therefore the intellectual principle is the form of man."[15] While never overlooking the role of volition in human being, man, who is made in God's image, should always allow reason to govern his will. Inasmuch as man is essentially rational, the proper telos of his life is the knowledge of God. The free exercise of human reason is necessary but not sufficient for salvation. Writing at the height of the church's power, Aquinas argues that revealed knowledge, which must supplement the natural knowledge of God, is available only through participation in Catholic rituals. Since grace must be added to nature for renewal to be complete, salvation depends upon membership in the true Christian community. More specifically, grace is mediated to individuals through the channels of the sacraments administered by official representatives of the church. The efficacy of the sacraments depends upon the office rather than the person; that is, it is objective and not subjective. The sacrament necessary for salvation is Baptism, which washes away original sin. This ritual cleansing prepares the believer for the Eucharist, which, according to the doctrine of transubstantiation, allows one to participate in the ritual repetition of Christ's redemptive sacrifice. Within this schema, the individual's relation to God is never direct but is always mediated by the church hierarchy. As we will see in more detail below, Luther called into question this principle, which was the foundation of the church's power.

Aquinas's rational and systematic theology seemed perfectly consistent with an orderly world, and thus, his theological vision provided a schema that lent life meaning and purpose for many people in the High Middle Ages. By the fourteenth century, however, natural, social, and religious factors intersected to upset the medieval equilibrium and push Europe toward the edge of chaos. In the middle of the fourteenth century, a pandemic of the bubonic plague, or Black Death, swept across Europe killing at least twenty-five million people. The medieval history of the plague offers a cautionary tale about the impact of climate change in an era of globalization. The Black Death appears to have originated on the Central Asian steppe and spread to Europe with unexpected speed. In anticipation of issues considered in the final chapter, it is important to note that historians and scientists now believe that a temperature increase of approximately one degree Celsius resulted in "a series of ecological upheavals—storms, floods and earthquakes—and these disturbances may have forced the rodents out of their holes and into contact with humans."[16] The plague traveled by land along trade routes and by sea to ports along the Mediterranean coast. By 1348, it had reached England, and by 1349 it extended as far as Scandinavia, bringing extraordinary devastation in its wake. Burgeoning cities were suddenly decimated, and the fabric of society began to unravel. Agriculture, manufacturing, and trade were disrupted and universities shut down. As the number of workers decreased, the value of their labor increased. The plague, in other words, created a labor shortage that contributed to the breakdown of feudalism. When manors started to compete for serfs, workers were able to sell their services to the highest bidder. Individuals were no longer members of a secure hierarchical structure but were thrown back on their own resources. Greater freedom and increased mobility brought more uncertainty and insecurity. By the middle of the fourteenth century, the world no longer seemed as rational and orderly as Aquinas had assumed, and people were searching for new ways to make sense of life.

Just when the church was needed most, it was embroiled in internal conflicts that diminished its authority. During the Great Schism (1378–1417), two and for a while three men claimed to be pope. Problems were compounded because the removal of the Holy See from Rome to Avignon created suspicions about the independence of the papacy. Though often overlooked, these developments contributed to the rise of the nation-state. In many cases, secular rulers, who sought to wrest control from the church, favored national churches rather than the so-called church universal, over which they had no power. Rome could claim universal jurisdiction more easily than Avignon, which obviously meant French rule of the church. But the church's sojourn in Avignon broke the spell of its universal authority even after the pope returned to Rome. In addition to these political difficulties, financial pressures resulting from, inter alia, lavish spending during the church's "Babylonian Captivity" led to increased taxation and burdensome schemes designed to generate more revenue. As abuses became excessive, calls for reform first arose within monastic orders; Franciscans, who were devoted to poverty, and Augustinians, who counted Luther among their ranks, urged the church to mend its ways.[17] John Wyclif in England and John Hus in Bohemia openly resisted the centralized authority of the pope and the onerous power of Rome. Calls for reform both contributed to and were fueled by nascent nationalism across the continent.

By the time Luther nailed his Ninety-five Theses, entitled "Disputation on the Power and Efficacy of Indulgences," on the door of Castle Church in Wittenberg on October 31, 1517, there was a widespread recognition of the urgent need for reform.[18] Luther's theses were not necessarily revolutionary and were not intended to promote a break with the church. But an unexpected development, whose far-reaching significance only became evident retrospectively, transformed a local dispute into a global event. Printed copies of the Ninety-five Theses in Latin and German quickly spread throughout Germany and triggered a pamphlet war between Dominican and Augustinian theologians. Pope Leo initially saw the dispute as a local matter and charged the parties to settle the issue at a meeting in Heidelberg in 1518. But efforts to find a solution failed and the conflict only deepened. While Luther was preoccupied with the issue of grace, his opponents shifted the debate to the question of papal authority. This was a fateful development that made Luther's conflict with Rome all but inevitable. A series of increasingly contentious encounters culminated at the University of Leipzig in 1519, when Luther debated Johann Eck, who was at the time the most important theologian in central Europe. Eck outmaneuvered his opponent by getting Luther to admit that many of the beliefs of Hus were "completely evangelical and Christian."[19] Hus, who had been condemned as a heretic by the Council of Constance, was burned at the stake in 1415. One year after his debate with Eck, Luther himself was condemned for heresy by a papal bull, which he defiantly burnt in front of the gates of Wittenberg. The longer the controversy about papal and ecclesiastical power continued, the firmer Luther's position became, until he declared that both popes and councils could err. When he refused to recant at the Diet of Worms in 1521, the break with Rome became irreversible.

If reform was in the air throughout Europe, why did Luther rather than one of his predecessors become a revolutionary figure? What made Luther so influential was his recognition that the critical issues were not merely ecclesiastical and political but, more importantly, doctrinal and theological. For Luther, theological doctrines were deeply existential rather than merely scholastic abstractions. The personal crisis out of which his theology grew was a direct reflection of the social crisis of the time. When Luther spoke, others heard their own anxieties expressed. His dark night of the soul articulated the pervasive sense that things were falling apart and apocalyptic change was imminent. In his effort to make sense of his own experience by refiguring Paul and Augustine, Luther created a new schema that allowed people to comprehend and negotiate a world that seemed to be slipping toward chaos. In the process he discovered or, more precisely, invented the modern subject.

In formulating a new theological anthropology, Luther brought together two apparently contradictory strands in medieval theology: mysticism and nominalism. Though both traditions insist on the direct (i.e., unmediated) relation between God and self, they differ on the role of the will in religious experience. While the mystics who interested Luther insisted on a radical passivity that tends toward a monistic identification of the human and divine, nominalists argued for a radical voluntarism that leads to the dualism between God and self/world. These two trajectories intersect to create the contradictions and paradoxes characteristic of what eventually becomes modern subjectivity.

The widespread influence of Thomistic rationalism should not obscure the importance of Christian mysticism during the Middle Ages. It is possible to identify three strands of mysticism, each of which is associated with the faculties of affection, cognition, or volition, respectively. For mystics like Bernard of Clairvaux and Saint Francis of Assisi, the relation to God was primarily a matter of sentiment or the heart. Pious feelings issue in devotional activity and practical service. The Victorites Hugh and Richard, by contrast, developed a speculative mysticism in which the ascent to God passes through three stages: purgation, illumination, and union. The classic work of speculative mysticism is Saint Bonaventure's *Itinerarium Mentis in Deum*, in which the devotee

starts with an immediate awareness of God in the outer world and proceeds first to the innate knowledge of truth, beauty, and goodness and
then beyond to the illumination of the intellect by God, who is Truth
itself, Beauty itself, and Goodness itself. While Bonaventure's sensibility
is obviously very different from that of Aquinas, his vision is, in the final
analysis, reconcilable with Thomistic rationalism. For both, the goal of
life is the knowledge of God. This is not the case for voluntaristic mystics,
who emerged during the fourteenth century. In 1374, Gerhard Groote, the
son of a prosperous merchant living in Deventer, Holland, underwent a
conversion experience and began preaching throughout the Low Countries. His ministry eventually led to a movement known as the Devotio
Moderna, which anticipated many of Luther's criticisms of the church.
More important, Groote translated parts of the Bible into the vernacular
and encouraged laypeople to read it. He also urged people to cultivate a
more personal relationship to God by imitating Christ. Groote's followers formed the Brethren of the Common Life and carried his message
throughout Germany and as far as Poland. Through practical activities
of humble service to others, they sought personal union with God. Luther was aware of the work of the Brethren and was influenced by some
of the ideas included in the most important work produced by this
movement—The Imitation of Christ, traditionally attributed to Thomas à
Kempis and first published anonymously in 1418.

Around the same time, a distinctive form of mysticism began to
flourish in the Rhineland area of Germany. The most influential of these
mystics were Meister Eckhart, Jan van Ruysbroeck, and John Tauler (to
whom Luther was most attracted). Though differing in many ways, the
Rhineland mystics shared the belief that human beings have an immediate relation to God that can be discovered only by renouncing one's
will. This is an unusual kind of voluntarism in which the will is used to
overcome the will through the deliberate cultivation of a radical passivity in which God and man finally become one. Eckhart and Tauler used
the term Gelassenheit, which Heidegger later appropriated, to describe
the letting go of the will necessary for (re)union with God.[20] Rather than
knowledge, the goal of human striving is theosis, that is, the absorption
of the subject into the groundless abyss of divine being. The use of the
will to overcome the will is something like an existential enactment of
negative theology in which God is affirmed through the process of negation or, in this case, self-negation. While always remaining a thoroughgoing dualist who rejected every form of monism, Luther accepted
Tauler's insistence that God is all and man is nothing. In Luther's the-

ology, the *Abgrund* from which all emerges and to which all returns is refigured dualistically as God's omnipotent will. He develops his argument by drawing on the theological voluntarism of William of Ockham as elaborated by Gabriel Biel, whose students were Luther's teachers at the University of Erfurt.

In contrast to Aquinas, for whom God's will is always guided by his reason, Ockham argues that God's will is prior to and determinative of divine reason. With this seemingly simple reversal, Ockham brought about a theological revolution that simultaneously reflected and promoted the dissolution of the medieval synthesis, thereby preparing the way for both modernity and postmodernity. To understand the far-reaching implications of this often-overlooked figure, it is necessary to consider the interplay of the notions of God, self, and world in nominalist philosophy and theology.

For Ockham, God is above all else omnipotent will—he is absolutely free and as such is bound by nothing, not even divine reason. God, in other words, is free to act in ways that sometimes seem arbitrary and often remain incomprehensible. Within this theological schema, the ground of the universe is the productive will of God, and existence is his unfathomable gift. Not precisely irrational, the will of God is the condition of the possibility of reason as well as unreason and as such is finally unknowable. Faith, therefore, cannot be a matter of knowledge; indeed, one must believe *in spite of*, not *because of*, reason. If the universe (or the world) is the product of God's creative will, unguided by the divine Logos, the order of things is contingent or perhaps even arbitrary. Since the divine will is constantly active, there can be no certainty about the continuation or stability of the cosmic order. God can always undo what he has done, and thus, there can be no final certainty or security in the world. In an effort to avoid this frightful prospect without forsaking his radical voluntarism, Ockham distinguishes between God's *potentia absoluta* (absolute power) and *potentia ordinata* (ordained power). While God has the absolute power to do anything that is not self-contradictory, he freely chooses to limit himself by ordaining a particular order for the world. In different terms, divine will posits the codes by which the world is ordered and establishes the rules by which it operates; these codes and rules, however, are not themselves determined by any code or rule. Every worldly structure, therefore, presupposes something it can neither include nor exclude. It is important to note that this voluntaristic ontology leads to an empirical epistemology. Since whatever exists depends upon God's free will, knowledge must be a posteriori and inductive rather than a priori and deductive. The only way to know anything about the world is to begin with sense experience. Such knowledge, however, always remains incomplete because it is ultimately "grounded" in the abyss of divine freedom.

Ockham's anthropology is a mirror image of his theology and, accordingly, has two fundamental tenets: first, the anteriority and priority of the singular individual over the social group and, second, the freedom and responsibility of every individual subject. His position on these issues led to his most devastating critique of medieval theology and ecclesiology. The issue over which Ockham split with his predecessors is the seemingly inconsequential question of the status of universal terms. For scholastic theology, the universal idea or essence is ontologically more real than the individual and epistemologically truer than particular empirical experiences. According to this doctrine, which is known as realism, humanity, for example, is essential, and individual human beings exist only by virtue of their "participation" in the antecedent universal. Exercising his fabled razor, Ockham rejects realism and insists that universal terms are merely *names,* which are heuristic fictions useful for ordering the world and organizing experience, but which are not real in any ontological sense. This position eventually came to be known as nominalism (from Latin *nomen,* "name"). For nominalists, only individuals are real. In the case of human beings, individuals are not constituted by any universal idea or atemporal essence but form themselves historically through their own free decisions. The defining characteristics of human selfhood are individuality, freedom, and responsibility. According to nominalism, the whole, up to and including the human race, is nothing more than the sum of all the individuals that make it up.

Finally, Ockham's nominalism entails a new understanding of language and, most important, of the relation between words and things. Insofar as language is general, if not universal, and subjects as well as objects are singular, existing entities as such cannot as such be represented linguistically. Words and things fall apart, leaving us caught in a linguistic labyrinth from which there is no exit. In semiotic terms, signifiers, which appear to point to independent signifieds, actually refer to other signifiers. As linguistic beings, we traffic in signs, which do not refer to things but are signs of other signs. While appearing to represent the world, language is a play of signs unanchored by knowable referents. This web is not, however, seamless, because it presupposes as a condition of its possibility something that cannot be represented (i.e., the originary will of God). The most philosophically astute interpretation of Ockham's theology is a book entitled *Guillaume d'Ockham: Le sin-*

gulier, which was published by Jacques Derrida's son under the pseud-
onym Pierre Alféri. Ockham's analysis of language, he argues, exposes
the "realities" of metaphysics to be phantoms. Since this argument is
important not only for interpreting Ockham but also for understanding
postmodernism, I quote at length.

> So, what is the consistency of metaphysics? The thesis, which seems
> to be Ockham's and initially was very discretely publicized, is particu-
> larly remarkable. First of all, it must be noted that, if we consider the
> occurrences in the texts, metaphysics is like a ghost or phantom [*un
> fantôme*] in Ockham's work. . . . Indeed, what can be said about being?
> The transcendental extension of being merges with the uses of "is." If
> we disregard the differences between these uses, being is then univocal
> but undetermined; if we take them into account, it is then determined
> but equivocal. Among the numerous differences, the most striking
> is the one that runs between the use of "is" in which it is a question
> of the properties of *signs as signs* or the one in which it is a question of
> the properties of *things as things*. In the "Roses *are* red" and "The word
> 'rose' *is* universal," the verb "to be" does not mean the same thing.
> In the first case, one speaks in ordinary language, and what one says
> stems from empirical knowledge; while in the second case, one speaks
> in a metalanguage (indicated by the quotation marks [around 'rose']),
> and what is stated arises from a logical or a semiological knowledge.
> Yet, metaphysical discourse keeps on defying this opposition and tries
> to go beyond it. Thus, some sentences are typical of the discourse of
> metaphysics as for instance "White is an accident," "The animal is a
> genre/gender," "Being rational is man's difference," or, to quote Hegel,
> "The animal's death is the passage to genre/gender." These are proposi-
> tions in which, to say it neutrally, beings are designated in their associa-
> tion with abstract terms. But more precisely, abstract terms such as "ac-
> cident," "genre/gender," "species," or "difference" refer to the concepts'
> properties or to the signs as signs. They make it possible to define the
> referential play of the signs "white," "animal," "man," or "rational" in a
> metalanguage: this is the work of logic, which is above all a semiology.
> In this sense, *metaphysics is strictly and unilaterally subordinated to logic*.
> To talk about the use of "is" in such statements is equivalent to talk-
> ing about the referential play of the signs and of its rules, in the meta-
> language of logic.[21]

As this remarkable analysis suggests, Ockham's deconstruction of metaphysics leads to an understanding of language as an ungrounded play of
signs. Words are traces of what can never be represented and, as such, re-

main ghosts or phantoms of a real that has always already slipped away and yet is not precisely absent.[22]

Though the importance of his work is rarely acknowledged, many of the themes Ockham identified have been enormously influential throughout the Western tradition. In view of the lasting significance of his work, it is helpful to summarize the critical points in his schema.

1. Only individuals are real. God and self as well as all the entities in the world, therefore, must be individuals.
2. Groups and societies emerge from the interactions among separate individuals.
3. Reason and faith are not complementary but are opposites. God is a *deus absconditus,* who can never be fully fathomed. Since there can be no knowledge of God, faith and uncertainty are inseparable.
4. Knowledge is empirical and a posteriori, and reason, therefore, is inductive.
5. The order of the world as well as thought is contingent rather than necessary. The laws of nature and principles of thought are posited by a reality that can never be adequately comprehended.
6. Divine will is the groundless ground of all existence. This *Abgrund* is neither simply immanent nor transcendent and, thus, is neither exactly present nor absent.
7. Existence is an incomprehensible gift of an Other whose abiding distance is incalculable.

In the course of the following chapters, the far-reaching implications of these insights will become increasingly clear. The Reformation Luther initiated and Calvin extended would have been impossible without Ockham's account of the interrelation of God's omnipotent will and the freedom and responsibility of the individual person. Less obvious but no less important, Ockham's empiricism prepares the way for modern science; his voluntarism points toward nineteenth-century romanticism as well as Nietzsche's will to power and Freud's and Lacan's unconscious; and his linguistic theories anticipate both British analytic philosophy and recent Continental semiology and poststructuralism.

Though Ockham's philosophy as it was developed by his followers was not reassuring, Luther recognized that it effectively expressed the inescapable uncertainties and anxieties of life in the late Middle Ages. Faced by instability and dissolution without, Luther turned inward in search of certainty and security. But his inner world proved just as confusing as the outer world; as we have seen, Luther was wracked by doubt and plagued by a profound sense of guilt. According to the medieval schema in which he had been schooled, reason and free will are necessary but insufficient for salvation. They could take a person so far but then had to be supplemented by revelation and faith, which were mediated by the church through the teaching of scripture by the magisterium of the church. In Luther's experience, however, the effort to fulfill the law only exposed the impossibility of a guilty sinner's ever doing so. Like a diseased tree that cannot bear healthy fruit, a corrupt individual cannot accomplish good deeds. Luther's personal experience drove him to distinguish between the civil and theological uses of the law. Since all human beings are sinners, the maintenance of social order requires civil law, which is universally binding. The theological use of the law, by contrast, involves the salvation of the individual rather than the management of life in this world. Though salvation is a free gift of God and as such cannot be earned through human striving, the will does have some role to play in the salvific process. The theological use of the law discloses the contradiction at the heart of human existence and thereby reveals the necessity of divine grace for redemption. Since the very effort to fulfill the law discloses the inability to do so, the law reveals that *I am not what I ought to be* and *I am what I ought not to be*. This experience is not merely negative, because it is the *praeparatio Evangelica* without which grace is impossible. Only when I realize that I can do nothing by myself do I become open to the possibility of grace. In this experience, the positive does not simply replace the negative but arises in and through the process of self-negation in which the subject apprehends itself as inwardly divided.[23]

I have noted that the key to Reformation theology is Luther's reinterpretation of Paul's notion of justification presented in Romans 1:17. In later years, Luther commented on the implications of his insight: "At last, God being merciful, as I thought about it day and night, I noticed the context of the words [Romans 1:17], namely, 'The justice of God is revealed in it; as it is written, the just shall live by faith.' Then and there, I began to understand the justice of God as that by which the righteous man lives by the gift of God, namely, by faith, and this sentence 'The justice of God is revealed in the Gospel' to be the passive justice with which the merciful God justifies us by faith, as it is written: 'The just lives by faith.'"[24] Luther's doctrine of salvation turns upon his distinction between active and passive righteousness. While active righteousness requires the fulfillment of the law, passive righteousness is a free gift from God. This interpretation of justification by faith alone brings together the voluntary passivity of the Rhineland mystics with the theological voluntarism of nominalist theology. Bound by self-incurred sin, nothing we do merits justification; if redemption occurs, it is the result of God's grace, that is, his *free* activity.

> But this most excellent righteousness, of faith I mean (which God through Christ, without works, imputeth unto us), is neither political nor ceremonial, nor the righteousness of God's law, nor consisteth in our works, but is clean contrary: that is to say, a mere passive righteousness, as the other above are active. For in this we work nothing, we render nothing unto God, but only we receive and suffer another to work in us, that is to say, God. Therefore it seemeth good unto me to call this righteousness of faith or Christian righteousness, the passive righteousness.[25]

Human beings can receive such righteousness because the forgiveness of sins has been accomplished once and for all by the sufferings of Christ. Through Christ, God establishes a *personal* relationship with each individual in which sins are forgiven by *imputing* Christ's righteousness to the sinner. The notion of imputed righteousness lies at the heart of Luther's theology. A person never becomes righteous in himself or herself but can only hope to become a forgiven sinner. "Thus a Christian man," Luther concludes, "is both righteous and sinner, holy and profane, an enemy of God and yet a child of God."[26] The Christian, in other words, is *simul iustus et peccator*—at the same time justified and sinner. So understood, the justified sinner is, in James's terms, *homo duplex*. Within Luther's schema, this belief is utterly paradoxical, and as such it cannot be established by rational argument but must be held against reason's protest.

With this notion of the divided subject, Luther identifies what eventually becomes the modern self. To understand what makes Luther's theology so revolutionary, it is necessary to examine the far-reaching implications of his account of subjectivity. First and foremost, faith is a *personal* relationship between an *individual* self and the *individual* God (*ens singularissimum*). The relation to God, therefore, does not need to be mediated by the church hierarchy of pope, bishops, and priests but can be direct. In contemporary terms drawn from theories of business management, Luther's soteriology does away with the middleman, or *disintermediates* the church, thereby undercutting its power. Never subject to ecclesiastical rules and regulations, salvation is a function of the absolute will of God, which is grounded in nothing other than itself.[27] Rather than depending on the authority and rituals of the church, God works through his Word, which is present in but not limited to scripture and sermon. In contrast to later Protestant scholastics and today's Fundamentalists, who tend to subscribe to biblical literalism, Luther never limits the freedom of God by restricting divine activity to the purportedly literal words of scripture. God acts whenever, wherever, and however he wills—where the Spirit is active, the Word is present. Bound by neither church nor book, God can act through anyone or anything. As a result of God's freedom, the priesthood is not limited to the ecclesiastical hierarchy but can extend to anyone. This belief is the basis of the Protestant doctrine of "the priesthood of all believers."

The relation to God is not only individual but also *private* or subjective. One of the distinguishing features of Luther's thought is its thoroughgoing dualism. The theological opposition between transcendence and immanence is reflected in the anthropological opposition between interiority and exteriority. The more deeply the self plumbs its inward depths, the more paradoxical subjectivity becomes. In contrast to Descartes's turn to the subject, which issues in the transparency of the ego and the lucidity of self-consciousness, Luther's inward turn leads to a contradictory subject that is irreducibly obscure. Far from calling faith into question, this obscurity makes it unavoidable. No one understood this aspect of Luther's theological anthropology better than Kierkegaard. The paradoxical subject of faith reflects the Absolute Paradox, which is its object: just as Jesus Christ is fully man and fully God, so the believer is simultaneously sinner and justified. In the moment of faith, the believer confesses: *I am what I am not.* This claim can be read in two ways: first, through my free actions, I have sinned, and therefore, I am not actually what I am essentially; and second, though I am a sinner, nevertheless I am justified. There are no outward signs or objective criteria by which to verify these beliefs.

While Kierkegaard captured the essence of Lutheran faith in his well-known dictum "truth is subjectivity," it was Luther's other major modern heir who first identified this critical principle in Lutheran theology. In his *Philosophy of History*, Hegel explains the importance of the Reformation for "the modern time":

> While the individual knows that he is filled with the Divine Spirit, all the relations that sprang from that vitiating element of externality . . . are *ipso facto* abrogated: there is no longer a distinction between priests and laymen; we no longer find one class in possession of the substance of Truth, as of all spiritual and temporal treasures of the church; but the heart—the emotional part of man's Spiri-

tual nature—is recognized as that which can and ought to come into possession of the Truth; and this subjectivity is the common property of *all mankind*. Each has to accomplish the work of reconciliation in his own soul. Subjective Spirit has to receive the Spirit of Truth into itself, and give it a dwelling place there.[28]

If truth is subjectivity, then subjectivity is truth. The insights of Hegel and Kierkegaard suggest that the reduction of truth to (self-)certainty does not begin with Cartesian rationalism as Heidegger insists. Rather, it was Luther who discovered the subjectivity of truth and truth of subjectivity in the inner paradoxes and contradictions of a self that is never simply itself but is always at the same time something other than what it is. This divided self becomes the infinitely restless subject of modernity. Even though Lutheran subjectivity is inseparable from divine "altarity"[29] and, therefore, remains inwardly heteronymous, this inward turn eventually leads to the self-legislating autonomous subject without which the political revolutions of the modern era would have been impossible.

A final aspect of Lutheran theology proved decisive for later developments. Luther's insistent dualism leads to his doctrine of two kingdoms: the kingdom of God and the kingdom of the world. This polarity is closer to Augustine's opposition between the City of God and the City of Man than it is to Joachim's tripartite structure and its progressive interpretation of history. Since the world is created but fallen, human beings must live simultaneously *coram mundo* and *coram Deo*. At times this dualism approaches a Manichaean struggle between God and the devil, which Luther describes in graphic language calculated for its rhetorical effect: "Thanks be to the good God, who can so make use of the Devil and his wickedness, that it must all serve for our good; otherwise (were it up to his wicked will) he would quickly slaughter us with his knife, and stink us and stab us with his dung. But now God takes him into His hand and says: 'Devil, you are indeed a murderer and a wicked spirit, but I will use you for my purpose, and all that depends on you, shall be my manure-dung for my beloved vineyard.'" Nowhere is the devil more cunning than in his use of money as a seductive lure for those whose faith is weak. "Money," Luther preaches, "is the word of the Devil, through which he creates all things the way God created through the true word." What most disturbed Luther about the church of his day was its acceptance of and accommodation with the corruption and materialism of nascent capitalism. He goes so far as to charge: "the God of the Papists is Mammon."[30] If money is the instrument of the devil, the pope is an agent of Satan. The material excesses of the medieval papacy led to financial improprieties that were indefensible in the eyes of the young Augustinian monk. Money was always a theological issue for Luther. His attack on the sale of indulgences involves an alternative interpretation of the economy of salvation. In the most memorable of the Ninety-five Theses, Luther declares: "There is no divine authority for preaching that the soul flies out of purgatory immediately the money clinks in the bottom of the chest."[31] The unholy alliance between church and capital was a sign that the time for a radical transformation of both church and society had arrived.

Appearances to the contrary notwithstanding, Luther's relation to the world actually remained thoroughly ambivalent. No matter how powerful the forces of darkness become, he insists that Christians still bear responsibilities for life in the world. In some ways Luther's attitude toward the world was more positive than medieval Catholicism's subordination of the secular to the sacred.[32] This can be seen in two of the most significant changes he introduced. First, as I have noted, Luther affirmed the priesthood of all believers. Since Spirit moves where it will, God can speak through anybody. This pivotal doctrine leads to what can best be described as the *deregulation* and *decentralization* first of religious and eventually of political authority. No longer trickling from the top down in a hierarchical structure, authority now is distributed laterally, as it were, and emerges from the bottom up. This structural transformation, as we will see below, is inseparable from the sixteenth-century information and communications revolution, which, in turn, prepared the way for the network revolution in the latter half of the twentieth century. Second, Luther did not accept the requirement of priestly celibacy. Citing Paul in Titus 1, he maintains that "a pastor shall not be compelled to live without a lawful wife."[33] The rejection of celibacy implies that monasticism is not a higher calling than the ordinary life of faith. To serve God one does not need to withdraw from the world but can become ever more deeply involved in the world. Luther expressed this conviction in his doctrine of calling or earthly vocation. John Dillenberger effectively summarizes this important point:

> The ministry is functionally, not ontologically, distinct. It implies no special status. The higher and lower callings, as in the prior distinctions between monks and the laity, are abolished. Luther does not mean that all possible callings are equally honorable. But ministers, cobblers, or magistrates may equally serve God in the exercise of their responsibilities. We men all, whatever our calling or station, face with confidence the conflicts and ambiguities of life and hope to be used by God as vessels to redeem the time. This is possible because through

the gift of faith we have learned to trust not in our own virtue but in Him who rules over all and who alone can bring good out of evil.[34]

Anticipating postmodern theologians and artists, Luther collapses high into low by associating the sacred with the profane in a way that transforms the value of worldly endeavor.

The opposition between the kingdom of God and the kingdom of the world is isomorphic with the antithesis between interiority and exteriority. While the Christian has obligations and responsibilities in the outer world, faith remains a private affair.[35] To a world teetering on the edge of chaos, Luther's defiance of medieval authority and hierarchy proved to be the tipping point for the emergence of a new cultural, political, and economic order. The effects of Luther's writings and activities were disproportionate to anything he imagined or intended. In 1524–25, German peasants rebelled against princes and nobles under the banner of Luther's Christian freedom in what became the most important European uprising prior to the French Revolution. Frustrated by Luther's social and political conservatism, two of his erstwhile followers, Andreas Bodenstein von Karlstadt and Thomas Müntzer, fanned the flames of rebellion by providing theological justification for social and political revolt. The peasants' concerns were worldly rather than religious—they demanded the abolition of class privileges and the granting of voting rights. Before the struggle had ended, more than a hundred thousand people had died. Luther's response was to attack rather than defend the uprising. In his infamous treatise "Against the Robbing and Murdering Hordes of Peasants," he declared that Christian freedom is inward and, therefore, can never justify social rebellion. Citing Paul in Romans 13:1–2, he counseled submission to secular authority: "Every person must submit to the supreme authorities. There is no authority but by act of God and the existing authorities are instituted by him; consequently anyone who rebels against authority is resisting a divine institution, and those who so resist have themselves to thank for the punishment they will receive."[36] Lutheranism never recovered from this capitulation; Calvinism, however, is a different story. The revolution that Luther began in a remote corner of Germany became global in Calvinism.

THE INVISIBLE HAND

The relatively minor theological differences between Luther and Calvin prove less important for the emergence of modernity than their contrasting interpretations of the social, political, and economic consequences of their respective religious visions. Calvin carefully and exhaustively worked out the implications of Luther's fundamental insight about justification by faith alone and by so doing systematized, institutionalized, and internationalized Protestantism. Without Luther, there would not have been a Reformation; without Calvin, Protestantism would not have changed the world.

The context that shaped Calvin's thought and the people to which it was addressed differed significantly from Luther's spiritual, intellectual, and social world. While Luther never lost his peasant roots, Calvin was raised in a commercial urban culture where increasing literacy led to growing cultural sophistication. Trained as a lawyer rather than a monk, he had greater appreciation for the law than Luther and, while at the University of Paris, studied classical languages as well as humanists from Virgil to Erasmus. His first published work was devoted to Seneca's treatise on clemency. Reflecting an appreciation for the classics that was completely alien to Luther, Calvin borrowed the famous opening lines of his summa, *The Institutes of the Christian Religion*, from Cicero: "Nearly all the wisdom we posses, that is to say, true and sound wisdom, consists of two parts: the knowledge of God and of ourselves."[37] While Calvin's God is every bit as mysterious and at times even more terrifying than Luther's God, and his assessment of the human condition is, if anything, darker, his acceptance of humanism suggests a more positive view of the world than is characteristic of Lutheranism. Alister McGrath goes so far as to argue: "Calvinism proved capable of engaging with western culture to the point at which, perhaps more than any other modern version of Christianity, it was able to transform it from within. The Calvinist was encouraged to engage directly with the world, rather than retreat from it."[38]

By the 1520s and 1530s, pressure for reform was building in France. Increasing literacy among the emerging urban bourgeoisie led to escalating anticlericalism and growing criticism of the church. The reform for which people were looking "must not, however, be thought of in purely spiritual terms. Social and economic factors conspired to point to the need for change, creating propitious circumstances for any revolutionary movement which appeared capable of offering social and economic, as much as religious, reform."[39] While Luther's words resonated with people suffering through the breakdown of the old order, Calvin's words found their audience among the rising middle class that was forging the new world order. As late as the 1540s, many in France still did not think

the acceptance of Lutheranism required the rejection of papal authority. This situation quickly changed, however, with the publication of the
French edition of Calvin's *Institutes* in 1541. A year later Parisian authorities banned all of his works, and the persecution of Protestants broke out
across France. Calvin, along with thousands of others, fled to Geneva,
where he carried on his struggle.

William Bousma concludes his important biography by arguing that
there are "two Calvins, coexisting uncomfortably within the same historical personage."

> One of these Calvins was a philosopher, a rationalist and a schoolman
> in the high Scholastic tradition represented by Thomas Aquinas, a
> man of fixed principles, and a conservative. For this Calvin, Christian-
> ity tended toward static orthodoxy, a Christian was a person endowed
> with certain *status*. This philosophical Calvin, peculiarly sensitive to
> the two contradictions and dilemmas of an eclectic culture and sin-
> gularly intolerant of what we now call "cognitive dissonance," craved
> desperately for intelligibility, order, certainty. . . . The other Calvin
> was a rhetorician and humanist, a skeptical fideist in the manner of
> the followers of William of Ockham, flexible to the point of opportun-
> ism, and a revolutionary in spite of himself. This Calvin did not seek,
> because he neither trusted nor needed, what passes on earth for intel-
> ligibility and order; instead, he was inclined to celebrate the paradoxes
> and mystery at the heart of existence.[40]

In terms of the word/deed polarity, the former Calvin gives priority to
word over deed and the latter privileges deed over word. These two alternatives correspond respectively to the structuring-stabilizing and
destructuring-destabilizing moments of religion. The contrasting sides
of Calvin's thought issue in two very different strands in the Reformed
tradition: on the one hand, the scholasticism embodied in Protestant
orthodoxy and Puritanism and, on the other hand, the spiritualism expressed in Anabaptism and Pietism.

While Luther once infamously declared reason "a whore," Calvin's
legal and humanist training impressed upon him the importance of
reason in managing and regulating human affairs. Though his methods
were different, he shared the systematic urge with medieval scholastic
theology. The trinitarian structure of the mature version of the *Institutes*
provided the organizing schema for the systematic formulation of the
foundational principles of Reformed Protestantism. This work had an
unexpected and rarely noted impact on French language: Calvin's *Insti-*

tutes did for the French language what Luther's translation of the Bible did for German.[41] Calvin's work, McGrath notes, is "widely regarded as the 'first monument of French eloquence.'" "It is often suggested that during the seventeenth century the French language developed abstract, denotational and analytic qualities (often described as *clarté* and *logique*)." But how, McGrath asks, "did *la clarté française*, so characteristic of writers of the French Classical period (such as Descartes and Pascal) develop?" His answer is as unlikely as it is insightful: "We would like to suggest that Calvin may be regarded as a precipitating factor in this important development, partly on account of his involvement in the general trend to popularize the highly intricate abstractions of Christian theology, and partly on account of his personal contribution to shaping the language."[42] This process of popularization began with Luther's crucial decision to extend the Reformation beyond the confines of the church proper by switching from lecturing and debating in Latin to preaching and campaigning before a growing public in German. Later Reformers appropriated and expanded Luther's tactics. "The Reformation witnessed the laying down of a major challenge to existing understandings of the way that the Bible could and should be read, to the structures of the church, and to Christian doctrine. Time and time again, the reformers appealed over the heads of the clergy and theologians to the people. The people, they insisted, must decide. The Swiss Reformation, in which a public disputation between evangelicals and Catholics in the vernacular was followed by a plenary vote by the assembled body of citizens on whether to accept the Reformation, reflects this principle."[43]

The contrasting ways in which Luther and Calvin interpreted Ockham's philosophy led in two different directions. Luther's exclusive emphasis on God's omnipotent will issued in an empirical epistemology, which still informs British political theory as well as analytic philosophy. Calvin, by contrast, did not ignore this arational voluntarism but placed much more emphasis on the rationality and lawfulness of God's *potentia ordinata*. This line of reasoning eventually led to Continental rationalism and political theory, which contributed significantly to the French Revolution.

The same principles that promoted philosophical rationalism also laid the groundwork for Protestant neoscholasticism. Borrowing the logical rules elaborated by the French logician Peter Ramus, theologians developed formulaic interpretations of scripture and rigid rules of conduct. Deepening conflicts between Catholics and Protestants as well as between Lutherans and Calvinists led to the proliferation of

creeds, which effectively reduced faith to belief in a series of propositions. As belief was rationalized, the role of human activity in the world
changed. The heart of the Reformation, I have insisted, is the faith that
salvation comes by grace rather than works. Unable to achieve salvation
through one's own efforts, individuals anxiously sought signs of God's
favor. Worldly success, Calvin told his followers, can provide assurance
that we are saved but can never be the cause of salvation. This distinction is, however, subtle and in practice easily leads to the conviction that
redemption can be earned through good works. When this belief is combined with Luther's doctrine of earthly vocation, the result is the dis-
cipline and "inner worldly" asceticism that Weber correctly argued are
essential to the growth of capitalism. Combining rationalism and moralism, ambitious pastors spread the faith through self-help pamphlets
designed to tell people how to win salvation. What is lost in all of this is,
of course, the freedom of Spirit that was critical for both Luther and Calvin. Religion degenerates into religiosity and thereby provides stability
at the price of vitality. In anticipation of issues to be considered later, it
is important to note that one of the reasons Protestantism has remained
so resilient in America is that rationalism and spiritualism have always
remained in tension with each other. When the rigidities of Puritans of
any stripe become overwhelming, the repressed returns in awakenings
great and small.

For many people in northern Europe in the late sixteenth and early
seventeenth centuries, Calvinism provided an effective schema for navi-
gating the turbulent transition to nationalism and capitalism. Rational
calculation was critical not only to the economy of salvation but also to
the burgeoning capitalist economy. While Luther condemned mercantilism as the work of the devil, Calvin saw capitalism as part of God's
providential plan. When extended beyond the religious life, rationalism
and legalism created the conditions for the instrumental logic and disciplinary regime without which capitalism could not have flourished. By
encouraging the spread of literacy, Protestantism helped people develop
skills that would become increasingly useful in the early modern period. In addition to providing a schema for rationalizing and moralizing
life, Calvin made a fateful decision about money that literally changed
the face of the earth: he accepted the practice of usury. Prior to Calvin,
both Catholics and Protestants condemned usury and insisted that the
only legitimate way to make money was through human labor or the
sale of things. This might have been adequate for an agrarian economy
but proved restrictive for the growing international markets that were

emerging in the early modern period. There can be no capitalism unless the monetary sign is detached from physical stuff—be it the labor-
ing body or the material object. By accepting usury, Calvin embraced
the principle that money (i.e., signs) can make money (i.e., signs) and
thereby prepared the way for new investment instruments and financial
institutions. As we will see, eighteenth-century Scottish Calvinists appropriated the Protestant notions of subjectivity and providence to create the model of the market that continues to govern economic theory
and financial practice. Though rarely noted, the ghost of religion haunts
today's financial markets.

These revolutionary political and economic transformations would
not have been possible without Calvin's elaboration and subtle revision
of several of Luther's foundational principles. The issue over which Calvinism and Lutheranism split was the Eucharist. As we have seen, in
medieval Catholic theology, the individual's salvation is mediated by
the church universal through the rituals of Baptism and the Eucharist.
According to the doctrine of transubstantiation, when the words of the
priest are spoken in Holy Communion, the elements of bread and wine
are actually transformed into the body and blood of Christ. This ritual
involves the reenactment of the sacrifice through which Christ becomes
present here and now. Since Luther believed that faith hinges on the subjective relation between God and self rather than the participation in an
objective ritual, he could not accept the Catholic interpretation of the
Last Supper. While rejecting the doctrine of transubstantiation, however, he continued to insist that Christ is somehow *really present* in the
rite. For Calvin and the Reformed tradition, the Eucharist is not a ritual
repetition of what occurred *in illo tempore* but is a commemorative event
in which participants recall what took place at the death and resurrection of the historical figure of Jesus. Calvin rejected Luther's notion of
real presence as an unjustified compromise with Catholicism.

To appreciate the implications of this seemingly arcane theological
debate for later developments within as well as beyond ecclesiastical and
theological circles, it is helpful to translate it into the semiotic terms implicit in nominalism's theory of language. According to the doctrine of
transubstantiation, the signifier (bread and wine) and the signified (body
and blood of Christ) are one and, thus, are indistinguishable. Luther denied the complete identity between signifier and signified but affirmed
the real presence of Christ in the ritual. The signified, therefore, is still
rendered present through the signifier. Calvin radicalized Luther's position by decisively breaking the bond between signifier and signified.

Table 2. Semiotics of the Eucharist

Catholicism	Lutheranism	Calvinism
Sign/thing identical	Sign/thing distinct but inherently related	Sign/thing separate

Christ is not present; rather, the ritual points beyond itself to a past historical event. In different terms, the referential structure of the sign presupposes that the signified "transcends" the signifier. From this point of view, to collapse the signifier into the signified is to commit the ultimate sin of idolatry. These three interpretations of the Eucharist entail alternative notions of the sign (table 2). The movement from Catholicism through Lutheranism to Calvinism, then, involves the drifting apart of signifier and signified, or word and thing. We will see in later chapters that at the end of a very long trajectory, this process culminates in the disappearance of the real referent in a play of floating signs mediated by the information and telematic networks of contemporary culture.

As these remarks suggest, Calvin's theology is in some ways even more dualistic than Luther's. God is radically transcendent and the world is sunk in an abyss of sin and corruption. Human beings, therefore, are *totally* dependent on God's grace not only for salvation but for all aspects of life. In developing his theology, Calvin accepts Luther's soteriology and systematically develops its implications. Belief in salvation by grace rather than works, Calvin argues, presupposes an all-powerful creator God who is radically free and completely unconstrained by external circumstances. Instead of a one-time event, creation is an ongoing process in which God constantly brings the universe into being and governs its course. The doctrine of creation, therefore, necessarily entails the doctrine of providence. "To make God a momentary Creator, who once for all finished his work," Calvin explains, "would be cold and barren, and we must differ from profane men especially in that we see the presence of divine power shining as much in the continuing state of the universe as in its inception. . . . For unless we pass on to his providence—however we may seem both to comprehend with the mind and to confess with the tongue—we do not yet properly know what it means to say: 'God is Creator.'"[44] Providence does not merely guide the general course of things but extends to each event and every individual. From the beginning of time, the direction of the world has been predestined in God's omniscient gaze. Within this theological framework, there is no such thing as fortune or chance, because everything "is directed by God's ever-present hand." God's hand is not, of course, always visible; to the contrary, God's plan is "secret" because "the true causes of events are hidden to us."[45] The hand of providence, in other words, is *invisible;* though never properly present, God is never absent from creation.

Calvin's elaboration of Luther's divided subject pushes Protestantism to the point where it reverses itself and inadvertently prepares the way for the secularity of the modern world. As we will see in more detail in chapter 4, God can disappear in two ways: on the one hand, God can become so transcendent that he is functionally irrelevant, and on the other, the divine can become so immanent that God and world are one. By pushing God's transcendence to the limit, Calvin unwittingly affirms divine immanence. If God is everything and I am nothing, then my deeds are never merely my own but are always also the expression of divine providence operating through me. Paul's Epistle to the Galatians proves decisive: "For through the law I died to the law—to live for God. I have been crucified with Christ: the life I now live is not my life, but the life which Christ lives in me" (2:20). In other words, when I act, Christ acts through me. The affirmation of human impotence and divine omnipotence leads to the unexpected identification of God with self and by extension world. At this point, the logic of opposition reverses itself in a logic of identity and creates the implosion of the sacred and the profane.

The collapse of transcendence into immanence leads to the second side of Calvin's theology. Calvin, like Luther, became a revolutionary in spite of himself. Just as Luther's notion of Christian freedom led to the Peasants' Revolt, so Calvin's doctrine of providence prepared the way for the transformative spiritualities of the radical Reformation. In contrast to Protestant neoscholasticism, which bound Spirit to literal scripture, formulaic creeds, and rational codes of conduct, radical Reformers ranging from Anabaptists, Moravians, and Pietists to Quakers, Methodists, and Baptists reaffirmed the freedom of Spirit and the unmediated relation between the individual self and God. At the end of the eighteenth century, these two strands of Reformed theology—rationalism and spiritualism—came together in the American and French Revolutions.

PRIVATIZATION, DECENTRALIZATION, DEREGULATION

The emergence of the new notion of subjectivity in Protestantism led to the privatization, decentralization, and deregulation of religion, which ran directly counter to the centralization and universalization of authority that the church hierarchy had imposed during the High Middle Ages. These developments, in turn, contributed to the information and communications revolution that began with print and continues in today's network culture. As religion was privatized and every believer became a priest, the centralized hierarchical authority of the church broke down and authority was distributed among individual believers. Rules and regulations no longer were imposed from above but now emerged from the bottom up through individuals who were separate but equal. These changes were brought about by and promoted literacy and education. Literacy never would have developed so quickly and spread so widely in northern Europe and America without the Protestant principle of *sola scriptura*. During the early Middle Ages, literacy was confined almost exclusively to the clergy and the Bible was in Latin. While this situation began to change during the Renaissance, it was the coemergence of printing and the Reformation that transformed the way in which information was produced, distributed, and consumed in the early modern period. According to Myron Gilmore, "the invention and development of moveable type brought about the most radical transformation in the conditions of intellectual life in the history of western civilization. It opened new horizons in education and in the communication of ideas. Its effects were sooner or later felt in every department of human activity."[46] Paper and printing had been invented centuries earlier in China, but social and cultural events did not create the conditions favorable to their explosive growth until the sixteenth century in Europe. The Reformation played a decisive role in these developments. From the beginning, printing and Protestantism were bound in a mutually reinforcing relationship of supply and demand: printing supplied the materials for the spread of the Word, and the spread of the Word created the demand for more printed materials. Lutheranism, Arthur Dickens argues, "was from the first the child of the printed book, and through this vehicle Luther was able to make exact, standardized and ineradicable impressions on the mind of Europe. For the first time in history a great reading public judged the validity of revolutionary ideas through a mass-medium which used the vernacular languages together with the arts of the journalist and the cartoonist."[47] Luther's protest never would have become a world-historical event without the printing press. Indeed, Luther was the first best-selling author and arguably the first media celebrity in the West; between 1517 and 1520, thirty of his works sold an astonishing 300,000 copies.[48] In his informative book *Printing, Propaganda, and Martin Luther*, Mark Edwards calculates: "If we assume conservatively that each printing of a work by Luther numbered one thousand copies, we are talking about an output for Luther alone of 3.1 million copies during the period 1515 to 1546."[49]

This scale of production and distribution required the creation of an unprecedented technological infrastructure. Though Marco Polo brought block-print technology to Europe from Asia in the thirteenth century, most religious manuscripts were produced and reproduced by hand in monastic scriptoria well into the fifteenth century. Gutenberg developed a punch-and-mold system in which replaceable letters were arranged in a type tray that could be used to mass-produce printed pages. In retrospect, it is clear that this printing press was the prototype for the method of mechanical reproduction, which eventually would create modern industrialism. Early printers were by necessity entrepreneurs eager to find profitable products and to create expanding markets where they could be sold. From their earliest days, Protestantism and capitalism have been inseparable. Bibles, religious pamphlets, prayer books, and self-help books were the most profitable printed works for much of the sixteenth century. To promote their products, printers developed novel advertising strategies ranging from handbills and book inserts to posters promoting popular trade and book fairs. As the Reformation spread to different cities and countries, entrepreneurs developed new trade routes and distribution networks. When markets grew and diversified throughout northern Europe, they opened lines of communication, which facilitated the relatively rapid dissemination of new ideas. As ideas spread in these emerging networks, their effects frequently were reinforced and amplified. This is what made Luther's writings, and especially his translation of the Bible from the Vulgate into the vernacular, so explosive within and beyond the walls of the church.

Throughout the Middle Ages, Jerome's fourth-century Latin translation from the Greek and Hebrew remained authoritative. The church's justification for the use of the Vulgate was twofold: first, it honored traditional liturgy, and second, the Latin language protected esoteric mysteries and sacred truths from profanation. The actual reasons for this practice were much more worldly—restriction of scripture to Latin and limitation of its proper interpretation to the magisterium increased the power of the church and reinforced the hierarchy between clergy and laity. During the late fifteenth century, translations into the vernacular began to appear in Germany and elsewhere. Prior to the Reformation, the church discouraged but did not forbid translations. But concern about the implications of biblical translations grew and, in 1485, the archbishop of Mainz, where Gutenberg had published his Bible in 1452, issued a warning alerting people to the dangers of rendering sacred texts in "incorrect and vulgar German." To underscore this point, the ecclesiastical authorities began to require the licensing of all German vernacular translations.[50] Such efforts, however, were too little too late—the Word was out.

By the time Luther published the first edition of his translation of the Bible in 1534, there were already eighteen German editions—fourteen in High German and four in Low German. The extraordinary success of Luther's translation was due to its style as well as the circumstances in which it appeared. Luther never lost touch with his peasant roots, and much of his political success can be attributed to his abiding bond with commoners, which is reflected in his language. As the writings collected in *Table Talk* make abundantly clear, Luther's rhetoric is consistently earthy and often vulgar, if not obscene. While criticized by representatives of the church hierarchy, this style resonated with ordinary people and contributed to the popularity of his message. But Luther's words would not have spread without print and the new networks it created. Eisenstein correctly argues that Protestantism was

> the first movement of any kind, religious or secular, to use the new presses for overt propaganda and agitation against the established institution. By pamphleteering directed at arousing popular support and aimed at readers who were unversed in Latin, the reformers unwittingly pioneered as revolutionaries and rabble rousers. They also left "ineradicable impressions" in the form of broadsides and caricatures. Designed to catch the attention and arouse the passions of sixteenth-century readers, their anti-papists cartoons still have a strong impact when encountered in history books today.[51]

The rapid development of printing technology prepared the way for the swift spread of Luther's gospel by creating a growing number of literate consumers. As if anticipating the principles of supply-side economics, the increase in the supply of printed material increased the demand for it, which, in turn, led to the further increase in supply.

The consequences of the coemergence of printing and the Reformation are still being felt today. The translation of the Bible into different languages facilitated the spread of Protestantism. William Tyndale, described by Jack Miles as "a linguistic genius who may be said to have seen the English language as a whole for the first time," published his epoch-making English translation of the New Testament in 1526. At the time of his execution in Belgium in 1536, Tyndale had completed his translation of about half of the Old Testament.[52] Born into a prosperous family of merchants, Tyndale's translation of the Bible was inspired by his belief in the common man and democratic principles. This impulse lies at the foundation of English Puritanism and, through English Protestantism, has shaped American mass culture.[53] As Protestantism expanded from country to country in northern Europe and eventually to America, printers and publishing houses quickly followed. The acceptance of the religious significance of scripture led to reading instruction for both children and adults first in the home and church-related organizations and later in social institutions and public schools. In 1642 the Massachusetts Bay Colony passed a law requiring all children to be taught how to read; thirty-two years later the colony passed the first public-schooling law. By the second half of the eighteenth century, literacy rates in Massachusetts were as high as 90 percent. While Puritan New England was a particularly striking example of these trends, similar patterns can be discerned among Protestants elsewhere.[54] The growth of literacy encouraged the further privatization and decentralization of religion. The home hearth became the private altar around which the family gathered.

Breaking the church's monopoly on literacy had important consequences that extended far beyond religion. People who knew how to read were able to make the transition from agrarian to mercantile and later to industrial society much more effectively. Printed materials were not, of course, limited to religious texts but also included maps, calendars, schedules, business textbooks, and tables for weights, measures, and currency conversion, which all contributed to industrial development and economic expansion. By encouraging literacy and numeracy, Protestantism created the educated workforce early capitalism required.

The Catholic reaction to these developments proved decisive for generations to come. As the Reformation spread, uneasiness about the use of the vernacular and the growth of literacy deepened. In 1515, at the Lateran Council, Pope Leo X issued a censorship decree that "applied to all translations from Hebrew, Greek, Arabic and Chaldaic into Latin and from Latin into the vernacular."[55] Protestantism and literacy were so closely associated that the church felt that, to contain the former, it had to restrict the latter. Additional edicts directed against Bible printing were issued throughout the 1520s and were backed up by the Inquisition. In 1546, at the Council of Trent, the Catholic Church reaffirmed the primacy of the Vulgate, thereby ensuring lay ignorance and obedience rather than promoting literacy and education. In 1559 Pius IV's reaffirmation of the prohibition of Bible printing and reading in his first papal Index put an end to additional translations of the Bible and drastically limited the spread of literacy in Catholic countries for two centuries. One of the most important effects of these developments was to curtail the growth of industrialism and capitalism in Catholic countries. As mercantilism gave way to industrialism, capitalism became much stronger in northern than in southern Europe. The effects of the division between north and south that grew out of these religious doctrines and policies can still be seen in Europe, as well as North and South America today.

The advent of print compromised ecclesiastical authority in other unexpected ways. Though they disagreed on many issues, Erasmus and Luther were both convinced about the importance of translating and publishing the Bible into as many languages as possible. During the Renaissance, humanists rediscovered and reappropriated Greek and Hebrew. As interest in ancient languages increased, new research tools like dictionaries, grammars, and reference works began to appear. In 1516, Erasmus published what might well have been the most important book in the sixteenth century—*Novum Instrumentum*. In this bilingual work, Greek and Latin versions of the biblical text appeared in columns side by side. Luther and Tyndale both drew on Erasmus's work in their translations of the Bible. Though Erasmus never became a Reformer, it is no exaggeration to insist that *Novum Instrumentum* made the Reformation possible. As scholars honed their new linguistic skills by studying translations of the Bible, they discovered numerous problems with Jerome's Vulgate version of scripture. In this way, printing created the conditions for historical and critical biblical scholarship, which eventually would shake the foundation of faith. When the Catholic Church reaffirmed the Vulgate, they chose to ignore questions raised by serious students of the Bible. As we will see in chapter 5, by the nineteenth century, these problems became even more severe for Protestants whose faith was bound to the validity of the written Word.

While these developments proved decisive for later history, the implications of print are even more complicated than these remarks suggest. In ways that are not immediately obvious, print not only individualizes and deregulates but also standardizes and regulates scripture, creedal codes, and disciplinary practices. The contrasting tendencies to individualize and to standardize correspond to the voluntaristic destabilizing and rationalistic stabilizing sides of Calvinism. The propensity of print to standardize and regulate has economic, linguistic, and political implications. The economic impact of print can be seen in the eventual development of new currencies and the formation of novel disciplinary techniques. Changes in currencies always presuppose new technologies: just as there could be no metal currencies without the requisite mining and metallurgy technologies and there can be no virtual currencies without information-processing machines and networks, so there could be no paper currencies apart from technologies for the production of paper and printing. Paper currency was first introduced in China in 910 CE and was used by Venetian goldsmiths during the Middle Ages, but the invention of printing allowed it to spread rapidly. Printing created the conditions for standardization and regulation of currencies and thereby facilitated the development of networks of exchange that made it possible for markets to expand beyond local and even national boundaries. But printing also introduced a subtle yet important change in the nature of money: with paper currency, the token of exchange shifts from valuable material to a sign with no intrinsic worth. Once the distinction between stuff and sign had been made, it was all but inevitable that the signified and the signifier would eventually drift apart and the economy would eventually become a play of signs.

The emergence of industrial capitalism presupposes not only the development of new technologies and educated workers but also the standardization and regulation of human behavior, which would not have been possible without printing. It is no accident that the famous Strasbourg clock was created in the city with a thriving printing industry to which Calvin fled from France to escape persecution. Before the widespread use of mechanical clocks, printed calendars and schedules had already begun the process of rationalizing human behavior in ways that would change work and transform the economy. Just as print had been the *preparatio Evangelica* for Luther, so the standardization and regulation of life prepared the way for industrialization.

In addition to changing the way people lived, print changed the way they thought and spoke. The paradoxical tendencies of print can be seen clearly in its impact on language. As Calvin's *Institutes* profoundly influenced the French language, so Luther's translation of the Bible transformed German. The propensity of print to cultivate individuality should not obscure the ways in which it standardizes language as well as personal habits and social customs. The standardization of language leads to the gradual eclipse of local dialects as well as the regulation of idiosyncratic usages. This development had serious political implications that extended far beyond the church. Throughout Europe, the standardization of language and its fixation in print created the conditions for the rise of nationalism.

> Studies of dynastic consolidation and/or of nationalism might well devote more space to the advent of printing. Typography arrested linguistic drift, enriched as well as standardized vernaculars, and paved the way for the more deliberate purification and codification of all European languages. Randomly patterned sixteenth-century type-casting largely determined the subsequent elaboration of national mythologies on the part of certain separate groups within multi-lingual dynastic states. The duplication of vernacular primers and translations contributed in other ways to nationalism. A "mother's tongue" learned "naturally" at home would be reinforced by inculcation of a homogenized print-made language mastered while still young, when learning to read. . . . Particularly after grammar schools gave primary instruction in reading by using vernacular instead of Latin readers, linguistic "roots" and rootedness in one's homeland would be entangled.[56]

The two most powerful agents of national identity are language and currency. As we saw in chapter 1, society and culture are codependent: society presupposes cultural ideals, and cultural schemata grow out of social relations. When local dialects give way to shared language, social relations are reconfigured. Patrick Collinson shrewdly observes: "Everywhere, the vernacular Bible was the most important vehicle for what we may call cultural nationalism."[57] This transformation was not, of course, limited to culture; cultural nationalism inspired and informed other forms of nationalism. In later chapters I will explore the ways in which the extension of the sixteenth-century information and communications revolution in the digital and network revolutions of the late twentieth century leads to the acceleration of the process of globalization, which unravels and rewires the relations among language, currency, and the nation-state.

Technological innovations change not only natural, social, political, and economic systems and structures but also transform perceptual and cognitive schemata. The ways in which we apprehend the world are not hardwired in the brain but change with the modes of production and reproduction. The development of mechanical technologies deployed in print issued in new disciplinary regimes for sensation and thought. Though rarely noted, printing and linear point perspective emerged at approximately the same time. In his groundbreaking study of Renaissance

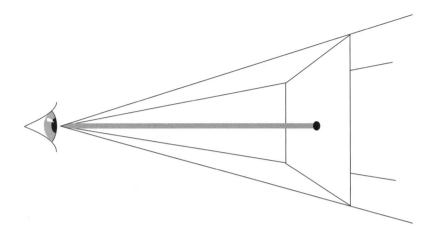

Figure 12. Visual Pyramid by Leon Battista Alberti, *Della pittura*, 1435–36.
(http://www.cs.brown.edu/stc/summer/viewing_history/
viewing_history_8.html)

art Samuel Edgerton first demonstrated that the key to the discovery of
linear perspective was recognition of the vanishing point, which made
it possible to construct a visual pyramid with its organizational grid. As
early as 1425, Filippo Brunelleschi had discovered the vanishing point
through a series of complicated experiments with mirrors designed for
the Baptistery of Florence. Based on his results, he proceeded to develop
techniques for painting realistic pictures and passed this information
on to other artists. Leon Battista Alberti refined Brunelleschi's instructions in his highly influential *Della pittura* (1435–36) (fig. 12). During the
Renaissance, questions about the eye and vision were more metaphysical than physical. The perspective rules formulated by Brunelleschi and
Alberti were accepted by artists because they "gave their depicted scenes
a sense of harmony with natural law, thereby underscoring man's moral
responsibility within God's geometrically ordered universe."[58] This new
geometric space foreshadowed the modern Cartesian grid, which literally transformed the world. This grid became the structural foundation
for administrative and cognitive regulation through the Enlightenment
and down to the present day. But linear perspective also involves the
countertendency of individualization, which we have discovered in both
Reformation theology and print technology. In addition to establishing
the similarity between the divine and the human eye, linear perspective

contributes to the constitution of a new subject, which is isomorphic with the individual self in Luther's theology. Perspective individualizes sight in idiosyncratic vision that informs the individual subject. Samuel Edgerton explains how print facilitated this epochal change:

> It should not be overlooked that almost coincidental with the appearance and acceptance of linear perspective came Gutenberg's invention of moveable type. Together these two ideas, the one visual, the other literary, provided perhaps the most outstanding scientific achievement of the fifteenth century: the revolution in mass communication. Linear perspective pictures, by virtue of the power of the printing press, came to cover a wider range of subjects and to reach a larger audience than any other representational medium or convention in the entire history of art. It is fair to say that without this conjunction of perspective and printing in the Renaissance, the whole subsequent development of modern science and technology would have been unthinkable.[59]

In this way, print actually contributed to the transformation of the way people see and, by extension, interpret the world.

In our investigation of the formation and operational logic of schemata, we discovered that perception and cognition are codependent and, therefore, mutually condition each other. The reconfiguration of the visual field recasts the structures of cognition and vice versa. On the one hand, the visual pyramid individualizes vision to create perspective, which, when translated into cognitive terms, eventually leads to Kierkegaard's subjectivism and Nietzsche's perspectivism. On the other hand, the visual pyramid and organizational grid create a taxonomic imperative, which leads to the comprehensive systematization of reality developed in different ways by the French Encyclopedists and Hegel's *Encyclopedia of the Philosophical Sciences*. Extending the empiricism inherent in the voluntarism of nominalistic philosophy and Protestant theology, linear perspective reinforces the insistence on the collection of data by the investigation of individual phenomena, which are then arranged according to principles defined in various schemata. These organizational structures can range from the popular *Wunderkabinet*, museums, and textbooks to sophisticated scientific theories. Print once again plays a mediating role in these developments. "The decisions made by early printers," Elizabeth Eisenstein explains,

> directly affected both tool-making and symbol-making. Their products reshaped the powers to manipulate objects, to perceive and think

about varied phenomena. Scholars concerned with "modernization" or "rationalization" might profitably think more about the new kind of brainwork fostered by the silent scanning of maps, tables, charts, diagrams, dictionaries and grammars. They also need to look much more closely at the routines pursued by those who compiled and produced such reference guides. These routines were conducive to a new *ésprit de système*.[60]

During the modern period, this *ésprit de système* changes the world into its own image. The far-reaching implications of this new transformation did not become evident until the end of the eighteenth century.

This examination of the Reformation offers ample evidence for the ways in which natural, social, cultural, and technological systems and networks coemerge and coevolve. As its consequences spread through emerging information and communications networks, Luther's personal crisis was amplified until it led to a revolution that ushered in the modern age. If, as Hegel argues, the essence of the Reformation is that man in his very nature is destined to be free, then what began in Wittenberg in the sixteenth century continued in Philadelphia and Paris in the eighteenth century.

CHAPTER THREE

Subjectivity and Modernity

FREEDOM AND REPRESENTATION

Modernity and revolution are inseparable. As order breaks down, societies drift toward the edge of chaos until they reach the condition of self-organized criticality, at which point local events can trigger global changes. Since nature, society, and culture are codependent and coevolve, a change in any of these systems leads to changes in the others. The Protestant revolution prepared the way for subsequent revolutions that created the modern world. Though historical circumstances vary, all of these revolutions rest upon the interrelated principles of freedom and representation, which must be understood religiously, aesthetically, and politically. Caught in feedback loops that are increasingly complex, ideas change history as much as history shapes ideas. Luther's divided subject becomes the restless subject of modernity, which realizes itself through the two most characteristic institutions of the modern world: democracy and the free market. What begins as a theological revolution becomes a political revolution, which, in turn, inspires the philosophical and aesthetic revolution that eventually culminates in twentieth-century secularity. In this chapter, I will consider the explicit and implicit political and cultural impact of Protestantism throughout the modern period. As we will see, many institutions and cultural practices that define modernity would not have taken the form they did without Luther's decisive turn to the subject and the unexpected events it unleashed. By translating Protestant theological principles into philosophical concepts, Kant elaborated a notion of the free subject, which simultaneously reflected the age of revolution in which he lived and set the trajectory for religion, politics, and art that eventually helped to transform the world. The site of this intersection is his analysis of the imagination in which he develops competing interpretations of freedom and representation that both reflect different theological traditions and anticipate alternative versions of postmodernism.

In his *Athenaeum Fragments*, published in Jena between 1798 and 1800, Friedrich Schlegel writes: "The revolutionary desire to realize the kingdom of God on earth is the elastic point of progressive civilization and the beginning of modern history. Whatever has no relation to the kingdom of God is of strictly secondary importance."[1] The tipping point of history for Schlegel and his fellow artists, writers, and philosophers, who gathered in Jena during the remarkable decade of the 1790s to create nothing less than the program for subsequent modernity, was the French Revolution. This event, which Hegel labeled "world-historical," simultaneously inspired and frustrated romantic artists and idealist philosophers. While revolutionary dreams culminated in the Reign of Terror, questions about the most effective way to bring social and political change became urgent. When religion and politics failed to realize what many imagined as the kingdom of God on earth, artists and philosophers fashioned new strategies, which more than two centuries later continue to shape our world. In his classic study *Natural Supernaturalism: Tradition and Revolution in Romantic Literature*, M. H. Abrams effectively summarizes these developments. "To put the matter with the sharpness of drastic simplification: faith in an apocalypse by revelation had been replaced by faith in an apocalypse by revolution, and this now gave way to faith in an apocalypse by imagination or cognition. In the ruling two-term frame of Romantic thought, the mind of man confronts the old heaven and earth and possesses within itself the power, if it will but recognize and avail itself of the power, to transform them into a new heaven and new earth, by means of a total revolution of consciousness."[2] While romantics and idealists insist that in order to change the world it is first necessary to transform human consciousness, their critics counter that such a point of view simply perpetuates religious illusions, thereby making real change impossible. Four decades after Schlegel's *Fragments* appeared, Marx published his "Contribution to the Critique of Hegel's *Philosophy of Right*" in the *Deutsch-französische Jahrbücher* (1844), in which he traced the revolutions that inaugurated the modern world back to Luther, whose theological principles form the foundation of Hegel's philosophy.

Even from the historical standpoint theoretical emancipation has a specific importance for Germany. In fact Germany's *revolutionary* past is theoretical—it is the *Reformation*. In that period the revolution originated in the brain of a monk, today in the brain of a philosopher.

Luther, without question, overcame servitude through devotion but only by substituting servitude through *conviction*. He shattered faith in authority by restoring the authority of faith. He transformed the priests into laymen by turning laymen into priests. He liberated man from external religiosity by making religiosity the innermost essence of man. He liberated the body from its changes because he fettered the heart with chains.

As we have seen, Luther's ambivalence about the revolutionary forces he unleashed was already evident in his own day. As Marx points out, "the Peasant War, the most radical event in German history, came to grief because of theology."[3] But Luther could neither contain nor control the transformation of reformation into revolution. Though Marx was very critical of Luther's limitation of freedom to inwardness and subjectivity, he never lost sight of Luther's importance for his own thought as well as for the subsequent course of history.

Although Luther remained devoted to a transcendent God, his insistence on the inwardness of faith led to his rejection of both church hierarchy and authoritative tradition. Since the locus of authority is the individual, power flows from the bottom up rather than from the top down. Over the course of time, Luther's divided subject gradually evolved into the modern subject, which is autonomous and thus self-legislating. The political stakes of this transformation can be seen in the formative revolutions of the modern era. In tracing the theological genealogy of the American and French Revolutions implied in their founding documents, it quickly becomes apparent that the differences between the religious climates in France and America during the late eighteenth century were as important as the similarities.

Alexis de Tocqueville once observed: "I do not know if all Americans have faith in their religion—for who can read to the bottoms of their hearts?—but I am sure that they believe it necessary to the maintenance of republican institutions. This opinion does not belong only to one class of citizens or to one party, but to the entire nation; one finds it in all ranks."[4] From its earliest days, America has always been a *religious* nation. Not all the early settlers came to America with the intention of staying; some saw their sojourn in the wilderness as necessary to complete the Reformation Luther and Calvin had started in Europe. Once they accomplished their mission, they planned to return to England to implement the new world order they believed they were predestined to create. Having absorbed the internationalism of Calvinism, the first generation of religious leaders who came to America remained in touch with events in Geneva, Strasbourg, Frankfurt, and Leiden.[5] The schema they used to interpret their mission was drawn largely from the Old Testament. In his second inaugural address, Jefferson invoked the image of the Exodus to describe the American experiment: "I need, too, the favor of that Being in whose hands we are, who led our forefathers, as Israel of old, from their native land, and planted them in a country flowing with all the necessaries and comforts of life; who has covered our infancy with his providence, and our riper years with his wisdom and power."[6] By the time the Pilgrims landed in 1620, the colony in Jamestown had failed, primarily because settlers had been unable to create an adequate government. Determined not to commit the same mistake, religious dissidents heading for Massachusetts developed what can best be described as a political theology. The heart of Puritan theology is the notion of the covenant, which is the basis of the Mayflower Compact, which William Bradford formulated in 1620.

> Having undertaken, for the Glory of God and advancement of the Christian Faith and Honor of our King and Country, a Voyage to plant the First Colony in the Northern Parts of Virginia, do by these presents solemnly and mutually in the presence of God and one of another, Covenant and Combine ourselves into a Civil Body Politic, for our better ordering and preservation and furtherance of the ends aforesaid; and by virtue hereof to enact, constitute and frame such just and equal Laws, Ordinances, Acts, Constitutions and Offices, from time to time, as shall be thought most meet and convenient for the general good of the Colony, unto which we promise all due submission and obedience.[7]

The doctrine of the covenant, which originated in the Old Testament, presupposes the nominalist distinction between *potentia absoluta* and *potentia ordinata*. Though God is omnipotent, he freely limits his absolute power in two ways: first, by establishing the laws that govern the natural world and, second, by entering into a binding agreement with human beings. The Mayflower Compact makes it clear that this covenant extends beyond the God-self relation to the relations between and among individual human beings. Perry Miller explains how covenant theology fulfills the requirement of any effective religious schema by providing life with meaning and purpose.

> That the illimitable sovereign of the universe should relate himself to His creatures not only as absolute power but as voluntarily abiding by the stated rules of His regime offered a solution to all difficulties, not only theological but cosmological, emotional and (most happily) political. This idea was the basis of both church polity and of social theory. Starting from the premise that a regenerate person, entering the Covenant of Grace, is taken into legal compact with God (this being available to him because God and Christ had, in a previous compact between themselves, the Covenant of Redemption, provided the foundation), federal theologians worked out a corollary that God likewise enters into covenant with a group as a unit. The two covenants—personal and public—were "branches" of the same, and yet distinct: saints dwelling alone may be in the Covenant of Grace without participating in a pledged society; a society may achieve this honor though (many or most) of its citizens are not gracious. Over and above His contracts with persons, God settles the social terms with a band of men, which thereupon becomes committed, as a political entity, to a specifically enunciated political program.[8]

The extension of the covenant from the bond between God and the individual to his relation to the group as a whole was critical for the emerging self-understanding of the nation. In 1630, John Winthrop formulated the principle of American exceptionalism, which still forms the foundation of national identity and shapes foreign policy:

> the Lord will be our God and delight to dwell among us, as his owne people, and will commaund a blessing upon us in all our wayes, soe that wee shall see much more of his wisdome power goodnes and truthe then formerly wee have beene acquainted with, wee shall finde that the God of Israell is among us, when tenn of us shall be able to resist a thousand of our enemies, when hee shall make us a prayse and glory, that men shall say of succeeding plantacions: the lord make it like that of New England: for wee must Consider that wee shall be as a Citty upon a Hill, the eies of all people are uppon us.[9]

It should be clear that this formulation of covenant theology involves a significant revision of the pivotal Reformation doctrine of salvation. While God freely restricts his power by cutting a deal with humanity, once the covenant is established, salvation depends on individuals living up to their end of the bargain. In this way, covenant theology provides the justification for the rigid moralism and disciplinary practices usually associated with Puritanism. Strict obedience leads to personal and national prosperity, and disobedience brings "war, epidemic or ruin."[10]

The guiding principles of the American Revolution were *theologically* grounded. Mark Noll points out that "the revolutionary assault on authority" arose from the "fear of abuses from illegitimate power and nearly messianic belief in the benefits of liberty."[11] Though human sin made government unavoidable for maintaining social order, the commitment to "utopian individualism" tended to encourage policies of minimal government regulation.[12] The widespread suspicion of authority shared by many early settlers had further implications that continue to shape social, political, cultural, and intellectual life today. The denial of ecclesiastical authority did not, of course, imply the rejection of authority as such; rather, the locus of authority shifted from church hierarchy to the Word of God. Many of the Protestants who founded this country insisted that, for the Word to be authoritative, it had to be unambiguous. In many, though not all, cases, the refusal of the authority of church hierarchy led to the acceptance of the unquestionable authority of the literal meaning of scripture. "The assumption that people could see clearly and without ambiguity what the Bible said, and that this biblicist knowledge qualified one to judge connections between moral cause and moral effect," Noll points out, "was the common person's counterpart to the Enlightenment confidence displayed by intellectual elites who employed learned formal moral philosophy for the same ends. Democratic biblicism undercut trust in traditional interpretations of Scripture with the same force that they were being leveled by a reliance on philosophical common sense. In both cases, confidence in present abilities overmastered confidence in what was handed on from the past. In both cases, a liberated modern self was the starting point for biblical interpretation."[13]

In America, unlike much of Europe, anti-authoritarianism also led to anti-elitism as well as anti-intellectualism. In the "New World," elites and intellectuals of every stripe tended to be viewed as poseurs who should be exposed as such. The corollary of this anti-elitism and anti-intellectualism is the veneration of common sense and plain style, which leads, inter alia, to literalisms that reach far beyond the words of scripture. There is a close relation between the plain style of radical Protestant sects like the Anabaptists, Mennonites, and Dunkards and the commonsense morality of the Scottish Enlightenment as well as the veneration of linguistic simplicity that extends from medieval nominalism to contemporary British and American analytic philosophy. Well into the nineteenth century the preoccupation with plain style led to a pronounced antipathy toward art, which was often derided as a "frill." This word gained currency because the Cavaliers, the Anglicans of the Restoration period, wore frills and French silks. The opposition to anything "fancy" is connected with antipathy to the core meaning of "fancy," namely, "fantasy"—the imagination, fiction, the invented. Facts, plain facts, were what mattered, and it was supposed that God was among them.[14] The common denominator of these seemingly disparate traditions is a shared resistance to any kind of excess—linguistic or otherwise—and the suspicion of pleasures related to whatever is not useful or is unnecessary. When less is more, language as well as life should be as neat, clean, and proper as the fashionless fashion of simple black and white.

The theological principles that guided the lives of the early settlers are clearly evident in the opening lines of the Declaration of Independence: "We hold these truths to be self-evident, that all men are created equal, that they are endowed by their Creator with certain unalienable Rights, that among these are Life, Liberty and the pursuit of Happiness. That to secure these rights, Governments are instituted among Men, deriving their just powers from the consent of the governed."[15] Human rights, then, are originally granted by God and the purpose of government is to secure and defend these rights. The representatives of the colonies return to these foundational principles when they conclude the Declaration by "appealing to the Supreme Judge of the world for the rectitude of our intentions" and express "a firm reliance on the protection of divine Providence." Though the precepts of Calvinism reflected in these lines were still influential in 1776, two-thirds of those who signed the Declaration were Anglican laymen with deist tendencies. Jefferson and Franklin had obviously been influenced by the French Enlightenment, but Locke's natural theology and political theory were also very important for some of the most influential founders. The contrast between English and French deism can be seen in the differences between the Declaration of Independence and the Declaration of the Rights of Man and of the Citizen (1789). The abiding importance of these differences is largely responsible for the divergent roles of religion in America and France today.

Deism, which is based on reason rather than revelation, is the belief in a transcendent God, who first creates the world and establishes the laws by which it operates and then withdraws to let it run on its own. In England, deism grew out of late medieval nominalism. Since God's free will is constrained by nothing other than itself, the world and its laws are contingent. The will of God is not completely unknowable but can be read in two books: scripture and nature. British and French deism agree on these basic principles but disagree in their interpretations of Christianity: in England deism and Christianity remained complementary and in France they became antithetical. As the work of mechanical reproduction spread beyond the printing press, the world itself appeared to be a machine. In the 1660s, Robert Boyle went so far as to describe the natural world as "a great piece of clock-work." The most precise image of this mechanistic universe was, he argued, the Strasbourg clock: "The several pieces making up that curious engine are so framed and adapted, and are put into such a motion, that though the numerous wheels, and other parts of it, move several ways, and that without any thing either of knowledge or design; yet each part performs its part in order to the various ends, for which it was contrived, as regularly and uniformly as if it knew and were concerned to do its duty."[16] The combination of the empirical epistemology implicit in the voluntarism of nominalism and the mechanistic interpretation of deism prepared the way for the rise of modern science.

Nowhere is the importance of deistic theology for science more evident than in the work of Isaac Newton. Alexander Pope captured the attitude of many of his contemporaries toward Newton when he wrote:

> Nature and Nature's law lay hid in night,
> God said: "Let Newton be," and all was light.[17]

One of Newton's most enduring contributions to intellectual history was his effort to redefine the proper domain of reason and to articulate the appropriate method by which reason should operate. Ernst Cassirer points out that throughout much of the history of the West, "truly 'philosophical' knowledge had seemed attainable only when thought, starting from a highest being and from a highest, intuitively grasped certainty, succeeded in spreading the light of this certainty over all derived being and all derived knowledge."[18] Beginning with metaphysical first principles that are implicitly or immediately known, one seeks to arrive at the concrete particulars of everyday experience by means of careful deduction. For Newton, the proper course of rational inquiry is precisely the reverse. Drawing on a uniquely British tradition dating back to Ockham, and more recently elaborated in the scientific work of Francis Bacon and Robert Boyle, Newton maintained that reason must always begin with an analysis of concrete empirical experience rather than a priori principles. After carefully observing and precisely recording data of experience, scientists attempt to formulate general principles or laws to account for their observations. When possible, controlled experiments should be carried out to confirm scientific conclusions. By following this method, one discovers the logic of the facts of experience. Repeated observation enables scientists to ascertain mathematical principles that explain observed data. The inductive method of establishing universal principles from particular experiences displaced the deductive method of determining particularities from universal or abstract notions and exerted enormous influence throughout the Enlightenment. A person as different from Newton in interests and in character as Voltaire could agree that inquiry should never "begin by inventing principles according to which we attempt to explain everything. We should say rather: Let us make an exact analysis of things. . . . When we cannot utilize the compass of mathematics or the torch of experience and physics, it is certain that we cannot take a single step forward."[19]

Two interrelated themes identified by Newton continued to be important throughout the eighteenth century. The first was the *principle of universality*. Later thinkers found Newton's ability to define one law under which all phenomena could be subsumed to be one of the most compelling features of his work. Newton showed that though the motions of distant planets and the falling of an apple seem to be qualitatively different, they are actually different instances of a single law. In short, the laws of nature are universal and thus valid at all times and in all circumstances. For many during this era, the principle of universality was not only descriptive of the outer, objective sphere of nature but also prescriptive in the inner realm of man's intellectual, ethical, and religious life.[20] Since the universality of the laws of nature is mirrored in human reason, it is possible to discover the laws by which nature actually operates. Closely related to the principle of universality is the *principle of unity* or of *harmony*. The discovery of universal laws enables one to see unity where previously only differences or even conflicts were visible. For people committed to this foundational belief, every contradiction is merely apparent and finally dissolves when the underlying universal principles are uncovered. Unity, therefore, is ontologically more real and morally more compelling than difference. Pope once again captures the point in a memorable couplet in his poem "An Essay on Man."

> The general ORDER, since the whole began,
> Is kept in Nature, and is kept in man.

In the course of his career, Newton wrote more theological than scientific works. As I have suggested, the modern scientific view of the world that developed during the Enlightenment was largely rooted in the Christian vision of man and of his place in the universe. The belief that the world and its laws are created by God is a basic presupposition of Newton's inquiry. Roger Cotes prefaced the second edition of Newton's *Principia* by explaining:

> The true business of natural philosophy [i.e., science] is . . . to inquire after those laws on which the Great Creator actually chose to found this most beautiful Frame of the World, not those by which he might have done the same, had he pleased. . . . Without all doubt this world . . . could arise from nothing but the perfectly free Will of God directing and presiding over all. From this Fountain it is that those laws, which we call the laws of Nature, have flowed, in which there appear many traces indeed of the most wise contrivance but not the least shadow of necessity.[21]

Within this schema, natural laws are not inherent in the cosmos but are imposed on inert matter by a creative God who transcends the world. Though Newton's consistent aim was to reinforce, rather than undercut, Protestant Christianity, it quickly became apparent that the implications of his work exceeded the limits he tried to place upon it.

John Locke played a crucial role in the elaboration of the implications of Newton's vision for human self-understanding. Heeding Pope's admonition "The proper study of mankind is Man," Locke devoted his major philosophical work (*An Essay concerning Human Understanding*, 1690) to an investigation of how we know. By so doing, he placed the problem of epistemology at the center of philosophical debate for succeeding generations and thereby set the course that British philosophy has followed down to the present day. Rejecting any notion of innate ideas and all versions of a priori knowledge, Locke argues that knowledge in the proper sense of the term must always be grounded in sense experience. The mind begins as a *tabula rasa* and gradually accumulates simple ideas through sense experience, which are then connected and associated to form more complex ideas. Locke's empiricism is insistently nondialectical; ideas are as atomistic as the world they represent. Two consequences of his argument prove particularly important for later philosophy as well as political and economic theory:

1. Interpretive schemata emerge from but do not act back upon sense data.
2. Complex ideas and systems can always be reduced to the simple units from which they are constituted.

When taken together, these two axioms lead to a mode of analysis in which the task of inquiry is to reduce complexity to underlying or antecedent simplicity. Locke's elaboration of a full-blown empirical epistemology would seem to sever the link between science and faith that Newton tried to preserve. If, after all, knowledge proper rests upon concrete experience, it would seem to be impossible to know the infinite God. In a manner reminiscent of Aquinas, Locke argues that, far from undercutting the relation between faith and reason, his epistemological investigation actually forms the foundation upon which the reasonableness of faith can be established. At the most basic level, Locke held that, given the principles of knowledge as he had defined them, it is possible to prove rationally the existence of God. According to what eventually was labeled the cosmological argument, it is possible to argue from the world (effect) to the existence of God as its necessary and sufficient cause. Following this line of analysis, Locke concludes: "from the consideration of ourselves, and what we infallibly find in our own constitutions, our reason leads us to the knowledge of this certain and evident truth,—*That there is an eternal, most powerful, and most knowing Being.*"[22] During the eighteenth century, theologians developed a popular variation of this approach—the teleological argument—to argue from the order or design of the world to God as its necessary designer. In his influential book *Natural Theology, or Evidences of the Existence and Attribution of the Deity Collected from the Appearances of Nature* (1854), William Paley, whose writings profoundly influenced Darwin, imagines a person finding a watch lying on the heath: "This mechanism being observed (it requires indeed an examination of the instrument, and perhaps some previous knowledge of the subject, to perceive and understand it; but being once, as we have said, observed and understood,) the inference, we think, is inevitable; that the watch must have had a maker; that there must have existed, at some time, and at some place or other, an artificer or artificers, who formed it for the purpose which we find it actually to answer; who comprehended its construction, and designed its use."[23] It is important to note that in this schema, order once again is external and imposed from without rather than internal and emergent from within.

For Locke, however, such rational argumentation did not exhaust the domain of faith. In the fourth book of his *Essay concerning Human Understanding*, he made a distinction that proved fateful for later philosophical and theological reflection:

> By what has been before said of reason, we may be able to make some guess at the distinction of things, into those that are according to,

above, and contrary to reason. 1. *According to reason* are such propositions whose truth we can discover by examining and tracing those ideas we have from sensation and reflection; and by natural deduction find to be true or probable. 2. *Above reason* are such propositions whose truth or probability we cannot by reason derive from those principles. 3. *Contrary to reason* are such propositions as are inconsistent with or irreconcilable to our clear and distinct ideas.[24]

The religious believer does not deny truths defined "according to reason," nor does he or she assert anything "contrary to reason"; nevertheless, revelation does disclose truths that, while not contrary to reason, are nonetheless "above reason."[25] This in-between sphere above but not contrary to reason is the realm of faith proper. Locke summarizes his position on this pivotal issue: "Faith . . . is the assent to any proposition, not thus made out by the deductions of reason, but upon the credit of the proposer, as coming from God, in some extra ordinary way of communication. This way of discovering truths to me, we call *revelation*."[26] Accordingly, reason and faith (or revelation) form an alliance: reason establishes certain truths of faith, and revelation discloses truths above, but not contrary to, reason. It soon became apparent, however, that this was not an alliance between equals—reason had the upper hand. In the final analysis, Locke concludes: "*reason must be our last judge and guide in everything*."[27] He developed the implications of his position in one of his most influential books, *The Reasonableness of Christianity* (1695). Through careful reflection, Locke insisted, the reasonableness of *all* aspects of Christian faith can be clearly established.

Just as the medieval synthesis began to dissolve as soon as it was formed, so Locke's alliance between reason and faith quickly unraveled. In the years immediately following the publication of his major works, the confidence in human reason waxed and the dependence on divine revelation waned. Revealed religion gradually was replaced by a completely rational, natural religion. The beginning of the dissolution of Locke's reconciliation between reason and revelation is evident in John Toland's *Christianity Not Mysterious*, published only one year after *The Reasonableness of Christianity*. In many ways Toland's influential work seems to support Locke's arguments. He admitted that revelation might serve a useful function but insisted that "what is once reveal'd we must as well understand as any other Matter in the World, *Revelation* being only of use to enform us, whilst the Evidence of its Subject perswades us."[28] In spite of apparent similarities between their viewpoints, Toland was much more suspicious of revelation than Locke. Indeed, he went so far as to deny that revelation can disclose any truths above or beyond reason: "From all the Observations, and what went before, it evidently follows that Faith is so far from being an implicate of Assent to any thing above Reason, that this Notion directly contradicts the Ends of Religion, the Nature of Man, and the Goodness and Wisdom of God."[29] The implications of the growing doubt about divine revelation became explicit in the book that represents the culmination of British deism—Matthew Tindal's Christianity as Old as Creation (1730). Tindal argues that there is "an exact Agreement between Natural and Reveal'd Religion; and that the Excellency of the Latter consists in being a Republication of the Former."[30] Christianity, then, teaches nothing we cannot discover by the free exercise of reason. On the one hand, reason and natural religion supplant revelation and Christianity; on the other hand, these developments extend the internalization of authority and the nascent autonomy implicit in Protestantism. Since each person possesses universal reason or has an implicit knowledge of the principles of natural religion, reliance on external authority (e.g., divine revelation, the church, or the Bible) is unnecessary. If people have courage to use their own reason, external authority becomes superfluous. Though reason increasingly infringed on the territory of revelation, British deists remained reluctant to take the final step of completely overthrowing religion. Things were different in eighteenth-century France.

Although profoundly influenced by the work of Newton and Locke, thinkers of the French Enlightenment tended to radicalize what they inherited from England.[31] This tendency was due in part to France's distinctive religious and political situation. Unlike England, where the Puritan revolution had already occurred, France had yet to undergo its revolution. The ancien régime retained considerable power and managed to thwart social and political change. In religious matters, the Catholic Church continued to exercise considerable control over the lives of most people. Moreover, there was a strong bond between the church and wealthy families of the French aristocracy, whose sons and daughters often assumed positions of responsibility within the ecclesiastical hierarchy. The combination of the church's wealth and its alliance with upper social classes made it appear to be an institution of privilege that opposed social change. This impression was deepened by the church's persistent effort to suppress disturbing intellectual inquiry. Most French Catholics in the eighteenth century were still convinced that the Catholic Church was the final arbiter of truth. The faithful held truth to be supernaturally ordained and preserved by an unbroken apostolic succession

dating back to Jesus' original followers. To doubt the authoritative proc-
lamations of the church was heresy, which was censored and at times
violently repressed. As late as 1757 a law was passed that condemned to
death any person who expressed "irreligious" opinions. Less extreme,
though no less significant, was the fact that those persons who were not
members of the Catholic Church had no recognized religious or civil status. Opposition to social change and intellectual progress created deep
conflicts between the church and many of Europe's most creative and
thoughtful citizens.

While many of the philosophes drew freely on the writings of Locke
and Newton, the version of deism that became the standard religion of
revolutionary France differed significantly from its British counterpart.
The French tended to be radically anticlerical and, thus, rejected any reconciliation between natural religion and Christianity. Voltaire spoke for
many in his generation when he wrote in *Les idées républicaines, par un
member d'un corps:*

> The most absurd of despotisms, the most humiliating of human na-
> ture, the most contradictory, the most deadly, is that of priests. Of
> all priestly dominations, that of the priests of Christianity is beyond
> question the most criminal. (V)
>
> When our bishop, who is there to serve and not to be served, to
> comfort the poor and not to devour their substance, to teach the cat-
> echism and not to dominate, dared, in a time of disorder, to call him-
> self the prince of a town of which he should be the shepherd, he was
> clearly guilty of rebellion and tyranny. (VI)[32]

When Voltaire famously proclaimed, "*Écrasez l'infame*," the target of his
attack was Christianity or more precisely Catholicism; his radical followers took this declaration as a call to arms, against the established
religio-political order.

In Baron Paul d'Holbach's celebrated essay *The System of Nature* (1770),
French atheism and materialism reached their most militant expression. Recalling arguments developed by Hume and anticipating critics a
century later, religion, he maintained, is the product of an ignorant and
fearful imagination. To support this contention, d'Holbach developed a
theory of projection to account for the origin of the idea of God. Arguing
that priests, anxious to retain power over the people, perpetuated the fiction of an almighty and jealous God, d'Holbach called upon his readers
to recognize that continued religious belief was keeping them in servitude to the church and was the major obstacle to intellectual and moral

progress. Religion is contrary to human nature and stands in the way of human happiness. However, since man creates religion, he can also destroy it. If human fulfillment is to be reached, the Christian schema of man as a creature of God who, by his own free action, has fallen into sin must be replaced by the image of an independent, rational being who has freed himself from the domination of an otherworldly, irrational God. While radicalizing British deism, d'Holbach nonetheless understood his position to be the logical extension of Newton's insights. Newton had discovered and verified universal laws of nature but had been unable to give up his belief in the Creator God. For d'Holbach, there was no need of a transcendent Creator to account for the world—nature, he insisted, is a self-regulating system governed by *inherent* natural laws. It is not even necessary to postulate God to start the world going, for matter is not, as Newton and British deists thought, inert; to the contrary, motion flows necessarily from matter.

While Newton's confidence in human reason was based in his faith in God's lawful behavior, for the philosophes, confidence in human reason and faith in God were inversely proportional. This difference has important political implications. Whereas American revolutionaries understood their revolt as an extension of their "errand into the wilderness," the French Revolution was inseparable from the negation of Christianity. The ostensible overthrow of Christianity did not, however, mean the end of religion; while turning away from the Christian God, leaders of the Revolution embraced the religion of reason. This concession grew out of their recognition that, though historical forms of religion are inadequate, symbolic networks nonetheless remain necessary for establishing the meaning and purpose without which life becomes unbearable for many people. To meet these needs, they created a humanistic religion replete with rituals devoted to the goddess Reason staged in Nôtre Dame. The new era inaugurated by the Revolution was marked by the institution of a new calendar in which A.D. 1789 became year 1 and traditional religious holidays and festivals were replaced by "reasonable" equivalents. To ensure the dissolution of Christendom, church lands were confiscated and auctioned to those who could afford to pay, thereby creating a new land-owning class that became increasingly conservative over the years. A decisive turning point for the Catholic Church during the revolutionary period occurred when the National Assembly passed the Civil Constitution of the Clergy on July 12, 1790. This statute was designed to bring the church into conformity with the structure and administrative organization of the state. These developments were met with violent opposition, which eventually led to civil war.[33]

The naturalistic civil religion at the heart of the French Revolution informs the Declaration of the Rights of Man and of the Citizen. This document begins by echoing opening lines of the Declaration of Independence: "Therefore the National Assembly recognizes and proclaims, in the presence and under the auspices of the Supreme Being [*Être Suprême*], the following rights of man and of the citizen." After this perfunctory reference, the Supreme Being is never again mentioned and the providential Creator, who figures so prominently in the American Declaration, never appears in the French counterpart. The thin veneer of religion is used to justify and legitimize beliefs and actions that are grounded in reason, nature, and, most important, humanity. This is evident in the first three articles.

1. Men are born and remain free and equal in rights. Social distinctions may be founded only upon the general good.
2. The aim of all political association is the preservation of the natural and imprescriptible rights of man. These rights are liberty, property, security, and resistance to oppression.
3. The principle of all sovereignty resides essentially in the nation. No body nor individual may exercise any authority which does not proceed directly from the nation.

Instead of insisting that these rights are given by the sovereign will of the Creator, representatives of the National Assembly declare that they are granted through the sovereignty that "resides essentially in the nation." In other words, the nation is substituted for the church, and the rights of the individual are, largely, the rights of the citizen. The foundational principle of this Declaration as well as the entire Revolution is formulated in Article 6:

> Law is the expression of the general will. Every citizen has a right to participate personally, or through his representative, in its foundation. It must be the same for all, whether it protects or punishes. All citizens, being equal in the eyes of the law, are equally eligible to all dignities and to all public positions and occupations, according to their abilities, and without distinction except that of their virtues and talents.[34]

The notion of the general will is, of course, borrowed from Rousseau's *Social Contract* (1762). The political significance of this principle should not obscure its theological roots and philosophical implications. In Rousseau's political theory, the will of God in effect becomes *la volonté générale*, which is simultaneously universal and particular. This will is autonomous and, therefore, self-legislating. Since all persons are representatives of this general will, every individual is essentially free. Freedom and representation—political and, as we will see, artistic—are inseparable: freedom expresses itself in representatives as well as representations, and both representatives and representations are grounded in the groundless ground of freedom. The constitutive attributes of the general will are identical to the characteristic traits of the traditional Christian God the revolutionaries sought to overthrow. *La volonté générale* is "indivisible," "infallible," and "indestructible." Through a dialectical reversal, the transcendent disappears and becomes incarnate in the general will of the people—*vox dei* becomes *vox populi*.

Rousseau's notion of the general will discloses a voluntarism at the heart of French rationalism, which, in turn, points to the abiding, though rarely recognized, significance of Protestantism not only for the American but for the French Revolution as well. Bloody religious wars and sustained political repression did not completely destroy Protestantism in France. Even after the infamous Saint Bartholomew's Day Massacre (1572) and the revocation of the Edict of Nantes (1685), French Huguenots continued to exercise covert as well as overt influence throughout French society and culture. It is also important to recall that Calvin was French, and although the Reformation ultimately failed in France, *The Institutes of the Christian Religion* had a profound impact on French thought and culture. While the French Revolution obviously would have been impossible without the Enlightenment, Calvin's theology and political theory played an important role in shaping the course of events. We have already seen that both *la clarté française* and the logical method characteristic of the writings of modern writers and French rationalism are indebted to the rigors of Calvin's writings and their elaboration in Protestant scholasticism. It is also important to recall that Rousseau was born in Geneva in 1712 to a Calvinist watchmaker. Although he converted to Catholicism and left Geneva in 1838, he always maintained his connection with the city and in 1754 returned to Geneva to recover his citizenship. In spite of the change in his religious affiliation, Calvinism left a deep and often-unrecognized impression on his understanding of social organization and political theory. In *The Social Contract,* he comments: "Those who think of Calvin only as a theologian know very little of the full extent of his genius. Our wise edicts, in the framing of which he played a large part, do him no less honor than his *Institutes*. Whatever changes time may bring to our religious observances, so long as the love of country and of liberty is a living reality with us, the memory of that great man will be held in veneration."³⁵ Rousseau's translation of the sovereign will of the transcendent God into the sovereign will of the people repeats the dialectical reversal, which we have discovered at the heart of Calvin's theology. When the Creator God is so powerful that everything is a representation of his free will, divine and human action become indistinguishable. The far-reaching implications of this dialectical reversal become clear in the course of the nineteenth century.³⁶

FIGURING SUBJECTS

In a memorial essay for Kant written in 1804, Schelling explained the close relationship between Kantian philosophy and the French Revolution:

> The claim that only the great event of the French Revolution gained him the general public regard that his philosophy alone would never have earned is nothing less than fictitious. A few of his enthusiastic adherents, not without perceiving some special work of fate, marveled at the coincidence of these two revolutions, which, in their eyes, were equally important. They did not realize that it was one and the same long-developing spirit that, in accordance with the distinctive features of the two nations and circumstances, expressed itself in one case in a real revolution and in the other in an ideal one.³⁷

Schelling's remark anticipates Marx's claim four decades later that, "in politics, the Germans have *thought* what other nations have *done*."³⁸ Whether philosophy anticipates or follows politics, it is clear that significant change is never simply a function of material conditions but always presupposes the emergence of new ideas. Though they interpreted the relation between person and state or between citizen and nation somewhat differently, French and American revolutionaries found the idea of the freedom of the individual subject politically transformative.

In 1784, Kant published a brief but influential essay entitled "What Is Enlightenment?" in which he stresses the interrelation of reason and freedom. "Enlightenment is man's release from his self-incurred tutelage. Tutelage is man's inability to make use of his understanding without direction from another. Self-incurred is this tutelage when its cause lies not in lack of reason but in lack of resolution and courage to use it without direction from another. *Sapere aude!* 'Have courage to use your own reason!' That is the motto of enlightenment."³⁹ This definition of enlightenment turns on his distinction between heteronomy, which derives from the Greek *hetero*, "other," plus *nomos*, "law," and autonomy, which derives from *auto*, "self," plus *nomos*. While heteronomy involves determination by another (e.g., God, sovereign, parent, or teacher), autonomy is the self-determination or self-legislation through which the subject gives itself the law. Far from arbitrary, free actions are, from this point of view, both rational and normative. Though reason is deployed both theoretically (in thinking) and practically (in acting), Kant insists on the primacy of the practical. Reason and will are inseparable: reason is essentially an *activity*, and if activity is free activity, it must be reasonable. In the Second Critique, Kant underscores the primacy of practical reason by arguing that freedom is the pivotal notion for his entire philosophy: "The concept of freedom, in so far as its reality is proved by an apodictic law of practical reason, is the keystone of the whole architecture of the system of pure reason and even of speculative reason."[40] Freedom, however, proves to be a complex keystone because it harbors an irreducible ambiguity. The more closely one examines Kant's argument, the clearer it becomes that freedom involves not only autonomy but also what can best be described as *an-archy*. In this context, the term *an-archy* does not mean the absence of form and thus disorder, confusion, or chaos. Rather, an-archy suggests the absence (*an*, "without") of any beginning (*arkhe*) and by extension the lack of an originary foundation. That which is anarchic is groundless. While Kant does not always seem to recognize the significant implications of his argument, his critical philosophy demonstrates that autonomy presupposes an-archy, which is the nonfoundational foundation or the groundless ground of the law that the self-legislating subject gives to itself. As we will see in detail below, autonomy and anarchy intersect in the activity of the imagination through which the interplay of word and deed deepens the contradictions of subjectivity. To understand the importance of these two aspects of freedom, it is necessary to consider why autonomy is impossible apart from anarchy.

The notion of autonomy is the structural principle around which all three critiques are organized. The theoretical and practical deployments of reason are isomorphic: a universal principle of reason is brought to bear on particular sense data. While theoretical reason organizes the sensible manifold of intuition through a priori forms of intuition and categories of understanding, practical reason controls idiosyncratic sensible inclinations through universal moral principles. Kant's analysis of reason is a critical response to the unexpected conclusions reached by representatives of the French and British Enlightenment. By radicalizing the empirical method, which begins with nominalist philosophy and is extended in Newtonian science, philosophers effectively undercut the two foundational principles of the eighteenth-century political and intellectual revolutions: freedom and reason. D'Holbach did not stop with his criticism of religion but proceeded to extend the principles of Newtonian science to human beings. The result was the unholy alliance of atheism, materialism, and determinism, which became emblematic of the French Enlightenment. If Newton is right, d'Holbach argues, no part of the universe is exempt from the rule of law. Not only the movement of planets and apples but also human thought and action are determined by universal natural laws. From this point of view, freedom is a chimera—thinking and willing are determined by laws that cannot be broken or suspended. A French doctor named Julien Offray de La Mettrie gave this deterministic picture of human life popular expression in a book with the title *Man a Machine* (1747). A devout disciple of Newton, La Mettrie used the scientific method to argue that human thought, feeling, and action can be reduced to the machinic operations of physiological processes. In words befitting a country renowned for its gastronomic excellence, he argues: "The human body is a machine, which winds itself up, the living image of perpetual motion. Food nourishes the movements which fever excites. Without food, the soul pines away, goes mad, and dies exhausted. It is a candle whose light flares up the moment before it goes out. But nourish the body, pour into its veins invigorating juices and strong liquors; then the soul, taking on their strength, arms itself with a proud courage, and the soldier whom water would have made flee, now made bold, runs joyously to death to the sound of drums."[41] La Mettrie's vision of man leaves no room for human freedom—thought and action are nothing more than symptoms of bodily functions.

The eclipse of reason and freedom by materialism and determinism was not limited to France. In Scotland, Hume's radicalization of empiricism as Newton and Locke had defined it led to skeptical conclusions about knowledge of both the world and God. In *A Treatise of Human Nature* (1738–40), Hume develops a radically empirical epistemology in which the difference between sense impressions and ideas is quantitative rather than qualitative. From this perspective, culture in all of its complexity can be reduced to the simplicity of sense data. In this context, Hume's most important argument is his insistence that a consistent empirical epistemology calls into question the objective validity of the principle of causality. Causality, like every other idea, is grounded in sense experience.

> The only connexion or relation of objects, which can lead us beyond the immediate impressions of our memory and senses, is that of cause and effect; and that because 'tis the only one, on which we can found a just inference from one object to another. The idea of cause and effect is deriv'd from experience, which informs us, that such particular objects, in all past instances, have been constantly conjoin'd with each other: And as an object similar to one of these is suppos'd to be immediately present in its impression, we thence presume on the existence of one similar to its usual attendant.[42]

Far from a universal objective law of nature, causality is a subjective habit of mind. This argument proved decisive for later developments within and beyond the bounds of philosophy. The experience of the repeated conjunction of two events leads people to assume that there is a necessary connection between them. "When two *species* of objects have always been observed to be conjoined together," Hume argues, "I can *infer*, by custom, the existence of one wherever I *see* the existence of the other; and this I call an argument from experience."[43] There is, however, no warrant for the movement from particular past experiences to a universal law, which determines that these events must always occur together. All that can reasonably be claimed is that in the past, whenever one event occurred, the other always followed. What appear to be universal natural laws are, then, nothing more than extrapolations of past subjective experience. When carried to its logical conclusion, Hume's argument leads to skepticism about the lawful character of the outer world as well as the relation of an individual's private experience to the experience of others.

The implications of Hume's reconstruction of the principle of causality were no less far-reaching for religious matters.[44] Many believers who sought to defend religion during the Enlightenment usually conformed to the temper of the era by framing their arguments in terms of empirical evidence and adhering to the rules of inductive reasoning. The two most popular arguments for the existence of God—the cosmological and the teleological argument—presupposed the objective validity of causal law, which Hume calls into question. If causality is subjective habit rather than objective law, then belief in the existence of God cannot be established by rational argument. In *Dialogues concerning Natural*

Religion, which Hume withheld from publication until after his death in 1776, he methodically takes apart the empirical justification for Christianity as well as natural religion. Far from rational, religion, he concludes, arises from irrational sensations, inclinations, and impulses.[45]

Kant's three critiques are directed at the triple threat of skepticism, determinism, and atheism. His critical philosophy prepares the way for the defense of religion in terms of moral activity rather than theoretical speculation. Every aspect of his argument is organized around a series of binary oppositions, which he both articulates and attempts to reconcile:

Autonomy / Heteronomy
Freedom / Determinism
Reason / Sensibility
A priori / A posteriori
Universality / Particularity
Objectivity / Subjectivity
Obligation / Inclination
Form / Matter

Kant's immediate successors were divided between those who thought he had not gone far enough and those who thought he had gone too far in formulating a comprehensive philosophical system that could mediate these oppositions. The former argued that his reconciliation of opposites remained incomplete, and the latter insisted that his effort to synthesize these opposites was misguided because it obscured the irreducible contradictions and inescapable aporiae inherent in thought and life. The unresolved tensions in Kant's work set the terms of debate in the nineteenth century and continue to influence critical reflection and practice down to the present day.

It has frequently been observed that Kant's "Copernican revolution" is the theoretical equivalent of the political revolution in France. Rarely noted but no less important is the fact that one of Kant's most significant philosophical innovations was his translation of ontology into epistemology. To understand the implications of this development, it is necessary to trace the religio-philosophical genealogy of Kant's epistemology all the way back to Plato and early Christian apologists. In Plato's myth of origin, the world is created by a Demiurge who brings together unchanging forms with the undifferentiated flux of matter. Within this framework the activity of creation is a process of *formation* through which order is brought to chaos. Early Christian apologists, eager to

demonstrate that their religion did not involve unsophisticated superstition, which was politically subversive, reinterpreted fundamental
theological principles in terms of Platonic philosophy. Instead of an intermediate being situated between eternity and time like the Demiurge,
the Christian God, they argued, is the eternal creator of the world. For
these apologists, Platonic forms become the mind of God, or the Logos,
which is understood as the eternal Son of the divine Father. Inasmuch
as the Father always creates through the Son, the world is an expression
of the divine Logos and is, therefore, logical, reasonable, or, in a more
recent idiom, Logocentric. Human reason is the reflection of the Logos
through which people can comprehend the world God has created.

In Kant's account of theoretical reason, Platonic forms and the divine
Logos become the forms of intuition and categories of understanding,
and the undifferentiated flux of matter becomes the sensible manifold of
intuition. Just as Platonic forms and the divine Logos are universal and
unchanging, so the forms of intuition and categories of understanding
are a priori rather than a posteriori and are therefore universal. Alternatively, Kant's epistemology can be expressed in terms of contemporary
information theory: the mind is programmed to process data. Knowledge results from the synthesis of the universal forms of intuition and
categories of understanding and the particular data of sense experience.
This information processing brings order to chaos by unifying the multiplicity of data we are constantly experiencing. The agency through
which this synthesis occurs is the imagination—*die Einbildungskraft*.
"Now, since every appearance contains a manifold," Kant argues, "and
since different perceptions therefore occur in the mind separately and
singly, a combination of them, such as they cannot have in sense itself,
is demanded. There must therefore exist in us an active faculty for the
synthesis of this manifold. To this faculty I give the title, imagination.
Its action, when immediately directed to perceptions, I entitled apprehension. Since imagination has to bring the manifold of intuition into
the form of an image, it must previously have taken the impressions up
into its activity, that is, have apprehended them."[46] Since the imagination articulates objects, it is the necessary condition of the possibility
of knowledge and as such is *transcendental*. To fulfill this function, the
imagination must operate at the edge or on the border *between* understanding and sensation. Kant writes: "Obviously there must be some
third thing, which is homogeneous on the one hand with the category,
and on the other hand with the appearance, and which thus makes the
application of the former to the latter possible. This mediating represen-

tation must be pure, that is, void of all empirical content, and yet at the same time, while it must be in one respect *intellectual*, it must in another be *sensible*. Such a representation is the *transcendental schema*."[47] Kant describes the operation of the imagination as the "schematization of the categories." In a manner reminiscent of the transcendent Demiurge who brings form to chaos and the transcendent God who creates through his Logos, the imagination deploys transcendental schemata to organize experience and thereby create the world in which we dwell.[48]

For Kant, all knowledge is synthetic and thus presupposes unification at every level. The data of experience are first processed through the forms of intuition (i.e., space and time) and then organized to conform to the categories of understanding through the transcendental imagination. The diverse objects of understanding are, then, unified through what Kant labels the three interrelated Ideas of reason—God, self, and world. Since these Ideas do not arise from and cannot be verified by sense experience, they do not constitute knowledge. Their function is regulative rather than constitutive; that is, they are useful heuristic devices but do not necessarily tell us anything about the world.

Kant was convinced that his analysis of reason provided a response to Humean skepticism and thereby secured the possibility of knowledge. Since the categories of understanding are universal, the knowledge they yield is objective. The data of experience are different but everybody processes them the same way. The principle of causality, for example, is not the result of arbitrary subjective habit but expresses the necessary structure of the human mind. It is clear, however, that such "objectivity" remains subjective because it tells us nothing certain about the way things really are in themselves. Kant's most incisive critics argued that, instead of establishing the conditions of the possibility of knowledge, he actually exposed the conditions of the *impossibility* of knowledge. Kant responded by insisting that this limitation is really an advantage. By limiting knowledge of the world, he thought he had made room for the rational affirmation of the freedom of the self and the existence of God.

Kant's argument in *Critique of Practical Reason* (1788) is strictly parallel to his argument in *Critique of Pure Reason* (1781). Reason is one, though its deployment is triune. In moving from theory to practice, the universal categories of understanding become the universal moral law, and the sensible manifold of intuition becomes multiple sensory intuitions and conflicting sensual desires. The "fundamental law of pure practical reason," Kant argues, is "to act that the maxim of your will could always hold at the same time as a principle establishing a universal law." He takes this law to be "a fact of reason," which is "plain to all."[49] Just as the First Critique is devoted to ascertaining the conditions of the possibility of knowledge, so the Second Critique seeks to establish the necessary presuppositions of moral activity. In his definitive study *Between Kant and Hegel*, Dieter Henrich writes: "Kant had already shown that the concept of mind as the subject of knowledge is not possible without the idea of a world that laws govern. Thus a certain concept of the mind implies a conception, an 'image' of the world. We don't have a concept of mind unless we see that the concept of the world is already implied in the self-understanding of the mind. In sum, to develop a conceptual framework for the interpretation of the mind that is based only on mental activity leads directly to the insight that mental activity always implies a world within which such activity occurs."[50] The exercise of practical reason entails a moral *Weltanschauung*, which, Kant maintains, is impossible apart from three postulates: freedom, God, and immortality. Freedom, I have noted, is for Kant "the keystone of the whole architecture of the system of pure reason and even of speculative reason." While the limitation of causality and, by extension, determinism to a law of the mind preserves the possibility of freedom, the fact of the moral law implies its actuality. In Kant's terms, "freedom is the *ratio essendi* of the moral law" and the moral law is "the *ratio cognoscendi* of freedom."[51] If the subject is not free, moral activity is impossible. In this context, Kant defines freedom as autonomy:

> The autonomy of the will is the sole principle of all moral laws and of duties conforming to them; heteronomy of choice, on the other hand, not only does not establish any obligation but is opposed to the principle of duty and to the morality of the will.
>
> The sole principle of morality consists in independence from all material law (i.e., a desired object) and in the accompanying determination of choice by the mere form of giving universal law, which a maxim must be capable of having. That independence, however, is freedom in the negative sense, while this intrinsic legislation of pure and thus practical reason is freedom in the positive sense. Therefore, the moral law expresses nothing else than the autonomy of the pure practical reason, i.e., freedom.[52]

In moral activity, the individual agent regulates personal inclinations and desires through the universal moral law. For an action to be moral, the will cannot be influenced by either desired objects or external pressures but must be determined by nothing other than itself.

While moral action cannot be determined by an object, it is nonetheless unavoidably intentional and, therefore, necessarily entails an object or, more precisely, an objective. The sole legitimate object of moral action is the *summum bonum*, which Kant defines as happiness proportionate to virtue. "Happiness is the condition of a rational being in the world, in whose whole existence everything goes according to wish and will. It thus rests on the harmony of nature with his entire end and with the essential determining ground of his will." If happiness is the conformity of will and world, it can be brought about only by a being wise enough to discern moral intention and powerful enough to control the natural world. God alone meets these requirements. Moral activity, therefore, presupposes a moral governor who actualizes "the Kingdom of God in which nature and morality come into harmony." It is important to note that, although Kant's God is a moral governor, he is not himself a moral being, because God's duty and desire are never in conflict. In terms Nietzsche uses in a different, though related, context, God is "beyond good and evil." Human beings, by contrast, are moral because they never are what they ought to be. Echoing Luther's account of the divided subject, Kant's moral agent confesses: I am what I am not. The best for which such a divided self can hope is infinite progress in moral development, which is impossible apart from personal immortality. Summarizing the import of the three postulates of practical reason, Kant concludes: "If, therefore, the highest good is impossible according to practical rules, then the moral law, which commands that it be furthered, must be fantastic, directed to empty imaginary ends, and consequently inherently false."[53] Taken together, freedom, God, and immortality provide a schema in which moral action appears to be reasonable, and the world, therefore, makes sense.

Kant realized that his interpretation of reason in both its theoretical and its practical deployments deepens the contradictions of subjectivity by interiorizing the conflict between the various binary opposites he articulates. With the movement from heteronomy to autonomy, universality, which had been externally imposed, is inwardly legislated. In the Third Critique, devoted to aesthetic judgment, Kant attempts to mediate these oppositions through the notion of inner teleology. In contrast to every form of utility and instrumentality, in which means and ends are externally related, inner teleology involves what Kant describes as "purposiveness without purpose," in which means and ends are reciprocally related in such a way that each becomes itself in and through the other and neither can be itself apart from the other. Kant illustrates this idea by describing the interplay of whole and part in the work of art. "The parts of the thing combine of themselves into the unity of a whole by being reciprocally cause and effect of their form. For this is the only way in which it is possible that the idea of the whole may conversely, or reciprocally, determine, in its turn, the form and combination of all the parts, not as cause—for that would make it an art product—but as the epistemological basis upon which the systematic unity of the form and combination of all the manifold contained in the given matter become cognizable for the person estimating it."[54] Though not immediately obvious, this formulation of inner teleology marks a tipping point in cultural and social history whose ramifications are still emerging. In hindsight it is clear that the nineteenth century began with the 1790 publication of the *Critique of Judgment*. The distinction between external and internal teleology is the philosophical articulation of the transition from a mechanical to an organic schema for interpreting the world. What Kant discovered is the *principle of constitutive relationality, in which identity is differential rather than oppositional*. The immediate implications of this insight were worked out by romantic artists and idealistic philosophers during the closing decade of the eighteenth century and the early years of the nineteenth century. But the significance of Kant's insight is even more far-reaching. In later chapters I will consider how the structure he identifies not only defines modern and postmodern art but also operates in today's information networks and financial markets and anticipates current theories of biological organisms as well as the nature of life itself. For the moment, it is sufficient to note that Kant offers two examples of inner teleology—living organisms and beautiful works of art. I will consider the question of life in chapter 7; here I will concentrate on art.

The Third Critique extends the principle of autonomy from theoretical and practical reason to the work of art understood as both the process of production and the product produced. In contrast to art produced for the market, which is utilitarian and as such has an extrinsic purpose, fine art is not produced for any external end but is created for its own sake. Never referring to anything other than itself, high art is art about art and is, therefore, self-referential and thus self-reflexive. But while seeming to be completely autonomous, the structures of self-referentiality and self-reflexivity are considerably more complicated than they initially appear because they presuppose something they cannot assimilate. The interruption of the self-referential circuit of reflexivity exposes aporiae, which are the condition of creativity. The pivot upon which this analysis turns is the interplay of the imagination and representation in the production of self-consciousness. In Kant's account of the imagination, the theology of the word and the theology of the deed come together in a notion of emergent creativity that prepares the way for the death of the transcendent God.

For the young writers, artists, and philosophers gathered in Jena in the years immediately after the publication of the Third Critique, Kant's critical philosophy opened the possibility of completing what began in France by shifting the revolutionary struggle from politics to philosophy and poetry. In a world without adequate social, political, and economic institutions and ravaged by the early stages of industrialization, writers and critics sought to overcome personal alienation and social fragmentation by cultivating new forms of unification and integration. Kant glimpsed the possibility of a unity that nourished, rather than repressed, differences in his account of the reciprocity of inner teleology but was unable to carry his argument through to its necessary conclusion. Given the limitation of knowledge established in the First Critique, he was forced to restrict his notion of beauty to a regulative idea, which might or might not describe the way things really are in the actual world. Since the work of art figures reconciliation as nothing more than an unrealizable idea, it actually deepens the oppositions and fragmentation it is designed to overcome. To accomplish what both the French and the Kantian revolutions leave undone, romantics and idealists argue, it is necessary to realize the Idea by transforming the world into a work of art. As apocalypse by revolution gave way to apocalypse by imagination and cognition, consciousness turned inward and became self-conscious. In pushing itself to its limit, however, autonomous self-consciousness becomes an-archic. That is to say, the subject discovers that it has emerged from a groundless ground that it can never fathom. This fissure creates the opening for the postmodern critique of modernism. Contrary to expectation, the transition from autonomy to an-archy, which is the condition of the possibility of postmodernism, passes through Hegel's speculative system.

Kant's successors realized that the inner teleological or self-referential structure he identified discloses the self-reflexive structure of self-consciousness. In self-consciousness, the subject turns back on itself by becoming an object to itself. Self-as-subject and self-as-object are reciprocally related in such a way that each becomes itself through the other, and neither can be itself apart from the other. The structure of self-relation constitutive of self-conscious subjectivity presupposes the activity of self-representation (fig. 13). Though it is not immediately obvious precisely at the point where self-consciousness seems to be complete, it approaches its constitutive limit. Henrich identified the crucial

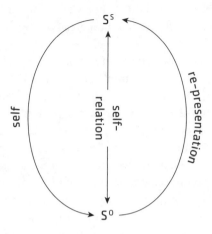

Figure 13. Self-Consciousness

question in commenting on Fichte's reading of Kant: "We might cast this question another way: Will ontological discourse always make use of the premise that something can be said about the mind that is not of the mind, and that the mind can say something that is of the mind about what is not of the mind, so that the two discourses can never be derived from one another—or even from a third discourse, thereby precluding any fully intelligible linear formulation?"[55] Henrich implies that the impossibility of explaining self-consciousness through linear models does not necessarily mean that the self-reflexivity of self-consciousness is circular. To the contrary, when consciousness turns back on itself, it discovers a lacuna without which it is impossible but with which it is incomplete. The pressing question is: Where does that which the self-conscious subject represents to itself come from? If self-as-subject and self-as-object are codependent, neither can be the originary cause of the other. The activity of self-representation, therefore, presupposes a more primordial presentation, which must originate elsewhere. This elsewhere is the limit that is impossible to think but without which thinking is impossible. "Thinking," as Jean-Luc Nancy explains in another context, "is always thinking on the limit. The limit of comprehending defines thinking. Thus thinking is always thinking about the incomprehensible—about this incomprehensible that 'belongs' to every comprehending, as its own limit."[56] This limit is the edge of chaos where order simultaneously dissolves and emerges. To understand what occurs along this border, it is necessary to consider the dynamics of representation in more detail.

The question of representation—*Vorstellung*—runs through all three critiques. In the First Critique, Kant argues: "A concept [*Begriff*] formed from notions [*Notio*] and transcending the possibility of experience is an idea [*Idee*] or concept of reason."[57] In the exercise of practical reason, Ideas that lie beyond experience and hence remain regulative are actualized as they become practically effective in moral activity. But postulates can no more be experienced than ideas and, therefore, yield no knowledge even though they are rational. An Idea or a postulate, Rodolphe Gasché explains, "is a representation by a concept of the concepts that serve to represent representation with consciousness."

> Representation here translates the German *Vorstellung,* a term Kant uses to designate the operation by which the different faculties that constitute the mind bring their respective objects before themselves. Yet when Kant claims that in spite of the impossibility of intuitively representing (and thus knowing) the ideas, they nonetheless play a decisive role in the realm of cognition, or that in the moral realm they acquire an at least partial concretization, he broaches the question of the becoming present of the highest, but intuitively unpresentable representation that is the idea. This is the problem of the *presentation,* or *Darstellung,* of the idea, and it is rigorously distinct from that of representation. The issue is no longer how to depict, articulate, or illustrate something already present yet resisting adequate discursive or figural expression, but of how something acquires presence—reality, actuality, effectiveness—in the first place. The question of *Darstellung* centers on the coming into presence, or occurring, of the ideas.[58]

Coming into presence (*Darstellung*) is the condition of the possibility of re-presentation (*Vorstellung*). But how does such "presencing," or presentation, occur?

In his analysis of Hegel's concept of experience, Heidegger suggests a possible answer to this question when commenting on Hegel's claim that "science, in making its appearance, *is* an appearance itself."

> The appearance is the authentic presence itself: the *parousia* of the Absolute. In keeping with its absoluteness, the Absolute is with us of its own accord. In its will to be with us, the Absolute is being present. In itself, thus bringing itself forward, the Absolute is for itself. For the sake of the will of the *parousia* alone, the presentation of knowledge as phenomenon is necessary. The presentation is bound to remain

turned toward the will of the Absolute. The presentation is itself a *willing* [emphasis added], that is, not just a wishing and striving but the action itself, if it pulls itself together within its nature.[59]

This remarkable insight complicates Hegelianism in a way that opens it up *as if* from within. Far from a closed system, which as a stable structure would be the embodiment of the Logos, the Hegelian Absolute here appears to be an infinitely restless will that wills itself in willing everything that emerges in nature and history and wills everything that exists in willing itself. Heidegger explains the implications of this reading of Hegel when he interprets the inconceivability of freedom in Kant's philosophy in a way that points toward his own account of the groundless ground of Being: "The only thing that we comprehend is its incomprehensibility. Freedom's incomprehensibility consists in the fact that it resists com-prehension since it is freedom that transposes us into the realization of Being, not in the mere representation of it."[60]

The interplay of *Darstellung* (presentation) and *Vorstellung* (representation) occurs through the activity of *Einbildungskraft*—imagination. The etymology of *Einbildungskraft* is important for Kant's argument as well as for its elaboration by his followers. *Bild* means "picture," "image," "likeness," or "representation," and *Bildung* means "formation," "forming," "generation," and, by extension, "culture," as well as "education." The verb *bilden* means "to form," "fashion," "shape," "mold," or "construct." Finally, *ein* means "one." *Einbildungskraft*, then, is the activity of formation or construction by which something is fashioned into a unified image or representation. The multiple nuances of *Einbildungskraft* are captured in the English word *figure*. *Figure*, which, as I noted in the development of my theory of religion in chapter 1, is both a noun and a verb and derives from the Latin *figura* (form, shape, figure). In addition to "form" and "shape," *figure* means the outline or silhouette of a thing as well as a pictorial or sculptural representation. A figure also refers to a diagram, pattern, design, and number. The verb *to figure* means "to shape or form something," "make a likeness of," "depict," "represent," and "adorn with design or figures." In mathematics, to figure is to calculate or compute. Finally, *to figure* can mean both "to take into consideration," "solve," "decipher," "comprehend" and, in a more recent twist, "to fail to solve," "decipher," "comprehend," as in "Go figure!" Figuration, by extension, refers to the act of forming something into a particular shape. What makes the words *figure, figuring,* and *figuration* so interesting and useful is the intersection of the three threads of meaning: form (object), forming (activity), and comprehending and/or failing to comprehend (thinking or reflecting). Kant's account of the imagination involves all three of these meanings—the imagination figures in all three senses of the word.

While Kant clearly and consistently distinguishes the theoretical and practical uses of reason, we have noted that he insists on the "primacy of practical reason." Cognition presupposes volition, but willing does not necessarily presuppose thinking. The imbrication of thinking and willing lies at the heart of the imagination. In his analysis of aesthetic judgment in the Third Critique, Kant offers a definition of the imagination that proved decisive for many later writers, artists, philosophers, and theologians: "If, now, imagination must in the judgment of taste be regarded in its freedom, then, to begin with, it is not taken as reproductive as in subjection to the laws of association, but as productive in exerting an activity of its own (as originator of arbitrary forms of possible intuitions)."[61] The imagination, then, involves two interrelated activities, which Kant describes as productive and reproductive. In its productive modality, the imagination figures forms that the reproductive imagination combines and recombines to create the schemata that organize the noisy data of experience into comprehensible patterns. Inasmuch as the imagination (Ein-bildung-skraft) is the activity of formation (bilden/Bildung), it is, in effect, an in-formation process. Information and noise, as we have already discovered, are not opposites but are codependent: information is noise in-formation and new information disrupts old patterns to create noise.

The imagination both creates schemata that organize experience and disrupts and dislocates stabilizing structures (fig. 14). The figures that the productive imagination forms are *arbitrary* insofar as they are not determined by other figures but are *freely* formed and thus original. Freedom, in other words, is the condition of the possibility of the imagination and, therefore, of knowledge as well. Fichte was the first to recognize implications of this interpretation of the imagination that Kant himself did not fully realize. In *The Science of Knowledge*, he argues:

> Our doctrine here is therefore that all reality—*for us* being understood, as it cannot be otherwise understood in a system of transcendental philosophy—is brought forth solely by the imagination. . . . Yet if it is now proved, as the present system claims to prove it, that this act of imagination forms the basis for the possibility of our consciousness, our life, our existence for ourselves, that is, our existence

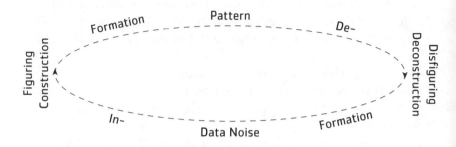

Figure 14. Imagination

as selves, then it cannot be eliminated unless we are to abstract from the self; which is a contradiction, since it is impossible that what does the abstracting should abstract from itself.

I will return to the seemingly outrageous claim that the imagination is the basis of all reality in the next section. At this point, it is important to understand why consciousness presupposes the imagination. The argument once again turns on the relation between *Darstellung* and *Vorstellung*. Theoretical and practical reason are impossible apart from representations. Re-presentation, however, is impossible apart from antecedently given data (Latin *datum*, "something given"; from *do*, *dare*, "to give"). The question, then, becomes: What gives? How does *Darstellung* occur? How do representations *emerge*? How are figures figured? According to Fichte, presentation is an act that "occurs with absolute spontaneity," and therefore, *Darstellung* is "grounded" in freedom. Such freedom is not the freedom *of* subjectivity but the freedom *from* subjectivity through which both subjectivity and objectivity are posited or given.

Autonomy is self-grounded, but an-archy is groundless. It "is not the diffraction of a principle, nor the multiple effect of a cause, but is the an-archy—the origin removed from every logic of origin, from every archaeology."[62] Heidegger describes the an-archy of freedom glimpsed in the presentational activity of the imagination as an abyss. In *Kant and the Problem of Metaphysics*, he explains: "In the radicalism of his questions, Kant brought the 'possibility' of metaphysics to the abyss. He saw the unknown. He had to shrink back. It was not just that the transcendental power of the imagination frightened him, but rather that in between [the two editions of the First Critique] pure reason as reason drew him increasingly under its spell."[63] This abyss, or *Abgrund*, from which all determination emerges is the groundless ground that is indistinguishable from nothing. Such an unfathomable ground is the no-thing on which every foundation founders. Hegel explains the relationship between nothingness and freedom: "In its highest form of explication nothingness would be freedom. But this highest form is negativity insofar as it inwardly deepens itself to its highest intensity; and in this way it is itself affirmation—indeed absolute affirmation."[64] Negativity is affirmative insofar as it is the condition of creative emergence of everything that exists. Just as God creates freely *ex nihilo*, so the productive imagination creates freely out of nothing.

In Kant's doctrine of the imagination, theology becomes anthropology in a way that subverts the simple opposition between word and deed or structure and event. As word issues from will, so structure emerges through event. This process is (the) infinite. Spirit, Hegel argues, "is not an inert being but, on the contrary, is absolutely restless being, pure activity, the negating or ideality of every fixed determination of the understanding; not abstractly simple but, in its simplicity, at the same time distinguishes itself from itself; not an essence that is already finished and complete before its manifestation, hiding itself behind its appearances, but an essence that is truly actual only through the determinate forms of its necessary self-manifestation."[65] This interpretation of the will further deepens the contradictions of subjectivity. Since the will "is actual only through the determinate forms of its necessary self-manifestation," it can be itself only in and through its particular instantiations. While Kant's analysis brings together universality (i.e., categories and the moral law) and particularity (sense data and sensible inclinations), Hegel demonstrates that, inasmuch as the will is inescapably active, the universal (will) is *in itself* particular (i.e., determinate) and particulars (determinations) are *in themselves* universal (i.e., instantiations of the will). So understood, the subject can be itself only by *not* being itself. When interpreted in this way, the will is not a unified self-identical ground but is the play of differences that can be itself only by always being other than itself. The noncoincidence of the self with itself issues in its infinite restlessness. Heidegger brings the argument full circle by *not* closing the loop of self-reflexivity: "This original, essential constitution of humankind, 'rooted' in the transcendental power of the imagination, is the 'unknown' into which Kant must have looked if he spoke of the 'root unknown to us,' for the unknown is not that of which we simply know nothing. Rather, it is what pushes against us as something disquieting in what is known."[66] The analysis of the transcendental power of the imagination "reveals" the concealment at the heart of subjectivity. Contrary to the promises of Descartes, the inward turn of consciousness discloses the irreducible obscurity rather than the transparency of the self.

This obscurity harbors the *radical* temporality of subjectivity. The time of the subject is radical because it involves an uncanny past that is not a modality of the present. The past of *Darstellung* is not a past present but is a past that was never present because it is always already past. Maurice Blanchot describes this "outside of time in time" as the space of literature in which the work of art emerges:

> In this time what appears is the fact that nothing appears. What appears is the being deep within being's absence, which is when there is nothing and which, as soon as there is something, is no longer. For it is as if there were no beings except through the loss of being, when being lacks. The reversal, which, in time's absence, points us constantly back to the presence of absence—but to this presence as absence, to the absence as its own affirmation (an affirmation in which nothing is affirmed, in which nothing never ceases to affirm itself with the exhausting insistence of the indefinite)—this movement is not dialectical. Contradictions do not exclude each other; nor are they reconciled. . . . In time's absence what is new renews nothing; what is present is not contemporary; what is present presents nothing but represents itself and belongs henceforth and always to return. It isn't but comes back again. It comes already and forever past, so that my relation to it is not one of cognition, but of recognition, and this recognition ruins in me the power of knowing, the right to grasp. It makes what is ungraspable inescapable.[67]

This absence of time is the nothingness that haunts subjectivity. This past that was never present eternally returns as the future that never arrives to disrupt the present that never is. In this way, the originary absence of the past is the condition of the inescapable openness of the future. Since the past is never accessible, the present is never present, and the future is never closed, subjectivity is infinitely restless.

With this understanding of the interplay of the imagination, temporality, and subjectivity, it is necessary to return to the question of self-consciousness. Self-consciousness, I have argued, is self-reflexive and as such necessarily entails self-representation. Our investigation of the imagination now makes it possible to answer the question that we encountered at the limit of self-consciousness: Where does that which the self-conscious subject represents to itself come from? Since subject and object are codependent, the subject cannot give itself the object without which self-consciousness remains impossible. The presence of the object of self-representation must be given through the process of presentation or presencing, which cannot be effected by the self posited by it. As the condition of the possibility of presence, presencing is never present as such—nor is it absent. *The present, understood both temporally and spatially, is always a gift or present pre-sent by (the) nothing that is (not) present.* This no-thing gives by withholding, shows by hiding, approaches by withdrawing. Since that which is never present cannot be re-presented, representation includes as a condition of its possibility "something" that remains irreducibly unrepresentable. Expressed in terms of figuration: inasmuch as figuring can never be figured, every figure is always disfigured as if from within.

If self-consciousness requires self-representation and representation is inevitably implicated with the unrepresentable, then the possibility of self-consciousness depends upon something it can never comprehend. The incomprehensible or unrepresentable is not simply outside or the opposite of consciousness and self-consciousness. To the contrary, as the condition of the possibility of (self-)representation, the unrepresentable is "inside" as an "outside" that cannot be assimilated. Schelling underscores this important point:

> All *thinking* and presentation in us is [sic] therefore necessarily preceded by an *original activity*, which, *because it precedes* all thinking, is to that extent absolutely *undetermined* and *unconfined*. Only once an opposing element is present does it become a restricted and, for that very reason, a *determinant* (thinkable) activity. . . . Our whole knowing, and with it Nature in all its multiplicity, arises out of unending approximations to this X, and only in our everlasting struggle to determine it does the world find its continuance. Our entire enterprise will be nothing but a progressive attempt to determine this X, or rather, to follow out our own mind in its never-ending productions. For in this lies the secret of our mental activity, that we are necessitated forever to approach a point which forever eludes every determination. It is the point upon which all our mental endeavor is directed, and which, for that very reason, continually recedes the closer we try to approach it. Were we ever to have reached it, the whole system of our mind—this world which finds its continuance only in the conflict of opposing endeavors—would sink back into nothingness, and the final consciousness of our existence would lose itself in its own infinitude.[68]

In the depths of interiority lies hidden an Other that can never be known. Though nothing is closer to consciousness, this Other is not personal but remains an unnamable anonymity that shadows subjectivity.

This interior exteriority further complicates the structure of self-relation inherent in self-consciousness. Kierkegaard, who was influenced by Schelling, exposes the "altarity"[69] implied but never explicitly acknowledged in Hegel's account of subjectivity. Turning Hegel's language back upon itself, Kierkegaard identifies the aporia of self-reflexivity. "A human being is spirit. But what is spirit? Spirit is the self. But what is the self? The self is a relation that relates itself to itself or is the relation's relating to itself in the relation; the self is not the relation but is the relation's relating itself to itself. A human being is a synthesis of the finite and the infinite, of the temporal and the eternal, of freedom and necessity, in short, a synthesis. A synthesis is a relation between two. Considered in this way, a human being is still not a self." Kierkegaard's argument suggests that the previous diagrammatic representation of the structure of self-representation must be revised (fig. 15). In Kierkegaard's terms Self-as-Subject (S^s) and Self-as-Object (S^o) are joined in a relation that is their "negative unity." Insofar as each becomes itself in and through the other and neither can be itself apart from the other, S^s is not S^o and S^o is not S^s. "Such a relation that relates itself to itself, a self," Kierkegaard maintains, "must either have established itself or have been established by another." Since the relation and the *relata* are codependent, neither can posit the other. Self-relation, therefore, presupposes a third, which posits the relation as such. Kierkegaard concludes: "If the relation that relates itself to itself has been established by another, then the relation is indeed the third, but this relation, the third, is yet again a relation and relates itself to that which established the entire relation."[70] In relating itself to itself, the self inevitably but unknowingly relates itself to an Other, which is neither present nor absent.

With the emergence or, more precisely, withdrawal of the Other "within" the self, Luther and Calvin's *Deus absconditus* becomes the *subjectus absconditus*, which is implicit in modernism and becomes explicit in postmodernism. Far from blocking representation and self-representation, the unrepresentable is the origin of its infinite excess. Infinite obscurity is what makes endless creativity possible. In *Thomas the Obscure* Blanchot poetically expresses the direction of the trajectory I have been tracing:

Now, in this night, I come forward bearing everything [*le tout*] toward that which infinitely exceeds the all. I progress beyond the totality that

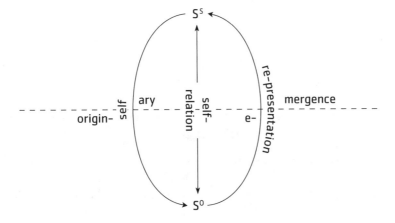

Figure 15. Self-Conscious Subjectivity

I nevertheless tightly embrace. I go on the margins of the universe, boldly walking elsewhere than where I can be, and a little outside my steps [*mes pas*]. This slight extravagance, this deviation toward that which cannot be, is not only my own movement leading me to a personal madness, but the movement of the reason that I bear within me. With me the laws gravitate outside the laws, the possible outside the possible. O night, now nothing will make me be, nothing will separate me from you. I adhere marvelously to the simplicity to which you invite me. I lean over you, equal to you, offering you a mirror for your perfect nothingness [*néant*], for your shadows that are neither light nor absence of light, for this void that contemplates. . . . I am the origin of that which has no origin. I create that which cannot be created.[71]

Perfect nothingness . . . shadows . . . neither light nor the absence of light . . . origin of that which has no origin. The unnamable bears many names: origin of that which has no origin, groundless ground, abyss, freedom, imagination, creativity. For Nietzsche, the plenitude of this void is the nonplace of the birth of tragedy: "something quite incommensurable: a certain deceptive clarity and, together with it, a mysterious depth, and infinite background. The clearest figured trailed after it a comet's tail, which seemed to point to something uncertain, something that could not be wholly elucidated."[72] The uncertainty of this mysterious depth is, as Heidegger has shown, the infinite background that is the origin of the work of art.

WORLD AS WORK OF ART

In his *Opus Posthumous*, Wallace Stevens offers an ironically unpoetic description of the imagination.

> Proposita: 1. God and the imagination are one. 2. The thing imagined is the imaginer.
> The second equals the thing imagined and the imaginer are one.
> Hence, I suppose, the imaginer is God.

If God and the imagination are one, the imagination is not only a faculty of the creative subject but also responsible for the creation of the objective world. The world, therefore, is the product of the creative imagination as it expresses itself in poetry. Poetry, then, is not merely a literary genre but is the "substance" of all things visible and invisible. "The theory of poetry," Stevens claims, is, therefore, "the theory of life."[73] In reaching this conclusion, Stevens follows Nietzsche, whom he never stopped reading and rewriting.

Infamous for his declaration of the death of God, Nietzsche is one of the most misunderstood writers in the history of Western philosophy. Commentators and critics consistently overlook the profoundly theological and religious dimensions of his thought. The son and grandson of German pastors, Nietzsche remained profoundly ambivalent about his Lutheran heritage. On the one hand, he regards Pauline Christianity, which lies at the heart of Luther's theology, as the negation of the form of religion originally introduced by Jesus. On the other hand, he sees in Luther's notion of the death of God the possibility of negating the negation of Christianity in a way that would reveal Dionysus or the Anti-Christ to be the contemporary embodiment of Jesus. What critics and commentators invariably overlook is that Nietzsche qualifies his proclamation of the death of God. The God who dies, Nietzsche declares, is the transcendent *moral* God: "At bottom, it is only the moral god that has been overcome. Does it make sense to conceive a god 'beyond good and evil'? Would a pantheism in this sense be possible? Can we remove the idea of a goal from the process and affirm the process in spite of this?"[74] Nietzsche devoted his life to attempting to answer these questions. If God is dead, what are the meaning and purpose of life? Perhaps, Nietzsche muses, life is its own purpose. Indirectly appropriating Kant's account of the inner teleology of the beautiful work of art, he challenges the reader to embrace purposeless process. The death of the moral God creates the possibility of the birth of the divine artist whose creative activity is beyond good and evil. In his early work, *The Birth of Tragedy*, Nietzsche writes, "throughout the book I attributed a purely aesthetic meaning—whether implied or overt—to all process: a kind of divinity if you like, God as the supreme artist, amoral, recklessly creating and destroying, realizing himself indifferently in whatever he does or un- does, ridding himself by his acts of embarrassment of his riches and the strain of his internal contradictions." This process has two sides or moments, which Nietzsche labels Apollonian and Dionysian. While the Apollonian is "the *principium individuationis*," which establishes "just boundaries," the Dionysian transgresses fixed limits and tends "toward the shattering of the individual."[75] In terms of the definition of religion I developed in chapter 1, the Dionysian disrupts and dislocates the stabi- lizing structures that the Apollonian de(-)limits. If God is "the supreme artist," then the world and human subjects are works of art. Radicalizing Kant's account of genius as resulting from the displacement of the un- moved mover or the Creator God from heaven to earth, Nietzsche main- tains that human creativity is the incarnation of divine creativity: "Only as genius in the act of creation merges with the primal architect of the cosmos can he truly know something of the eternal essence of art. For in that condition he resembles the uncanny fairy tale image, which is able to see itself by turning its eyes. He is at once subject and object, poet, actor, and audience."[76] Since art is both Apollonian and Dionysian, its es- sence is duplicitous: it simultaneously creates and destroys, structures and destructures, figures and disfigures.

Though Nietzsche never makes the point explicitly, these two sides of artistic production are actually elaborations of Kant's contrast between the beautiful and the sublime. In his most concise formulation of this critical distinction, Kant writes: "The beautiful in nature is a question of the form of an object, and consists in limitation, whereas the sublime is to be found in an object even devoid of form, so far as it immedi- ately involves, or else by its presence provokes a representation of *un- limitedness*, yet with a super-added thought of its totality."[77] The beauti- ful, then, is associated with form, limit, and figure, and the sublime with formlessness, the unlimited, and the unfigurable. So understood, beauty and the sublime are not merely opposites but are codependent. "The beautiful resides in form as such, in the form of form, if one can put it this way, or in the figure that it makes. The sublime resides in the tracing-out, the setting-off, and seizure of form, independently of the figure this form delimits."[78] De-limitation simultaneously limits and unlimits—it both delineates or articulates and erases or subverts the boundary or margin that articulation presupposes. What cannot be articulated cannot be represented; it can, however, reveal itself by hiding itself in and through the process of disfiguring seemingly stable figures. Disfiguring presents the unpresentable without which representation is impossible. The interplay between the beautiful and the sublime in the work of art reflects the two sides of the imagination as isomorphic with the two moments of religion and the two types of theology I have previously described. These formal parallels become clear when they are graphically represented.

RELIGION	THEOLOGY	IMAGINATION	WORK OF ART	INFORMATION
Pattern/ structure	Word Structure	Figure	Beautiful	Pattern
Disruption/ dislocation	Deed Event	(Dis)figuring	Sublime	Noise

In chapter 7, I will analyze the metastructure that constitutes and coordinates these seemingly disparate phenomena.

To understand the implications of the interpretation of the world as a work of art, it is necessary to develop an expanded notion of the imagination. As I have noted, the philosopher Fichte and the poet Stevens argue that the imagination is the basis of objective as well as subjective reality. This puzzling claim begins to make sense if art is understood as essentially poetic. The word *poetic* derives from the Greek *poiesis* (*poiein*), which means a "making" or "creation." *Poiesis* is not limited to poetry in the traditional sense but involves all productive and creative activity. Inspired by the Third Critique but convinced that it did not go far enough, romantic philosophers and poets extended Kant's analysis of the imagination beyond the bounds of the human until it became a creative cosmic principle. Schlegel makes this point concisely in his *Athenaeum Fragments*: "No poetry, no reality. Just as there is, despite all the senses, no external world without the imagination."[79] The Jena romantics identified three different but related aspects of poetry:

1. The restricted literary meaning of poetic literature in verse or prose.
2. A faculty of the mind that mediates sensation, understanding, and reason.
3. A cosmic principle informing the entire universe.[80]

As the expression of the productive imagination, *poiesis* is the "putting-into-form of form" or the figuring of figure. In *The Philosophy of Art,*

Schelling turns to the notion of genius to explain *poiesis:* "The real side of genius, or that unity that constitutes the informing of the infinite into the finite, can be called *poesy* in the narrower sense; the ideal side, or that unity that constitutes the informing of the finite into the infinite, can be called the art within *art.*" The work of art is not only the created product but, more importantly, the *creative process* through which any determinate form emerges. If the imagination is the activity of figuring, which de-limits figures, then it is, in effect, an in-formation process that occurs wherever figures are articulated. The so-called natural world is a work of art de-signed by an anonymous artist. Art in the more common sense of the term is, as Schelling suggests, "art within art" or, in Stevens's words, "every poem is a poem within a poem."

> The endlessly elaborating poem
> Displays the theory of poetry
> As the life of poetry. A more severe,
>
> More harassing master would extemporize
> Subtler, more urgent proof that the theory
> Of poetry is the theory of life,
>
> As it is, in the intricate evasions of as,
> In things seen and unseen, created from nothingness,
> The heavens, hells, the worlds, the longed-for lands.[81]

It is important to stress that this more inclusive notion of art implies an expanded notion of the imagination. Wherever forms are figured, the imagination is active. In other words, the imagination is not merely a subjective process but also the creative origin of the so-called natural world.

Insofar as objectivity and subjectivity emerge in and through the same in-formation process, they are isomorphic. The formal identity-within-difference of subject and object makes knowledge possible. If knowledge is to be something other than a projection or construction of human schemata, the structure and operation of the mind and the world must be the same. In knowing the world, the subject knows itself, and in the subject's self-consciousness, the world becomes aware of itself. Through the self-reflexivity of the subject, the figurative process of the world bends back on itself and manifests itself to itself. This is implied in Kant's account of genius: "*Genius* is the talent (natural endowment), which gives the rule to art. Since talent, as the innate productive activity of the artist, belongs to nature, we may put it this way: *Genius* is the innate mental aptitude (*ingenium*) *through which* nature gives rule to art."[82] Insofar as the activity of the genius is "natural," nature manifests itself to itself in the work of art. Such self-manifestation, however, is always incomplete and, thus, self-reflexivity is inevitably short-circuited. Since the groundless ground of the imagination can never be fathomed, knowledge and self-consciousness are necessarily incomplete and must constantly be revised and reformulated. Far from an insufficiency, the lacuna, which is constitutive of all knowledge and every figure, is infinitely generative. As Blanchot observes when commenting on Schlegel's *Athenaeum Fragments:* "The poet becomes the future of humankind at the moment when, no longer being anything—anything but one who knows himself to be a poet—he designates in this knowledge for which he is intimately responsible the site wherein poetry will no longer be content to produce the beautiful, determinate works, but rather will produce itself in a movement without term and without determination."[83] When the movement of the imagination is without term, the conversation becomes infinite.

The in-finity of the work of art is the unending process of its own production. The work (verb) of art is the creative activity through which determinate works (noun) of art emerge. As the formation of form or figuring of figure, art is the eternal process of creative emergence. Here production is autoproduction and as such is autotelic; the work of art, in other words, is purposeless or has no purpose other than itself. To affirm the world and oneself as works of art is to accept Nietzsche's challenge to embrace "process without goal." This creative process is both complete and incomplete—it is complete insofar as it always becomes *itself* in and through itself, and it is incomplete insofar as it can become itself only by becoming *other* than itself and, thus, never secures its own identity.

The structure of the creative imagination is isomorphic with the structure of the self-contradictory will. Since creativity is grounded in the groundless abyss of nothing, its expression is always new. As Schlegel insists: "creative art is still in the process of becoming, and it is even its essence proper never to obtain perfection, to be always and eternally new; no theory of art can exhaust it, it alone is infinite just as it alone is free."[84] The founding axiom of modernism—Make it new!—grows out of this interpretation of the creative imagination and, correlatively, of the self-contradictions of subjectivity. Since the imagination is what it is by becoming other than itself, it constantly "strives," "hovers," "oscillates" between opposites it simultaneously brings together and holds apart. As Novalis explains: "Being free means to waver between extremes that have to be united and also to be separated necessarily. From the light point of the wavering radiates all reality; object and subject exist through it, not it through them."[85] Another name for this oscillation is *altarity*. The neologism *altarity* harbors three implications that are important in this context. First, altarity specifies the endless alternation through which binary and dialectical differences are articulated in such a way that their oppositions are overcome. Second, *altarity* names the unnamable "outside" that is "inside" every system, structure, and schema as its necessary condition. As such, it is the irreducible trace that marks and remarks the openness and incompletion of seemingly closed systems. And third, *altarity* suggests a dimension of sacrality, which is neither simply transcendent nor immanent but is an immanent transcendence that disrupts and dislocates systems, structures, and schemata that seem to be secure.[86]

The immanent transcendence of altarity transforms human agents into vehicles of a creative process that is more encompassing than their individual activity. The artist, as Nietzsche observes, is the *medium* through which "the True Subject celebrates His redemption in illusion." This True Subject is the incarnation of the transcendent Creator who dies and is reborn in the creative imagination of the artist. While Nietzsche restricts the genuine work of art to the activity of the genius, Schlegel prepares the way for Marcel Duchamp and Andy Warhol when he declares: "Everyone is an artist whose central purpose in life is to educate his intellect." Education (*Bildung*) is cultivation (*Bildung*). To educate oneself is, therefore, to cultivate oneself, and to cultivate oneself is, in effect, to become God. Schlegel continues: "Every good human being is always progressively becoming God. To become God, to become human, to cultivate oneself are all expressions that mean the same thing."[87] Cultivation occurs through the imagination. Coleridge, who heard Fichte's lectures in Jena and transmitted German philosophical idealism and romanticism to British romantics and American transcendentalists, reformulates Kant's doctrine of the imagination in a way that translates theology into anthropology and vice versa: "The *imagination*, then, I consider either as primary, or secondary. The primary *imagination* I hold to be the living Power and prime Agent of all human Perception, and as repetition in the finite mind of the eternal act of creation in the infinite I AM. The secondary Imagination I consider as an echo of the former, coexisting with the conscious will, yet still as identical with the primary in the *kind* of its agency, and differing only in *degree* and the *mode* of its operation."[88] Whereas the primary imagination is emergent, the secondary imagination is recombinant. In different terms, the imagination involves both the activity of figuring through which schemata emerge and the activity of recombining and reconfiguring schemata to adapt to changing circumstances. Though figuring cannot be represented, there is nonetheless a mimetic dimension to creative emergence. In a gloss on Kant's notion of art, Derrida describes a mimesis that is not simply a repetition of preformed figures:

> *Mimesis* here is not the representation of one thing by another, the relation of resemblance or identification between two beings, the reproduction of one product of nature by a product of art. It is not the relation of two products but of two productions. And of two freedoms. The artist does not imitate things in nature, or if you will, *natura naturata*, but the acts of *natura naturans*, the art of an author-subject, and, one could even say, of an artist-god; mimesis displays the identification of human action with divine action—of one freedom with another.[89]

With this notion of nonrepresentational mimesis, we return to the issue of freedom, which we have been exploring from the outset. Since our course has been long and complicated, it might be helpful to summarize it diagrammatically (table 3).

To complete this analysis, it will be necessary first to chart the way in which these trajectories issue in alternative versions of postmodernism and then to show how "the theory of poetry is the theory of life" by exploring the way in which word and deed—structure and event—intersect in emergent complex adaptive networks. The transition from modernism to postmodernism passes through the rise of secularity during the nineteenth century and first half of the twentieth. Secularity results from the evolution of autonomous subjectivity, whose genesis we have been following in this chapter.

Freedom, I have argued, is neither simple nor monolithic but is inwardly divided and, thus, irreducibly complex. Though the modern subject is self-legislating, autonomy presupposes an originary givenness, which is groundless and hence an-archic. In relating itself to itself through the activity of self-representation, the creative subject relates itself to an altarity, which, as a condition of its own possibility, is not simply heteronomous. The "inward" disruption of altarity issues in the infinite restlessness of desire. Appearances to the contrary notwithstanding, desire that is vital never strives for fulfillment; to the contrary, creative desire desires desire. Such desire is the pulse of life. In turning back on itself, the uncanny self-reflexivity of desire holds open the open without which creative emergence is impossible. When desire no longer

Table 3. Word and Deed

	WORD	DEED	
	Transcendent Forms	Omnipotent Will	
Platonism	Forms	*Potential absoluta*	Nominalism
	Demiurge	*Potential ordinata*	Ockham
	Matter		Protestantism
			Luther
			Calvin
Christian	Mind of God	Covenant Theology	Puritanism
Apologists	Logos		
	Structure of Consciousness	Structure of Consciousness	Rousseau
Kant	A priori forms	Imagination	Fichte
	Imagination	Emergent Figuring	F. Schlegel
	Schematization	*Darstellung* presentation	Schopenhauer
	A posteriori experience	Poiesis	Nietzsche
		Recombinant Figuring	Freud
		Vorstellung representation	
		Mimesis	

desires satisfaction, it becomes revolutionary. This is Schlegel's point when he declares: "The revolutionary desire to realize the kingdom of God on earth is the elastic point of progressive civilization and the beginning of modern history."[90] Here faith in an apocalypse by imagination gives way to faith in an apocalypse by revolution, which, in turn, is displaced by faith in an apocalypse by imagination and cognition. In coming centuries, this revolutionary imagination is destined to transform the world.

CHAPTER FOUR

Religious Secularity

IMMANENCE AND TRANSCENDENCE

Susan Jacoby begins her informative book *Freethinkers: A History of American Secularism* with an epigram written by Robert Green Ingersoll on July 4, 1876: "We have retired the gods from politics. We have found that man is the only source of political power, and that the governed should govern." Jacoby proceeds to explain:

> On the centennial anniversary of the signing of the Declaration of Independence, Robert Ingersoll, the foremost champion of freethought and the most famous orator in late-nineteenth-century America, paid tribute in his hometown of Peoria, Illinois, to the "first secular government that was ever founded in this world." Also known as "the Great Agnostic," Ingersoll praised the framers of the Constitution for deliberately omitting any mention of God from the nation's founding document and instead acknowledging "We the People" as the supreme governmental authority. This unprecedented decision, Ingersoll declared, "did away forever with the theological idea of government."[1]

Nearly a century and a half later, it has become clear that Ingersoll's selective account of the past led to a misreading of the future. "The theological idea of government" has not disappeared but is perhaps more powerful than ever. Ingersoll is not alone in his misinterpretation of the trajectory of so-called secularity. Since the early 1970s, we have been in the midst of what might be called the Fourth Great Awakening, which was unanticipated by virtually all of the most sophisticated cultural critics.[2] This religious revival is not limited to the United States but is a *global* phenomenon whose causes and implications have yet to be adequately understood. Continuing confusions about the relationship between religion and secularity make the last half of the twentieth century and our current situation impossible to understand.

Secularity and its cognate *secularization* are notoriously vexed terms. The current sense of these words can be traced to the Treaty of Westphalia (1648), in which *secularity* was used to designate "the conversion of an ecclesiastical or religious institution or its property to sovereigns, princes or lay people." By extension, *secular* came to mean "belonging to this world or its affairs as distinguished from the church and religion; civil, with the meaning of non-ecclesiastical, non-religious or non-sacred."[3] During the first half of the twentieth century, theologians, philosophers, and social theorists developed detailed analyses of the interrelation of secularity and secularization, on the one hand, and modernity and modernization, on the other. Peter Berger summarizes what by the 1960s had become a consensus widely shared by both defenders and critics of religion:

> By secularization we mean the process by which sectors of society and culture are removed from the domination of religious institutions and symbols. When we speak of society and institutions in modern Western history, of course, secularization manifests itself in the evacuation by the Christian churches of areas previously under their control or influence—as in the separation of church and state, the expropriation of church lands, or in the emancipation of education from ecclesiastical authority. When we speak of culture and symbols, however, we imply that secularization is more than a socio-structural process. It affects the totality of cultural life and of ideation, and may be observed in the decline of religious contents in the arts, in philosophy, in literature and, most important of all, in the rise of science as an autonomous, thoroughly secular perspective on the world.[4]

A teleological notion of history rooted in the very religious tradition whose death knell Berger claims to toll is implicit in this explanation of secularity. Modernization and secularization, according to this argument, are inseparable: as societies modernize, they become more secular. Moreover, this process, many argued, is inevitable and irreversible. It is important to stress that this line of analysis is not merely descriptive but also normative—the disappearance of religion tends to be regarded as a mark of human progress. When explicitly articulated, different versions of the philosophy of history that underlie this theory of modernization chart the movement from the primitive to the modern, the infantile to the mature, instinct to reason, superstition to enlightenment, and bondage to freedom. Within any such schema, the so-called return of the religious during the latter half of the twentieth century and opening decade of the new millennium can only be regarded as a regression that threatens to plunge the world into a new primitivism made all the more dangerous by the destructive potential of modern technology. Faced with this prospect, secularists declare war on religion by repeating Voltaire's call to arms: *Écrasez l'infame!*

Many religious believers and secularists actually agree about the relation between modernization and secularization but disagree in their assessment of it. Instead of a sign of progress, the faithful tend to see the eclipse of religion as a regression that leads to the chaos of moral relativism and inevitably ends in pernicious nihilism. The only way to counter this destructive downward trajectory, they insist, is by returning to the religious absolutes and fundamental moral values without which life has neither meaning nor purpose. It is a mistake to see the many contemporary forms of religiosity as a reversion to premodern modes of belief and conduct because, as we will see in detail in chapter 6, neofoundationalism is a distinctively postmodern phenomenon.

Religionists and secularists are mirror images of each other who share more than they are willing to admit; each reverses but does not displace the other. Although it is not immediately obvious, both perspectives rest on the same error. Bound by the exclusive logic of either/or, each side in this conflict sees religion and secularity as irreconcilable opposites. While choosing opposing sides, they are fighting the same battle. What neither secularists nor religionists realize is that secularity is a *religious* phenomenon—indeed, religion as it has developed in the West has always harbored secularity, and secularity covertly continues a religious agenda. In other words, secularity and religion are coemergent and codependent. It is, therefore, misleading to speak of a "return of" or "return to" religion. Religion does not return, because it never goes away; to the contrary, religion haunts society, self, and culture even—perhaps especially—when it seems to be absent. To trace the specter of religion in ostensibly secular culture, it is necessary to consider first the emergence of the Hebrew God in the spiritual milieu of the ancient Near East and then the seemingly esoteric Christian doctrines of the Incarnation and Trinity as they were formulated at the great church councils of the fourth and fifth centuries.

There can be no doubt that secularization is one of the symptoms of modernization. As we have seen, however, modernization is an extension of processes set in motion by the Protestant revolution. It is now necessary to consider how the transcendent, omnipotent God that lies at the heart of Protestantism grows out of ancient Jewish monotheism. Judaism's emergence in the midst of ancient Near Eastern societies, which were governed by cosmogonic myths and rituals, was no less revolutionary than Protestantism's reformation of Catholicism. Yahweh represents the eruption of a radically transcendent power in a world that had seemed to be ruled by immanent natural forces deemed divine. The polarity of immanence and transcendence both characterizes contrasting religious visions and defines the trajectory of their historical development in the West. To clarify the implications of these alternatives, it will be helpful to return to the typology of religious schemata developed in the first chapter. The foundational principle of immanence entails a monistic schema in which God, self, and world are different manifestations or expressions of the same underlying reality. Transcendence shatters monism by introducing a radical Other, which forms the foundation of the principle of oppositional difference constitutive of every dualism. The monistic and dualistic schemata illuminate the close relationship between religion and secularity by showing the contrasting ways in which God or the divine seems to disappear. In monism, God and the gods disappear by becoming indistinguishable from the world—when everything is sacred nothing is sacred. In dualism, God and the gods vanish by becoming so distant that they are inconsequential and thus disposable—when the divine is totally absent, nothing is sacred.

This typology, I have argued, makes it possible to compare schemata across different religious traditions as well as within single traditions. Details of the evolution of religious schemata vary from context to context, and thus, secularism assumes distinctive contours in different historical settings.[5] In tracing the religious genealogy of Western secularism, the monistic type will clarify the contours of the cosmogonic myths and rituals of ancient Egypt and Mesopotamia, and the dualistic type will help to define the distinctive characteristics of Jewish monotheism. Various versions of Christianity try to negotiate, which is not to say integrate, these extremes through the interrelated doctrines of the Incarnation and Trinity. But the negotiation of differential identity proves to be very difficult; oppositional differences invariably return to create conflicts that threaten to become destructive. The history of modern theology and religion grows out of the repeated "altarnation"

Table 4. Immanence and Transcendence

1. From deism to romanticism and idealism	Transcendence → Immanence
2. From liberalism to neo-orthodoxy	Immanence → Transcendence
3. From neo-orthodoxy to death of god	Transcendence → Immanence
4. From death of god to neo-foundationalism	Immanence → Transcendence

between the monism of immanence and the dualism of transcendence (table 4). The question that remains at the end of modernity is whether this alternation figures an immanent transcendence that subverts the nihilism of both belief and unbelief. To answer this question, it is necessary to return to the beginning of the beginning.[6]

The notion of the beginning has a beginning. Before the beginning nothing begins because everything returns eternally in cyclical rhythms that are both natural and divine. Beginning begins with the religion of ancient Israel, and this beginning disrupts cycles that seem to have neither beginning nor end. Describing what begins with the transcendent God of Israel, the distinguished archaeologist and historian Henri Frankfort writes:

> When we read in Psalm XIX that "the heavens declare the glory of God; and the firmament sheweth his handiwork," we hear a voice which mocks the beliefs of Egyptians and Babylonians. The heavens, which were to the psalmist but a witness of God's greatness, were to the Mesopotamians the very majesty of the godhead, the highest ruler, Anu. To the Egyptians the heavens signified the mystery of the divine mother through whom man was reborn. In Egypt and Mesopotamia the divine was comprehended as immanent: the gods were in nature. The Egyptians saw in the sun all that man may know of the Creator; the Mesopotamians viewed the sun as the god Shamash, the guarantor of justice. But to the psalmist the sun was God's devoted servant who "is as a bridegroom coming out of his chamber, and rejoiceth as a strong man to run a race." The God of the psalmist and the prophets was not in nature. He transcended nature and transcended likewise the realm of mythopoeic thought.[7]

While important social and political differences between Egyptian and Mesopotamian culture are reflected in their myths and rituals, the mythopoeic imagination cultivated in these societies developed a vision of the world whose deep structure is shared. It appears that cosmogonic myths first emerged in societies as they made the transition from dispersed tribes to more centralized and hierarchical social and political structures. The distinctive characteristics of such cosmogonic schemata become clear by considering the interrelation of God (or, more precisely, the gods), self, and world. The divine, human, and natural realms are integrated in such a way that each is an embodiment of the other. Natural forces and cycles provide the primary symbols and metaphors for interpreting life. While the ancient Near East underwent gradual urbanization from the middle of the fourth to the first millennium BCE, the size of cities remained relatively small and people maintained a close relationship with nature. The foundational myths of these cultures explain how the world and human societies arise from and are regulated by cyclical natural processes represented by multiple deities. Analyzing the widely influential ancient Babylonian narrative *Enuma elish* and its lingering traces in Genesis 1:2, Mircea Eliade explains the significance of aquatic symbolism in cosmogonic myths:

> The waters symbolize the universal sum of virtualities; they are *fons et origo*, "spring and origin," the reservoir of all possibilities of existence; they precede every form and *support* every creation. One of the paradigmatic images of creation is the island that suddenly manifests itself in the midst of the waves. On the other hand, immersion in water signifies regression to the preformal, reincorporation into the undifferentiated mode of pre-existence. Emersion repeats the cosmogonic act of formal manifestation; *immersion* is equivalent to a dissolution of forms.[8]

The cosmos emerges through a figurative process that forms the virtual into the actual. The *Enuma elish* is a particularly rich text because it integrates cosmogony and theogony in a way that explains the origin of human society while at the same time grounding political authority in sacral kingship. In his insightful and provocative book *Order and History: Israel and Revelation*, Eric Voegelin distinguishes three stages in the cosmogony.[9] In the first stage, nothing exists but the primordial waters known as Apsu ("the sweet-water abyss") and Tiamat ("salty sea water"). The second stage is marked by silt accumulating at the border between sweet and sea water. Along this margin, the paired differences and oppositions that structure the cosmos progressively emerge. As the silt increases, sweet and salt water, represented by Lahmu and Lahamu, are distinguished from the horizon and heaven, represented by Anshar and Kishar.[10] The articulation of the horizon allows for the differentiation of heaven, Anu, from earth, Ea, who, in turn, gives birth to the all-important god Marduk. With the theogony complete, tensions and conflicts among different gods eventually break out. The third stage in the cosmogonic process recounts Marduk's rise to supremacy and the creation of human beings to serve the gods by doing their work. Marduk appears as a powerful storm god, who establishes order by slaying the sea monster Tiamat. He then proceeds to create the universe from the dismembered body of the goddess. As an expression of their appreciation, the gods join forces to build a temple for Marduk in Babylon; this magnificent structure is the center of the cosmos and as such serves as the *axis mundi*. The political hierarchy of the society reflects and is grounded in its divine counterpart. The king, whose authority derives from his identification with Marduk, serves the gods by maintaining order in the cosmos.

At the most obvious and least interesting level, the *Enuma elish* is a political document intended to explain, legitimize, and preserve a specific social structure. By grounding history in nature, which is believed to be divine, contingent sociopolitical institutions appear to be natural and thus necessary. At a deeper level, however, the *Enuma elish* is a remarkably sophisticated account of the emergence of order in all dimensions of life. It anticipates both Plato's cosmogony as well as Kant's translation of it into the epistemological activity of the imagination. In all cases, the primordial waters figure what cannot be figured in the determinate forms that structure the world, and order emerges through the articulation of dialectical or binary opposites. The distinctive characteristic of monistic schemata, as I have stressed, is that God(s), self, and world are all embodiments or expressions of a single reality. Voegelin stresses this important point when commenting on the *Enuma elish*: "The cosmogony . . . is not a 'creation' but a growth of the cosmos through procreation of gods and struggles between their generations. The gods themselves are bodily the structural parts of the cosmos."[11] Creation, then, is not a deliberate act but is a natural process of procreation, which is, in effect, the emanation of the divine first into a hierarchical plurality of deities and then into a hierarchical cosmos. Inasmuch as cosmogony brings to completion theogony, human beings are not autonomous but exist only to the extent that they *participate* in the divine-natural totality. As part of the cycle of nature, creation is not a once-and-for-all event but is repeated annually. In the course of the year, the pristine order of the cosmos gradually drifts toward the edge of chaos until it reaches the tipping point, where it dissolves and must be restored. As extensions of the gods, human beings are responsible for maintaining order through the performance of archetypal rituals, which repeat the original cosmogonic act. Once order has been restored, the cycle starts over again.

In the first chapter, I argued that religion is a complex adaptive network of symbols, myths, and rituals that both give life meaning and purpose and disrupt, dislocate, and disfigure every stabilizing structure. While it should be clear that this cosmogonic myth serves both of these functions, it is important to note precisely how this is accomplished. Within this schema, human life has meaning and purpose insofar as it is understood to be a repetition of a divine prototype. Meaning, in other words, is not really temporal or historical but is derived from recurrent natural rhythms. Indeed, inasmuch as the future is prefigured before the beginning, it is actually always already past. If everything is programmed in advance, nothing new occurs; creation is not creative but is the eternal return of the same. In the absence of creativity—be it divine or human—change remains superficial. From this point of view, the challenge is not to "make it new" but to repeat the old.

All of this changes with the irruption of the transcendent God in the midst of the divine-natural cosmos. Although the founding event of Israel was God's call to Abraham, the far-reaching implications of the special role Israel believed it was called to play in history did not begin to become clear until God instructed Moses to gather the Hebrew clans and lead them from bondage in Egypt and journey into the desert. This event, which proved to be of world-historical proportions, seemed so insignificant at the time that it was not even recorded in the official records of the Egyptian authorities. The religion of Israel was as different from the religion of its neighbors as the desert is from rivers and the sand is from water. A place of wandering, temptation, and tribulation, the desert is haunted by loss and absence. In fleeing Egypt, the ancient Hebrews went into the desert to find themselves through their relation to an Other they could neither imagine nor know. As narrated by the writers of the Hebrew Bible, the emergence of this radical Other introduced a series of structured oppositions, which, when elaborated, constitute a new religious schema:

God / World
One / Many
Creator / Creature
History / Nature
Revelation / Reason

Inward / Outward
Chosen / Not Chosen
Faithful / Infidel

The Jewish God is first and foremost One. In contrast to the polytheism characteristic of ancient Near Eastern cultures, Jews are radical monotheists: there is only one God and that God himself is one. Second, and equally important, this God is the sole Creator of the world. Creation is a free and deliberate act of a powerful agent rather than an emanation of the gods. The created order is, therefore, contingent rather than necessary.[12] Far from a recurrent natural process, creation is a unique event that brings into being what never before has been. This event marks the beginning of the beginning, which is the condition of both divine and human creativity. If the new is cosmologically or ontologically impossible, creativity is illusory. Created in the image of God, human beings are free and responsible individuals. As creatures, they are not embodiments or expressions of a divine reality but independent agents whose actions have decisive consequences. The relation between God and self is covenantal rather than ontological—God elects Israel to be his chosen agent in the world and by so doing sets his people apart from all others. As Moses explained to Israel in the desert, election carries the obligation of fulfilling the Law that God establishes.

> Now, Israel, listen to the statutes and laws which I am teaching you, and obey them; then you will live, and go in and occupy the land which the Lord the God of your fathers is giving you. You must not add anything to my charge, nor take anything away from it. You must carry out all the commandments of the Lord your God which I lay upon you.
>
> You saw with your own eyes what the Lord did at Baal-peor; the Lord your God destroyed among you every man who went over to the Baal of Peor, but you who held fast to the Lord your God are all alive today. I have taught you the statutes and laws, as the Lord my God commanded me; these you must duly keep when you enter the land and occupy it. You must observe them carefully, and thereby you will display your wisdom and understanding to other peoples. (Deuteronomy 4:1–6)

The establishment of the covenant marks the transition from cosmic or natural religions to a religion organized around the supposed *historical* interaction of God and his people. Frankfort summarizes the implications of this important development:

Not cosmic phenomena, but history itself, has here become pregnant with meaning; history had become a revelation of the dynamic will of God. The human being was not merely the servant of the god as he was in Mesopotamia; nor was he placed, as in Egypt, in a preordained station in a static universe, which did not need to be—and, in fact, could not be—questioned. Man, according to Hebrew thought, was the interpreter and the servant of God; he was even honored with the task of bringing about the realization of God's will. Thus man was condemned to unending efforts which were doomed to fail because of his inadequacy. In the Old Testament we find man possessed of a new freedom and a new burden of responsibility.[13]

This vision of the interplay of God, self, and world constitutes a new religious schema. The meaning and purpose of life are no longer established by the ritual repetition of prefigured forms and programs but now are forged in the midst of time and space through events that are genuinely free and thus creative. While every individual is responsible for his or her own actions, he or she is also a member of a community, which develops through its ongoing relation to God. Accordingly, meaning and purpose are prospective or teleological rather than merely retrospective or archaeological. More precisely, meaning is constituted through personal and cultural narratives that unify past and present in terms of the anticipated future. The tripartite structure that eventually becomes characteristic not only of Christian history but of virtually all historical narratives in the West can already be discerned in the story of the Exodus. Egypt represents "the land of bondage" from which ancient Israel flees. The desert is not the final destination but is the space of erring, which eventually leads to the Promised Land, that is, Canaan. Past and present assume meaning and purpose through their relation to the future toward which the Jewish people are always moving. This future, however, proves to be as elusive as the transcendent God who calls his people toward it.

In retrospect, it is clear that the emergence of the religion of Israel began a long process in which God becomes increasingly transcendent. In Deuteronomy, Yahweh says to his people:

> "The commandment that I lay on you this day is not too difficult for you, it is not too remote. It is not in heaven, that you should say, 'Who will go to heaven for us to fetch it and tell it to us, so that we can keep it?' Nor is it beyond the sea, that you would say, 'Who will cross the sea for us to fetch it and tell it to us, so that we can keep it?' It is a thing

very near you, upon your lips as in your heart ready to be kept." (Deuteronomy 30:11–12)

By the time of Second Isaiah, God has withdrawn into the remote heavens:

> For my thoughts are not your thoughts,
> And your ways are not my ways.
> This is the very word of the Lord.
> For as the heavens are higher than the earth,
> So are my ways higher than your ways
> And my thoughts higher than your thoughts. (Isaiah 55:8–9)

In the Wisdom tradition, common throughout the ancient Near East, the highest god, El, is the creator and guarantor of order. Before Israel, which claimed him as its own, he was nobody's national god. His distance was the condition of his impartiality and universality. The gods Marduk and Baal, who had much in common with Yahweh in spite of their important differences, were disrupters and destroyers of order. Over time, the latter of these two understandings of God tended to lapse into desuetude. The hope remained that Yahweh would return to action as of old, but in the interim the deity who continued to matter was a god of wisdom. Torah itself began to fuse with wisdom. As God withdraws, the world becomes, in Weber's famous term, "disenchanted." The divine is no longer present but now remains absent even when he seems to speak or intervene in history. The transcendence of God is closely related to other processes and developments, which become important over the course of the next two millennia: abstraction, unification, legalization, rationalization, universalization, standardization, and regulation. When God withdraws into transcendence, he gradually becomes so abstract that he can be neither represented nor conceived. Turning back on itself in reflection, the human mind glimpses its own power to abstract from everything particular and concrete in its conception of divine transcendence. The absence of God and the gods creates the necessity for laws to regulate nature and rules to provide a clear rationale for conduct. Since there is only one God in Jewish monotheism, he has the power to establish laws that are universal. Though circumstances change, the universality of laws leads to the standardization of natural processes and human behavior. The more distant God becomes, the more autonomous laws appear until God no longer seems necessary for the orderly functioning of the universe. At this point, God effectively disappears, and the world develops without divine guidance or intervention.

INCARNATION AND TRINITY

The emergence of transcendence in the ancient Near East began a process of withdrawal that eventually led to a divine absence that was the functional equivalent of the death of God. Christianity reverses this trajectory with a God who actually becomes embodied in time and space. As transcendence is emptied into immanence, God once again dies, and nature, as well as history, eventually is sacralized, or resacralized. Christianity is not, of course, the simple negation of Judaism; to the contrary, Christians believe their God to be the same as the God of what they label the Old Testament.[14] Like Jews, early Christians were monotheists devoted to the transcendent God, who is the sole creator of the universe. The fundamental difference between Christianity and Judaism concerns the status of the historical person named Jesus. Whereas Jews believe Jesus stands in a long line of religious prophets who are human, most Christians are convinced that Jesus is the Messiah, who, as the unique Son of God, is divine. The unyielding insistence on divine transcendence makes it impossible for Jews to accept the divinity of Jesus or any other finite being. While disagreeing with Judaism on this critical issue, Christianity's commitment to monotheism creates difficulties for belief in the divinity of Jesus. If Jesus is divine, how can God be One? The fate of Christianity and, by extension, the history of the West turns on this question.

When expectations for the imminent return of Jesus were disappointed, the early Christian community was forced to rethink its commitments and reformulate its beliefs. As Christians began to turn their attention from hope for the future to the realities of the present, they found themselves immersed in an extraordinarily complex social, cultural, and spiritual world. Although the rule of Augustus (emperor from 27 BCE to 14 CE) brought the Roman Empire a period of peace and optimism between eras of decline and decay, the initial centuries of Christian history were, for the most part, times of social and political unrest. Augustus's success lay in his effort to reverse the movement away from the ideal of republican principles for which Rome had stood that had started with Julius Caesar's (100–44 BCE) assumption of dictatorial power. He attempted to return significant power to the Roman Senate and to serve as a representative of the people. This political program was part of Augustus's overall aim of bringing peace and stability to an empire that had long been at war. In many ways, Augustus's efforts were successful; a semblance of republican government again was achieved, and peace came to the empire. Augustus's successors, however, were less skillful in preserving the shaky peace. Times of relative tranquility were punctuated with violence and repression. The inability of later rulers to maintain the delicate balance established by Augustus was especially evident in the crisis of the third century. During this period, the very social and moral fabric of Roman society seemed on the verge of unraveling. Under internal siege at the hands of Roman warlords and faced with external attack by raiding barbarians, the empire's fragile stability crumbled. As conditions worsened, Christians became the target of persecutions, which at first were local and sporadic, but as the problems of the empire worsened, attacks grew more severe. In 177, Marcus Aurelius proclaimed that Christians were a menace to the empire and should be tortured to death. By the middle of the third century, the political and social crisis of the empire resulted in Decius's (emperor, 249–51) systematic persecution of Christians. The beginning of the fourth century brought Emperor Diocletian's (284–305) prohibition of practicing Christianity under penalty of death.

In an effort to defend themselves against charges of superstition, atheism, moral laxity, and sedition, Christian apologists recast their beliefs in terms of Greek philosophy as it had been developed primarily in Platonism and Neoplatonism. The result was a conjunction of Christian theology and Platonic philosophy that created tensions that were never completely resolved. During the formative years of Christianity, Jewish monotheism and Platonism combined to create a notion of God that made it virtually impossible to affirm both the divinity of Jesus and the unity of God. The major church councils of the fourth and fifth centuries were devoted to establishing what became the orthodox interpretation of Jesus. While agreement eventually was reached, the full implications of creeds approved by the Councils of Nicaea (325), Constantinople (381), and Chalcedon (451) did not become clear until the nineteenth century. When fully elaborated, the doctrine of the Incarnation requires the doctrine of the Trinity. The doctrine of the Trinity, in turn, implies a theology of nature, history, and culture that comes to completion in the notion of divine life as a process of creative emergence.

As we will see, it is a mistake to relegate the esoteric doctrines of Christology and the Trinity to "the dustbin of history," which is the domain of historians and theologians. The debates of the fourth and fifth centuries have shaped subsequent history and thought in ways that could never have been anticipated at the time. Indeed, what eventually become modernism and postmodernism in the West cannot be adequately understood apart from their *theological* genealogy. This claim admittedly will appear outlandish and, therefore, will be resisted by some. If, however, readers are willing to suspend their disbelief and engage in rethinking of traditional theology in light of later developments and in reinterpreting modernism and postmodernism through classical theology, unexpected insights will, I believe, emerge.

The central doctrine of Christianity is Christology; indeed, without the Incarnation there is no Christianity. To affirm the incarnation of God in the historical person of Jesus is to believe that the real, however it is figured, is not elsewhere but is, in some sense, present here and now. The problem theologians and church officials faced was to find a way to affirm the divinity of Jesus while at the same time preserving the unity of God. Coming up with a rational solution to this problem was virtually impossible because of the way unity and identity were understood at the time of the early church councils. Rather than an inclusive or dialectical notion of unity and identity, Platonism and then-current monotheism presupposed an exclusive idea of unity in which plurality, multiplicity, and difference are irreconcilable with identity. Since something is *either* one *or* many—*either* identical *or* different—it cannot be both at the same time. And yet, the identity of identity and difference or unity of unity and multiplicity is precisely what the acceptance of monotheism and divinity of Jesus requires. If Jesus were God, God, it would seem, cannot be one but must be at least two. After all, how can God—or anything else—be one and more than one at the same time? The problem is compounded by the belief that the unity of God entails his immutability; if God were one, he cannot change, and correlatively, whatever changes cannot be God. The commitment to an exclusive notion of unity and identity leaves only three possible alternatives for the Father-Son relationship:

1. The Father and Son are identical, which violates the principle of non-contradiction and, therefore, seems irrational.
2. The Father and Son are different, which is reasonable but theologically problematic.
3. The Father and Son are somehow identical in their difference, which would resolve the problem but requires a new notion of reason.

The solution to this conundrum eventually turns out to be the unlikely claim that God is not merely one but is three-in-one. The implications of the complex relation between the doctrine of the Incarnation and the doctrine of the Trinity are not immediately obvious; indeed, it took

Table 5. Trinitarian Controversy

RELATION OF FATHER TO SON			
IDENTITY	IDENTITY-WITH-DISTINCTION		DIFFERENCE (SUBORDINATION)
Monarchianism	Alexander		Arius
Sabellius Patripassionism Modalism	Council of Nicaea (325)		
Marcellus	Athanasius (*homoousion*)	Semi-Ariana (*homoiousion*)	Radical Arians
			Dissimiliarians (*anomoean*)
	Constantinople (381)		

over a century and a half to resolve the problem in other than a perfunctory way, and even then few understood the importance of the issue
(table 5).

In the fourth century, these abstruse theological debates had serious
political consequences. By this time, the situation of the Christians had
changed dramatically. No longer a persecuted minority, Christianity had
become the privileged religion of the empire with the "conversion" of
Constantine at the battle of the Milvain Bridge in 312. While the Edict of
Milan (313) granted religious freedom to all citizens, Constantine's policy
gradually shifted from religious neutrality to policies favoring Christianity. His motives, however, were more political than religious—Constantine thought Christianity could provide the foundation for the political integration of the entire empire. His rule in the West was secure,
but the Eastern Empire was governed by his brother-in-law, Licinius,
whose policy of complete religious tolerance led to instability in 321,
when a dispute broke out between Alexander, the bishop of Alexandria,
and Arius, who was a presbyter in his church. While the focus of the
controversy was the status of the Son's relation to the Father within the
Godhead, the dispute had much wider implications. Alexander's chief
concern was soteriological; salvation, he argued, is impossible if Jesus
is not divine. Though not uninterested in redemption, Arius, who was
a radical monotheist, was primarily concerned with the preservation
of the absolute transcendence, unity, and immutability of God. If Jesus

were God, he countered, the immutable would be mutable, which is both a logical and a theological contradiction. Over the next three years, a series of councils and synods and a variety of political maneuvers failed to settle the issue. In 324 the uneasy truce between the Western and Eastern Empires broke down. Constantine defeated, exiled, and eventually ordered Licinius killed on trumped-up political charges. The triumphant emperor initially dismissed the theological controversy as "a trifling and foolish dispute about words" but, when the conflict threatened to undercut his political gains, quickly sought a resolution of the issue. On May 20, 325, Constantine convened a general church council in Nicaea for the purpose of reaching a theological consensus that would ensure the stability of the empire. He soon realized, however, that his hope for a quick resolution of the issue was an idle fantasy.

Both parties in the dispute traced their positions back to Origen, who had been the head of the catechetical school in Alexandria. Deeply influenced by Greek philosophy, Origen appropriated Platonism and Neoplatonism to interpret the Christian faith. In *On First Principles*, which is the first Christian summa, he developed a comprehensive, though not always consistent, theology, which he expanded into a philosophy of the universe. His writings remain fraught with tensions and plagued by unresolved contradictions; indeed, these contradictions are precisely what made his thought so influential. Opposing sides in disputes could justifiably appeal to the authority of Origen to support their positions. On the critical issue of the relation between the Son and the Father, Origen at some points maintains that the Son is equal to the Father but elsewhere insists that the Son is subordinate to the Father. In some contexts he insists that the Son is "coeternal and without beginning: As regards the power of his works, then, the Son is in no way whatever separate or different from the Father, nor is his work anything other than the Father's work, but there is one and the same movement, so to speak, in all they do; consequently the Father has called him an 'unspotted mirror,' in order to make it understood that there is absolutely no dissimilarity between the Son and the Father."[15] To underscore this important point, he introduced a term that became central in subsequent debates—*homoousion*, which means of the same essence or substance. *Homoousion* eventually is distinguished from *homoiousion* (of like essence or substance) and *anomoean* (of different essence or substance). In other passages, however, Origen contradicts the claim that the Father and Son are equal by arguing that there is a hierarchy within the Godhead as well as within the created order:

The God and Father, who holds the universe together, is superior to every being that exists, for he imparts to each one from his own existence that which each one is; the Son, being less than the Father, is superior to rational creatures alone (for he is second to the Father); the Holy Spirit is still less, and dwells within the saints alone. So that in this way the power of the Father is greater than that of the Son and that of the Holy Spirit, and that of the Son is more than that of the Holy Spirit, and in turn the power of the Holy Spirit exceeds that of every other holy being.[16]

Those who insisted on the equality or identity of the Father and Son came to be known as right-wing Origenists and those who maintained that the Son is subordinate to the Father were labeled left-wing Origenists.

The Arians were left-wing Origenists, who believed that the only reasonable position is the subordination of the Son (the historical Jesus) to the Father (the transcendent immutable God). Right-wing Origenists, by contrast, insisted on the complete identity of the Son and the Father. To preserve monotheism while at the same time affirming the divinity of Jesus, right-wing Origenists argued that the Father, Son, and Holy Spirit are not ontologically different but are different modalities of the same substance. The technical name of this point of view is Modalistic Monarchianism and its chief representative was Sabellius. In Sabellius's own words: "The same is the Father, the same is the Son, the same is the Holy Spirit. They are three names, but names for the same reality." In such a theology God the Father inevitably suffers, and critics who were devoted to divine impassibility labeled Sabellius's position Patripassionism. For Arius and his followers, the claim that God suffers is blasphemous. To avoid "contaminating" the eternal God with the vicissitudes of temporality, they argued, there can be no substantial identity between the Father and the Son. The Son not only is subordinate to the Father but is actually a creature. In a letter defending his beliefs written to Eusebius of Nicomedia around 318, Arius confesses:

What is it that we say, and think and have taught, and teach? That the son is not unbegotten, nor a part of the unbegotten in any way, nor [formed out] of any substratum, but that he was constituted by [God's] will and counsel, before times and before ages. . . . We are persecuted because we say, "The Son has a beginning, but God is without beginning." For this we are persecuted, and because we say "He is [made] out of things that were not." But this is what we say, since he is neither a part of God nor [formed] out of any substratum.[17]

Though he resists admitting the conclusion, Arius actually denies the Incarnation. If God were to become flesh and suffer, he would no longer be God, but if the Son is subordinate to the Father, there is no Incarnation.

For Alexander and his followers, to deny the Incarnation is to deny the possibility of salvation. It is, therefore, urgent to establish the full divinity of Jesus. In the years leading up to the Council of Nicaea, Athanasius, whose name means "man of immortality," became the chief spokesperson for the Alexandrian position. Athanasius explains his differences with the Arians:

> if the Son were a creature, man had remained mortal as before, not being joined to God; for a creature had not joined creatures to God, as seeking itself one to join it; nor would a portion of the creation have been the creation's salvation, as needing salvation itself. To provide against this also, He sends His own Son, and He becomes Son of Man, by taking created flesh. . . . For, the Word being clothed in flesh, as has many times been explained every bite of the serpent began to be utterly staunched from out it; and wherever evil sprung from the motions of the flesh, to be cut away.[18]

In other words, unless God becomes incarnate, salvation is impossible. To counter what he regarded as the pernicious subordinationism of the Arians, Athanasius insists on the *substantial* identity of the Father and the Son. Appropriating the term Origen had introduced, he argues that the Father and Son are *homoousios*—of the same substance. When the Council of Nicaea finally convened in a highly charged political atmosphere, representatives sided with Alexander and Athanasius and explicitly rejected the Arian position. The Trinitarian structure of the Nicene Creed asserts without explaining that the divinity of the Son does not compromise the unity and eternity of God:

> We believe in one God, Father, Almighty, maker of all things, visible and invisible,
>   And in one Lord Jesus Christ, begotten of the Father uniquely, that is, of the substance of the Father, God of God, Light of Light, true God of true God, begotten, not made, consubstantial with the Father, through whom all things were made, both things in heaven and those on earth, who for us men and for our salvation came down and was incarnate, [and] became man; he suffered and rose on the third day, ascended into heaven, and is coming to judge living and dead,
>   And in the Holy Spirit.[19]

The Council of Nicaea did not, however, settle the controversy; disputes running so deep are never resolved quickly. In the years following the council, the differences among opposing parties became even more pronounced. When Constantine died in 337, the tenuous unity of the empire threatened to dissolve in a theological dispute that had become thoroughly politicized. Though many sought to fashion a compromise that would appease everyone, Athanasius was tenacious in his defense of the creed. His chief concern always remained salvation. In his treatise *On the Incarnation of the Word*, he concisely summarizes the gist of his position: "For he [God] was made man that we might be made God; and he manifested himself by a body that we might receive the idea of the unseen Father; and he endured the insolence of men that we might inherit immortality."[20] In 381, the Council of Constantinople reaffirmed the Nicene Creed and condemned all surviving Arians. While this council brought to a close one of the most protracted and important theological disputes in the history of Christianity, important questions about the person of Jesus were left unanswered.

The debates surrounding the Council of Nicaea were so preoccupied with establishing or denying the divinity of the Son that the status of Jesus' humanity remained unclear. Shortly after the theological crisis seemed to have been resolved, contentious disputes once again erupted. The exclusive view of unity and identity again left only three options:

1. Jesus is fully God but not fully man.
2. Jesus is fully man but not fully God.
3. Jesus is fully God and fully man.

The two poles in these debates were represented by theologians and churchmen from Alexandria, who affirmed the divinity but denied the humanity of the Son, and those from Antioch, who affirmed the humanity but denied the divinity of the Son (table 6).

Since Alexandrians were more concerned with the heavenly than the earthly, they were drawn to mystical spirituality and tended to read scripture allegorically. Apollinaris, one of the staunchest supporters of the Alexandrian position, argued that, since human being is temporal, transient, and corruptible and divinity is eternal, unchanging, and incorruptible, it is impossible for them both to be fully present in a single undivided being. The question, then, is how the divine and the human can be united. For Apollinaris it is philosophically impossible for both the divine and the human to be fully present in a single undivided being. The only reasonable position, he believed, is for one nature to be completely present and the other nature only partially present. Since the

Table 6. Christological Controversy

DIVINE		DIVINE AND HUMAN	HUMAN
Monophysitism		Dyophysitism	Monophysitism
Alexandria Allegorical Mystical		Orthodoxy	Antioch Literal Historical Ethical
Apollinaris Apollinarianism	Cyril of Jerusalem	Gregory of Nazianzus Council of Ephesus (431)	Nestorius Nestorianism
Eutyches		Pope Leo	
Ephesus (449)		Council of Chalcedon (452) Against: Apollonarianism Nestorianism Monophysitism	
	Leontius of Byzantium		

divine nature cannot be incomplete and thus imperfect, human nature must be partially present in Jesus Christ. Apollinaris concludes that the divine is present as Jesus' mind but that his body remains completely human. "For God incarnate in human flesh keeps His own active energy, Mind being untouched by animal and bodily passions, and guiding the body and its movements divinely and sinlessly; not only unconquered by death but destroying death. And he is true God, the incorporeal appearing in flesh, perfect in true and divine perfections, not two persons, not two natures."[21] This position and its opposite (i.e., that the Son was fully man but not fully God) are known as Monophysitism (i.e., one nature). In subsequent debates, it became clear that Apollinaris's denial that Jesus Christ is two natures—both divine and human—is also tantamount to the rejection of the Incarnation.

It is important to recognize the implications of this Christology. Although not explicitly expressed, the denial of the Son's full humanity is a negative judgment about the created order and bodily existence. This position is consistent with the oppositional logic that underlies the exclusive notion of identity and unity. The logic of either/or issues are dualisms that can be neither reconciled nor mediated. During the formative years of Christianity, esoteric traditions that traced their roots to ancient Zoroastrianism were very popular throughout the region. Manichaeism and different forms of Christian and non-Christian Gnosticism attracted many followers and were for a while serious rivals of Christianity. Though the details of myths and rituals differ, all of these movements shared a view of God as radically transcendent and the world as utterly corrupt. Human beings are exiled in a world of darkness and seek to escape to the realm of pure light. Traces of these traditions can be detected in Alexandrian Christology, which denies that divinity can be fully embodied in humanity. Throughout the history of Christianity, versions of Manichaeism and Gnosticism repeatedly appear and claim to be the true version of the faith. But nothing is farther from the vision of life implicit in the doctrines of the Incarnation and the Trinity than such otherworldly dualisms.

Antiochean Christology is the polar opposite of the Alexandrian position. In contrast to the mystical and allegorical propensities of Alexandrian Christology, Antiocheans tended to be more literal, interested in the historical figure of Jesus, and devoted to Jesus as an ethical model for life in the world. As the controversy about the relation between divinity and humanity in Jesus continued, the focus shifted to the question of whether Mary was the mother of God (i.e., *theotokos*). To counter Apollinaris's tendency to absorb Jesus' humanity in divinity, Nestorius argued that since like can give birth only to like, Mary is the mother of the man Jesus but not of the divine Word, or Logos: "If anyone wishes to use this word *theotokos* with reference to the humanity which was born, joined to God the Word, and not with reference to the parent, we say that this word is not appropriate for her who gave birth, since a true mother should be of the same essence as what is born of her."[22] While Apollinaris tended to deny the humanity in order to affirm the divinity of Christ, Nestorius tended to deny the divinity in order to affirm the humanity of Christ. What neither could imagine was that Jesus Christ could be *fully divine* and *fully human*. Yet this is precisely what is required for salvation according to what finally became Christian orthodoxy. Gregory of Nazianzus, who played a central role in the debate, made the crucial point concisely: "For that which he has not assumed he has not healed." Gregory condemned both Apollinaris's denial of the full embodiment of divinity in humanity and Nestorius's rejection of the full divinity of the human person named Jesus. Though it took many years of theological argument and political maneuvering, the church eventually accepted Gregory's position. This understanding of the relation between the Father and the Son is formulated in the creed approved at the Council of Chalcedon:

> Following therefore the holy Fathers, we confess one and the same our Lord Jesus Christ, and we all teach harmoniously [that he is] *the same perfect in Godhead, the same perfect in manhood, truly God and truly man, the same of a reasonable soul and body, consubstantial with the Father in Godhead, and the same consubstantial with us in manhood,* like us in all things except sin; begotten before ages of the Father in Godhood, the same in the last days for us; and for our salvation [born] of Mary the virgin *theotokos* in manhood, one and the same Christ, Son, Lord, unique; acknowledged in *two natures without confusion, without change, without division, without separation, different natures being by no means taken away because of the union, but rather the distinctive character of each nature being preserved,* and [each] combining in one Person and hypostasis.[23] (emphasis added)

Here at last is the formulation of the hypostatic union, which still remains orthodox Christology: one person, two natures—fully God and fully man. To proclaim, however, is not to explain; the acceptance of the formula did not end the debate. Disputes have continued to simmer and at times have broken out, creating deep divisions that in some cases have led to lasting schisms.

One of the reasons for the lingering confusions is that the philosophical assumptions underlying the critical categories cannot express the insights theologians and churchmen were struggling to articulate. The intent of the creed is clear but its language is not. The church fathers wanted to affirm the full divinity and full humanity of the Son. It is important to recall that theological claims not only are about God but also entail beliefs about self and world. To embrace the full divinity and humanity of Jesus is to affirm that the real can be embodied in time and space, and therefore, nature and history are themselves in some sense real rather than illusory or merely apparent. Confusions inevitably arose because the language at the disposal of early church theologians made it virtually impossible for them to express the complexities of their vision. This is evident in the key terms in the creed:

> . . . **consubstantial** with the Father in Godhead, and the same **consubstantial** with us in manhood. . . . two **natures** without confusion, without change, without division, without separation, different **natures** being by no means taken away because of the union, but rather

the distinctive character of each **nature** being preserved, and [each] combining in one Person and **hypostasis.**

The terms that caused all the problems were *hypostasis, substance,* and *nature.* The words *hypostasis* and *substance* express similar metaphysical presuppositions inasmuch as they both draw a hierarchical distinction between surface and depth. While depth is essential, surface is accidental. *Hypostasis* literally means "that which lies beneath as the basis or foundation." In a similar manner, *substance* designates "that which stands *(stare)* beneath *(sub)*." Accordingly, substance is "the essential *nature* of anything; the primary or basic element that receives modifications."[24] The distinction between hypostasis or substance and accident is isomorphic with the distinction between unity and multiplicity as well as identity and difference. Within this schema, unity and identity underlie and thus are the foundation of multiplicity and difference. The issue once again turns on the question of unity and identity, on the one hand, and multiplicity or difference, on the other.

In a little-known book titled *The Doctrine of the Trinity,* Leonard Hodgson describes what I have defined as the difference between exclusive and inclusive views of unity in terms of the distinction between arithmetical and organic unity. While the criterion of arithmetical unity is "the absence of multiplicity," organic unity "exists as a complex differing of constituents."

> The idea of unity in our minds is primarily an arithmetical idea: the criterion is the absence of multiplicity. Here one is one and three are three; what is one is not three and what are three are not one. But we have long been acquainted with unities which are not so simple. There is, for example, aesthetic unity, the unity of a work of art. And there is organic unity, the unity of a living creature. In both of these the unity is far from being simple. It does indeed exclude certain kinds of multiplicity, such as a distracting multiplicity of interests in a work of art, or a lack of coordination in the activities of a living creature. But it can only exist at all by virtue of the presence of another kind of multiplicity, the multiplicity of varied elements, which constitute the work of art or the living creature.[25]

The problem with the orthodox formulations of the doctrines of the Incarnation and the Trinity is that they attempt to express organic unity in arithmetical terms. The inevitable result is a contradiction that seems to shatter reason. Confronted with such a contradiction, many believers over the centuries have felt that the best response is to embrace Tertullian's well-known dictum *Credo quia absurdum*. From this point of view, it is impossible to think that the infinitely and qualitatively different God has become incarnate in the particular historical figure of Jesus. The Incarnation is a *coincidentia oppositorium*, which, in Kierkegaard's memorable phrase, is the Absolute Paradox. "The paradox," he explains, "unites the contradictories, and is the historical made eternal, and the Eternal made historical." "It is easy to see, though it scarcely needs to be pointed out, since it is involved in the fact that reason is set aside and faith is not a form of knowledge; all knowledge is either a knowledge of the eternal, excluding the temporal and historical as indifferent, or it is pure historical knowledge. No knowledge can have for its object the absurdity that the eternal is historical."[26]

But what if unity and identity are inclusive rather than exclusive— complex rather than simple? Though Hodgson does not refer to Kant, his account of the unity characteristic of natural organisms and works of art is clearly reminiscent of the notion of inner teleology developed in the Third Critique. As we discovered in chapter 3, post-Kantian philosophers and poets extended Kant's argument to develop a notion of the modern subject, which is prefigured in Luther's theological anthropology. It now becomes apparent that this entire trajectory is inseparable from the theological disputes of the fourth and fifth centuries. But the far-reaching implications of the Incarnation and Trinity for the modern period did not become clear until Hegel developed his system.[27] This is not to suggest, of course, that the doctrines of Christology and the Trinity were not the subject of heated arguments over the centuries. But the terms of debate precluded an adequate resolution of the issues. A decisive turning point was reached when Hegel developed his dialectical interpretation of spirit to account for the contradictions inherent in Luther's account of subjectivity. In the preface to the *Phenomenology of Spirit*, Hegel takes the category that is central to the Trinitarian and Christological controversies—*substance*—as his point of departure: "In my view, which can be justified only by the exposition of the system itself, everything turns on grasping and expressing the True, not only as *Substance*, but equally as *Subject*."[28] When the True is finally grasped as subject, God becomes fully embodied in nature as well as history and both self and world are completely transformed. This transformation reverses the interrelated processes of desacralization and disenchantment by revealing the sacred in the midst of what had seemed profane. With this twist, secularity appears to be the fulfillment rather than the simple negation of religion.

SELF-EMBODIMENT OF GOD

In the *Philosophy of History*, Hegel makes a remarkable claim when commenting on the importance of the Christian notion of God: "God is thus recognized as *Spirit* only when known as triune. This new principle is the pivot upon which world history turns."[29] What makes the notion of the Trinity so important for Hegel is his belief that it reveals the dynamic structure of all reality. The Trinity, in other words, not only represents the inner life of God but also discloses the truth about the self and world. When rationally comprehended, the Trinity reveals that God, self, and world are three-in-one and one-in-three—each becomes itself in and through the other, and none can be itself apart from the others. Self and world emerge in and through the self-embodiment of God, and God is real only by becoming incarnate in self and world. In this movement, transcendence negates itself in an immanence that always remains incomplete.

We have already discovered the reversal of transcendence in immanence at the heart of the Protestant tradition. In an effort to establish the omnipotence of the Creator God and the absolute dependence of the human creature, Calvin effectively identified divine and human activity. Without ever mentioning Calvin, Hegel captures the logic of this critical reversal in his analysis of what he aptly labels "unhappy consciousness."[30] For unhappy consciousness, the real is always elsewhere—in this case, God remains remote in his transcendence, and human beings are trapped in a world of despair, darkness, and death. Hegel describes the dilemma faced by unhappy consciousness in terms of the opposition between the changeable and the unchangeable. Bound to the vicissitudes of time, unhappy consciousness longs for the permanence of eternity. This "yearning," Hegel maintains, marks the inward turn of consciousness that leads to redemption and eventually to freedom:

> What we have here, then, is the inward movement of the pure heart, which *feels* itself as agonizingly self-divided, the movement of an infinite yearning [*Sehnsucht*], which is certain that its essence is such a pure heart, a pure *thinking* which *thinks* of itself as a *particular individuality*, certain of being known and recognized by this object, precisely because the latter thinks of itself as an individuality. At the same time, however, this essence is the unattainable beyond which, in being laid hold of, flees or, rather, has already flown.[31]

As a particular subject, the believer is separate from and set over against the transcendent object to which it is devoted. This moment of opposi-

tion, which is a condition of the subject's self-consciousness, is, however, unstable and reverses itself in seeking complete self-expression.
When it is effective, devotion is not merely passive but manifests itself
in "desire and work [*Begierde und Arbeit*] devoted to God." In anticipation of issues to be considered in the next section, it is important to
note the complexity of this notion of desire: *Begierde* also means "wish,"
"longing," "craving," "appetite," "concupiscence," and "lust." Through
the Incarnation, these experiences are, contrary to expectation, transformed into embodiments of divine activity. Though ostensibly gifts to
God from the believer, desire and labor are actually gifts (*Gabe*, "gift,"
"present," "donation," "offering") to unhappy consciousness from the
unchangeable. Just as Calvin asserts the identity between the creature
and the Creator in and through the very activity designed to affirm their
infinite difference, so desire and labor of unhappy consciousness lead to
a dialectical reversal that establishes its identity-in-difference with the
unchangeable.

> The active force appears as the *power* in which actuality is dissolved;
> for this very reason, however, the consciousness to which the intrinsic
> or essential Being is an 'other,' regards this power, which it displays in
> its activity to be the beyond of itself. Instead, therefore, of returning
> from its activity back into itself, and having obtained confirmation of
> its self-certainty, consciousness really reflects this activity back into
> the other extreme, which is thus exhibited as a pure universal, as the
> absolute power from which the activity started out in all directions,
> and which is the essence both of the self-dividing extremes as they at
> first appeared, and of their interchanging relationship to itself.
>
> The fact that the unchangeable consciousness *renounces* and *sur-
> renders* its embodied form, while, on the other hand, the particular
> individual *gives thanks* [for the gift], i.e., *denies* itself the satisfaction
> of being conscious of its *independence*, and assigns the essence of its
> action not to itself but to the beyond, through these two movements
> of *reciprocal self-surrender* of both parts, consciousness does, of course,
> gain a sense of its *unity* with the Unchangeable.[32]

As this important passage suggests, oppositional difference gives way to
relational identity: changeable/unchangeable, subject/object, time/eter-
nity, particular/universal, desire/reason, works/grace, secular/sacred,
man/God are no longer opposed but now are recognized as codependent.
Paul's words echo in Hegel's argument: "the life I now live is not my life
but the life of Christ in me" (Galatians 2:20).

Hegel sees his entire philosophical vision prefigured in Luther's theology. This association might seem unlikely since, as we have seen, Luther's thought is characterized by a dualism sometimes bordering on Manichaeism. It is undeniable that Luther often described the kingdom of God as the irreconcilable antithesis of the kingdom of the world. But his thought is more subtle and complex than even he at times realized. In practice, there is a very close relationship between the two kingdoms, which, when fully elaborated, effectively reconciles the religious and the secular. It is no exaggeration to insist that modern secularity as it has developed in the West would have been impossible without Lutheran Protestantism. The key to this development is Luther's doctrine of calling—*Beruf*. Though salvation depends on grace rather than works, every person is called to fulfill the responsibilities of his or her station in the world.[33] This understanding of Christian duty is implicit in Luther's rejection of the church's hierarchical authority and insistence on the priesthood of all believers. Christian faith does not draw one from the world into the cloister but sends one into the world to serve God in everyday life. For Luther, the Christian calling is most closely related to family and work—or in Hegel's terms "*Begierde und Arbeit*," which, we will see, Freud translates as "*Liebe und Arbeit*." Gustav Wingren summarizes Luther's position:

> A vocation is a "station," which is by nature helpful to others if it be followed. It is important to emphasize the fact that vocation is not confined to an occupation, but includes also what Betcke calls biological orders: father, mother, son, daughter. Every attempt to differentiate between the sphere of the home, where personal Christian love rules, and the sphere of the office, where the more impersonal rules of vocation hold sway, immediately runs afoul of Luther's terminology. The life of the home, the relation between parents and children, is vocation, even as is life in the field of labor, the relation between employer and employee.[34]

This understanding of vocation discloses tensions at the heart of Lutheranism, which lead to very different conclusions. On the one hand, as we have discovered, Luther's privatization of faith issues in an opposition between interiority and exteriority that makes faith an entirely private matter. As faith becomes private, the public sphere is gradually secularized until church and state become separate. On the other hand, Luther's doctrine of Christian calling erodes the opposition between the public and the private by investing worldly activity with religious value. Through his or her activity in the world, the Christian becomes the agent or vehicle of God. It is important to stress that Christian calling is not limited to positions of power and prestige but extends to every station in life no matter how low or ordinary. This reconciliation of the religious and the secular is actually an extension of the Incarnation, which collapses high and low in a way that redeems what once had seemed to be profane. In an effort to express the implications of this notion of calling, Luther uses the richly suggestive image masks of God—*larvae Dei*. Always aware of his peasant roots, Luther writes: "All our work in the field, in the garden, in the city, in the home, in struggle, in government—to what does it all amount before God except child's play, by means of which God is pleased to give his gifts in the field, at home and everywhere? These are the masks of our Lord God, behind which he wants to be hidden and to do all things. . . . God bestows all that is good on us, but you must stretch out your hands and lay hold of the horns of the bull, i.e., you must work and lend yourself as a means and a mask of God."[35] When my work is God's work, the will of man and the will of God are one or, more precisely, are identical in their difference. Just as God can disappear by becoming too transcendent or too immanent, so religious activity can disappear by becoming completely private or by becoming indistinguishable from worldly engagement. In either case the result is the same: secularity is revealed to be inseparable from religion.

This conclusion is exactly what makes the Reformation so important for Hegel. Within his schema, world history is marked by the steady march of freedom. As one moves from east to west, there is a progression from a condition in which only one is free, through a situation in which some are free, to a state in which all are free. The Reformation marks a tipping point in the emergence of the modern world when freedom becomes—or is supposed to become—universal. Describing this transition, Hegel writes:

> We spoke above of the *relation that the new doctrine sustained to secular life* and now we have only to exhibit that relation in detail. The development and advance of Spirit from the time of the Reformation onwards consist in this, that Spirit, having now gained the consciousness of its freedom, through that process of mediation, which takes place between man and God—that is, in the full recognition of the objective process as the existence of the Divine essence [*göttlichen Wesens*, "divine essence, substance, being"]—now takes it up and follows it out in building up the edifice of secular relations. That harmony [of objective and subjective will], which has resulted from the painful struggles of history, involves the recognition of the secular [*Weltliche*]

as capable of being an embodiment of Truth, whereas it had been formerly regarded as evil only, as capable of Good, which remained in the life to come.[36]

To understand how truth becomes embodied in the secular, it is necessary to return to the interrelation of the Incarnation and the Trinity.

As we have seen, Truth, according to Hegel, first appears sensually in artistic images and religious representations and then is articulated in philosophical concepts. Representation (*Vorstellung*) and concept (*Begriff*) differ substantively but not formally or structurally. At the level of *Vorstellung*, the beautiful work of art and the Trinity are isomorphic: both represent the structure of self-referentiality or self-reflexivity in which apparent opposites are reciprocally related in a way that renders them coemergent and codependent. These figures of self-reflexivity disclose the structure of self-conscious subjectivity, which, for Hegel, is infinite and absolute. This is why he insists that it is necessary to grasp the True, "not only as *substance*, but equally as *subject*." Hegel was not, however, the first to recognize the similarity between self or, more precisely, self-consciousness and the Trinitarian God. In his seminal treatise *On the Trinity*, Augustine attempts to explain how something can be simultaneously three and one by drawing an analogy between God and self-consciousness. The sixth chapter of book 9 bears the intimidating heading

> The three are one, and also equal, viz. the mind itself, and
> The love, and the knowledge of it. That the same three
> Exist substantially, and are predicated relatively.
> That the same three are inseparable. That the
> Same three are not joined and commingled
> Like parts, but that they are of one
> essence, and are relatives.

Augustine proceeds to explain his point: "But as there are two things, the mind and the love of it, when it loves itself; so there are two things, the mind and the knowledge of it, when it knows itself. Therefore the mind itself, and the love of it, and the knowledge of it, are three things, and these three are one; and when they are perfect they are equal."[37] This is a remarkable text because it identifies constitutive relationalism at the very heart of the Christian notion of God. There is no Father without the Son and no Son without the Father; Spirit fashions a unity that constitutes and sustains differences. When philosophically understood, this is precisely the inclusive notion of identity for which the church fathers, other than Augustine, were searching for but never able to formulate. It took more than fifteen hundred years for the significance of Augustine's insight to emerge. If God is triune, constitutive relationalism is the structure or substance of all reality and as such is divine.

Hegel was the first to understand the far-reaching implications of epistemological and ontological relationalism. From one point of view, his entire philosophy is an explication of the meaning of the Incarnation and the Trinity. When interpreted speculatively, these doctrines reveal the truth not only about God but also about self and world. Hegel realizes that unless God is triune, the Incarnation is impossible: "The reconciliation believed to be in Christ has no meaning if God is not known as triune, if it is not recognized that he *is* but is at the same time the other, the self-differentiating, the other in the sense that this other is God himself, and has in himself the divine nature, and that the sublation of this difference, of this otherness, this return, this love, is spirit."[38] If Jesus is God and God is One, then the Christian God must be triune, three-in-one and one-in-three. This relational structure is not static but is thoroughly dynamic. Indeed, at one point Hegel goes so far as to appropriate Aristotle's term to describe God as "spirit, absolute activity, *actus purus*, i.e., subjectivity, infinite personality."[39] The Trinity reveals God to be a self-engendering and self-organizing creative process or, in Hegel's speculative terms, "God is this, to differentiate himself from himself, to be an object to himself, but in this differentiation, to be absolutely self-identical with himself—this is spirit."[40]

In this threefold relation, the Son is at once other than and one with the Father, and the Father is simultaneously other than and one with the Son. Each sees himself in the other and becomes himself through the other. God, Hegel explains, "beholds himself in what is differentiated; and when in his other he is united only with himself, he is there with no other but himself, he is in close union only with himself, he *beholds* himself in his other."[41] The complexities of this self-reflexive relationship are easier to grasp in diagrammatic form (fig. 16). This relation between the Father and Son is possible only if their unity and identity are inclusive rather than exclusive. The name of this self-engendering relational activity is Spirit, which now appears to be Holy. The divine activity in and through which God, self, and world become actual involves three moments figured as Incarnation, Crucifixion, and Resurrection. Through this threefold process, oppositional differences give way to differential identity. The abstract transcendent God, whom Nietzsche labeled "the moral God," dies and is reborn in the human figure of Jesus, who is also divine. This particular individual is, then, crucified and resurrected

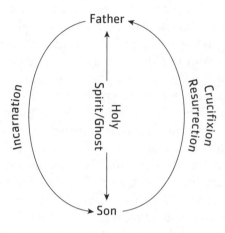

Figure 16. Trinity

as an integral member of a universal community, which emerges in a global process. Oppositional difference is negated when the transcendent God dies in the incarnate Christ and the individual subject dies in the crucified Jesus:

> For it is *this* suffering and death, this sacrificial death of the individual for all, that is the nature of God, the divine history, the being that is utterly universal and affirmative. This is, however, at the same time to posit God's negation; in the death the moment of negation is envisaged. This is an essential moment in the nature of spirit, and it is this death that must come into view in this individual. It must not then be represented merely as the death of *this individual*, the death of this empirically existing individual. Heretics have interpreted it like that, but what it means is rather that *God* has died, that *God himself* is dead. God has died: this is negation, which is accordingly a moment of the divine nature, of God himself.[42]

The Incarnation is the negation of the radically transcendent God, and the Crucifixion is the negation of the isolated individual deemed divine. The Resurrection represents the double negation that issues in the sublation of opposites in a relation of identity-in-difference and difference-in-identity. In this way, death is not merely negative but is ever duplicitous—negation is negated in the infinite process of life.[43]

This truth can be realized only when the individual subject recognizes itself in the divine object. The triadic structure of Father-Son-Spirit is isomorphic with the triadic structure of self-consciousness:

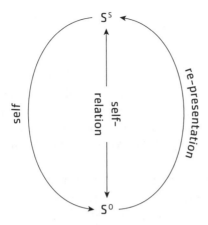

Figure 17. Self-Consciousness

self-as-subject (Father), self-as-object (Son), and the interrelation of the two (Spirit). Self-consciousness presupposes self-representation— in the self-reflexivity of self-consciousness, the self re-presents itself to itself. To grasp this important point, it is helpful to recall our diagrammatic representation of the structure of self-consciousness (fig. 17). In a manner strictly parallel to the relation of Father and Son through Spirit, self-as-subject and self-as-object are reciprocally related in such a way that each becomes itself through the other and neither can be itself apart from the other. The complexity and vitality of this relationship cannot be represented in the simple and static language of substance but must be grasped in terms of dynamic subjectivity.

A few lines after Hegel claims that his overriding philosophical concern is to express the True as subject rather than only as substance, he offers his most explicit and concise definition of the concept of subjectivity that informs his entire system:

> Further, the living substance is being which is in truth *subject*, or, what is the same, is in truth actual only insofar as it is the movement of positing itself, or is the mediation of its self-othering with itself. This substance is, as subject, pure, *simple negativity,* and is for this very reason the division [*Entzweiung*] of the simple; it is the doubling [*Verdöpplung*], which sets up opposition, and then again the negation of this indifferent diversity and of its antithesis [the immediate simplicity]. Only this self-*restoring* sameness, or this reflection in otherness within itself—not an *original* or *immediate* unity as such—is the True.

It is the process of its own becoming, the circle that presupposes its end as its goal [Zweck], and having its end also as its beginning; and only by being worked out to the end is it actual.[44]

The self-contradictory subject identified by Luther and elaborated by Kant and post-Kantian poets and philosophers reaches conceptual clarity in the triadic structure of Hegelian subjectivity. This subject, like the triune God, is inwardly differentiated yet unified. Never static, this identity-in-difference involves an activity that is, in Hegel's terms, an *actus purus*.

It is important to note that the triplicity of subjectivity is both synchronic and diachronic; the structure as well as the development of the subject is triune. *In principio*, the subject is an undifferentiated unity or simple identity, which is completely abstract and utterly indeterminate. This corresponds to the theological modality of transcendence, which, in human terms, is the moment prior to any specific action. In order to become actual, this indeterminacy must be negated through particular actions. In a manner reminiscent of the struggle between Tiamat and Marduk, the splitting of the subject is an inward doubling, which introduces differences that disrupt primal identity. Initially these differences appear to be an "indifferent diversity"; that is, each determination seems to be separate and isolated. In the third moment, this indifference is negated (i.e., negation is negated), and unity, which initially appeared to exclude difference, is revealed as necessarily including difference. At this point, substance becomes subject; far from an underlying identity that grounds otherwise-indifferent differences, subjectivity is the vital interplay in and through which differences arise and pass away. "Only this self-*restoring* sameness, or this reflection in otherness within itself—not an *original* or *immediate* unity as such—is the True." Bending back on itself from its self-determination in specific actions, the subject returns to itself with a difference or with differences. No longer an "original or immediate unity," its identity is now differential and thus complex rather than simple. When understood in this way, the structure of subjectivity is isomorphic not only with the Trinitarian God but also with the beautiful work of art as Kant defined it. According to the principle of relationalism in which identity is differential rather than oppositional, parts and whole are reciprocally related in such a way that each becomes itself through the other and neither can be itself apart from the other.

By translating artistic images and religious representations into phil-

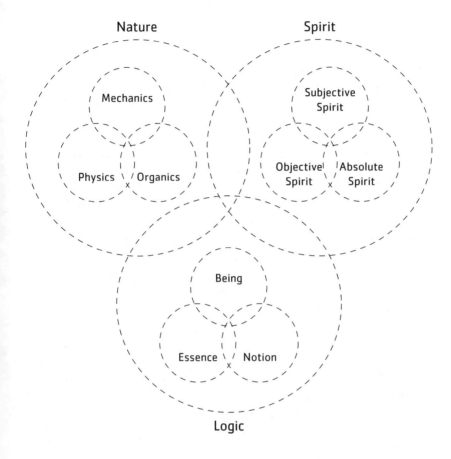

Figure 18. Hegel's System

osophical concepts, Hegel believes he has ascertained the structure or logic of all reality: subjectivity is infinite or absolute. In his speculative system Hegel refigures the romantics' poetic vision by showing how the transcendent creator God dies and is reborn as the infinite creative process that endlessly emerges in space and time. In the theological language Hegel is attempting to translate, the world is really the self-embodiment of God, and thus, whatever exists is an incarnation of divine reality. Whether considered synchronically or diachronically, part and whole are isomorphic or, in a more contemporary idiom, fractal. At the most comprehensive level, the tripartite structure of the system—Logic, Nature, Spirit—conforms to the threefold structure of subjectivity (fig. 18). The unfolding of the system through natural evolution and historical and cultural development conforms to the three-part narrative Joachim of Floris first formulated in his economic rendering of the Trinity. For Hegel, as for Joachim, the long march of history is characterized by the spread of freedom throughout the world. The third era, the age of Spirit, marks the culmination of this process; at this point, freedom no longer is limited to a few but now is enjoyed by everyone. As freedom spreads, the kingdom of God arrives on earth and history comes to an end.

But this is a strange end—indeed, it is an end without end. Just as self-consciousness discovers its irreducible incompleteness at the moment it seems to achieve fulfillment, so history encounters its inescapable openness at the very moment it approaches what seems to be its end. The issue once again turns on the question of freedom. Freedom, we have discovered, is duplicitous—it involves both autonomy and an-archy. While autonomy issues in the self-referentiality and self-reflexivity characteristic of closed structures and systems, an-archy is the groundless ground that keeps every structure and system open. The nothingness of this abyssal *Abgrund* haunts Hegel's system and opens it to complexities he could not recognize. The trace of this nothingness is the ellipsis that decenters the circle and transforms it into an ellipse.[45]

When Hegel is read against the grain, it appears that his system necessarily includes a strange excess it can neither incorporate nor comprehend. This openness, which appears by withdrawing at the moment of closure, engenders the infinite restlessness of the negative, which we have already glimpsed in the work of art. For Hegel, as for his fellow Jena romantics, the world remains a work of art even when it is philosophically comprehended. This work of art is not merely a finished product but is, more importantly, a process that is its own end or purpose. Since the end is endless, the process through which it approaches is neither complete nor incomplete. Inasmuch as the poetic subject can become itself only through the activity of negation in which it becomes what it is not, subjectivity is never complete—nor is it simply incomplete. Far from a lack, this incompleteness is what makes infinite creativity possible. When the transcendent Creator becomes emergent creativity, the sacred and secular become one while remaining two.

> The instinct for heaven had its counterpart:
> The instinct for earth, for New Haven, for his room,
> The gay tournamonde as of a single world
>
> In which he is and as and is are one.
> For its counterpart a kind of counterpoint
> Irked the wet wallows of the water-spout.[46]

THEOLOGY AND THEORY

Hegel's reconciliation of the secular and the sacred proved unstable; in the years immediately following his death in 1831, his followers split into opposing camps, which David Strauss quickly labeled right-wing and left-wing Hegelians. While right-wing Hegelians appropriated his speculative system to defend a theistic version of traditional Protestantism, critics on the left argued that Hegel had inadvertently demonstrated that religious beliefs and practices are epiphenomenal and as such can be understood only by reducing them to more basic economic, social, and psychological processes. Some right-wing Hegelians were influential during the 1830s and 1840s—especially in Denmark—but their work has been of little lasting significance. Left-wing Hegelians, by contrast, played an important intellectual and political role throughout the nineteenth and twentieth centuries. Representatives of the Hegelian Left argued that consciousness, always symptomatic of something other than itself, is "false consciousness" if not properly interpreted. Through an unexpected reversal, Hegel's absolute knowledge led to what Paul Ricoeur has aptly described as "the hermeneutics of suspicion."[47] Ricoeur identifies three primary representatives of this mode of interpretation: Marx, Freud, and Nietzsche. In attempting to decode human consciousness, these writers developed theories of religion that continue to frame the terms of much critical debate today. While these theories appear to reinforce the interplay between modernity and secularity, more careful consideration suggests a theological dimension that continues to haunt their theoretical reflections. Though each critic approached religion from a different angle, their theories are structurally similar. Furthermore, each of these theoretical perspectives turns out to be internally inconsistent. Far from a shortcoming, these inconsistencies actually enrich their analyses in unexpected ways that lend them continuing significance. By bringing together without integrating theologies of the Word and theologies of the Deed, Marx, Freud, and Nietzsche formulated theories whose self-contradictions, we shall discover, created openings for alternative critical trajectories to emerge during the latter half of the twentieth century.

One of the most radical conclusions of Hegel's system is that reason as well as all human culture evolves historically. Neither eternal nor unchanging, notions of truth, beauty, and goodness are historically contingent and thus inescapably relative. From this point of view, the Enlightenment commitment to the principle of universality becomes suspect. The historical relativity of culture does not, according to Hegel, preclude the possibility of absolute knowledge. Rather than a specific epistemological position, absolute knowledge involves the apprehension of the complex process in which determinate forms of knowledge and specific institutions emerge and pass away through their ongoing interrelations. In this historical process, the only thing that is not relative is, paradoxically, the relativity of specific figures of the world and determinate shapes of consciousness. Hegel's left-wing followers and critics were quick to realize the implications of this argument, and nowhere was this insight more important than in the interpretation of religion. This first became apparent when a heated controversy broke out about the historical status and reliability of the Bible in the years immediately following Hegel's death.

We have already seen that early translations of the Bible, many of which were the product of Protestantism's preoccupation with the Word of God, raised questions about the historical accuracy of scripture as early as the sixteenth century. Erasmus's multilingual edition of the Bible exposed many inconsistencies in the Vulgate, which had been accepted as normative since the fourth century. But Erasmus was not alone; in 1520, the Reformer Andreas Bodenstein von Karlstadt published *On the Canonical Scriptures,* in which he argued that Moses could not possibly have written the Pentateuch as it exists in its present form. During the modern era, biblical criticism became more sophisticated and rigorous while at the same time becoming less indebted to dogmatic assumptions. Needless to say, the centrality of the Bible for Protestant religiosity made the stakes of any criticism of the Bible very high. When Spinoza issued his *Tractatus Theologico-politicus* (1670) anonymously under the imprint of a fake publisher, the Reformed Council of Amsterdam quickly condemned the book. Spinoza, who was one of the first to use empirical methods, treated the Bible no differently than other historical or natural phenomena. Four years after the church's action, the Court of Holland banned the printing, sale, and distribution of Spinoza's work. By the time of the Enlightenment, critics questioned not only the historical accuracy but even the moral value of the Bible. At the end of the eighteenth century, Lessing published the Wolfenbüttel fragments (1774–78), which included selections from Hermann Reimarus's *Apologie oder Schutschrift für die vernünftigen Verehrer Gottes.* Devoted to the principles of rationalism as Christian Wolff had defined them, Reimarus defended a form of natural religion that was at odds with the revealed religion of the Bible. More important, he sought to expose historical and factual inaccuracies in the Bible and even went so far as to question the moral integrity of both the apostles and the people who wrote the Gospels. As might be expected, the militant anticlericalism, materialism, and atheism of the French En-lightenment led to even more hostile attacks on the Bible. Pierre Bayle's *Critical and Historical Dictionary* (1697) marked a tipping point in biblical criticism. Bayle, as Franklin Baumer points out, was

> one of the first to dissolve the traditional distinction between "sacred" and "profane" history. Up to this time, secular historians normally stopped short of "sacred" history, i.e., the events described in the Holy Scripture and the subsequent history of the church. Bayle, however, had no such compunctions about invading that sphere, stripping it of its providential aura, and in general treating it as though it operated through the same laws as any other history, or indeed nature itself. He expressed incredulity of biblical chronology, he cast doubt on the accuracy of Christian records, he pointed out the similarity between biblical and pagan stories, he cut Old Testament heroes like Abraham and David down to human size, he planted doubts about the miracle stories. In his hands "sacred" history from the time of Christ to the Reformation fared, if anything, even worse. His clear inference was that there was nothing providential at all about the record, that if there was such a thing as Providence, Christians should be ashamed of it, that the victory in so-called "sacred" history usually went to the priests and theologians, which is to say, the devil.[48]

Left-wing Hegelians accepted many of the criticisms of religion de-veloped by Enlightenment critics but shifted the terms of debate by moving beyond the traditional oppositions between reason/faith and natural/supernatural. Though they disagreed about many things, these Hegelians shared a philosophy of history in which modernity entails the progressive displacement of religion by reason. The arguments they de-veloped to support their positions eventually led to the theory of secu-larization that became extremely influential more than a century later. The two most important works of biblical criticism to come out of this school of thought were both published in 1835: Wilhelm Vatke's *Biblical Theology Delineated Scientifically: The Religion of the Old Testament Developed according to the Canonical Books*, and David Friedrich Strauss's *The Life of Jesus*. Vatke argued that the history of Israelite religion developed in three dialectical stages, which move progressively from paganism (i.e., nature religion, in which most people are slaves), through prophetic religion (i.e., ethical religion in which individuals are free), to theocratic legal-ism (i.e., the Bible's Deuteronomistic and Priestly sources, in which the ethical is formulated in abstract laws). This "progression," Vatke argued, eventually prepared the way for Christianity.[49] Strauss extended this speculative/historical analysis to the New Testament by appropriating Hegel's distinction between religious representations and philosophical concepts. He argued that biblical texts are not historical narratives or implicit truths of reason but are the product of a "primitive mentality," which expressed itself "naturally" in myths. Neither historically accurate nor rationally coherent, the Bible is a mythological reflection of a form of awareness that is both primitive and infantile. Strauss's questioning of the factual veracity of Scripture ignited a heated controversy, which led to a quest for the historical Jesus that still continues today. For many Protestants, the viability of faith depends on the historical reliability and literal accuracy of the Bible. As we will see in the next chapter, the acceptance of so-called scientific biblical criticism became one of the distinguishing features of religious modernism and played a major role in the rise of Fundamentalism during the early decades of the twentieth century.

The issue of history as it is framed in Hegel's philosophy, however, involves considerably more than the historical accuracy of the sacred texts in one or two particular traditions. If culture, like everything else, evolves, then religions have histories and, therefore, must have historical beginnings. In the wake of Hegel's effort to reconcile the sacred and profane, the question of the origin of religion became urgent.[50] Perhaps, some argued, "profane history" provides the key to decode the secrets of "sacred history." As critics developed theories to explain religion, they became preoccupied with its origin, which must be understood both diachronically and synchronically. On the one hand, "origin" designates the initial emergence of religion in ancient or so-called primitive history (diachronic), and on the other hand, "origin" refers to the persistent underlying causes or conditions of religious beliefs and practices (synchronic). Though not immediately evident, these two aspects of the notion of origin turn out to be inseparable. Since the historical origins of religion (diachronic) are inaccessible, critics argued, it is necessary to examine the way religion originates in the present world (synchronic). In arguments that are undeniably circular, analysts projected origin back in time in order to explain the historical evolution of religion up to the present. It is important to note that there is an unresolved tension between these two meanings of "origin." If the causes of religion operate in the same way anywhere and anytime, then these causes are actually ahistorical rather than historical. Throughout the latter half of the nineteenth century, abiding causes underlying historical phenomena were interpreted alternatively in socioeconomic, psychological, and aesthetic terms.

The accounts of the origin of religion that directly and indirectly set the terms for all subsequent theories are all versions of the hermeneutics of suspicion. This approach to cultural phenomena translates the philosophical distinction between appearances and reality into what Marx describes as the difference between superstructure and infrastructure. Such binaries are not, of course, equivalent but are hierarchical—the latter term is consistently privileged over the former: superstructure (appearance) can be understood only in terms of the infrastructure (reality). Marx argues:

> In the social production of their life, men enter into definite relations that are indispensable and independent of their will, relations of production, which correspond to a definite stage of development of their material productive forces. The sum total of these relations of production constitutes the economic structure of society, the real foundation, on which rises a legal and political superstructure and to which correspond definite forms of consciousness. The mode of production of material life conditions the social, political, and intellectual life process in general. It is not the consciousness of men that determines their being, but, on the contrary, their social being that determines their consciousness.[51]

In addition to being formulated spatially as surface and depth, the distinction between superstructure and infrastructure can also be expressed temporally as the difference between the primitive and the modern. When these binaries frame analysis, interpretation involves reducing surface to depth by tracing the modern to the primitive.

This ostensibly "secular" interpretive strategy is actually an extension of theological hermeneutics dating back to the appropriation of Platonic philosophy by early Christian apologists. In the hermeneutics of suspicion, the functional equivalents of Platonic forms and the Christian Logos constitute the foundational structures that ground cultural superstructures. As we have seen, the forms, which initially transcended the Demiurge, were first transformed into the Word, which is the mind of God, and then drifted downward to become *imago Dei* as the structure of human consciousness. At the final stage of their descent, the forms and the Logos slip below the surface to become the infrastructures grounding the processes of both self and world. Surface is no longer explained in terms of the heavens as it had been for millennia but now is interpreted through the depths. Though everything seems different, nothing *fundamental* changes because interpretation remains logocentric.

This inversion of transcendent forms into underlying structures is reflected in Marx's famous claim to turn Hegel on his head by transforming speculative idealism into dialectical materialism. Marx deploys Hegel's account of self-consciousness to develop a dialectical analysis of the socioeconomic processes that "ground" human awareness. Just as self-consciousness comprises the three moments of being-for-self, being-for-other, and being-in-and-for-itself, so society is constituted through the three moments of externalization, objectification, and internalization. Peter Berger summarizes the standard Marxist account of this process in his influential account of the relationship between modernization and secularization. "Externalizing is the ongoing outpouring of human into the world, both in the physical and the mental activity of men. Objectivation is the attainment by the products of this activity (again both physical and mental) of a reality that confronts its original producers as a facticity external to and other than themselves. Internalization is the reappropriation by men of this same reality, transforming it once again from structures of the objective world into structures of subjective consciousness."[52] This argument derives from Hegel's analysis of the master-slave relation, which, in turn, can be traced to his interpretation of the origin of the transcendent God. Reversing the traditional God-self relation, man, Hegel argues, creates God in his own image and then becomes the indentured servant to the Other he has produced. Marx begins his critique of the *Philosophy of Right* by recasting Hegel's analysis of religion in his own materialistic terms:

> For Germany, the *criticism of religion* has been largely completed; and the criticism of religion is the premise of all criticism.
>
> The *profane* existence of error is compromised once its celestial *oratio pro aris et focis* has been refuted. Man, who has found in the fantastic reality of heaven, where he sought a supernatural being, only his own reflection, will no longer be tempted to find only the *semblance* of himself—a non-human being—where he seeks and must seek his true reality.
>
> The basis of irreligious criticism is this: *man makes religion;* religion does not make man. Religion is indeed man's self-consciousness and self-awareness so long as he has not found himself or has lost himself again.[53]

For Marx, religion is not eternal but originates in particular historical circumstances to address specific human needs. In contrast to his precursor Ludwig Feuerbach, for whom consciousness of this process of projection and reification is sufficient to overcome religion, Marx insists that religion will not disappear until the conditions that make it necessary are alleviated. Extending Hegel's interpretation of religion to the process of production, Marx argues that men and women create and perpetuate their bondage through their own labor. By producing products over which they seem to have no control, workers become slaves to masters they create. The harder one works to get out of bondage, the more wealthy and hence powerful the master becomes and, correspondingly, the weaker the worker becomes. To break this cycle, which perpetuates alienation, Hegelian theory must become Marxist practice. Tracing his revolutionary program back to Luther by way of Hegel, Marx, we have noted, declares: "In fact Germany's *revolutionary* past is theoretical—it is the *Reformation*. In that period the revolution originated in the brain of a monk, today in the brain of a philosopher." But, Marx continues, "it is not enough that thought should seek to realize itself; reality must also strive towards thought."[54] The *Communist Manifesto* is a call to arms for this revolution.

Marx's revolutionary program not only depends on Hegel's account of religion but also presupposes a thinly disguised secularization of traditional Judeo-Christian theologies of history. In this narrative of redemption, capitalism represents the fallen condition of sin, which must be overcome by destroying private property and the selfishness it promotes. In a revealing footnote on the first page of the *Manifesto*, Marx posits a primitive form of communism, which existed prior to capitalism.

> In 1847, the prehistory of society, the social organization existing previous to recorded history, was all but unknown. Since then, Haxthausen discovered common ownership of land in Russia, Maurer proved it to be the social foundation from which all Teutonic races started in history, and by and by village communities were found to be, or to have been, the primitive form of society everywhere from India to Ireland. The inner organization of this primitive Communistic society was laid bare, in its typical form, by Morgan's crowning discovery of the true nature of the *gens* and its relation to the *tribe*. With the dissolution of these primeval communities, societies begin to be differentiated into separate and finally antagonistic classes.[55]

Commentators have consistently overlooked the significance of this textual supplement. For all its declared radicalism, Marx's revolutionary program presupposes an interpretation of history that is strictly parallel to orthodox Judeo-Christian theology, romantic poetry, and idealistic philosophy. In terms of Hegel's dialectical logic, capitalism is the negation of the primal unity, which characterized primitive communism. To restore lost harmony, this negation must be negated through the creation of a socialist society in which the good of each (i.e., the individual) is the good of all (i.e., the universal). This negation of the negation promises to bring what is in effect the kingdom of God to earth.

While Freud's and Nietzsche's analyses of religion present different accounts of its origin, the structure of their arguments is virtually identical to Marx's position. Freud translates Marx's distinction between superstructure and infrastructure into the difference between what he labels the manifest and latent content of the mind, as well as of social and cultural institutions. He formulates the hermeneutical model that guides all his work in *The Interpretation of Dreams* (1900). In a passage that has proven decisive for many cultural critics, Freud explains the difference between latent dream-thoughts and manifest dream-content by drawing an analogy between dream interpretation and translation: "The dream-thoughts and dream-content are presented to us like two versions of the same subject-matter in two different languages. Or, more properly, the dream-content seems like a transcript of the dream-thoughts into another mode of expression, whose characters and syntactic laws it is our business to discover by comparing the original with the translation."[56] In this schema, the unconscious is, as Jacques Lacan insisted, "structured like a language." Just as it is necessary to know vocabulary and grammar to translate a text, so it is necessary to know the significance of the elements in a dream and the rules by which they are combined to decode the dream-content. The problem with interpreting dreams is that, by their very nature, unconscious desire must "speak" indirectly. Like the transcendent God, the unconscious can show itself only by hiding; its revelation, therefore, is a concealment and its concealment a revelation. In a manner reminiscent of a seasoned rabbi, the psychoanalyst interprets the word of the Other, which now sounds from the depths rather than from the heavens. Once again, God does not simply disappear but slips underground, where the repressed lurks awaiting the propitious moment for its return.

When Freud wrote *The Interpretation of Dreams*, he understood the personality in terms of the binary opposition between consciousness and unconsciousness. By the time he arrived at his mature position, he had become convinced that the personality is triadic—it comprises the id, ego, and superego. Like Plato's charioteer trying to control horses stampeding in different directions (reason, appetite, will), the ego struggles to negotiate the conflict between the raging desires of the id and the moral dictates of the superego. For Freud, as for both orthodox theology and Hegel, the trinitarian structure of the personality is both synchronic and diachronic. The three different aspects of the subject are not given but must be cultivated (*bilden, Bildung*) in a process whose trajectory is isomorphic with the emergent structure it produces. In its original condition, there is no differentiated individual ego—immediate desires rule the personality. This situation begins to change when the rules and norms of the social group are internalized to form the superego. Reenacting Kant's moral struggle, the ego tries but inevitably fails to resolve the conflict between obligation (i.e., the social) and inclination (i.e., the individual). Torn between personal desires and the Law of the Father, Freud's subject, like Luther's guilty sinner, is inwardly divided or split and, thus, inherently self-contradictory.

The three aspects of subjectivity unfold through three stages: oral, anal, and genital. The general direction of the development of the personality is from undifferentiation through differentiation and conflict back to undifferentiation. In Freud's schema, this process is driven by the dialectical interplay of Eros and Thanatos. The oral stage of development is an extension of intrauterine life, in which self and world are one—mother and infant form a single organism. All desires are fulfilled immediately *in utero*, but the trauma of birth disrupts this original harmony. In a manner reminiscent of Marduk's slaying of Tiamat, the breaking of the waters and severing of the umbilical cord result in the infant's "fall" into time and space. Once separated from the mother, there is an inevitable delay between desire and fulfillment; this temporal deferral marks the beginning of the process of differentiation and hence individuation. As theologians and philosophers from Augustine to Kierkegaard and Heidegger have argued, time and self are inseparable—subjectivity, in other words, is inescapably temporal. According to Freud, individuation is a long, slow process. After the initial separation has occurred, the differentiation between self and Other remains minimal during the oral stage. While the details of Freud's argument need not concern us here, it is important to note the role the will plays in negotiating the conflict between desire and law. Infants and so-called primitives, Freud argues, are uninhibited and seek the closest approximation to immediate gratification that is possible. As individuals mature, however, they gradually learn to control desires by conforming to social regulations. Revising or perhaps reversing the Enlightenment myth of progress, Freud argues that the history of civilization is marked by increasing repression and hence growing discontent. Denied direct expression, desires go underground but never disappear. Though not immediately apparent, the dynamics of these developments can also be expressed in the abstract terms of Hegel's speculative dialectic. The individual first emerges in the process of negating the undifferentiated matrix of its origin and then achieves further individuation through the exercise of the will. Volitional activity inevitably leads to conflicts, which simultaneously seek expression and resolution through sexuality and aggression. Though tension can be reduced, conflicts cannot be fully resolved apart from death. The death of the individual is the negation of the negation (i.e., the differentiated individual) and entails return to the original undifferentiated matrix. This threefold nature of the structure and development of the personality frames Freud's interpretation of religion. Increasing repression creates growing tension, which must be released through circumscribed rituals that allow for a regulated return of the repressed. What makes such rituals dangerous is the possibility that desires will rage out of control, thereby disrupting or destroying the lives of individuals and groups.

Over the course of his career, Freud repeatedly turned his attention to religion. Indeed, religion was never far from his mind, and many of his most telling insights about it were offered when he seemed to be discussing something else. Freud's comments are not always consistent and vary considerably, from the simplistic theory of projection presented in *The Future of an Illusion* to the seminal psychosocial analysis in *Totem and Taboo*. A lifelong fascination with Rome led him to use archaeological metaphors to describe the analytic process he applies to both individuals and cultures. These images reveal more than even Freud realized. In *Civilization and Its Discontents*, he writes:

> It is hardly necessary to remark that all these remains of ancient Rome are found dovetailed into the jumble of a great metropolis which has grown up in the last few centuries since the Renaissance. There is certainly not a little that is ancient still buried in the soil of the city or beneath its modern buildings. This is the manner in which the past is preserved in historical sites like Rome.
>
> Now let us, by a flight of imagination, suppose that Rome is not a human habitation but a psychical entity with a similarly long and copious past—an entity, that is to say, in which nothing that has come into existence will have passed away and all the earlier phases of development will continue to exist alongside the latest one.[57]

From this point of view, psychoanalysis is, in effect, the archaeology of the mind. In this schema, the only way to understand the manifest is to excavate memories until one unearths the latent. In this archaeological enterprise, to dig down is to go back. Since Freud agrees with Hegel's insistence that the development of the individual repeats the development of the race or, in terms more consistent with Darwinian evolution, ontogeny recapitulates phylogeny, the depths reveal the origin of both the individual and the race as a whole.

A few pages before invoking the image of Rome, Freud reports that a friend had responded to *The Future of an Illusion* by suggesting that religion is the result of an "oceanic feeling" associated with the mother rather than originating in the relation to the father. Freud admits that the conditions of the original emergence of the ego lend this theory a certain plausibility.

> Originally the ego includes everything, later it separates off an external world from itself. Our present ego-feeling is, therefore, only a shrunken residue of a much more inclusive—indeed, an all-embracing—feeling which corresponded to a more intimate bond between the ego and the world about it. If we may assume that there are many people in whose mental life this primary ego-feeling has persisted to a greater or lesser degree, it would exist in them side by side with the narrower and more sharply demarcated ego-feeling of maturity, like a kind of counterpart to it. In that case, the ideational contents appropriate to it would be precisely those of limitlessness and of a bond with the universe—the same ideas with which my friend elucidated the "oceanic" feeling.

After further deliberation, however, Freud rejects this theory and returns to his initial hypothesis, according to which religion results from "the feeling of infantile dependence" and the correlative "need for a father's protection."[58] The relation to the father, like everything else in life for Freud, is fraught with ambiguity and ambivalence. After encountering the tendency of patients to repeat traumatic experiences, Freud was forced to admit that the psyche cannot be completely explained in terms of the pleasure principle, whose aim is the reduction of tension. In *Beyond the Pleasure Principle*, he concludes that there are two, not one, basic instincts: Eros and Thanatos. Though appearing to be opposites, love and death are actually dialectically related in such a way that each one turns into the other. Eros brings together individuals in a union that, when complete, negates their separation by destroying their differences.

Thanatos, by contrast, *"is an urge inherent in organic life to restore an earlier state of things,* which the living entity has been obliged to abandon under the pressure of external disturbing forces; that is, it is a kind of organic elasticity, or, to put it another way, the expression of the inertia inherent in organic life."[59]

To understand the implications of this argument, it is necessary to see how Freud's theory of the instincts grows out of his appropriation of Newton's principle of equilibrium. Interpreting life on the model of mechanical systems, Freud maintains that organisms remain in a state of equilibrium unless they are disturbed *from the outside.* Once disequilibrium occurs, the organism seeks to restore balance and thus return to the condition of equilibrium. Insofar as the satisfaction of desire reduces tension and restores equilibrium, it leads to inertia or, in terms of information theory, entropy, which ultimately results in the death of the organism. In an effort to delay this inevitable end, the death instinct becomes "negentropic" by turning outward in aggression directed against others. In hostile activity, the subject asserts and defends itself by negating the Other. As Hegel realized, however, aggression is always ambiguous and ultimately becomes self-defeating—hostility toward the Other is at the same time the identification with the Other. Violence, in other words, is erotic, and love inevitably harbors hostility. Thanatos and Eros eventually become indistinguishable—the end of both love and death is the return of differences into the unity from which they originally emerged.

> Those instincts are therefore bound to give a deceptive appearance of being forces tending towards change and progress, whilst in fact they are merely seeking to reach an ancient goal by paths alike old and new. Moreover, it is possible to specify this final goal of all organic striving. It would be in contradiction to the conservative nature of the instincts if the goal of life were a state of things that had never been attained. On the contrary, it must be an *old* state of things, an initial state from which the living entity has at one time or another departed and to which it is striving to return by the circuitous paths along which its development leads. If we are to take this as a truth that knows no exception that everything living dies for *internal* reasons—becomes inorganic once again—then we shall be compelled to say that *"the aim of all life is death"* and, looking backwards, that *"inanimate things existed before living ones."*[60]

This complex interplay between Eros and Thanatos lies at the heart of the Oedipus complex and forms the basis of Freud's most provocative interpretation of the origin and function of religion. Weaving together his theory of psychosexual development and Darwin's speculation about the primal horde, Freud develops a myth of origin to explain the historical emergence and continuing function of religion. By prohibiting the fulfillment of the son's erotic desire for the mother, the father provokes both hostility and envy. The resulting emotional ambivalence is expressed in the son's aggression toward the father. In desiring his death, the son seeks to take the father's place; hostility toward the father is at the same time identification with the father. Through an act of literary imagination, Freud stages his psychodrama as an actual historical event. Drawing on Darwin, he speculates that at the beginning of history, a band of brothers joined together to slay the primal father and, thus, gain access to the mother and the other women he controlled. To ensure their bond of shared guilt, all the brothers were required to participate in the sacrifice, which culminated in the consumption of the body of the dead father. This ritual process involves three seemingly contradictory moments: first, the acting out of the hatred of the father; second, the unification of the guilty sons; and third, the identification of the sons with the father. Expressed in religious language with which we are by now familiar, the father dies and is reborn by literally becoming incarnate in the sons.

While admitting the fictive character of his narrative, Freud is convinced that it reveals the psychological and historical truth of Christianity. The myth of origin discloses the latent hidden in the manifest by interpreting the present in terms of the past. Reenacting the totemic ritual with which human civilization began, the ritual of the Eucharist provides the safe confines within which primitive desires can be simultaneously expressed and regulated. In orthodox Christology, Jesus, we have discovered, is fully God and fully man. Freud interprets Christianity as the displacement of a religion of the Father (Judaism) by a religion of the Son. Inasmuch as Jesus is one with the Father, his crucifixion is the death of the Father through which the Son becomes the object of worship. The Eucharist, then, is the repetition of the victory over the Father through which the faithful become guilty:

> The very deed in which the son offered the greatest possible atonement to the father brought him at the same time to the attainment of his wishes *against* the father. He himself became God, beside, or, more correctly, in place of, the father. A son-religion displaced the father-religion. As a sign of this substitution the ancient totem meal was revived in the form of communion, in which the company of brothers

consumed the flesh and the blood of the son—no longer the father—obtained sanctity thereby and identified themselves with him. Thus we can trace through the ages the identity of the totem meal with animal sacrifice, with the anthropic human sacrifice and with the Christian Eucharist, and we can recognize in all these rituals the effect of the crime by which men were so deeply weighed down but for which they must nonetheless feel so proud. The Christian communion, however, is essentially a fresh elimination of the father, a repetition of the guilty deed.[61]

But guilt is not the only aftereffect of the transgression; participation in the Eucharist renders believers not only guilty but also divine. In the Eucharist, the community of the faithful repeats the death and rebirth of God. Just as the primitive sons identified with the father by eating his dead body, so the believers identify with the Son, who is the Father, by eating his body and drinking his blood. In different terms, when the host (Latin *hostia*) is consumed, the believing subject becomes one with the object of belief. The Eucharist is, then, the ritual reenactment of the self-embodiment of God through which the transcendent deity dies and is reborn in the believing community. The agent of this (re)union is the Holy G-host (Latin *ghostis*) or Spirit (*Geist*), now deemed divine. When understood in this way (though there is, we shall discover, another way to understand this story), Freud's hermeneutics of suspicion extends Hegel's dialectical process by repeating without acknowledging Nietzsche's death of God.

Freud once admitted that he had stopped reading Nietzsche because he feared he would be too influenced by him. His concerns were well founded because Nietzsche anticipated many of Freud's most important insights. Freud concludes *Totem and Taboo* by citing a line by Goethe that both echoes and reverses the opening verses in the Gospel according to John:

> It is no doubt true that the sharp contrast that *we* make between thinking and doing is absent in both of them [i.e., primitives and neurotics]. But neurotics are above all *inhibited* in their actions: with them thought is a complete substitute for the deed. Primitive men, on the other hand, are *uninhibited*: thought passes directly into action. With them it is rather the deed that is a substitute for the thought. And that is why, without laying claim to any finality of judgment, I think that in the case before us it may safely be assumed that "in the beginning was the Deed."[62]

This is, in many ways, a strange text because no one since Kant, Fichte, Schlegel, Schelling, and Schopenhauer had done more to demonstrate that thinking *is* acting than Freud. Freud implicitly invokes the voluntaristic tradition extending back to Ockham in which deed informs word as its necessary yet incomprehensible condition. For Nietzsche, the deed that is always already in the beginning is the *will to power*.

To understand the persistence of theology in theory, it is helpful to situate these theories of the origin and function of religion on the axis of theological and philosophical alternatives that we have been following (table 7). As will become clear below, Marx, Freud, and Nietzsche can be read in both foundational and nonfoundational ways. On the one hand, they extend the theology of the word by arguing that cultural superstructures can be reduced to economic, psychological, and aesthetic infrastructures, and on the other hand, they reinscribe the theol-

Table 7. Theology of Theory

	WORD	**DEED**	
Platonism	Transcendent Forms	Omnipotent Will	
	Forms	*Potential absoluta*	Nominalism
	Demiurge	*Potential ordinata*	Ockham
	Matter		Protestantism
			Luther
			Calvin
Christian Apologists	Mind of God	Covenant Theology	Puritanism
	Logos		
Kant	Structure of Consciousness	Structure of Consciousness	Rousseau
	A priori forms	Imagination	Fichte
	Imagination	Emergent Figuring	F. Schlegel
	Schematization	*Darstellung* presentation	Schopenhauer
	A posteriori experience	Poiesis	
		Recombinant Figuring	
		Vorstellung representation	
		Mimesis	
	Foundational Theories	Non-foundational Theories	
Marx[1]	Socio-economic	Socio-economic	Marx[2]
Freud[1]	Psychological	Psychological	Freud[2]
Nietzsche[1]	Aesthetic	Aesthetic	Nietzsche[2]

ogy of the deed by admitting without ever directly acknowledging that these infrastructures are inevitably incomplete.[63]

I have already considered Nietzsche's early formulation of his position in the account of the world as a work of art. As the supreme artist, God is "amoral, recklessly creating and destroying, realizing himself indifferently in whatever he does or undoes."[64] The creative-destructive interplay between the Apollonian (individuation) and Dionysian (dissolution) rhythms in this process corresponds to the tension between the ego and the id. By the end of his life, Nietzsche had elaborated his expansive aestheticism to form a vision that can only be described as religious. In the concluding aphorism of his posthumous *Will to Power*, he waxes ecstatic:

> This world: a monster of energy, without beginning, without end; . . . enclosed by "nothingness" as by a boundary; not something blurry or wasted, not something endlessly extended, but set in a definite space as a definite force, and not a space that might be "empty" here or there, but rather as force throughout, as a play of forces and waves of forces, at the same time one and many, increasing here and at the same time decreasing there; a sea of forces flowing and rushing together, eternally changing, eternally flooding back, with tremendous years of recurrence, with an ebb and flood of its forms . . . a becoming that knows no satiety, no disgust, no weariness: this, my *Dionysian* world of the eternally self-creating, the eternally self-destroying, this mystery of the world of twofold voluptuous delight, my "beyond good and evil," without goal. . . . *This world is the will to power—and nothing more!* And you yourselves are also this will to power—and nothing more![65]

As the clouds of madness slowly gathered, Nietzsche increasingly identified with Dionysus and began signing his fragmentary writings "The Crucified," "Dionysus," or the "Anti-Christ." Though analysts usually dismiss this practice as symptomatic of growing dementia, these strange pseudonyms actually reveal the dialectical structure that underlies all of Nietzsche's thought.

Every interpretation of Nietzsche's proclamation of the death of God as a nihilistic rejection of religion is wrong. Unwittingly following Hegel, whom he unjustifiably dismissed, Nietzsche correctly insisted that it is not unbelief but belief in the transcendent God that is nihilistic. As Hegel's analysis of unhappy consciousness shows, if the real is elsewhere (i.e., transcendent), it can be affirmed only by negating the world as we know it. In Nietzsche's dialectical analysis, the nihilism of transcendence was introduced by Paul rather than Jesus. Invoking a distinction that became commonplace after the rise of historical biblical criticism, Nietzsche distinguished the religion *of* Jesus from the religion *about* Jesus. Nietzsche insisted that Jesus never preached about a distant God or proclaimed an otherworldly kingdom but rather "demonstrates how one must live in order to feel 'deified'—and how one will not achieve it through repentance and contrition for one's sins: 'sin is of no account' is his central judgment." This message is, in effect, a realized eschatology in which "'Bliss' is not something promised; it is there if you live and act in such and such a way." Paul, however, "reversed" Jesus' message by setting sinful human beings against a transcendent God and promising their reconciliation only in the afterlife: "He understood what the pagan world had the greatest need of, and from the facts of Christ's life and death made a quite arbitrary selection, giving everything a new accentuation, shifting the emphasis everywhere—he *annulled* primitive Christianity as a matter of principle."[66] Since the gospel of Paul is the negation of the gospel of Jesus, the only way to restore primitive Christianity is to negate this negation through the death of "the moral God." "The concept of 'God,'" Nietzsche declares, "was until now the greatest objection to existence. We deny God, we deny the responsibility in God: only thereby do we redeem the world." If the Christ of faith is the negation of the religion of the historical Jesus, then the Anti-Christ is the negation of the negation in which primitive Christianity returns in the guise of Dionysus. Far from nihilistic, this double negation is radically affirmative of life in all its ambiguity, uncertainty, and complexity. Saying, "No to No," Dionysus, the Anti-Christ, says, "Yes to life even in its strangest and hardest problems. The will to live rejoicing over its own inexhaustibility."[67] In Nietzsche's Dionysian world, one rediscovers Hegel's insight: "The True is thus the Bacchanalian revel in which no member remains sober; yet because each member collapses as soon as he drops out, the revel is just as much transparent as simple repose."[68]

Nietzsche's interpretation of religion brings our analysis of secularity full circle but does not close the issue. I have argued that the history of religion in the West involves the alternation between transcendence and immanence. God repeatedly disappears by becoming either too absent or too present. In the wake of Enlightenment deism and atheism, the withdrawal of God is reversed through a process that extends the Incarnation through natural and historical processes. Though the interpretations of the details of this process change, the structure remains the same (table 8). In all variations of this schema, historical development—be it personal, social, or cultural—is an archaeoteleological process in which the implications of the beginning become explicit only at the end. The

Table 8. Narrative of Redemption

Creation	Fall	Redemption
Garden	World	Kingdom
Union	Opposition	(Re)Union
Identity	Difference	Identity-in-Difference
Primitive Communism	Capitalism	Modern Communism
Oral	Anal	Genital
Jesus	Christ	Anti-Christ
Primitive Christianity	Christianity	Modern (Dionysian) Christianity

meaning of this process can be decoded by those who know its foundational structures and their operational logic. But at this moment of apparent closure, an unanticipated opening "appears" to disrupt the return by which the circle had seemed to complete itself. Logocentric structures betray faults that imply without revealing the groundless ground they presuppose but cannot incorporate. This opening marks an *excess* that must always be inscribed differently. For Nietzsche, the "Dionysian world of the eternally self-creating, the eternally self-destroying," involves an "exuberance" that is "beyond good and evil." He makes this point by recasting the notion of genius. Whereas Kant regards the genius as a figure for the autonomy of self-reflexivity in which the subject emerges from and returns to itself, Nietzsche sees in the genius an expenditure without return that disrupts every economy of exchange that appears to be balanced and complete. "The genius, in work and deed, is necessarily a squanderer: that he squanders himself, that is his greatness. The instinct of self-preservation is suspended, as it were; the overpowering pressure of overflowing forces forbids him any such care or caution. . . . He flows out, he overflows, he uses himself up, he does not spare himself—and this is a calamitous, involuntary fatality, no less than a river's flooding the land."[69] The excess Nietzsche detects overflows not only his own argument but also the schemata Marx and Freud construct to contain it.

Though he attempted to ignore it, Marx eventually was forced to admit that not everything could be explained in terms of the principle of equilibrium that lies at the heart of modern economic theory. There is something that inevitably eludes the binary logic of exchange and pushes systems away from equilibrium and toward the edge of chaos. This strange something, Marx concludes, is closely related to art and religion. In the chapter on money in his *Grundrisse*, he writes:

> Among all the peoples of antiquity, the piling-up of gold and silver appears at first as a priestly and royal privilege, since the god and king of

commodities [i.e., money] pertains only to gods and kings. Only they deserve to possess wealth as such. This accumulation, then, occurs on one side merely to display overabundance, i.e., wealth as an extraordinary thing, for use on Sundays only; to provide gifts for temples and their gods; to finance public works of art. . . . Later in antiquity, this accumulation becomes political. The *state treasury*, as reserve fund, and the temple are the original banks in which this holy of holies is preserved.

Such ancient practices do not disappear in capitalist economies, where they seem to make no sense. The calculated efficiency of the insistent utilitarianism that is characteristic of the modern bourgeoisie is contradicted by useless, irrational practices that can be traced to "primitive" rituals. Marx sees the ostentatious display of wealth as a spectacle whose end is nothing other than itself:

Like the accumulation of gold, etc. as ornament and ostentation among semi-barbarians. But a very large and growing part of it is withdrawn from circulation as an object of luxury in the most developed bourgeois society. . . . As representative of general wealth, it is precisely its retention without abandoning it to circulation and employing it for particular needs which is proof of the wealth of individuals; and to the degree that money develops in its various roles, i.e., that wealth as such becomes the general measure of worth of individuals, [there develops] the drive to display it. . . . The point being that it is *not* used as money; here the form antithetical to circulation is what is important.[70]

Marx realizes that such practices cannot be explained in terms of the utilitarian logic that makes economic sense. How can this impractical activity be understood? Such practices serve no purpose and make no sense in terms of the economic logic that Marx believes forms the foundation of all cultural practices. What he resists considering because to do so would call his whole theory into question is that serving a purpose and making sense might be precisely what such activities are designed to avoid.

When approached from a psychoanalytic perspective, the excesses of ostentatious display bespeak complex desires, which are inconceivable in terms of closed equilibrium systems of exchange. Freud suspects but cannot bring himself to admit that the divided subject is in the final analysis *irreducibly* obscure. Desire, we have discovered, never shows itself directly but always reveals itself by concealing itself. *The Interpretation of Dreams* expresses Freud's dream of interpretation in which he wagers that the manifest content of dreams can be completely decoded. But he loses his bet—this dream, like all dreams, cannot be fulfilled, because the codes necessary for deciphering dreams are inevitably cracked. By turning Freud's hermeneutics of suspicion back on his own text, one discovers, not the transparency of self-reflexivity, but a fault in the mirror of reflection. If desire can show itself only by hiding, then the circle of self-consciousness is never complete but is always decentered like a duplicitous ellipse rather than a transparent circle. What is most important lies—always lies—at the periphery rather than the center, at the margin rather than in the body of the work. In analyzing one of his own dreams, Freud glimpses a blind spot that simultaneously resists and solicits interpretation. Acknowledging what he would rather ignore, he supplements his narrative with a "revealing" footnote that effectively subverts his analysis. "I had a feeling that the interpretation of this part of the dream was not carried far enough to make it possible to follow the whole of its concealed meaning. If I had pursued my comparison between [sic] the three women, it would have taken me far afield. There is at least one spot in every dream at which it is unplumbable—a navel, as it were, that is its point of contact with the unknown."[71] This remarkable admission implies that every interpretation is incomplete because consciousness is doubled by an unconscious that not only is unknown but remains unknowable. As the point of contact with the unknown, the navel of the dream is the trace of the unrepresentable that every representation presupposes but cannot re-present. Far from a lack, the repetition of this point is the ellipsis that shows the hiding of the infinite restlessness of desire through which the world is created and re-created.

By developing theoretical analyses of the origin and function of religion, Marx, Freud, and Nietzsche extend the transformation of transcendence into immanence begun in romantic poetry and Hegelian philosophy. While intending to reduce the divine to the human, these hermeneuticists of suspicion actually remain haunted by the ghost of religion they struggle to dispel. When read against the grain, their socioeconomic, psychological, and aesthetic theories of religion imply an irreducible alterity in the midst of immanence and the presence it is supposed to realize. Kierkegaard was the only nineteenth-century writer to recognize the inescapability of a radical difference. However, his preoccupation with his relentless attack on Hegelianism led him to pose his critique of the dialectical reversal of God's transcendence in terms of oppositional differences, which reinscribe the very position Hegel had already overcome. It is, therefore, necessary to reread Hegel's both/and through Kierkegaard's either/or and vice versa to formulate a position that *neither* collapses differences into identity *nor* reifies differences into irreconcilable opposites. This neither/nor opens a new space where the religious imagination can develop critical reflections and constructive arguments that will be more effective in emerging network culture. Symbolic networks, I have argued, assume specificity through their interrelations with other cultural systems as well as with natural, social, and technological factors. In the next two chapters, I will examine how theology, philosophy, and art emerge from the confines of church, university, and museum to transform the political, economic, and technological landscape. These changes, in turn, have led to radical theologies and ideologies that threaten to bring the world to the brink of collapse. At the edge of chaos lurks not only danger but also the prospect of creative emergence, which harbors the only hope that remains.

CHAPTER FIVE

Eclipse of the Real

DEATHS OF GOD

The December 11, 1968, edition of the *New York Times* carried a front-page story on the death of the Swiss theologian Karl Barth at the age of eighty-two.[1] Edward Fisk opened his long article with an account of Barth's humble beginnings:

> In 1919 an unknown Swiss country pastor gave the world a rather unpre-tentious-sounding book entitled *The Epistle to the Romans*. He had had difficulty finding a publisher but, as a fellow theologian later put it, the volume "landed like a bombshell on the playground of theologians."
>
> The young pastor was Karl Barth and his commentary on Romans was one of those events that happen only rarely in a discipline such as theology—when a revolutionary idea falls into the hands of a giant who possesses the powers not only to utter it but also to control its destiny.
>
> In this case the idea was the radical transcendence of God. At a time when theologians had reduced God to little more than a projection of man's highest impulses, Dr. Barth rejected all that human disciplines such as history or philosophy could say about God and man. He spoke of God as the "wholly other" who entered human history at the moment of His own choosing and sat in judgment on any attempt by men to create a God in their own image.

Rereading Paul amid the smoldering ruins of World War I, Barth pronounced a resounding *"Nein!"* to every form of theological liberalism and all versions of what was labeled *Kulturprotestantismus*.

To understand the importance of Barth's theological innovation, it is necessary to return once again to Jena at the turn of the nineteenth century. It has become customary to mark the beginning of modern theology with the publication of Schleiermacher's *Speeches on Religion* in 1799, a work that remains the definitive Romantic interpretation of religion. In a move that proved decisive for all later theologians and critics, Schleiermacher shifted attention from the transcendent God to human beings' experience by arguing that religion is primarily concerned with feeling rather than thinking or acting. While theoretical reflection and moral action presuppose a separation between subjectivity and objectivity, religious experience, which closely approximates aesthetic awareness, involves the apprehension of an "original unity," which is antecedent to and a condition of all difference and opposition. Anticipating Freud a century later, Schleiermacher uses erotic imagery to evoke what he cannot properly describe:

> The first mysterious moment that occurs in every sensory perception, before intuition and feeling have separated, where sense and objects have, as it were, flowed into one another and become one, before both turn back to their original position—I know how indescribable it is and how quickly it passes. But I wish that you were able to hold on to it and also to recognize it again in the higher and divine religious activity of the mind. Would that I could and might express it, at least indicate it, without having to desecrate it! It is as fleeting and transparent as the first scent with which dew gently caresses the waking flowers, as modest and delicate as a maiden's kiss, as holy and fruitful as a nuptial embrace; indeed, not *like* these, but it *is itself* all of these.[2]

When understood in this way, religious experience is supposed to restore momentarily the primal unity that is inevitably lost when consciousness and self-consciousness emerge.

Schleiermacher emphatically rejects the notion of a personal God because it introduces an opposition between the human and the divine, on the one hand, and between self and world, on the other. In a manner reminiscent of some of the religions of the ancient Near East, which we have considered, Schleiermacher's God is immanent in the cosmos. "Every finite thing," he insists, "is a sign of the Infinite, and so these various expressions declare the immediate relation of a phenomenon to the Infinite and Whole."[3] Borrowing the poetic vision of his fellow Romantics—the Schlegels, Hölderlin, and Novalis—Schleiermacher describes "the harmony of the universe, the wondrous and great unity," as "the eternal work of art." Within this Infinite whole, differences and diversity are epiphenomenal—the real is One and One is real: "Recall how in religion everything strives to expand the sharply delineated outlines of our personality and gradually to lose them in the Infinite in order that we, by intuiting the universe, will become one with it as much as possible. . . . Try to surrender your life out of love for the universe. Strive to annihilate your individuality and to live in the One and in the All; strive to be more than yourselves so that you lose little if you lose yourselves."[4] In this moment of union, differences collapse in a primal identity and Alpha and Omega become One.

While Schleiermacher's refocusing of attention from the transcendent God to human experience was decisive for the emergence of modern theology, his preoccupation with feeling and aesthetics found little resonance in the nineteenth century. The distinction between left-wing Hegelians, who reduced religion as well as the rest of culture to underlying psychological, social, and economic processes, and right-wing Hegelians, who defended orthodox Christianity, omitted the middle ground that defines modern liberal theology. It is important to note the precise meaning of *liberal* in this theological context. In contrast to economic and political forms of liberalism, which privilege the individual and resist regulatory intervention of any kind, theological liberalism is defined by a commitment to reconciling religious faith with reason as it is expressed in the natural and social sciences. Consistently devoted to the centrality of ethical activity in human life, liberal theology tends to be politically progressive and, through the first half of the twentieth century, remained open to various forms of socialism. While theological liberalism welcomes modernity, it must not be confused with theological modernism. In the course of the nineteenth century, liberalism became associated with Protestantism and modernism with Catholicism and Anglicanism. Within Catholic circles, modernism is often limited to the progressive theological views developed during the pontificates of Leo XIII and Pius X. What liberalism and modernism share is a resistance to biblical literalism and dogmatic traditionalism.

Since its earliest days, one of the distinguishing features of liberal theology has been the acceptance of historical critical methods for studying the Bible. As we have seen, left-wing Hegelians like Strauss and his followers used biblical criticism to undercut Christianity by calling into question the historical accuracy of the text. For more moderate critics, new methods of historical analysis provide resources for defending what they regard as a form of Christianity suitable for the modern world. In contrast to Schleiermacher's preoccupation with aesthetics, the most influential of these critics tend to understand religion in terms of morality. They combine a Kantian interpretation of morality with a Hegelian view of history shorn of its speculative excesses to form a progressive theology of history in which the kingdom of God is understood as an ethical commonwealth that steadily emerges on earth.

For these nineteenth-century liberal theologians, the primary critical task was to distinguish the faith of Jesus from the church's belief in Christ. The first noteworthy proponent of this approach to scripture was Ferdinand Christian Baur, leader of the Tübingen school and teacher of Strauss. Baur appropriated Hegel's tripartite philosophy of history to argue that biblical sources disclose a decisive conflict between "Jewish Christianity" (particularity) and "Gentile Christianity" (universality), which eventually are reconciled even if not completely harmonized in the third moment of historical development. To understand the dynamics of this process, Baur argues, it is necessary to move beyond the Bible by tracing the way ecclesiastical dogma both developed from and distorted "Jesus' self-consciousness." While Baur's most influential followers shared his critical vision, most of them rejected his commitment to Hegelianism. His student Albrecht Ritschl, who became the most important Protestant theologian of his generation, appropriated Baur's historical and critical method to recast the Reformation doctrine of justification by faith alone in terms he believed were compatible with modernity. The most significant modification that Ritschl and his fellow liberals made was to reinterpret Luther's view of the kingdom of God by reformulating the doctrine of vocation in ethical terms, which called for the transformation of social, political, and economic structures. While Luther believed that the kingdom of God is inward and cannot be outwardly expressed, in *Justification and Reconciliation*, Ritschl argues that God's grace frees the individual *from* guilt and anxiety and *for* Christian service in the world. By faithfully fulfilling one's "secular vocation" through love of one's neighbor, the kingdom of God, which is a "moral society of nations," is progressively realized.

On the all-important issue of Christology, Protestant liberals tend to be more Antiochean than Alexandrian; that is, they are more interested in the humanity of Jesus than in the divinity of Christ. While there are subtle and sometimes important differences in their theological positions, liberals agree that Jesus is best understood as a moral exemplar. This view is most concisely expressed by Ritschl's student Adolf von Harnack in his widely influential book *Das Wesen des Christentum* (1900), which was translated as *What Is Christianity?* (1903) and became quite influential in the United States. Harnack begins by noting the direction of biblical criticism since Strauss's *Life of Jesus*: "Sixty years ago David Friedrich Strauss thought that he had almost entirely destroyed the historical credibility not only of the fourth but also of the first three Gospels as well. The historical criticism of two generations has succeeded in restoring that credibility in its main outlines." The task of criticism, according to Harnack, is to separate "the kernel" from "the husk" by stripping away accretions of Greek metaphysics from the message of the historical Jesus. The essence of Jesus' message as it is presented in the synoptic Gospels is simply "the Fatherhood of God and the brotherhood of man." Though proclaimed by the historical Jesus, this message is "timeless." Summarizing the content of this eternal gospel, Harnack writes:

> If, however, we take a general view of Jesus' teaching, we shall see that it may be grouped under three heads. They are each of such a nature as to contain the whole, and hence it can be exhibited in its entirety under any one of them.
> *Firstly, the kingdom of God and its coming.*
> *Secondly, God the Father and the infinite value of the human soul.*
> *Thirdly, the higher righteousness and the commandment of love.*[5]

Far from passive bystanders awaiting the apocalypse, the faithful are active agents whose love contributes to the arrival of the earthly kingdom in which the universal brotherhood of man becomes a reality.

The acceptance of historical criticism and preoccupation with an ethical interpretation of the kingdom of God and, correlatively, a progressive view of history were not limited to Europe but enjoyed considerable support in America throughout the nineteenth century and during the first decade of the twentieth century. One of the leading figures in the emergence of Protestant liberalism was William Ellery Channing, who agreed with the need to reconceive the kingdom of God as an ethical community but was considerably more critical of the foundational principles of Reformation theology than his German counterparts. Having been raised in a strict New England Calvinist family, he eventually became a Unitarian and rejected the notions of the total depravity of human beings as well as their complete dependence on God. He acknowledged human shortcomings but remained convinced that people are free and have an "inherent capacity" for moral action. By formulating these basic theological and anthropological principles, Channing took his place at the head of a long line of influential Protestant liberals, which, a century later, included leading figures like A. C. McGiffert, Harry Emerson Fosdick, Shailer Mathews, and Henry Nelson Wieman.

At the time Harnack was writing and lecturing about the essence of Christianity, an important variation of Protestant liberalism was emerging in the United States. Problems resulting from rapid industrialization and urbanization created the conditions for the emergence of the Social Gospel movement, whose chief spokesperson was Walter Rauschenbusch. The son of a Westphalian Lutheran minister, Rauschenbusch worked for eleven years in a tenement section of New York City, where he daily encountered poverty and human suffering that convinced him that capitalism had to be regulated if not eliminated. In sermons and books, he developed what he described as "a theology for the social gospel" in which he presented a well-wrought political program in a religious vision that combined personal piety with social activism. Though agreeing that the doctrine of the kingdom of God should be interpreted as an ethical commonwealth, Rauschenbusch was more radical than other European and American liberals because he insisted that capitalism eventually must be replaced with a form of socialism based upon Christian moral principles. "The Kingdom of God," he argues,

> is humanity organized according to the will of God. Interpreting through the consciousness of Jesus, we may affirm these convictions about the ethical relations within the Kingdom: Since Christ revealed the divine worth of life and personality, and since his salvation seeks the restoration and fulfillment of even the least, it follows that the Kingdom of God, at every stage of human development, tends toward a social order which will best guarantee to all personalities their freest and highest development. . . . This involves the redemption of society from private property in the natural resources of the earth, and from any condition in industry, which makes monopoly possible. The reign of love tends toward the progressive unity of mankind, but with the maintenance of individual liberty and the development of nations to work out their own national peculiarities and ideals.[6]

Rather than the fallen realm of sin and corruption, history is the stage for humankind's gradual progress toward a just and equitable society in which greed and competition give way to benevolence and cooperation. This social ideal cannot be realized without the vigilant oversight and deliberate guidance of individuals committed to the common good.

By the time Rauschenbusch published *A Theology for the Social Gospel* in 1917, the scheme for interpreting God, self, and world developed in Protestant liberalism seemed naïve if not pernicious. Barth was one of the first to realize that liberalism died in 1914. The horrors of war-ravaged Europe made the liberal belief in both the immanence of God and the imminent arrival of the kingdom of God on earth through the moral actions of people who are basically good and intrinsically ethical seem little more than a cruel joke. In declaring *"Nein!"* to *Kulturprotestantismus,* and the political and economic order it promoted, Barth echoed Luther's world-transforming proclamation at the Diet of Worms: "Here I stand, I can do no other." While liberalism claimed to be an ethical vision designed to create a just society, its moral failure drove Barth to reject its pretensions. Liberalism, he concluded, actually exacerbated the problems it claimed to solve. In August 1914, ninety-three of Germany's cultural leaders signed the "Manifesto of the Intellectuals," in which they proclaimed their support for Kaiser Wilhelm II's war policy. Barth was shocked and dismayed: "Among these intellectuals I discovered to my horror almost all of my theological teachers whom I had greatly venerated . . . I suddenly realized that I could not any longer follow either their ethics and dogmatics or their understanding of the Bible and of history."' He concluded that the only fitting response to the unholy alliance between religion and politics was a radical break with liberal theology. Modern theology, he decided, had been misguided ever since Schleiermacher turned his gaze from the heavens to the earth and proclaimed that God, man, and world are one. The belief that God is immanent in the universe and that the kingdom of God emerges historically through human actions commits the sin of idolatry by confusing the Infinite with the finite. Returning to the Swiss Calvinism in which he was raised, Barth declared that God is "infinite and qualitatively different" and, as such, remains "Wholly Other." Barth was convinced that divine transcendence, far from being nihilistic, as Nietzsche insisted, is the condition of the possibility of social criticism and, thus, makes political resistance and sociopolitical transformation possible. Unlike many of his colleagues in the university and the church, Barth remained politically engaged throughout his life. When the National Socialists attempted to promote their teachings in German churches, he led the resistance to such practices. In an act designed to defy the political capitulation of his teachers, Barth drafted the Barmen Confession (1934), which declared that the church was not subject to temporal powers. When two hundred Protestant leaders and pastors signed this document, it became clear that a significant change was occurring and that Barth was its most influential leader. With his influence growing, a Nazi court convicted Barth of "seducing the minds of his students" in 1935; he was fired from his professorship at the University of Bonn and expelled from Germany.

Barth's experience left him with no doubt that far from remaining true to the foundational principles of Christianity, modern religion had actually become an expression of human sin. The relativity implicit in historicism made normative judgments impossible and deprived people of any firm basis upon which to make moral distinctions. To respond to this religious and moral crisis, which had led to social and political disaster on a massive scale, Barth turned to thinkers and writers who had been overlooked by modern philosophy and theology: Fyodor Dostoyevsky, Franz Overbeck, Johann Christian Blumhardt, Christoph Blumhardt, and, above all others, Søren Kierkegaard. Rejecting every form of philosophical idealism, Romanticism, and religious socialism, Barth argued that the kingdom of God does not develop progressively through human activity but is the result of a divine intervention that interrupts historical continuity. Once again a new theological departure is marked by a return to Paul—Barth, however, reads Paul through Kierkegaard. In the preface to the second edition of *The Epistle to the Romans* (1921), he writes:

> If I have a system, it is limited to a recognition of what Kierkegaard calls the "infinite qualitative difference" between time and eternity, and to my regarding this as possessing negative as well as positive significance: "God is in heaven, and thou art on earth." The relation between such a God and such a man, and the relation between such a man and such a God, is for me the theme of the Bible and the essence of philosophy. Philosophers name this *Krisis* of human perception—the Prime Cause: the Bible holds at the same crossroads—the figure of Jesus Christ.[8]

To counter what he regarded as the deleterious effects of Protestant liberalism, Barth developed what came to be known as neoorthodoxy. As his theology evolved, the difference between transcendence and immanence turns into their irreconcilable opposition. By bringing together Luther's doctrine of two kingdoms and Calvin's emphasis on human depravity, neoorthodoxy articulates a vision of life bordering on Manichaeism. In the midst of smoldering ruins created by what was supposed to have been the most advanced civilization in history, Barth concluded that, rather than making steady progress toward a more just and humane world, humankind is so corrupt that people can do absolutely nothing to redeem themselves:

> The man who boasts that he possesses something which justifies him before God and man, even if that something be his own insecurity and

brokenness, still retains confidence in human self-justification. No, the solid ground upon which the law of works stands must be completely broken up. No work, be it most delicately spiritual, or be it even a work of self-negation, is worthy of serious attention. In fact, our experience is that which we have not experienced; our religion consists in the dissolution of religion; our law is the complete disestablishment of all human experience and knowledge and action and possession.

From this perspective, religion is not humanity's greatest accomplishment but its most profound sin, because it encourages individuals to "forget the qualitative distinction between man and God, and, thus, encourages them to believe they can contribute to their own salvation or even to the dawning of the Kingdom."[9] The infinite gap separating the human and the divine cannot be bridged by man but can be crossed only by God.

The radical otherness of God complicates his relation to humanity. While never compromising God's omnipotent will, Barth's theology is thoroughly Christocentric: God reveals himself decisively in Jesus Christ. If, however, God is infinite and qualitatively different from man, then how can he be revealed in a finite human being? Rejecting Hegel's dialectical reconciliation of the divine and the human, Barth turns to Kierkegaard's account of the exclusive relationship of opposites. If opposites are not implicitly identical, then a *coincidentia oppositorium* cannot be implicitly rational but must be utterly paradoxical—the greater the opposites, the more profound the paradox. In Barth's schema, there is no greater opposition than that between God (the Infinite) and man (the finite). In terms borrowed from Kierkegaard, he concludes that by bringing together these opposites, the Incarnation becomes "the Absolute Paradox."

[I]n Jesus revelation is a paradox, however objective and universal it may be. That the promises of the faithfulness of God have been fulfilled in Jesus the Christ is not, and never will be, a self-evident truth, since in Him it appears in its final hiddenness and its most profound secrecy. The truth, in fact, can never be self-evident, because it is a matter neither of historical nor of psychological experience, and because it is neither a cosmic happening within the natural order, nor even the most supreme event of our imaginings. Therefore, it is not accessible to our perception: it can neither be dug out of what is unconsciously within us, nor apprehended by devout contemplation, nor made known by the manipulation of occult psychic powers.

Like Yahweh suddenly shattering the cosmic myths of the ancient Near East, Barth's transcendent God breaks into the historical process that moderns had believed continuous and progressive. In a manner reminiscent of the Freudian unconscious, the wholly other God can be revealed only through concealment. "In Jesus," Barth argues, "God becomes veritably a secret: He is made known as the Unknown, speaking in eternal silence."[10] Because God is known as the Unknown, faith cannot be a matter of knowledge but must be a free decision, which involves a radical risk. Citing Luther, while echoing Kierkegaard, Barth writes:

> "Therefore when God makes alive, He kills; when He justifies, He imposes guilt; when He leads us to heaven, He thrusts us down into hell" (Luther). The Gospel of salvation can only be believed in; it is a matter for faith only. It demands choice. This is its seriousness. To him that is not sufficiently mature to accept a contradiction and rest in it, it becomes a scandal—to him that is unable to escape the necessity of contradiction it becomes a matter for faith. Faith is awe in the presence of the divine incognito; it is the love of God that is aware of the qualitative distinction between God and man and God and the world.

Instead of drawing believers into an ethical community, the Absolute Paradox drives the individual into isolation and confronts him with an impossible decision with eternal consequences. Barth sees Kierkegaard's lesson in Paul's Epistle to the Romans: "As an apostle—and only as an apostle—he stands in no organic relationship with human society as it exists in history: seen from the point of view of human society, he can be regarded only as an exception, nay, rather as an impossibility."[11]

Barth's critique of Protestant liberalism repeats without significantly advancing Kierkegaard's critique of Hegel and Hegelianism. Kierkegaard's writings, which eventually became very influential, were largely ignored until they were translated into German in the early decades of the twentieth century. By that time, world history made the categories of dread, despair, corruption, and estrangement appear to be well-suited for theological reflection and cultural criticism. Just as Barth saw *Kulturprotestantismus* as symptomatic of a morally and religiously bankrupt society, so Kierkegaard regarded Hegelianism as symptomatic of a comfortable Christendom that betrayed Christianity's original message. For Kierkegaard, social and cultural criticism was inseparable from philosophical and theological criticism. He realized, however, that Hegel's principle of dialectical inclusion through the process of negation precluded the possibility of directly criticizing his purportedly all-inclusive system and the society it rationalized. If the structure of the Absolute is double negation, then to oppose the Hegelian system is, in fact, to support it. Therefore, instead of overtly attacking Hegel, Kierkegaard proceeded covertly and indirectly by turning the system back on itself to expose lacunae it is designed to overcome. This strategy is in effect deconstruction *avant la lettre*. We have already seen this approach at work in the way Kierkegaard defines the structure of self by redoubling Hegel's dialectic of self-consciousness. By rendering reflexivity reflexive, Kierkegaard exposes unassimilable altarity in the midst of subjectivity. In his pseudonymous writings, he uses a similar strategy to develop an alternative phenomenology of spirit, which appropriates the structure of Hegel's dialectic to subvert his conclusion. In Kierkegaard's scheme there are three "stages on life's way": Aesthetic, Ethical, and Religious. As one moves from the first to the last stage, there is a progression from inauthenticity to authenticity. Like Hegel's system, this dialectic of existence can also be used to classify different theological and philosophical positions. Kierkegaard places Hegel's speculative philosophy and Schleiermacher's religion of art at the aesthetic stage and sees Kant's moral philosophy and theology as the paradigm of the ethical stage. None of these perspectives, he argues, adequately identifies and describes the requirements of religious faith.

Kierkegaard presents his most dramatic exploration of the view of faith that both twentieth-century neoorthodoxy and deconstruction find so persuasive in *Fear and Trembling* (1843). In this seminal work, he develops his argument through an imaginative reading of Abraham. Though rarely noted, Kierkegaard's argument bears an uncanny resemblance to Hegel's argument in "The Spirit of Christianity and Its Fate," which was not published until 1907. As we have seen, Hegel inscribes his analysis of Abraham in a three-part dialectic represented by Greek, Jewish, and Christian religion. This progression conforms to the standard Romantic and idealist movement from a condition of undifferentiation through differentiation, which becomes opposition, to the reconciliation of opposites in which self and society are unified. Depicted as the embodiment of "the spirit of self-maintenance in strict opposition to everything," Hegel's Abraham represents the transitional stage between the loss and recovery of unity. In this early work, Hegel follows other Jena philosophers and poets by maintaining that opposition is overcome when difference returns to the identity from which it emerges.[12] Echoing Schleiermacher's erotic language, which he eventually came to regret, Hegel writes: "Thus specifically does Jesus declare himself against personality, against the view that his essence possessed an individuality opposed to that of those who had attained the culmination of friendship with him (against the thought of a personal God), for the ground of such an individuality would be an absolute particularity of his being in opposition to theirs. A remark about the unity of lovers is also relevant here (Matthew 19:5–6): Man and wife, these twain, become one, so that they are no longer two."[13] For Kierkegaard, by contrast, such a lack of difference is the mark of inauthenticity and as such must be negated. Through his faith in the radically transcendent God, Kierkegaard's Abraham embodies the *principium individuationis*, and as such is the figure of authentic selfhood. To make this argument, Kierkegaard appropriates the first two moments in the Hegelian dialectic but rejects the third moment of reunion or reconciliation. As a person moves from the aesthetic through the ethical to the religious, there is a progressive differentiation of and opposition between the self and God, world, and other selves (table 9).

Consistently privileging deed over word, Kierkegaard's theology and anthropology are thoroughly voluntaristic—God and self define themselves through the free exercise of the will. For human beings, in the absence of decision, there is no self or, more precisely, the self remains completely indeterminate. At the aesthetic stage, the subject has yet to emerge from immediacy (Schleiermacher) and reflection (Hegel). Differentiation begins to occur with the exercise of the will at the ethical stage. Through the process of socialization, the emerging subject incorporates the norms and rules that are supposed to guide the will. While this is a significant stage in human development, the expression of individuality remains constrained by general principles and universal codes. Only at

Table 9. Hegelian and Kierkegaardian Dialectics

Hegel	Greek		Jewish	Christian
	Monism		Dualism	Monism
	Undifferentiation		Differentiation / opposition	Reconciliation / reunion of opposites
Kierkegaard	Aesthetic	Ethical	Religious	
	Undifferentiation	Individual as expression of universal	Singular individual in opposition to all others	

the religious stage does the self achieve authenticity by becoming "the singular [Enkelt]." Kierkegaard, under the guise of Johannes de Silentio, maintains that faith is "the paradox that the single individual is higher than the universal—yet, please note, in such a way that the movement repeats itself, so that after having been in the universal he as the single individual isolates himself as higher than the universal. If this is not faith, then Abraham is lost, then faith has never existed in the world precisely because it has always existed."[14] This formulation of faith discloses the far-reaching implications of Luther's privatization of the God relationship. Just as Luther insists that the individual's relation to God does not have to be mediated by the church universal, so Kierkegaard argues that the individual relates to God *as an individual* rather than as a member of any community or group. The privacy of Luther's God relationship becomes the inwardness of Kierkegaard's faith, and the interiority of faith is as incommensurable with exteriority as God's transcendence is with immanence. Since faith is as hidden from the world as Christ's divinity is from his humanity, the "knight of faith," like "the God-Man," is completely "incognito." Indeed, the paradox of faith is the mirror image of the Absolute Paradox. In the Incarnation, the eternal becomes temporal, and in faith, the temporal moment is the occasion for eternal salvation. For Kierkegaard, as for Barth, faith is the free decision of a solitary subject or, in his well-known metaphor, a leap, which must be made in the absence of any assurance or certainty. Since the self defines itself through its decisions or, in different terms, existence precedes essence, temporal choices have eternal consequences. The claim of the historical figure of Jesus to be the eternal God poses a choice: *either* believe *or* be offended—there is no middle ground, no third alternative. Within this schema, the highest good is the individual's free choice in which he achieves or fails to achieve personal authenticity. While Kierkegaard's anthropology is thoroughly theological, its implications extend far beyond the domain of religion. As we will see, during the latter half of the twentieth century, commitment to individual freedom and the maximization of choice create a political ideology that issues in neoliberal economic policies that transform society.

Though not immediately apparent, Kierkegaard's existential dialectic harbors contradictions, which, when fully elaborated, reverse it. Since the decisions a person makes determine his or her eternal destiny, time assumes extraordinary significance. And yet, the most important decision—the leap of faith, which is supposed to change everything—transpires at a level of inwardness that *cannot* be outwardly expressed.

Faith, as Derrida later will insist, is a secret that can never be told. This radicalization of Luther's privatization of faith transforms truth into subjectivity—no longer a universal norm or objective reality, truth becomes the subject's inward transformation of itself. Imagining an encounter with a knight of faith, the pseudonymous Johannes de Silentio suggests that, in terms of worldly activity, nothing distinguishes the believer from the philistine: "I move a little closer to him, watch his slightest movement to see if it reveals a bit of heterogeneous optical telegraphy from the infinite, a glance, a facial expression, a gesture, a sadness, a smile that would betray the infinite in its heterogeneity with the finite. No! I examine his figure from top to toe to see if there may not be a crack through which the infinite would peek. No! he is solid all the way through. His stance? It is vigorous, belongs entirely to finitude; no spruced-up burgher walking out to Fresberg on a Sunday afternoon treads earth more solidly."[15] The most significant decision of life is, then, completely inconspicuous and utterly insignificant for ongoing life in the world.

This is not the conclusion Barth had anticipated when he invoked Kierkegaard to pass judgment on war-torn Europe. To the contrary, he had hoped that belief in the transcendent God would provide a critical perspective from which to resist worldly corruption. If, however, faith is so inward that it has no apparent consequences in the real world, it is a difference that ultimately makes no difference. Neoorthodoxy ends by repeating—albeit in an inverted way—the very death of God it is designed to challenge. When transcendence becomes so radical and faith so interior, the absence of the divine becomes indistinguishable from the death of God.

What began with the publication of Barth's *The Epistle to the Romans* in 1919 ended with the publication of Thomas J.J. Altizer's *The Gospel of Christian Atheism* in 1966. Shortly after this book appeared, *Time* magazine, as I have noted, published its Easter issue with a black cover bearing words printed in red: "Is God Dead?" Notoriety in the popular press transformed this new theological movement into a major media event.[16] In the America of the late 1950s and early 1960s, the horrors of world wars had quickly become a distant memory, and postwar prosperity had created a thriving consumer culture fueled by new media and technologies. Just as the utopian vision of Protestant liberalism became irrelevant with the outbreak of World War I, so the darkness of Kierkegaard's and Barth's vision seemed at odds with suburbia and the Age of Aquarius. Neoorthodox theologians rejected a Hegelian view

Table 10. Twentieth-Century Protestant Theology

PROTESTANT LIBERALISM	NEO–ORTHODOXY	DEATH OF GOD
Immanence	Transcendence	Immanence
Monism	Dualism	Monism
Identity	Difference / opposition	Identity

of history, but the course of twentieth-century theology actually conforms to the structure of Hegel's dialectic to a surprising extent. While neoorthodoxy is the negation of Protestant liberalism, the death of God theology is the negation of this negation, which restores, though at the same time changing, many of the most important principles of the first moment (table 10). When understood in this way, the most important European and American theological movements of the first half of the twentieth century repeat the dialectical encounter between Hegel and Kierkegaard. Liberalism, we have seen, takes two primary forms: in the first, the Infinite is immanent in the finite and religion is a feeling of primal unity, which closely approximates the enjoyment of art; in the second, a Hegelian view of history is synthesized with Kantian moralism to form a vision of the kingdom of God as an emerging ethical commonwealth. In both versions, God or his activity is immanent in the world and human beings are intrinsically good if not actually divine. The end of history is an organic whole in which every person becomes an integral member of an ethical community. Neoorthodoxy negates this schema by invoking Kierkegaard's notion of God as infinitely and qualitatively different. The opposition between God and humankind leads to other oppositions: faith/reason, Christianity/other religions, self/other, and interiority/exteriority. In the third moment, the death of God theology negates this negation and all the oppositions it poses by returning to Hegelian and Nietzschean immanence. But, as we will see, this dialectic remains incomplete. While effectively reversing neoorthodoxy's reversal of the principles of liberalism, the death of God theology does not carry its neo-Hegelian vision through to its logical conclusion and, therefore, remains symptomatic of a late modernism for which postmodernism remains alien.

"Death of God theology" appears to be an oxymoron—if, after all, God is dead, how can theology continue? In Altizer's dialectical vision, "true" theology is inescapably atheistic. God, however, does not simply disappear; rather, a particular notion of God—more specifically, neoorthodoxy's wholly other God—dies in an act of self-emptying that issues in a realized eschatology that totally transforms the present. Borrowing Nietzsche's description of the "moral God," who is the negation of the religious vision of Jesus, Altizer argues that the distant God of neoorthodoxy is "the *contradiction* of life, instead of being its transfiguration and eternal Yes!"[17] This Wholly Other is the God of Hegel's unhappy consciousness and Nietzsche's devoted Christian. Since this God is always elsewhere, believers can approach the divine only by withdrawing from the world as we know it. The death of the transcendent neoorthodox God is, therefore, the negation of the negation of life, which allows the true God of Jesus (rather than Christ) to be born anew. Altizer begins his best-known and most influential book by stating the principles that ground his entire theological enterprise:

> Today a new theologian is speaking in America, a theologian who is not so confident of the truth or certainty of faith, yet a theologian who is willing to discuss the meaning of faith. From the perspective of the theology of our century, the strangest thing about this new theologian is his conviction that faith should be meaningful and meaningful in the context of our world. . . . Refusing either to deny the Word or to affirm it in its traditional form, a modern and radical Christian is seeking a totally incarnate Word. When the Christian Word appears in this, its most radical form, then not only is it truly and actually present in the world but it is present in such a way as to be real and active nowhere else. No longer can faith and the world exist in mutual isolation, neither can now be conceived as existing independently of the other; thus the radical Christian condemns all forms of faith that are disengaged with the world. A given autonomous faith here reveals itself to be nonincarnate—and is judged to be a retreat from the life, the movement, and the process of history—with the result that faith must now abandon all claims to be isolated and autonomous, possessing a meaning or reality transcending the actuality of the world, and become instead wholly and inseparably embedded in the world.[18]

In denying the neoorthodox God, Altizer rejects all the oppositions that such transcendence engenders. In this way, the death of the otherworldly God issues in a worldly faith that deems the secular sacred and the sacred secular.

Refusing Barth's Christocentrism, Altizer develops a thoroughly Jesus-centric theology in which the central message of the Incarnation is that the transcendent Father actually dies and is reborn in the human figure of Jesus. Hegel, according to Altizer, was the first to apprehend the truth revealed in the Incarnation: "Despite the fact that Hegel has been damned by theologians for transposing faith into philosophical think- ing, it is only in Hegel that we may discover an idea of God or Being or Spirit, which embodies an understanding of the theological meaning of the Incarnation." In contrast to Kierkegaard and Barth, for whom the In- carnation is a once-and-for-all event in which eternity interrupts time, Altizer, following Hegel, maintains that the Incarnation is an ongoing process in which God completely "empties Himself," through a process known as *kenosis,* into the vicissitudes of history: "So long as the Chris- tian God continues to be known as transcendent and impassive, or as a primordial deity who is unaffected by the processes of time and history, he cannot appear in his uniquely Christian form as the Incarnate Word and the kenotic Christ. Thus the radical Christian reverses the orthodox confession, affirming that 'God is Jesus,' rather than 'Jesus is God'. . . . To say that 'God is Jesus' is to say that God has become the Incarnate Word, that he has abandoned or negated his transcendent form."[19] As Altizer makes clear in his best but most difficult work, entitled *The Self- Embodiment of God* (1977), this incarnational process conforms to Hegel's dialectic of historical development. In a style uniquely his own, he re- writes Hegel's Trinitarian dialectic as a five-act play based on the bib- lical narrative: Genesis, Exodus, Judgment, Incarnation, Apocalypse. The general structure of the story is the familiar movement from pri- mal unity through differentiation to the apocalyptic return to unity. The Incarnation is the negation of original unity, and the Crucifixion is the negation of this negation, which resurrects lost unity. The relentlessly abstract argument in this book lays bare the structural foundation of all of Altizer's writings. While his position remains remarkably consistent over the years, certain tensions gradually emerge, which disclose its shortcomings and point to necessary revisions. The most critical issues involve the precise meaning of the incarnational process and the nature of the redemptive unity that marks the end of history.

In the Incarnation, the transcendent God who had been absent from space and time becomes *totally present* in history. Two questions must be asked about Altizer's claim: first, where does this Incarnation actually occur? And second, how is "total presence" to be understood? Altizer's answer to the first question changes over the years. Perhaps it was youth- ful exuberance or the Dionysianism of the decade, but in the 1960s he stressed the bodily dimension of the Incarnation: "When the Incarnation is known as a dynamic process of forward movement, then it must be con- ceived as a progressive movement of Spirit into flesh."[20] There is, how- ever, always something peculiarly abstract—even disembodied—about

Altizer's notion of the body, and by the 1970s flesh gives way to speech. First "embodied" in Jesus' parabolic speech, the redemptive Word eventually is fully expressed in the Western literary tradition. In *History as Apocalypse*, Altizer traces the history of the Word from the Bible through the epic tradition extending from Dante and Milton through Blake to its culmination in Joyce's *Finnegans Wake*. This literary history, he argues, tells the story of the gradual unfolding of human self-consciousness. In a manner strictly parallel to Hegel's argument in "The Spirit of Christianity and Its Fate," Altizer charts the course of self-conscious subjectivity from its emergence in Greek religion through its expression in Judaism to its complete undoing in Christianity. In this schema, the death of God and the disappearance of individual subjectivity are two aspects of the same process. Altizer draws the unlikely conclusion that in the words of *Finnegans Wake* history reaches its end, as God, self, and world collapse into each other:

> That speech is the real presence of resurrection, and its full enactment is the total presence of Apocalypse, a presence in which the dark and negative passion of God becomes immediately at hand. And it is immediately at hand insofar as it is actually spoken. Then the total silence and emptiness of the original abyss becomes an immediately present chaos, but a chaos which is the cosmos when it [is] resurrected in language and word. This cosmos is the resurrected Christ, but a resurrected Christ who is inseparable and indistinguishable from the crucified Christ, for now the Christ of glory *is* the Christ of passion.[21]

Though Altizer has insisted for more than four decades that his theology is emphatically radical, the conclusion of his argument remains undeniably conservative in important ways. By limiting his analysis to *high* culture, he effectively denies the very incarnational principle upon which his whole position rests. What Altizer has never been able to accept is that the Incarnation actually collapses high and low into each other in such a way that the divine is embodied not only in high culture and the fine arts but also in nature as well as low, or popular, culture. In other words, Altizer cannot follow where Hegel surely would have dared to go—he is unwilling and unable to extend theological and philosophical argument to nature, history, and culture as a whole. The death of God theology, therefore, must become a radical a/theology that finds the divine implicated in both high culture and popular culture as well as in the practices and technologies that are transforming contemporary society.

The second problem with Altizer's theology involves his understanding of the apocalyptic presence with which history is supposed to end. While always insisting that his analysis culminates in a dialectical *coincidentia oppositorium*, pivotal texts in Altizer's corpus tell a different story. The crucial questions concern the status of difference and, correlatively, the nature of presence. In the chapter entitled "Apocalypse" in *The Self-Embodiment of God*, he writes:

> Hence difference, as difference becomes unsaid when it is fully spoken. But it is unsaid only in being actually unsaid. The silence of the unsaid is now actually spoken, and when it is fully spoken it passes into total speech. Total speech can only be the disembodiment, the actual negation, of difference. When speech is fully embodied in pure voice, it is disembodied from difference, or disembodied from all difference which is only difference. But that disembodiment from difference is also the full actualization of difference. Now difference is fully actual by having come to an end as difference, by having come to an end as a difference which is other and apart.[22]

In Altizer's apocalyptic vision, at the culminating moment of history as a whole, the differences constitutive of individuality are negated rather than sublated. In *Total Presence: The Language of Jesus and the Language of Today*, he summarizes this important point in less abstract but no less sweeping terms:

> Historically, actual solitude was born in the eighth century B.C.E. in Greece and Israel, and it was accompanied by a parallel birth at something like this time in India. This was a unique historical moment when an individual form of consciousness broke through the previous collective or corporate identity of consciousness, and did so in such a way as to make possible a truly individual act and enactment of consciousness. But ours is the time of the end of a unique and individual consciousness, and the end of that consciousness is the end of history as well, and the beginning of a posthistorical time when an integral and interior individuality will have disappeared.[23]

Altizer concludes *History as Apocalypse* by once again citing Joyce: "In that immediacy death is life, and 'Lff' is all in all."[24] At this point opposites meet and collapse into each other. By inverting Kierkegaard's and Barth's radical transcendence into his own version of Hegelian and Nietzschean immanence, Altizer ends by rendering difference indifferent. While for Kierkegaard and Barth faith becomes indifferent as a result of its radical interiorization in the isolated individual, for Altizer difference returns to identity, and absence gives way to a presence that is supposed to be "immediate and total."

But can such presence ever be totally present? Or, as we have come to suspect, does presence always presuppose a presencing that can never be present? Do oppositions like immanence/transcendence, presence/absence, and identity/difference represent exclusive alternatives or codependent differences that must be refigured otherwise? Neoorthodoxy and the death of God theology are mirror images of each other and are mistaken in opposite ways. The former's commitment to the exclusive logic of either/or obscures the codependence and coevolution of opposites, and the latter's preoccupation with identity and presence represses the altarity without which nothing can be what it is. *Neither* such monism *nor* such dualism is adequate to comprehend the complexities of emerging network culture.

CONSUMING IMAGES

The day before Bobby Kennedy was assassinated in June 1968, Andy Warhol was shot at his place of business, Andy Warhol Enterprises. Reflecting on the experience several years later in his book *The Philosophy of Andy Warhol (From A to B and Back)*, Warhol wrote: "Before I was shot, I always thought that I was more half-there than all-there—I always suspected that I was watching TV instead of living life. People sometimes say that the way things happen in the movies is unreal, but actually it's the way things happen to you in life that's unreal. The movies make emotions look so strong and real, whereas when things really do happen to you, it's like watching television—you don't feel anything."[25] The leading artist of his generation, Warhol was one of the most insightful interpreters of postwar consumer culture and the technologies that made it possible. He was among the first to understand that the collapse of the distinction between high and low culture was symptomatic of a transformation of the way in which the real—however it is conceived—had been figured for centuries. The eclipse of the real enacts the death of God in social, economic, political, and technological processes, which are, in turn, interpreted in semiotics and critical theory. Consumer capitalism, which lies at the heart of Warhol's art, marks the transition between industrial capitalism of the nineteenth and early twentieth centuries and finance capitalism of the latter half of the twentieth and early twenty-first centuries. Here as elsewhere a three-stage process is discernible (table 11).

Table 11. Society, Culture, and Theory

Capitalism:	Industrial	Consumer	Finance
Technology:	Mechanical	Televisual	Electronic / network
Semiotics:	Representation	Spectacle	Simulacrum
Theorists:	Walter Benjamin	Guy Debord	Jean Baudrillard

I will consider the first two stages of the process in this section and the third stage in the next section.

During the modern period, religion and art, we have discovered, were inseparable. While the founder of modern theology, Schleiermacher, and his fellow Jena Romantics tried to revitalize religion by interpreting it aesthetically, Hegel translated artistic images and religious representations into philosophical concepts. This important difference notwithstanding, nineteenth-century Romantics and idealists agreed that the death of the transcendent God issues in a realized eschatology in which the Infinite and the finite are reconciled through art. In ways that are not immediately evident, what began in Jena reached closure in Warhol's Factory. During the first half of the twentieth century, avant-garde artists attempted to carry out the Romantic program of transforming the world into a work of art. While liberal Protestants were proclaiming the progressive development of the kingdom of God on earth, prophetic artists in Europe and Russia were transforming this kingdom into an artistic utopia, which, they believed, could actually be realized. Though rarely noted, many of the radical artists in the early twentieth century were profoundly spiritual even if not overtly religious. One of the most important reasons for the failure to appreciate the spiritual significance of modern art has been neoorthodoxy's condemnation of all human culture as depraved or even sinful. For the artists who shaped the subsequent history of art and by so doing transformed modern society as a whole, the outbreak of World War I did not reveal the futility of human culture but, to the contrary, disclosed its critical importance for the restoration of psychological harmony and social order.

When artists directed their attention to psychosocial reformation, they faced a question that, we have seen, runs throughout the Western religious tradition: Does one change society by changing consciousness (as for believers in the church mystic and their "secular" counterparts— Freudians), or does one change consciousness by changing society (as for believers in the church militant and their "secular" counterparts— Marxists)? In the next chapter we will see that these alternatives return yet again in the 1960s counterculture. In this context, I will take Kandinsky as an example of the former position and Rodchenko as an example of the latter point of view. Kandinsky refigures Hegelian philosophy in artistic images, and Rodchenko translates Nietzsche's death of God into the "death of art," which Warhol then proceeds to make "real" by shattering the walls of the museum. When the intricacies of these relationships are traced, it becomes clear that the development of art in the twentieth century restages the dialectical interplay between transcendence and immanence that structures the history of Western theology and religion. When art becomes so abstract that it is practically irrelevant, it provokes efforts to develop socially useful art; conversely, when art becomes so worldly that everything seems to be art, strategies to create critical differences between art and non-art begin to emerge.

Kandinsky's *Concerning the Spiritual in Art* is one of the seminal texts of modernism. The argument is structured around the opposition between the debilitating materialism Kandinsky saw in early-twentieth-century life and the redemptive idealism he believed to be characteristic of abstract art. He begins the chapter entitled "Spiritual Revolution" with a criticism of what he labels "the materialist creed": "Today one of the largest of the lower segments has reached the point of using the first battle cry of the materialist creed. The dwellers in this segment group themselves around various banners in religion. They call themselves Jews, Catholics, Protestants, etc. But they are really atheists, and this a few either of the boldest or the narrowest openly avow. 'Heaven is empty,' 'God is dead.'"[26] Though it is no longer possible or desirable to resurrect the traditional theistic God, Kandinsky believes that, after the death of God, the artist must assume responsibility for promoting a spiritual transformation that will prepare the way for a sociopolitical revolution. In developing the spiritual vision informing his art, Kandinsky weaves together insights drawn from philosophical idealism, Russian Orthodoxy, and, most important, Theosophy. A syncretistic tradition originally founded by the Russian emigrant Helena Blavatsky, Theosophy is a monistic spirituality that represents a popularized version of nineteenth-century Romanticism and idealism. Kandinsky came to art by way of the law and philosophy. After studying law, economics, and politics at the University of Moscow, where he was for a time on the Faculty of Law, his political concerns deepened. He eventually became convinced that art was the most effective means to bring about the personal change necessary for social revolution. He left Russia, roamed around Europe for nearly a decade, and finally settled in Munich, where he became involved with the Blaue Reiter group. At this time, apocalyptic fervor was sweeping across Europe and Russia, and in 1911 Kandinsky along with Franz Marc wrote a manifesto that reflected the temper of the times: "A great era has begun: the spiritual 'awakening,' in the increasing tendency to regain 'lost balance,' the inevitable necessity of spiritual plantings, the unfolding of the first blossom. We are standing at the threshold of one of the greatest epochs that mankind has ever experienced, the epoch of great spirituality."[27]

Kandinsky describes the emergence of this New Age through a Russian Orthodox adaptation of the theology of history I have already traced from Joachim of Floris to Hegel. "According to the Russian Orthodox tradition," Marit Werenskiold explains, "Constantinople (Byzantium) was the 'Second Rome,' and when that city was conquered by the Muslim Turks in 1453, the succession as the 'Third Rome' passed to Moscow, the new and everlasting capital of Christianity. . . . For the Orthodox, the Old Rome represented the Father; the second Rome, Constantinople, symbolized the Son or the Logos; while the third Rome, Moscow, expressed the conviction that the entire collective life of the nation should be inspired by the Holy Spirit."[28] Kandinsky's paintings from this era make it clear that Moscow is the New Jerusalem where the kingdom of God will dawn on earth. Although the New Age has not fully arrived, Kandinsky invokes the authority of Blavatsky to express his full confidence that it is near: "The earth will be heaven in the twenty-first century in comparison with what it is now." The avant-garde artist rather than the religious prophet leads people from "the nightmare of materialism" to "the kingdom of the abstract." "The more abstract is form, the more clear and direct is its appeal. In any composition the material side may be more or less omitted in proportion as the forms used are more or less material, and for them substituted pure abstractions, or largely dematerialized objects. The more an artist uses these abstracted forms, the deeper and more confidently will he advance into the kingdom of the abstract. And after him will follow the gazer at his pictures, who will have gradually acquired a greater familiarity with the language of the kingdom."[29] For Kandinsky, abstract art provides a way to overcome the crass utilitarianism and materialism he believed were the causes of the problems plaguing society. By cultivating "the oneness of the 'human and divine,'" abstract art would bring about the personal transformation without which social change is impossible.

With the outbreak of World War I, Kandinsky was forced to flee Germany, and in 1915 he returned to Russia. During the early years of the

Russian Revolution, political leaders supported the avant-garde and sponsored the reorganization of artistic and cultural institutions. By 1921, Kandinsky was a member of the Visual Arts section of the People's Commissariat of Enlightenment and a year earlier he developed an educational program for the new Institute of Artistic Culture. The more deeply Kandinsky became involved in Theosophy, the more withdrawn from engagement with the practical world his art became. Drawing on a book entitled *The Meaning of Colors*, published in 1911 by the new leader of the Theosophical Society, Annie Besant, and her associate Charles Leadbeater, Kandinsky developed a theory of painting in which different colors are correlated with specific emotions. He became more and more preoccupied with bringing about inward emotional experience through art rather than with using art to inspire outward social and political change. As political debate in Russia grew more heated, criticism of his style of abstract nonrepresentational art grew. Realizing that his future was elsewhere, Kandinsky left Russia in 1921 and accepted a position at the Bauhaus, where he remained until the Nazis forced it to close.[30]

Established in 1919, the Bauhaus was created to realize the ideals of Weimar *Kultur* as they had been defined by philosophers and poets in Jena during the 1790s. In an early address to the students at the Bauhaus, Walter Gropius, the young architect appointed to direct this new institution, explained his vision for the *Künstlerkolonie*: "No large spiritual organizations, but small, secret, self-contained societies, lodges. Conspiracies will form which will want to watch over and artistically shape a secret, a nucleus of belief, until from the individual groups a universally great, enduring, spiritual-religious idea will rise again, which finally must find its crystalline expression in a great *Gesamtkunstwerk*. And this great total work of art, this cathedral of the future, will then shine with its abundance of light into the smallest objects of everyday life."[31] At this stage in his career, Gropius obviously shared Kandinsky's understanding of the relationship between the spiritual and the political. For Gropius, "the cathedral of the future" is the "cathedral to socialism." The unity of the total work of art simultaneously expresses and promotes social unity within the community and as such becomes the prototype for the transformation of society as a whole. In his "Program" for the Bauhaus, Gropius declares: "Let us create a new guild of craftsmen without the class distinctions that raise an arrogant barrier between craftsman and artist! Together let us desire, conceive, and create the new structure of the future, which will embrace architecture and sculpture and painting in one unity and will one day rise toward heaven from the hands of a million workers, like a crystal symbol of a new faith."[32] In the following years, Gropius's commitment to forging "a new unity" between art and architecture created the conditions for the emergence of modern architecture, which transformed more than the face of the world. By bringing together the idealism of Bruno Taut's and Paul Sheebart's *Glasarchitektur* with the practicality of Peter Behren's glass, iron, and concrete architecture, Gropius created what amounts to an architectural expression of Nietzsche's gay wisdom: "As a direct result of the growing preponderance of voids over solids," Gropius writes, "glass is assuming an ever greater structural importance. Its sparkling insubstantiality, and the way it seems to float between wall and wall imponderably as the air, adds a note of gaiety to our modern homes."[33] As we will see, the superficiality and insubstantiality of glass prefigure the disappearance of the real in the play of images reflected in store windows and on the screens of televisions and computer terminals.

Back in Russia, artists and architects committed to Marx's dialectical materialism and atheism were pursuing a program of social transformation without ostensible religious and spiritual trappings. Just as the necessity to rebuild Europe after World War I had forced a reconsideration of the utility of art, so the Russian Revolution (1917) had posed the question of the social responsibility of the artist with a new urgency. During the early years of the revolution, influential artists like Rodchenko remained committed to the principles of European abstraction, while Malevich and his followers promoted an aesthetic spirituality not unlike that of Kandinsky and his colleagues at the Bauhaus. Others, like Tatlin, were suspicious of any art bearing a resemblance to religion. In the years following the revolution, Russian constructivists emphatically rejected the foundational modernist principle of art for art's sake. Mayakovsky, who was the leading poet of the Russian Revolution and one of the founders of Russian futurism, spoke for many when he declared: "We do not need a dead mausoleum of art where dead works are worshipped but a living factory of the human spirit—in the streets, in the tramways, in the factories, workshops and workers' homes."[34] "Pure art," constructivists argued, must be replaced by "production art," in which studio and factory are united in revolutionary practice.

The tipping point for this shift came in September 1921, when Moscow's Institute for Artistic Culture (INKhUK) mounted a controversial exhibition entitled $5 \times 5 = 25$. The show included five paintings by five artists: Rodchenko, Alexandra Exter, Liubov Popova, Varvara Stepanova, and Alexander Vesnin. Rodchenko's contribution consisted of monochromatic paintings done in the three primary colors, but by the time the exhibition opened he had become suspicious of abstraction. In a statement released to coincide with the opening, Rodchenko, echoing Nietzsche's proclamation of the death of God and Marx's critique of religion, declares: "Art is dead! . . . Art is as dangerous as religion as an escapist activity. . . . Let us cease our speculative activity and take over the healthy bases of art—color, line, materials and forms—into the field of reality, of practical construction."[35] However, just as the death of God is not a simple negation but is a complex process in which the divine becomes incarnate when the profane is grasped as sacred, so art ends not because it disappears but when it appears everywhere. Art, in other words, dies when everybody becomes an artist and the world is finally transformed into a work of art.

For Rodchenko, the move from "speculative activity" to "practical construction" entailed a commitment to advancing the revolution by creating socially useful products. In an effort to transform "pure art" into "production art," he turned his attention to graphic design (i.e., advertising posters, books, and magazines), furniture design, information centers (i.e., kiosks), interior design, theater sets, and film. The trajectory of Rodchenko's career illustrates the course followed by many of the leading Soviet artists of the period. In the catalog accompanying the 1922 exhibition entitled The Constructivists: K. K. Medunetskii, V. A. Strenberg, G. A. Strenberg, the featured artists state that all artists "should now go into the factory, where the real body of life is made." Christian Lodder briefly summarizes the founding principles of constructivism: "the call for the artist to go into the factory; the recognition that the factory is the real creative force in the world; the impediment that conventional concepts of art and practicing artists represent to such a link between art and life, and therefore the call for their banishment; and the identification with a new political and social order."[36]

In Russian constructivism, the nascent socialism of the Bauhaus becomes a full-fledged commitment to creating a communist society. If, as Marx argues, there is a direct line from Luther's revolution through Hegel's philosophy to his own socioeconomic analyses, then the Russian Revolution, which appears to be materialistic and atheistic, actually has theological roots. While declaring pure art and religion impediments to achieving this goal, the constructivist program actually conforms to the implicit theological narrative Marx presents in The Communist Manifesto. Following the avant-garde agenda as it had been defined in Jena, constructivists sought to create a "social organism" that would embody the harmonious relation of parts and whole figured in the beautiful work of art. But whereas the Jena Romantics and idealists saw mechanization and industrialization as the cause of alienation, the constructivists were convinced that new technologies prepared the way for the arrival of the communist kingdom. "Russian Modernism," as Hubertus Gassner points out, "abandoned all opposition to the modernization of life affected by industrialization and mass production, and began to assume the functions of oil and engine in the machinery of progress. The stated goal was no longer just the reconciliation of consciousness and machine but the total alignment of human psycho-physical being to machine mechanisms and motions."[37] This attempt to integrate modernism and modernization was inspired by the conviction that social equality, economic justice, and political freedom could be realized only when artistic vision became practically effective by directing the forces of mass production and mass media. But, alas, this utopian venture reversed itself in its very pursuit: the search for economic justice was thwarted by the inefficiencies of centralized planning, the effort to establish social equality was hampered by rigid bureaucracies, and, most important, the quest for freedom led to extensive repression and mass suffering. As the revolution betrayed its ideals, artists betrayed their mission. Art, originally intended to be socially productive, became little more than political propaganda for a regime whose inadequacies and failures eventually led to its collapse.

Though the distance separating the factories of communist Russia from the Factory of Andy Warhol Enterprises seems to be more than geographical, there are surprising similarities between the practices of leading members of the Russian avant-garde and the strategies Warhol devised. In many ways, Warhol's activity in his Factory is an inverted image of the relation between art and industry in Russian factories during the 1920s. While Rodchenko, for example, took his artistic skills into the factory to produce advertising and packaging for everything from beer, candy, and biscuits to pacifiers, cigarettes, and galoshes, Warhol brought ads for everything from shoes, telephones, and televisions to soup cans, scrubbing pads, and cars into his Factory to be transformed into works of art. Like many leading artists of his generation, Warhol began his career as a commercial artist who did drawings for newspapers and magazine ads and designed display windows for department stores. Having become adept at using his skills in the fine arts to promote consumer products, he reversed his tactics and used consumer products— or, more precisely, their images—to create art. In this process, Warhol collapsed the distinction between high and low by using material from popular culture to create fine art. This strategy grew out of his sophisticated understanding of the relationship between art and business in consumer capitalism.

It is no accident that so many of the people who became the leading artists of the postwar period worked as window designers. A close relationship between art and department stores already existed by the middle of the nineteenth century. Noting this connection, Warhol quips: "All department stores will become museums and all museums will become department stores."[38] Walter Benjamin was the first to recognize the far-reaching implications of the changes in consumption that department stores introduced. While acknowledging that the modern department store traces its origin to oriental bazaars, Benjamin argues that nineteenth-century arcades were its immediate precursor. The arcades depended on the same technological innovation that made modern architecture possible. With the introduction of the glass-and-steel construction initially used by John Paxton in his Crystal Palace (1851), separate shops could be enclosed within the same space.[39] The arcades became the prototype for department stores, which Benjamin, following Louis Philippe, labeled "temples of commodity capital." The Paris opening of Bon Marché, designed by L. C. Boileu and Gustav Eiffel, in 1852 marked a new chapter in the economic history of the West. Five years later, Macy's opened in the United States. For Benjamin, the arcades were to modernity what cathedrals were to the Middle Ages—"Dream Houses: arcade as nave with side chapels."[40]

To understand the intricate relationship of art, business, and religion that Benjamin detects and Warhol thematizes critically and artistically, it is necessary to consider the role of image in consumer capitalism. While capitalism is predicated on expanding markets, there are unavoidable limits to growth, and new marketing strategies must, therefore, constantly be devised. There are basically two ways markets can grow—spatially and temporally: as geographical limits are reached, markets can continue to expand by accelerating the rate of product cycles. For this approach to succeed, it is necessary to create desire where there is no need. If people were to buy new cars or suits only when the old ones wore out, the economy would stall. To keep the economy moving by generating renewable demand, manufacturers introduced annual models and seasonal fashions, which they promoted through advertising methods that changed with new technologies. As the power of advertising increased, things were effectively transformed into their images in an economy of signs whose goal is endless circulation. In this way, consumer capitalism leads to the aestheticization of commodities, which, in turn, issues in the commodification of the work of art. These processes reflect the changing relation between commodity (thing) and image brought about by new technologies for the promotion and distribution of products.

Once again, glass plays an important role in modernization and modernism. Before glass became important in architectural design, it was used to create store windows where products could be displayed. This innovation led to a significant transformation of the exchange process. Prior to the emergence of department stores, the place of production and the place of purchase were usually the same—items were sold in small workshops where they were made. Prices were not fixed and the customer had to enter shops and engage in face-to-face negotiations with the producer and retailer. The invention of plate glass interrupted the immediacy of this exchange and began a long process that eventually transformed thing into image. With these developments, economic viability began to depend on effective visual display. Though store windows appeared in the United States as early as the 1840s, it was not until the turn of the century that window display became an art. From 1897 to 1902, Frank Baum, author of *The Wizard of Oz* (1900), edited a highly influential monthly journal entitled *The Show Window*, whose primary purpose was to advance "the arts of decoration and display." Using mechanical devices and electrical technology, Baum sought to create spectacular displays that would "arouse in the observer the cupidity and longing to possess the goods."[41] Initially, these windows were in small, locally owned shops, but they quickly spread to large stores in urban areas.

Department stores became possible only with the widespread deployment of mechanical means of reproduction. When craft and handwork gave way to mechanization and eventually industrialization, mass-produced copies replaced original products. To create mass markets for mass-produced commodities, advertising had to become more and more sophisticated. As technologies changed from print to radio, television, and eventually Internet, the transformation of thing into image accelerated.[42] With desire rather than need driving the economy, images designed to promote consumption themselves become consuming. Consumers do not simply purchase cars or suits; rather, they buy (into) the image that the product is supposed to represent. Through this process, the aura shifts from the work of art to the commercial product. Benjamin was one of the first to recognize the far-reaching significance of these developments. Commenting on signs printed on the windows of a shop selling umbrellas, he reflects: "Years of reckless financial speculation under Louis XVIII. With the dramatic signage of the *magasins de nouveautés*, art enters the service of the businessman."[43] Browsing the assorted entries in *The Arcades Project*, where Benjamin develops his insights, is like strolling through the Paris arcades, pausing to consider fragments displayed like so many products offered for purchase in department store windows and stalls.

Warhol realized that postwar America took these developments to an entirely different level. Consumed by consumption, the only thing Andy loved as much as TV was shopping. "Buying," he declares, "is much more American than thinking, and I'm as American as they come." But Warhol does not just buy, he also sells—sells art and himself by transforming his art and himself into a brand with a recognizable image. Explaining the "philosophy" behind his artistic practice, he writes: "Business art is the step that comes after Art. I started as a commercial artist, and I want to finish as a business artist. After I did the thing called 'art' or whatever it's called, I went into business art. I wanted to be an Art Businessman or a Business Artist. Being good in business is the most fascinating kind of art. During the hippie era people put down the idea of business—they'd say, 'Money is bad,' and 'Working is bad,' but making money is art and working is art and good business is the best art." Far from a useless object that exceeds productive networks of exchange as orthodox modernists insisted, the work of art, Warhol admits, is a valuable commodity and must be marketed as such. At one point, he goes so far as to suggest that his silk-screened sheets of money should be replaced with "the real thing": "I like money on the wall. Say you were going to buy a $200,000 painting. I think you should take that money, tie it up and hang it on the wall."[44] As high and low collapse into each other, art becomes money and money becomes art. This is simultaneously the realization and the parodic reversal of the avant-garde program of transforming the world into a work of art.

When Warhol turned his back on abstract expressionism by appropriating images from popular culture, he held up a mirror in which consumer capitalism could see itself reflected. In this economy, image is the currency of exchange. People as well as things become a matter (or nonmatter) of image—everything and everybody is for sale. Commenting on his fame, Warhol pokes fun at the category of Benjamin's that cultural critics take most seriously: "Some company was recently interested in buying my 'aura.' They didn't want my product. They kept saying, 'We want your aura.'"[45] Aura does not simply disappear with mechanical reproduction as Benjamin had thought but is transferred to the copy through electronic reproduction, which, as Warhol realizes, dematerializes the so-called original. When the store window becomes the television screen, the signified collapses into the signifier in a play of signs that has no end other than itself. This development marks the beginning of what Guy Debord labeled the "society of the spectacle."

Debord appropriates Hegel's account of alienation and Marx's analysis of religion to argue that the spectacle created by consumer capitalism causes human alienation. Media and advertising project a realm of "autonomous images" that represents an inversion of the actual lives most people lead:

> Philosophy, the power of separate thought and the thought of separate power, could never by itself supersede theology. The spectacle is the material reconstruction of the religious illusion. Spectacular technology has not dispelled the religious clouds where men had placed their powers detached from themselves; it has only tied them to an earthly base. The most earthly life thus becomes opaque and unbreathable. It no longer projects into the sky but shelters within itself its absolute denial, its fallacious paradise. The spectacle is the technical realization of the exile of human powers into a beyond; it is separation perfected within the interior of man.

Just as religion reconciles people to the inevitability of suffering by promising them a better life in the future, so consumer capitalism regulates behavior by holding out the prospect of a material utopia that remains an unrealizable dream for the masses. When money is God and the kingdom is the enjoyment of all the trappings of bourgeois life, "the spectacle is the guardian of sleep."[46] To awake from this slumber, it is necessary to strip image from reality by demystifying the spectacle through the exposure of its material base.

For Warhol, by contrast, there is no material base beyond the play of images; everything—even Andy himself—becomes image. At this point, the real disappears in image or, conversely, the image becomes our reality. When the image becomes real and the real becomes image, the world is effectively transformed into a work of art. Warhol exposes the unexpected implications of Duchamp's urinal: if everything is a work of art, then everyone is an artist. This is both the fulfillment and the end of art. Just as God dies by becoming so immanent that the profane is sacred and the finite is Infinite, so art ends when everyone is an artist and there is nothing that is not a work of art. The death of art that Rodchenko proclaimed is actualized in Warhol's art and the consumer economy it simultaneously reflects, promotes, and ironizes. When transcendence— be it religious or aesthetic—disappears, the oppositional hierarchies it founds and grounds collapse. Far from perpetuating human alienation, the consumerist utopia created in postwar America is, contrary to every expectation, the realization of the avant-garde's dream of transforming the world into a work of art, which brings what had been figured as the kingdom of God to earth. The most important principle of this kingdom is equality:[47]

> What's great about this country is that America started the tradition where the richest consumers buy essentially the same things as the poorest. You can be watching TV and see Coca-Cola, and you can know that the President drinks Coke, Liz Taylor drinks Coke, and just think, you can drink Coke, too. A Coke is a Coke and no amount of money can get you a better Coke than the one the bum on the corner is drinking. All the Cokes are the same and all the Cokes are good. Liz Taylor knows it, the President knows it, the bum knows it, and you know it.
>
> In Europe the royalty and the aristocracy used to eat a lot better than the peasants—they weren't eating the same thing at all. It was either partridge or porridge, and each class stuck to its own food. But when Queen Elizabeth came here and President Eisenhower bought her a hot dog I'm sure he felt confident that she couldn't have had delivered to Buckingham Palace a better hot dog than the one he bought her for maybe twenty cents at the ballpark. Because there *is* no better hot dog than a ballpark hot dog. Not for a dollar, not for ten dollars, not for a hundred thousand dollars could she get a better hot dog. She could get one for twenty cents and so could anybody else.

Deliberately ignoring new hierarchies created by consumer capitalism, Warhol, with biting irony, envisions a world in which commodities create social equality. This social leveling harbors important cultural implications: the distinction between high and low implodes, making the extraordinary ordinary and the ordinary extraordinary. Just as there are no better or worse Cokes or hot dogs, so there are no better or worse paintings. "You see," Warhol writes, "I think every painting should be the same size and the same color so they're all interchangeable and nobody thinks that they have a better or a worse painting. And if the one 'master painting' is good, they're all good. Besides, even when the subject is different, people always paint the same painting." In the absence of master artists and masterpieces, art is "just another job."[48] When art becomes an ordinary job, it is possible to see ordinary workers as artists. Here the principle of equality is no longer an abstract norm but becomes a social reality. If everyone as well as everything is equal, there is no need to dream of a distant beyond or to long for another world. In this realized eschatology, the kingdom is totally present here and now: "What you see is what you see."[49] It is what it is.

CULTIVATING DIVERSITY

I remember clearly the day our first television set arrived in 1952. It was designed to be the most prominent piece of furniture in a living room or family room—the small screen was mounted in a large wooden cabinet with a highly polished mahogany veneer. My parents, some friends, and I gathered around the dim glow it cast as if it were the new family hearth. Fuzzy images flickered into focus as my father adjusted the antenna mounted on the roof of the house. We eventually were able to watch one of the network talent shows that were so popular in the 1950s. My most vivid memory is not of the program or the Geritol ads but of my three-year-old brother seeing TV for the first time. He immediately rushed to the screen, jumped up and down screaming with delight, and repeatedly tried to stick his finger in the mouth of the woman who was singing on TV. As my parents and the neighbors who had come for the occasion laughed, his actions became more frenzied, and he rather than the TV program became the show. There was absolutely no doubt that he thought the image on the screen was a real person. The reason I remember this scene so well is that my father, who was a serious photographer, filmed the entire event. As the technologies have changed over the years, I transferred the film first to videotape and most recently to a DVD. The history of the image in the last half of the twentieth century is captured in the different versions of this episode.

Similar scenes were, of course, played out in millions of homes during the 1950s. Although the first regular television station was established in 1940 (WNBT in New York City) and CBS and NBC started commercial transmission in 1941, network telecasts did not begin until 1949. One of the reasons television developed so rapidly was that technologies initially created for military purposes during World War II were quickly released for commercial use shortly after hostilities ended. What made television so attractive to businesses was its capacity to expand advertising beyond anything that had previously been possible. The impact of this development was not merely economic but also social, political, and cultural. In the years immediately following the war, pent-up consumer demand fueled an economic revival, but by the late 1940s the economy was slowing down and new ways to promote products were needed. It seemed as if television had been invented to generate precisely such excessive desire for consumer products that people did not really need. In its early stages, network television functioned as an extension of the mechanical means of reproduction typical of industrialism. Nationwide advertising vastly expanded mass markets and led to growing product standardization. While promoting unprecedented choice, advertisers offered customers a limited menu of options. Regional and personal differences did not disappear, but the increasing uniformity of products brought greater social homogenization throughout the 1950s. The color might differ but the model remained the same. By 1960, gray flannel suits and Levittown had become emblematic of a sameness that a growing number of people found stifling.

Industrialization and the processes that promote it, however, are extremely complicated and are not merely hegemonic. Product standardization requires a division of labor, which creates social differentiation as well as stratification. During the 1960s, sameness began to give way to difference—philosophically, socially, politically, economically, and technologically. These differences were created, expressed, and promoted by new kinds of networks, which both supplemented and increasingly competed with TV networks. The information and communications revolution of the '60s radicalized the processes of privatization, decentralization, and deregulation, which, we have seen, began with the Protestant revolution. With the invention of personal computers and their eventual networking, reality literally changed. New kinds of networks brought with them a new infrastructure, which, by the turn of the century, had become global, and this worldwide web, in turn, changed the economy and with it much else. These technological innovations and economic transformations have led to the decline of the nation-state and the emergence of what can best be described as "the market-state." This new form of sociopolitical organization is fraught with contradictions, which inevitably create uncertainty, instability, and insecurity. Faced with a world that is ever more complex and volatile, many people turn to conservative forms of religion to find order, meaning, and purpose in life. However, just as the economic policies and strategies of the market-state increase the instability they are designed to overcome, so neofoundational religions deepen the very conflicts they claim to resolve. In the remainder of this chapter, I will examine the further eclipse of the real brought about by the network revolution in the latter half of the twentieth century, and in chapter 6 I will consider the return of the real in overt and covert forms of postmodern religion. In the final two chapters, I will offer a proposal for a theological alternative and ethical program that overcomes destructive oppositions while cultivating creative differences.

To untangle these complex trajectories, it is necessary first to trace the further eclipse of the real in nets that sometimes appear to be ethereal and then to analyze the unexpected relationship between Protestantism and the Internet revolution. In retrospect, it seems that my brother who mistook image for reality actually understood more about the world that was dawning than the adults who laughed at him. With the move from mechanical means of reproduction through the televisual to digital machines and networks, we discover, in the words of Wallace Stevens, that the "real and the unreal are two in one."[50]

Though Stevens and Warhol might appear to be an odd couple, they share an important insight about life in midcentury America. As Warhol suggests, when life is unreal and TV is real, image and reality merge. This interplay between thing and image reenacts the dialectical reversal of transcendence into immanence figured in the death of God and refigured in both Stevens's poetry and Warhol's pop art. This process passes through three stages, which are related to three different technologies. The separation of thing from image, we have seen, begins with advertising designed to sell mechanically manufactured products. Such advertising started with print distributed in newspapers, magazines, catalogs, and fliers and then developed into window displays, which became possible with the invention of plate glass. At these early stages, there is a referential relation between image and thing: the ad re-presents the product. With the shift from print to television, the thing withdraws farther and the gap between image and reality widens. *Television* means vision at a distance (Greek *tele*, "at a distance," "far off"). Ghostly images flickering on the screen are presumed to represent something that apparently is present elsewhere. As Debord argues, the traces of this absent presence create the spectacle that projects the utopia of consumer society. But the things themselves never appear, and the kingdom they promise is forever deferred. Just as radical transcendence reverses itself to become total immanence, so the withdrawal of the thing leaves nothing but the presence of the image, which now appears real.

What Warhol paints, Baudrillard theorizes: image and thing (or, in semiotic terms, signifier and signified) "implode." When TV no longer represents the real but *is* reality itself, reality is TV (image), and TV (image) is reality. By the beginning of the twenty-first century, reality TV made this explicit by doubling the reflexive loops of the spectacle. This marks the tipping point that turns the transition from the regime of representation to the era of simulation. In his influential essay "The Precession of Simulacra" (1978), Baudrillard writes: "Abstraction today is no longer that of the map, the double, the mirror or the concept. Simulation is no longer that of a territory, a referential being or a substance. It is the generation by models of a real without origin or reality: a hyperreal. The territory no longer precedes the map, nor survives it. Henceforth, it is the map that precedes the territory—PRECESSION OF SIMULACRA—it is the map that engenders the territory whose shreds are slowly rotting across the map."[51] According to Baudrillard, a simulacrum is a copy for which there is no original. Since the notion of the spectacle presupposes a distinction between image (appearance) and thing (reality), the precession of simulacra marks the end of the society of spectacle. In hyperreality, alienation is impossible because there is no real from which one can be alienated. The sign is always the sign of another sign, or, in terms of the structure of the sign itself, the signifier represents another signifier rather than the signified. Signs, therefore, are not grounded in real referents but float freely in a groundless play with other signs. This development involves a seismic shift in the way meaning is constituted: if no(-)thing anchors signs, then meaning is no longer referential but now is relational. The meaning of the sign, in other words, is not determined by its reference to an actual thing but is formed by its relation to other signs. Moreover, relational meaning is differential; in a manner reminiscent of Hegel's dialectical analysis, the identity of any sign is its difference from and hence relation to other signs. In the absence of difference, identity is completely indeterminate. As relations change and develop, meaning shifts in this play of signs—*nothing* is fixed or stable.

This linguistic revolution reflects theological developments that were occurring at the same time. The implosion of the signified and the signifier is the semiotic equivalent of the death of God through the kenotic process in which transcendence empties itself into immanence. Baudrillard is fully aware of the theological implications of his argument; indeed, he begins his analysis by putting theory into practice when he introduces his essay with what he claims to be an epigram from Ecclesiastes but whose translation has been so radically altered that it is in effect a fabricated quotation:

> The simulacrum is never what hides the truth—it is truth that hides the fact that there is none.
>
> The simulacrum is true.

Drawing an explicit connection between theology and semiotics, Baudrillard argues: "The transition from signs that dissimulate something to signs that dissimulate that there is nothing, marks the decisive turning point. The first implies a theology of truth and secrecy (to which the notion of ideology still belongs). The second inaugurates an age of simulacra and simulation in which there is no longer any God to recognize his own, nor any last judgment to separate true from false, the real from its artificial resurrection, since everything is already dead and risen in advance."[52] If God is Wholly Other, signs inevitably dissimulate—they show by hiding and reveal by concealing. Though never present as such, the Other is not merely absent—or so it seems. But what if there really is no such Other? What if the thing-in-itself is always already encoded, or in Hegel's terms, what if the thing-in-itself is a construct created by consciousness to mark its own limit? What if God is nothing more than a sign constructed to deny its status as sign and thereby ground all other signs? If this were the case, then the demystification of theological language would expose a polysemous play of signifiers that has neither ground nor foundation. Like the purposeless work of art, this play would have no end other than itself.

Culture, I have argued, can never be separated from socioeconomic processes. This is not to imply that culture is epiphenomenal and, thus, can simply be reduced to some more fundamental morphological base. To the contrary, cultural and socioeconomic processes are codependent—each conditions and is conditioned by the other, and therefore, neither can be what it is apart from the other. The emergence of what Baudrillard describes as hyperreality (i.e., the culture of simulacra) is coterminous with the changes in the economy made possible by new information and communications technologies. Extending the analysis first from theology to semiotics and then to economics, it becomes clear that one of the most important developments of the latter half of the twentieth century was the end of the gold standard. Going off the gold standard was the economic equivalent of the death of God. Gold functions in the economic system just as God functions in religious schemata: gold is a sign constructed to deny its status as sign and thereby ground the value of other monetary signs. The history of the global economy during the latter half of the twentieth century is inseparable from the changing fortunes of the gold standard. In an effort to restore order to the international monetary system after World War II, a modified version of the gold standard was instituted. The dollar was linked to gold at a fixed conversion rate and all other currencies were bound to the dollar. By 1971, the United States' gold reserves were not adequate to support this system; at the same time, international economic developments and domestic pressures were mounting for the Nixon administration to suspend the gold standard. Concerned about introducing too much volatility into global markets, Secretary of the Treasury John Connolly gave up the gold standard but instituted a system of fixed exchange rates. But this experiment failed and a year later the United States was forced to let the dollar float. With this development, the value of monetary signs was determined by their relation to other monetary signs. Baudrillard draws on Saussure's theory of language to explain the significance of these developments:

> A revolution has put an end to this "classical" economics of value, a revolution of value itself, which carries value beyond its commodity form into its radical form. This revolution consists in the dislocation of the two aspects of the law of value, which were thought to be coherent and eternally bound as if by a natural law. *Referential value is annihilated, giving the structural play of value the upper hand.* The systems of reference for production, signification, the affect, substance and history, all this equivalence to a "real" content, loading the sign with the burden of "utility," with gravity—its form of representative equivalence—all this is over with. Now the other stage of value has the upper hand, a total relativity, general commutation, combination and simulation—simulation, in the sense that, from now on, signs are exchanged against each other rather than against the real (it is not that they just happen to be exchanged against each other, they do so *on condition* that they are no longer exchanged against the real). The emancipation of the sign: remove this "archaic" obligation to designate something and it finally becomes free, indifferent and totally indeterminate, in the structural or combinatory play that succeeds the previous rule to determine equivalence. The same operation takes place at the level of labor power and the production process: the annihilation of any goal as regards the contents of production allows the latter to function as a code, and the monetary sign, for example, to escape into infinite speculation, beyond all reference to a real of production, or even to a gold-standard. The flotation of money and signs, the flotation of "needs" and ends of production, the flotation of labor itself—the commutability of every term is accompanied by speculation and a limitless inflation.[53]

When monetary signs are backed by nothing other than themselves, they are, like Warhol's silk screens, Cindy Sherman's photographs, and Robert Venturi's architecture, nothing more than signs of other signs.

While Baudrillard is an insightful commentator on these developments, his analysis is limited by his preoccupation with televisual, telematic, and virtual technologies. Having learned the lessons of McLuhan all too well, his message remains the media. Since he does not adequately recognize the far-reaching implications of information and network technologies, Baudrillard cannot understand the importance of finance capitalism, which emerged in the 1980s and dominated the 1990s. The year the gold standard was finally revoked was marked by other major developments in technology and finance that signaled a phase shift of historic proportions. The network revolution of the late twentieth century, I have argued, is an extension of the information and communications revolution of the sixteenth century. The intersection of Protestantism and print decisively contributed to forming the modern subject without which democracy and the free market would have been impossible. By privatizing, deregulating, and decentralizing religion, the Protestant revolution began the long process of transforming socio-economic structures and practices in ways that eventually created the conditions for the personal computer and Internet. These developments are inseparable from economic changes that are also tied to Protestantism. The most influential interpretation of markets was originally developed during the eighteenth-century Scottish Enlightenment by theorists whose interpretation of the world was decisively shaped by their Calvinist heritage. In the *Wealth of Nations* (1776), Adam Smith translates the notion of divine providence into the invisible hand of the market. Faith in the reliable guidance of this all-powerful hand has become the foundation of the market fundamentalism characteristic of neoliberal economic theory. In the contemporary market-state, the autonomous subject, which begins to emerge with the privatization of religion, becomes the hinge upon which history swings. But this subject, we have discovered, is self-contradictory—it is what it is not and is not what it is. Now it becomes apparent that the contradictions of modern and post-modern subjectivity are inseparable from contradictions inherent in the technologies of production and reproduction that simultaneously are shaped by and continuously transform Protestantism.

We have seen that Protestantism contributed to the rise of industrialism by encouraging literacy. As individuals learned to read so they could study scripture by themselves, they began to form the educated workforce modern industrial capitalism needed. The transformation of the relation to God from public participation in the rituals of the church universal to the privacy of the individual's personal relation to God initiated the breakdown of social hierarchies and, by so doing, hastened the emergence of free and responsible individuals. The interrelated processes of individualization and privatization led to economic, social, and political diversification and, correlatively, to greater religious pluralism.

There is, however, another, no-less-important side to the mechanical means of reproduction that created print culture. Print, we have seen, not only facilitates individualization and diversification but also promotes the standardization and regulation of language and, by extension, social policies and practices. There are, in other words, contradictory tendencies at work in print: on the one hand, it differentiates and deregulates in ways that lead to greater heterogeneity, and on the other hand, it standardizes and regulates in ways that lead to greater homogeneity. These conflicting tendencies point in different political and economic directions. I have already noted the role Luther's translation of the Bible played in standardizing the German language and marginalizing regional and local dialects. In this way, the development of a common language became a precondition for the emergence of the nation-state. A similar pattern can be seen in France, where Calvin's *Institutes* contributed significantly to *la clarté française*, which still remains so much a part of France's national identity. While modern nations obviously are multilingual, in its early stages nationalism was nourished by a common language. Standardization, however, is not a simple process; it always provokes resistance, which often turns into overt opposition. The tensions between standardization/regulation/homogeneity and differentiation/deregulation/heterogeneity continue down to the present day. During the first half of the twentieth century, the former tendencies were predominant, and in the second half, the latter tendencies became increasingly important. In terms of production processes, this distinction corresponds to the difference between mass production and mass customization; in terms of cultural processes, it is roughly parallel to the difference between modernism and postmodernism; and in terms of critical practices, it is equivalent to the difference between structuralism and poststructuralism. As the balance shifts from standardization and regulation to differentiation and deregulation, the nation-state starts to wane and the market-state begins to wax. This is not to imply that one tendency ever completely displaces the other; to the contrary, massification and demassification are coemergent and remain codependent. This ongoing interrelationship can be seen in the structure of markets and the operational logic of production.

The interplay between the standardization of products and differentiation of the workforce necessary for mass production lies at the heart of Smith's interpretation of the market. He begins the first chapter of his analysis, entitled "Of the Division of Labor,"[54] by writing: "The greatest improvement in the productive powers of labor, and the greater part of the skill, dexterity, and judgment with which it is any where directed or applied, seem to have been the effects of the division of labor."[55] The example he uses to make his point is his now-famous pin factory. By dividing the production process into separate repetitive tasks done by different people, efficiency increases exponentially. According to the utilitarian calculus informing Smith's argument, efficiency is the measure of rationality: what does not increase efficiency and thereby productivity is irrational. Though he understands rationality differently from many of his Enlightenment counterparts, he shares their belief in the progressive development of reason. Indeed, the philosophy of history implicit in Smith's economic analysis conforms to the familiar pattern we have discovered throughout the Western tradition. Progress is marked by growing differentiation, which increases efficiency and thus extends the reach of instrumental reason.

> The division of labor, however, so far as it can be introduced, occasions, in every art, a proportionable increase of the productive powers of labor. The separation of different trades and employments from one another, seems to have taken place, in consequence of this advantage. This separation too is generally carried furthest in those countries which enjoy the highest degree of industry and improvement; what is the work of one man in a rude state of society, being generally that of several in an improved one. In every improved society, the farmer is generally nothing but a farmer; the manufacturer, nothing but a manufacturer. The labor too which is necessary to produce any one complete manufacture, is almost always divided among a great number of hands.[56]

The movement from agrarian to industrial society entails the shift from unspecialized labor to differentiated trades. In Smith's schema, a mechanic, as well as a veterinarian, is a specialist who depends on others to supply what he does not produce. Since the separation of trades creates more efficiency and, correspondingly, more prosperity, the most advanced societies are the ones with the maximum differentiation of the workforce. The invisible hand of the market leads people to a world in which the greatest good is enjoyed by the greatest number. In this schema, divisions paradoxically nourish harmony, and as Darwin would learn from Smith, competition promotes the good of the whole.

Theory and practice, however, do not always coincide. The division of labor creates social differentiation, which, in turn, leads to a pluralization of the plausibility schemata available in a given society. The organizational structures required to produce standardized products, in other words, create diverse life-worlds, which are not always commensurate with each other. This socioeconomic process has a direct impact on religion. As different religious schemata proliferate and come into greater contact with each other, they are relativized: no one frame of reference has a monopoly on belief, and different religious groups are forced to compete with each other for followers. When this occurs, the principles of the market are extended to religious systems; religious leaders become spiritual entrepreneurs who must compete in the open market. In the next chapter, we will see that the same advertising and promotion strategies used to sell consumer products are deployed to market religion. Not only artists but also preachers follow the money—while Warhol and his fellow artists were commodifying art, Billy Graham and his fellow preachers were commodifying religion.

When the monopoly on religious schemata is broken and systems are relativized, beliefs that traditionally legitimized institutions tend to become questionable. In this way, economic development leads to what sociologists describe as a "crisis of legitimacy" or a "crisis of credibility" in which the foundations of cultural traditions and social institutions tremble and sometimes collapse. As objective truth fades in the mist of multiple truths, the locus of certainty becomes more and more subjective. Peter Berger effectively summarizes these developments:

> The pluralistic situation multiplies the number of plausibility structures competing with each other. *Ipso facto*, it relativizes their religious contents. More specifically, the religious contents are "de-objectivated," that is, deprived of their status as taken-for-granted, objective reality in consciousness. They become "subjectivized" in a double sense: Their "reality" becomes a "private" affair of individuals, that is, loses the quality of self-evident intersubjective plausibility—thus one "cannot really talk" about religion anymore. And their "reality," insofar as it is still maintained by the individual, is apprehended as being rooted within the consciousness of the individual rather than

in any facilities of the external world—religion no longer refers to the cosmos or to history, but to the individual *Existenz* or psychology.[57]

When this occurs, history finally catches up with Luther, Kierkegaard, and Nietzsche: truth becomes subjective or perspectival, and subjectivity is most fully realized in the interiority of the isolated individual.

As processes of privatization, deregulation, and decentralization extend from religion to the economy and back again, society is transformed. As always, cultural, economic, and social changes are inseparable from technological innovations. In the years after the end of World War II, more and more technology created for military purposes found commercial applications. The most important result of this development was the rapid rise of the computer industry. To appreciate just how recent these events are and how quickly the world has changed, it is helpful to recall a few important dates:

1951	First electronic digital computer (ENIAC)
	First mass-produced computer (Univac I)
1957	First high-level computer-programming language developed (FORTRAN)
1961	First paper on packet-switching theory
1964	First mass-produced computer operating system (IBM's OS/360P)
1965	First mass-produced minicomputer (PDP-8)
	First network between two computers
1968	First prototype for mouse and working hypertext
1969	APARNET goes online
1975	First computer for home use (Altair 8000)
1976	Apple I introduced
1977	Apple II, Commodore Pet, TRS-80
	500,000 computers in United States

It has become commonplace to describe the second half of the twentieth century in terms of a shift from a manufacturing to an information economy or from an industrial to a postindustrial society. While such analyses point to obvious changes, they are misleading because the information and communications technologies transform, rather than displace, industrialism. Furthermore, the tension between standardization and differentiation inherent in industrialization is also operative in information processes. The alternative trajectories that set the course for the following decades might be more effectively represented by the dif-

ferences between mainframe and personal computers. With the introduction of the personal computer in the 1970s, the nature of computing
and with it social, economic, and political structures changed. No longer
centralized and regulated, personal computers are distributed and are,
therefore, more difficult if not impossible to regulate. As technology
improved and prices rapidly fell, the monopoly on computer ownership
and access that the government, major companies, and wealthy institutions had enjoyed was broken. For early enthusiasts, this change was
revolutionary—the refrain "Power to the people!" became "Information
in the hands of the people!" If information is power, its free distribution is revolutionary. The real revolution, however, resulted, not from
the introduction of personal computers, but from the global networking
of all kinds of information-processing devices. The information revolution remained incomplete without the network revolution. Information
and network technologies also develop through a three-part dialectical
process:

Mainframe computers	Personal computers	Networked computers
Centralized	Decentralized	Connected

While the movement from the mainframe to the PC involves the individualization of computing and the distribution of information, the
connection of computers creates distributed networks in which each
machine is a node in relational webs that eventually become worldwide.
This emerging reality is not merely technological but also economic, political, ontological, and even theological: in network culture, to be is to
be connected (i.e., related).

To understand these developments, it is necessary to untangle the
intricate feedback loops among technology, politics, economics, and
religion during the latter half of the twentieth century. The technological innovations necessary for the emergence of network culture would
not have been possible without changes in the post-1960s political,
economic, and religious climate. The formation of a neoconservative
political consensus led to the promotion of neoliberal economic policies, which where justified by a neofoundational religious ideology. The
program of privatization, deregulation, and decentralization created the
conditions for the rapid deployment of new information and network
technologies, which, in turn, facilitated the spread of new political, economic, and religious agendas. These loops were possible and perhaps

inevitable because of the isomorphism between the ideological super-structure and the technological infrastructure. As mirror images of each other, policies and networks are mutually reinforcing. In this way, grow-ing networks create the conditions for the global expansion of the very policies that made them possible in the first place. While these changes began with the erosion of the New Deal during the 1960s, the drift to the right in the past several decades has occurred on both sides of the po-litical aisle. Though the financial economy of the 1980s and 1990s would have been impossible without Nixon's suspension of the gold standard, it was actually Carter who began the policy of deregulation, when he gave up federal control of the trucking and airline industries. By 1980, Reaganism in the United States and Thatcherism in Great Britain set in motion policies that continue to shape the political landscape and de-fine cultural values. After analyzing how changes in financial markets brought about by network technology contributed to the further eclipse of the real, it will be necessary to consider their political impact.

The new infrastructure created by networked computers altered the structure of the economy and transformed investment strategies. The two most important developments that led to these changes were the virtualization of money and the globalization of markets, both of which continue at an accelerating rate. According to Walter Wriston, former chairman of Citicorp, "In 1971, we switched from the gold standard to the information standard."[58] When currency becomes information and information is the coin of the realm, money, Martin Shubik points out, becomes "a network phenomenon."[59] But how is information to be un-derstood in this context? Gregory Bateson, who was an anthropologist as well as a leading figure in postwar discussions of cybernetics, defined information as "a difference that makes a difference."[60] Though there can be differences that communicate no information, there can be no information without differences. Information, in other words, is differ-ential and as such relational. As we have seen, the end of the gold stan-dard marked a shift from referential to relational values. Rather than be-ing determined by reference to gold, silver, or anything else, the value of monetary signs is determined by their relation to other monetary signs. Just as the meaning of words is determined by their places within a se-miotic system, so the value of currencies is determined by their places in financial networks. The most effective index of meaning in mon-etary systems is price—for those who know the language of finance, price communicates information. So understood, markets are in effect information-processing machines. In the late 1970s, these machines first shifted from analog to digital and then were wired. Financial networks began as local and private but quickly became global and public. Corporations discovered that the decentralized network structure originally developed by the military for defense purposes was more robust and reliable than the commercial systems that were publicly available. Instead of adapting to existing technologies, many businesses began to create proprietary systems known as local area networks (LANs). As spending increased, the influence of corporations on the direction of computer and network technology grew until it eventually extended from LANs to the Internet itself. At the same time, corporations successfully lobbied Congress not to regulate computers and networks. In exchange for granting these concessions, Congress put increasing pressure on business to make their networks available to more people. When computers and telecommunications technologies were interfaced, the nature of both changed. Money, information, news, and entertainment became thoroughly commutable, and eventually a finance-entertainment complex was superimposed on the military-industrial complex. Though connections were far from seamless, the interfacing of fiber-optic networks, cable TV, and satellite transmission created a global network in which spatial distance and temporal delay gave way to the here and now of simultaneity and "real" time. In this new world, money is time—only the quick survive.

It is important to note that the increase in connectivity does not inevitably lead to greater unity; to the contrary, the more interconnected the world becomes, the more evident the differences among peoples and cultures appear to be. Since differences often tend to become oppositions, the expansion of networks does not necessarily lead to stability but can actually create instability and even conflict. Increased connectivity, therefore, often issues in greater volatility in both financial and sociocultural networks. With the development of the so-called information economy and the globalization of networks, financial markets became more unstable. The growing volatility during the past three decades has made it necessary to devise new financial strategies to manage risk.

Risk, of course, lies at the heart of capital markets—indeed, without risk there is no prospect of financial gain. While risk can never be eliminated, it can be managed by distributing it among those who are more or less willing to bear it. Computers and networks, which created the problem, also provided the solution. To distribute risk, new financial instruments were required and these innovations were made possible by networked computers. The new financial instruments developed to manage financial instability have names as strange as the world they create: derivatives, futures, options, currency swaps, interest rate swaps, repos, mortgage-backed securities, collateralized mortgage obligations, notional capital, etc. With the emergence of such instruments, what used to be called "money" becomes less and less real and more and more virtual. Moreover, trading increasingly is done by computers rather than human beings. While buying and selling on the New York Stock Exchange for the most part continues to be a face-to-face auction on the "real" trading floor, NASDAQ, as well as many other exchanges around the world, is nothing more than computer networks. The prominent NASDAQ building with its signature digital sign in the middle of Times Square is not a "real" exchange but a studio for financial programs broadcast on network and cable television.

Just as the rapid development of network technology would not have been possible without neoconservative policies of deregulation, so the financial economy of the 1980s and 1990s would have been impossible without neoliberal economic policies. When Milton Friedman displaced John Maynard Keynes as the patron saint of economists, the banking industry and financial institutions were quickly privatized and deregulated. Since financial markets were increasingly dependent on telecommunications technology, the privatization and deregulation of phone companies played a vital role in the exponential growth of financial markets. These policies were not limited to the United States but were internationalized through the International Monetary Fund and the World Bank. Financial assistance and debt relief for developing countries became contingent upon opening up national telecommunications systems and financial institutions to foreign investment, which usually means American companies.

The virtualization of "money" and global wiring of the invisible hand created a financial economy that became more and more speculative as the twentieth century drew to a close. Changing tax policies combined with the transformation of investing to bring about a redistribution of wealth of unprecedented proportions. It has always been true that money makes money but never more so than during the past three decades. The reason for this is clear: in an agricultural or an industrial economy, money is made primarily by selling either material things or one's labor; in the network economy, by contrast, money is made with financial assets, which are not things but signs backed by other signs. In a process that makes the metallurgical techniques of alchemists seem primitive, financial wizards create gold out of immaterial signs circulating in networks that are nothing but ether. As velocity and volatility increase, Marx's observation becomes all the more prescient: "All that is solid melts into thin air."[61]

When money begets money, the economy increasingly favors people, institutions, companies, and countries that have significant financial assets. More than interest is compounded—the increase in wealth of those who already have money to invest becomes exponential, and correspondingly, the gap between the rich and the poor widens. Nevertheless, enough is never enough—individuals and companies frantically pursue excessive profits, and the economy becomes dangerously speculative. Though many factors contributed to this tendency, two of the most important were changes in attitudes toward debt and new forms of collateral. The generation that had lived through the Great Depression tended to regard debt not only as financially imprudent but as nothing less than sinful. For many individuals, the only justifiable reason to borrow money was to purchase a home or other necessities, and companies tended to borrow primarily to cover operating expenses and to invest in the physical infrastructure necessary for production. But all of this began to change in the 1960s, when consumer, corporate, and government debt became vital to the national and international economy. For the economy to continue to expand, individuals, companies, and countries had to spend more than they had. Far from avoiding debt, politicians and businesses began to promote it.[62] For individual consumers, the emergence of acceptable alternatives to cash payment erased the stigma that had long been associated with debt. Though some stores and companies had used layaway plans and payment cards for decades, nationwide credit cards were not introduced until the late 1950s. After starting with fee-based cards issued by Diners Club, American Express, and Carte Blanche, the credit card industry quickly became first national and then international. By 1970, there were two major cards: National Bank Americard (later Visa) and Master Charge/Interbank (later Master-Card). Not until the 1980 Monetary Control Act and the 1982 Garne–Saint Germaine Depository Institutions Act extended deregulation did plastic become ubiquitous. With credit available for the asking, consumers' calculation shifted from the cost of the product to the amount of the monthly payment, which included interest rates that could run as high as 21 percent. Needless to say, it was people without much money who used credit cards most frequently and, thus, became deeply indebted. Investors with significant financial assets stood to profit from the growing debt of others.

At the same time, business changed its attitude toward debt. For

CEOs and security analysts more concerned about short-term profits than long-term viability, the question was no longer whether a company had too much debt but whether it had too little. If money makes money, managers and investors reasoned, it seems to make sense to borrow money to invest in the stock market and other financial assets. Such practices were encouraged by the high inflation rates of the late 1960s and 1970s. Businesses and investors figured they could borrow money, invest it in securities, whose value they gambled would increase, and then repay the debt with money that had decreased in value over the duration of the loan. As the apparent prospect of profits grew, individuals, companies, and other financial institutions started taking out significant loans to invest in increasingly speculative markets. To encourage more investment, lending agencies changed their policies governing collateral. Prior to the emergence of the network economy and the new financial products it created, loans were secured by "real" assets with ascertainable value. Individuals taking out a mortgage, for example, secured the loan with the house they purchased, and a company borrowing money offered the factory, equipment, real estate, and inventory as collateral. With the shift to the speculative financial economy, however, lenders began to accept the securities purchased with the borrowed money as collateral for the loan. At the same time, businesses became much more highly leveraged—in other words, they borrowed more and more money with fewer and fewer *real* assets. Obviously, these strategies are reasonable only if markets continue to go up. Paul Samuelson once famously quipped: "You cannot lose more than you have to invest." But the speculative financial economy of the 1980s and 1990s proved him wrong: you *can* lose more than you have if you borrow money to play the market. As leverage increased and collateral all but disappeared, the economy became a house of cards. Everyone knew the game they were playing but few wanted to pick up the chips while the ante was growing. As signs grounded in nothing but other signs circulate in global networks with increasing velocity, the hard realities of economics seem to vaporize in strings of digits floating in cyberspace. When the global debt crisis erupted and the dot-com bubble burst in 1998, the party seemed to be over. The precipitous decline of markets around the world created financial instabilities that led to calls for a return to the fundamentals of investing, which echoed calls for a return to basic values and religious fundamentals that were occurring at the same time. But the effort to return to the real after its eclipse proved to be impossible; strategies that were developed to provide security and certainty exacerbated the very instability they were designed to control.

Before proceeding to examine the rise of neofoundational religion, it is necessary to consider some of the political implications of the interrelation between conservative religiosity and neoliberal economics. During the last several decades, economic and political issues have often been deeply influenced by conservative religious beliefs and agendas. Though the details of their theological visions vary, members of what I have described as the New Religious Right tend to be absolutistic: their world is divided between hostile oppositions that can be neither mediated nor reconciled. In many cases this Manichaean vision borders on the apocalyptic. During the 1980s, the age-old struggle between good and evil took the form of the conflict between democracy and capitalism, on the one hand, and socialism and communism, on the other. While his name was unknown to many preaching the neoliberal and neoconservative gospel in the early 1980s, the patron saint of these critics was Friedrich von Hayek, who received the Nobel Prize in Economics in 1974. Even though Hayek did much of his influential work before computers were used in business and finance, he was the first to understand that the economy is actually an information-processing machine that is structured like a distributed network. Indeed, he goes so far as to argue: "from the Scottish moral philosophers of the eighteenth century stem the chief impulses towards a theory of evolution, the variety of disciplines known as cybernetics, general systems theory, synergetics, autopoiesis, etc., as well as the understanding of the superior ordering power of the market system, and of the evolution also of language, morals, and law." In his influential book *The Fatal Conceit: The Errors of Socialism*, he elaborates and supports this remarkable claim in terms that indirectly echo Luther's criticism of the hierarchical authority and centralized organization of the Catholic Church:

> Meanwhile, among those who, in the tradition of Mandeville, Hume, and Smith, did study economics, there gradually emerged not only an understanding of market processes, but a powerful critique of the possibility of substituting socialism for them. The advantages of these market procedures were so contrary to expectation that they could be explained only retrospectively, through analyzing this spontaneous formation itself. When this was done, it was found that decentralized control over resources . . . leads to the generation of more information than is possible under central direction. Order and control extending beyond the immediate purview of any central authority could be attained by central direction only if, contrary to fact, those local managers who could gauge visible and potential resources were *also* currently informed of the constantly changing relative importance

of such resources, and could then communicate full and accurate details about this to some central planning authority in time for it to tell them what to do in light of all the other, different, concrete information it had received from other regional or local managers—who of course, in turn, found themselves in similar difficulties in obtaining and delivering such information. . . . Such a process thus remains one of making use of dispersed knowledge . . . , rather than unifying the knowledge of a number of persons.[63]

This seminal comment suggests that markets and networks display the same decentralized, distributed structure and, thus, have the same operational logic. As markets became more wired in distributed networks, the centralized planning and regulatory practices of communistic and socialistic systems became less effective.[64] Since distributed networks cannot be centrally manipulated or managed, the flow of information cannot be controlled well enough to maintain centralized authority. Hayek's analysis suggests that, when the Berlin Wall finally fell in 1989 and the Soviet Union collapsed shortly thereafter, it was not so much the result of Reagan's defense policy as the dissemination of information about world events and images of consumer culture through decentralized networks. When webs become worldwide, walls become permeable and eventually crumble.

In the eyes of many, the failure of communism and the success of democratic capitalism marked the advent of the long-awaited kingdom on earth. Developing an idiosyncratic reading of Hegel through the lens of Alexander Kojève, Francis Fukuyama, who for a while became the darling of neoconservatives, argued that "the triumph of liberal democracy" was nothing less than "the end of history." "What we may be witnessing," he opines, "is not just the end of the Cold War, or the passing of a particular period of postwar history, but the end of history as such: that is, the end of mankind's ideological evolution and the universalization of Western liberal democracy as the final form of human government." Since liberal democracy is, according to Fukuyama, "free of contradictions and irrationalities," its victory represents the final triumph of reason, which, he believes, is the destiny of the West.[65] Needless to say, subsequent history has proven this faith to be at best naïve.[66]

Philip Bobbitt presents a more balanced and sanguine interpretation of these developments in his monumental but unfortunately neglected book *The Shield of Achilles: War, Peace, and the Course of Human History*. The accelerating globalization brought about by new technologies, Bobbitt argues, is creating a new form of political organization that is displacing the modern nation-state. He labels this new phenomenon "the market-state." The distinction between the nation-state and the market-state is not parallel to the difference between communism or socialism and traditional liberal democracy. According to Bobbitt, during the first half of the twentieth century, both the Soviet Union and its satellites, as well as the United States and Western Europe, displayed the characteristics of the nation-state. It is also important to stress that the erosion of the nation-state does not necessarily lead to a decline in nationalism; indeed, in the short run, it actually results in more intense nationalism. Bobbitt summarizes the responsibilities that define the nation-state by tracing the historical developments that led to its emergence:

> The nation-state has accumulated various responsibilities. The legitimating promises of earlier, preceding constitutional forms are often inherited by successive archetypes as entrenched expectations and entitlements. The princely state promised external security, the freedom from domination and interference by foreign powers. The kingly state inherited this responsibility and added the promise of internal stability. The territorial state added the promise of expanding material wealth, to which the nation-state further added the civil and political rights of popular sovereignty. To all these responsibilities the nation-state added the promise of providing economic security and public goods.[67]

The nation-state, then, promises to protect territorial, military, economic, and cultural integrity, while at the same time providing entitlements and public goods and services. To meet these obligations, nation-states develop more or less elaborate systems of taxation, regulation, and administration. "The economic orthodoxy of nation-states," Bobbitt explains, "counseled state intervention in the national economy as a necessary means of achieving growth and other goals. Economic regulation was part of this orthodoxy and fitted the ethos as nation-states that relied so heavily on law."[68] Within this taxonomy, the United States during the first half of the twentieth century and the Soviet Union differed by degree rather than in kind.

By contrast, the market-state, or, in a more recent idiom, "ownership society," rests upon two fundamental principles: individual choice and market fundamentalism. Reagan and Thatcher represent the last leaders of the nation-state, and George W. Bush and Tony Blair are the first leaders of market-states. In this new political order, the state's primary responsibility is no longer to provide for the welfare of its citizens or to manage the economy in a way that leads to a more equitable distribution of wealth. Rather, supporters of the market-state "appeal to a new standard—whether their policies improve and expand opportunities offered to the public—because this new standard is the basis for a new form of the state."[69] To accomplish the goal of expanding opportunities, they believe, there must be less taxation, regulation, and administration. Accordingly, capital markets should be subject to less government control and labor markets should become more flexible and mobile. For transnational corporations, global concerns consistently trump national interests. Since capital tends to go where it is most wanted, the accelerating mobility of financial assets in global markets decreases the leverage of nation-states as well as the power of politicians. The responsibility of government shifts from providing for citizens' welfare to creating opportunities for individuals to succeed on their own. When fully developed, the market-state becomes what Bobbitt describes as "the entrepreneurial market-state":

> The Entrepreneurial Model tends to loosen the identification that citizens feel with the larger polity: autonomy and individual achievement are so prized and the consumption of particular goods so meaningful an act of self-definition that the citizens of these states "invent" their citizenships, identifying themselves with those subgroups within the state with whom they share a consumption pattern. . . . The basic ethos of the Entrepreneurial Model is libertarian: the conviction that it is the role of society to set individuals free to make their own decisions. This ethos counsels minimal state intervention in the economy as well as in the private lives of its citizens. Privatized health care, housing, pensions, and education as well as low taxes and low welfare benefits all characterize such states.[70]

By the beginning of the twenty-first century, this new orthodoxy was spreading quickly. An article entitled "In Bush's 'Ownership Society,' Citizens Would Take More Risk," published on February 2, 2005, in the *Wall Street Journal* summarizes the way in which the entrepreneurial model of the state is transforming political policy:

> President Bush's campaign to revamp Social Security is just the boldest stroke in a much broader effort: To rewrite the government's social contract with citizens that was born of Franklin Roosevelt's New Deal and expanded by Lyndon Johnson's Great Society.
> In what Mr. Bush calls an "ownership society," Americans would as-

sume more of the responsibilities—and risks—now shouldered by government. In exchange, the theory goes, they would get the real and intangible benefits of owning their own homes, controlling their retirement savings, and using tax credits or vouchers to shop for education, job training and health insurance. The emphasis would be on the individual, supplanting a 70-year-old approach in which citizens pool resources for the common good—and government doles out benefits.

What is most surprising is the extent to which even those who criticize this sociopolitical program accept its premises as well as the terms of debate in which these policy changes are cast. Part of what makes the vision of the market-state so powerful is the intersection of politics, economics, and religion. Far from secular, the market-state rests upon a foundational faith in the omniscience, omnipotence, and increasing omnipresence of the market. At the turn of the new millennium, God is not dead; rather, the market has become God in more than a trivial sense: human beings freely err but the market is never wrong. Just as Calvin's providential God weaves good out of evil, so the providential market redeems losses by creating ever-greater profits. The revolution that began with the processes of privatization, deregulation, and decentralization initiated in the Protestant Reformation and extended by the network revolution unexpectedly issues in the emergence of the entrepreneurial market-state.

The market-state, however, no more marks the end of history and the dawn of the kingdom than does liberal democracy. Current orthodoxies and the sociopolitical system they promote harbor contradictions that will lead to their negation and the emergence of new interpretive schemata and organizational configurations. The anthropological and theological assumptions of the market-state and ownership society are wrong: individuals *are not* radically autonomous and the market *is not* absolute. The ideology of individualism preached by believers in the market-state makes social cohesion all but impossible and pushes the notion of subjectivity that extends from Luther to Kierkegaard to the point of reversal. Far from singular monads, individuals are nodes in synchronic and diachronic webs of relation. Decisions, therefore, are never simply the acts of isolated subjects but always occur in coemergent networks where everyone as well as everything is codependent. The complexity of these relational networks points to the second mistake of market fundamentalists. The market does not transcend human beings like a distant deistic God who governs a world that appears to be a machine regulated by the equilibrium principle of Newtonian mechanics. To the contrary, the market is an emergent complex adaptive system in which deliberate human activity plays an integral role. Though individuals can never know the whole or where it is heading, they are not simply ignorant and totally blind; the trajectory of the overall system emerges through interactions based on the local knowledge of competing and cooperating agents. As I argued in the first chapter, nature, society, culture, and technology are bound in feedback and feed-forward loops that are mutually conditioning. Within these dynamic networks we can no more abdicate responsibility for the deliberate oversight of economic processes than we can leave everything in the hands of a transcendent providential God who seems to have died. The creative action so desperately needed in today's world is impossible without a different religious vision framed by a new interpretive schema.

CHAPTER SIX

Recovering the Real

COUNTERCULTURE

On May 2, 2005, *Time* published a special issue devoted to the new pope, Benedict XVI, with a lead article by David van Biema entitled: "The Turning Point: How the Upheavals of 1968 turned a Vatican II Reformer into an Ardent Conservative." The article begins with an interview of the liberal Catholic theologian Hans Küng, who had been instrumental in recruiting Josef Ratzinger for the theological faculty at Tübingen University in 1966. Having grown up in the small town of Marktl in southern Bavaria and become deeply involved in the church during the Nazi period, the future pope decided to join the priesthood and quickly rose through the ranks. At the relatively young age of thirty-five, Ratzinger became a theological adviser to Cologne's influential Joseph Cardinal Frings during the critical period of the Second Vatican Council (1962–65). Ratzinger was an enthusiastic supporter of policies intended to reconcile the church and the modern world and promoted efforts to balance papal authority by increasing the responsibility and power of ecclesiastical councils. But all of this changed abruptly in 1968 when student rebellion broke out in Tübingen as well as elsewhere in Germany and many other countries. According to van Biema:

> It was an authority issue: European teachers back then were regarded as almost godlike, and for someone used to that kind of status and Catholicism's rigid hierarchies, such an overturning of authority was traumatic; Ratzinger would later call it "brutal." But, says Wolfgang Beinert, assistant and friend of Ratzinger's at the time, there was also

guilt. Beinert says because Ratzinger had advocated—was known for advocating—a greater openness and loosening of ecclesiastical authority, the Tübingen strikes "triggered a huge fright. Ratzinger believed that he was in some way responsible, guilty of the chaos, and that the university and society and church were collapsing."[1]

The situation in Tübingen was further complicated by the Marxist ideology espoused by many of the student radicals. A lifelong student of Augustine's *City of God*, Ratzinger increasingly viewed history in oppositional terms: City of God/City of Man, Christianity/communism, spiritualism/materialism, relativism/absolutism, and so on. Due to his embrace of this schema, many erstwhile friends and colleagues, who supported radical sociopolitical change as well as ecclesiastical reforms, became his enemies. When Küng, for example, published a pointed critique of papal authority, *Infallible?* (1970), Ratzinger supported the official investigation that led to the revocation of his friend and mentor's license to teach Catholic theology. Ratzinger's newly articulated conservative theology and political ideology drew the attention of Pope John Paul II, who eventually appointed him to be the Prefect for the Congregation of the Doctrine of Faith. From this influential position, Ratzinger patrolled the borders of what he took to be orthodoxy and orthopraxis. In a remarkable document issued on August 6, 2000—"*Dominus Iesus:* On the Unicity and Salvific Universality of Jesus Christ and the Church"—he expressed his firm belief that the most pressing problems in the church as well as in society as a whole are caused by relativism and pluralism:

> The church's constant missionary proclamation is endangered today by relativistic theories which seek to justify religious pluralism, not only *de facto* but also *de iure.* As a consequence, it is held that certain truths have been superseded; for example the definitive and complete character of the revelation of Jesus Christ, the nature of Christian faith as compared with that of belief in other religions, the inspired nature of the books of Sacred Scripture, the personal unity between the Eternal Word and Jesus of Nazareth, the universality of the mystery of Jesus Christ, the universal salvific mediation of the Church.

The only remedy for this "relativistic mentality," he concludes, is "to reassert the definitive and complete character of the revelation of Jesus Christ."[2] Ratzinger presents what he takes to be the truth of Christianity in absolutistic terms, which, as we will see below, are ill-suited to life in the twenty-first century.

The trauma of 1968 extended far beyond the confines of Tübingen and other university campuses. It is no exaggeration to say that many of the conflicts rending the world at the beginning of the twenty-first century can be traced to the tumultuous decade of the sixties. Mark Kurlansky begins his informative study, *1968: The Year That Rocked the World*, by claiming: "There has never been a year like 1968, and it is unlikely that there will ever be one again. At a time when nations and cultures were still separate and very different—and in 1968, Poland, France, the United States, and Mexico were far more different from one another than they are today—there occurred a spontaneous combustion of rebellious spirits around the world."[3] Though any list is incomplete, it is helpful to recall just a few of the events that occurred during this remarkable year:

January 5	Benjamin Spock and William Sloan Coffin indicted on charges of conspiracy to encourage violations of the draft laws by a grand jury in Boston
January 23	North Korean patrol boats capture USS *Pueblo*
January 31	North Vietnamese launch the Tet offensive
February 2	Richard Nixon enters the New Hampshire primary
February 16	President Johnson announces the revocation of all draft deferments
March 12	Eugene McCarthy comes within 230 votes of beating President Johnson in the New Hampshire primary
March 16	My Lai massacre
April 4	Martin Luther King assassinated
May 3	United States and North Vietnam agree to begin peace talks in Paris
May	Student revolts in the United States, Europe, and Mexico
June 3	Andy Warhol shot
June 4/5	Robert Kennedy assassinated
June 27	Prague Spring
August 8	Republican National Convention, Miami Beach
August 26	Soviet Union invades Czechoslovakia
August 26	Democratic National Convention, Chicago
November 5	Richard Nixon defeats Hubert Humphrey
December 11	Karl Barth dies

1968 marked the culmination of the decade when the first postwar generation came of age. After suffering through years of war and depression, the world in which these young people grew up seemed to many adults remarkably prosperous and their lives unusually privileged. Although young people had more and wanted for less than had ever been imaginable for their parents, many remained haunted by the uncertainty accompanying the prospect of nuclear destruction and were plagued by the suspicion that material well-being could not ensure happiness. As the currents unleashed by the sexual revolution, the civil rights movement, and the antiwar movement intersected, world history seemed to be slipping toward the edge of chaos, and a major phase shift seemed about to occur. The impact of these events was made much more immediate by television. When the Beatles appeared on the *Ed Sullivan Show* in February 1964, they did not so much trigger a social upheaval as disclose the countercultural revolution that new technologies were already bringing about. A few weeks after the Beatles' appearance, Marshall McLuhan published a book that would prove prophetic—*Understanding Media: The Extensions of Man.* The world events of 1968 signaled the first global revolution created by information and telecommunications technologies.

Nowhere were these changes felt more keenly than on college and university campuses in Europe and the United States. As the postwar student population exploded, many universities began to resemble factories turning out graduates like so many products on an assembly line. With mounting domestic and international problems flashing across television screens daily, a growing number of students became disaffected and found little "relevance" in the work their teachers were asking them to do. The three central issues for restless young people in the sixties were authority, alienation, and authenticity: they resented and resisted authority, felt alienated from society, and passionately sought experiences they believed were authentic. Mike Nichols captured the sense of a disaffected generation in a single word: *"Plastics!"* In a world where everything seemed plastic, people desperately sought to recover the real.

Youth in universities across the globe labeled the cause of the problems they sought to remedy "The System." While it was rarely clear precisely what this term specified, it captured a widespread sense of invasive social and political structures that seemed both repressive and inescapable. Accordingly, for many young people in the sixties, the burning question became how to resist the system by cultivating experiences and activities designed to elude its control, if not overturn it. Though these criticisms tended to be more intuitive than analytic, the deliberately vague term *system* effectively captured the gist of analyses of modern society that influential sociologists, psychologists, and philosophers were developing at the same time. Paradoxically, the very system that brought unprecedented economic prosperity and material well-being also created a pervasive sense of anomie and alienation. For many critics, the proper name for this system was "the military-and-industrial complex." Social commentator Theodore Roszak argues that this system created a new form of social, economic, and political organization, which he labels "technocracy." "By technocracy," he explains, "I mean that social form in which an industrial society reaches the peak of its organizational integration. It is the ideal men usually have in mind when they speak of modernizing, updating, rationalizing, planning. Drawing upon such unquestionable imperatives as the demand for efficiency, for social security, for large-scale coordination of men and resources, for ever higher levels of affluence and ever more impressive manifestations of collective human power, the technocracy works to knit together the anachronistic gaps and fissures of the industrial society."[4] What makes this system so effective is that control is not only imposed externally but also internalized through the effective use of new media. A system so extensive and intensive does indeed seem to be inescapable.

On June 9, 1968—four days after Robert Kennedy was shot and a day after his funeral service in Saint Patrick's Cathedral in New York City and burial in Arlington National Cemetery—I graduated from Wesleyan University. Leonard Bernstein was to have delivered the graduation address but was unable to do so because he was too distraught from having played at Kennedy's funeral. Under the ominous clouds of a gathering thunderstorm, the world into which we were sent that morning seemed dangerously fragile. The Wesleyan I left that June day was very different from the university I had entered in the fall of 1964. I had grown up in a prosperous New Jersey suburb that was staunchly Republican. Though most people in the town preferred Rockefeller to Goldwater, they would never have considered crossing party lines to vote for a Democrat. Since my parents were high school teachers, I was never part of "the country club set," which controlled the politics and dominated the social fabric of the town. Religion was a part of my childhood and youth. As a compromise between the Lutheran tradition, in which my mother had been raised, and the Reformed Mennonite tradition of my father's family, we became members of the Westfield Presbyterian Church. At the time, this church was the largest Presbyterian church east of the Mississippi and was the preferred church of the local social elite. Vance Packard captured the ethos of the church in his widely acclaimed book *The Status Seekers* (1959):

> Three other denominations strongly favored by the two top social classes of America are the Presbyterians, Congregationalists and Unitarians. Corporate executives, for example, favor Presbyterian churches second only to Episcopal. They are six times as likely to be Presbyterians as are Americans at large. . . . The New York suburb of Westfield, New Jersey, is a wealthy "bedroom" town favored by Wall Street commuters and other nearby executives. Its Presbyterian church virtually overwhelms the center of town, with several structures built around a vast park. The church has to hold three services on Sundays, has four ministers and, at last report, needed a fifth. Wives of economic titans, who have homes staffed by servants, wait on table at church suppers.[5]

Though we were regular churchgoers, it was clear to me from a very early age that in our family, school was church and books were scripture. More Protestant than they ever realized, my parents always assumed that teaching was a vocation. It took me many years to understand that this is one of the primary reasons teaching has always been so important to me. There is, I believe, no more noble calling—and it *is* a calling—than teaching young people. It was not only *that* my parents taught but also *what* they taught that proved decisive for me. My mother taught American literature and was a painter; my father taught physics and biology and was a photographer. Their interests and values converged in their appreciation for nature. My mother most loved to teach the American transcendentalists—especially Emerson and Thoreau. In the heavily annotated anthology from which she taught, which is one of my most treasured possessions, she underscored the passage from Emerson's essay "Nature" that was her point of departure for discussing this chapter in America's literary history:

> It seems as if the day was not wholly profane in which we have given heed to some natural object. The fall of snowflakes in a still air, preserving to each crystal its perfect form; the blowing of sleet over a wide sheet of water, and over plains; the waving rye field; the mimic waving of acres of houstonia, whose innumerable florets whiten and ripple before the eye; the reflections of trees and flowers in glassy lakes; the musical streaming odorous south wind, which converts all trees to wind harps; the crackling and spurting of hemlock in the flames; or

of pine logs, which yield glory to the walls and faces in the sitting room—these are the music and pictures of the most ancient religion.

My parents' language was different, but their devotion was the same. Biology was my father's first intellectual love. In the depths of the Depression, he and my mother journeyed from the small Pennsylvania coal-mining town where they taught to Duke University to study botany and literature respectively. No matter where we hiked or hunted, my father not only could identify all the plants and trees but could also give their Latin names. From the time I was old enough to hold a hoe, he made me work in our large vegetable garden. I complained at the time but now realize the garden was his church and my classroom. Having eventually learned my lessons, I fully expect to be a landscape architect in my next incarnation. After he retired, my father led a campaign to preserve the last undeveloped area in our town as a natural park. Though the struggle was long and often heated, he prevailed and the park today bears his name. Like the garden in which I worked, the park became his classroom. My father developed an environmental curriculum with fieldwork and laboratory experiments for K–12, which the public schools still use. In a short book for students and teachers, he wrote:

> Man does not understand the way in which all life on earth is interrelated. It is essential for the thousands of species of animals and plants to live in harmony or balance in order for them to exist. If this balance does not occur, then various species will become extinct. . . . Most people never stop to study or understand the balance needed in nature. People may enjoy the beauty of flowers and butterflies or moths but despise snakes, which are needed to retain the balance of life. . . . With the increase in population, forests and all natural areas became fewer. With the loss of forests and other natural areas and with the increase in population, the problem of pollution of the air, water and soil becomes more critical. . . . Brightwood Park is a microcosm where many forms of life may be preserved for our benefit for future generations.

Poetry and prose. Literature and biology. A "secular" religion in which the world appears sacred. As painter and photographer, my mother and father both knew that word needs image as much as image needs word. Believing is not only a matter of thinking; it is also a matter of seeing. While they devoted their lives to books, they both realized that words were not sufficient for the lessons they sought to teach. In their religion, the world truly was a work of art. At a very young age, my mother encouraged me to learn to paint and helped me when I became frustrated; my father taught me how to take and process photographs. I will never know how deliberate these lessons were but have no doubt that I would not see the world the way I do without the cultivated eye they gave me.

This is some of the baggage I was carrying when I left for college in 1964. The Wesleyan I entered was as lily white as the suburb I left. There were only two people of color in my freshman class; by the time I graduated, 5 percent of the Wesleyan student body was African American. While this shift reflected changes taking place in the broader society, the more proximate cause was the commitment of several members of Wesleyan's Department of Religion to the civil rights movement. I majored in religion at Wesleyan because of a sermon I never heard. When I was searching for a fifth course my sophomore year, I decided to take a class with John Maguire. For more than a year the woman who is now my wife had been raving about a sermon Maguire delivered at a nearby college. At her urging, I enrolled in his course entitled Contending Approaches in Contemporary Protestant Theology, in which we read major works by Barth, Bultmann, and Tillich. Maguire was a charismatic teacher who had a remarkable ability to bring demanding texts to life by relating them to what was going on in the world at the time. A southerner with a knack for telling stories, Maguire was a close friend of Martin Luther King and Ralph Abernathy and brought them to campus regularly during my days at Wesleyan. He and William Sloan Coffin had led one of the first "freedom buses" south to participate in the civil rights movement. Their bus was overturned and burnt and the case went all the way to the Supreme Court. When Newark, which is near my home in Westfield, went up in flames a little more than a year later, nothing could have been more relevant than the lessons of Maguire and the writers he taught. After King created a split in the civil rights movement by joining the antiwar movement, Maguire presented one of the most cogent explanations and persuasive defenses of the moral reasons behind this strategy to members of the civil rights movement throughout the country. His arguments provided many students at Wesleyan and elsewhere with the framework for criticizing the escalating war and suggested a rationale for resistance when President Johnson revoked all draft deferments in February 16, 1968.

The more I studied, the clearer it became that the pressing social and political issues of the day not only involved complicated theological and ethical issues but also raised questions that lie at the heart of modern philosophy. In the fall of 1967, I took a course taught by Stephen Crites entitled Self-Alienation and Reconciliation in Hegel, Feuerbach, and Marx, and in the fateful spring of 1968, I followed it up with his seminar Kierkegaard's Dialectic of Existence. Though nothing would seem to be farther from the struggle in Southeast Asia and the turmoil on American and European campuses than the abstract writings of four nineteenth-century philosophers, I found that their work helped me to understand what was happening around me.

The conflict between Hegel's systematic philosophy and Kierke-gaard's existential individualism both prefigured and illuminated the tension between the system and the individual in the counterculture. It was Hegel, I discovered, who had philosophically articulated the dialectic of self-alienation that people who had never heard his name invoked, and it was Kierkegaard who developed an account of the authenticity of individual experience for which so many seemed to be searching. As my understanding of these philosophers deepened, I became impatient with the superficiality and facility of what passed for social criticism and political commentary. In two term papers on Hegel and Kierkegaard, I developed what became the foundation for everything I have since written. When recently rereading my paper for the Hegel seminar, pretentiously entitled "The Implications of the Difference between the Kantian and the Hegelian Conceptions of Reason and Understanding for the Proofs of the Existence of God," I was startled to discover an appendix in which I formulated the interplay of theology, psychology, and cosmology, which lies at the heart of the book you are now reading (table 12). What I was beginning to see even then was that Hegel and Kierkegaard are not merely two philosophers who are significant historically but are thinkers who remain important because they figure alternative forms of life that are still viable. Moreover, these two ways of being-in-the-world can be traced throughout the history of Christianity and define the contending poles of the counterculture I could not avoid.

Protests to the contrary notwithstanding, the counterculture was a *religious* movement. The culture wars and religious wars of the past two decades have demonized the sixties as a decadent period when individuals and society lost their way by slipping into the morass of relativism, which, critics argue, inevitably leads to nihilism. But this is a naïve and simplistic view, which is ideologically motivated and distorts both history and the rich diversity of religion. Religion, I have argued, is an emergent complex adaptive network of symbols, myths, and rituals that, on the one hand, figure schemata of feeling, thinking, and acting in ways

Table 12. Classification of Ideas of Pure Reason

Syllogistic inference:	Categories of relation	Most general relation of representations (A334, B391)	Unconditional unity postulated by pure reason (B380)	Classes of transcendental ideas (A334, B391)	Ideas of pure reason	Branches of speculative metaphysics
Categorical:	Substance	To subject	Something that is always subject and never predicate	Absolute unity of thinking subject	Permanent ego as substance: soul	Psychology
Hypothetical:	Causality	To objects as phenomena	Ultimate presupposition	Unity of the series of conditions of experience	Totality of causal sequences in phenomena: world	Cosmology
Disjunctive:	Community	To all things in general	Aggregate of members of the division of a concept as requires nothing further to complete division	Unity of condition of all objects of thought in general	Absolute perfection: God	Theology

that lend life meaning and purpose and, on the other, disrupt, dislocate, and disfigure every stabilizing structure. During the sixties, religion tended to be most creative when it disrupted stabilizing structures, which had become politically and personally repressive. The resistance to authority in multiple guises expressed the belief among many young people that the so-called System had betrayed not only them but also the very principles and values it ought to be defending. As the sense of alienation spread, the search for experience that counted as *real* became more frantic: sex, drugs, and rock and roll as well as authentic religious experience, which increasingly was found outside mainline churches, were alternative ways of fulfilling a shared need. The religious language of redemption and salvation was translated into the language of personal fulfillment and social liberation. Though the terms changed, the questions remained the same as have been asked throughout the history of Christianity: Is liberation primarily personal or social? In other words, must one change consciousness to change society or change society to change consciousness? During the sixties, those who followed the ancient way of mystics attempted to change consciousness through drugs, music, meditation, and religious practices, which usually were non-Western. Those who followed the way of the church militant sought liberation through political action, which ranged from nonviolent movements for reform, often inspired by Western religious traditions, to calls for radical change by violent means if necessary. Theorists of this period often interpreted the former approach in terms of Freud and the latter in terms of Marx. With a cultural revolution unfolding from the streets of Berkeley, Cambridge, and Paris to Mao's China, the preoccupation with synthesizing Freud and Marx was of more than theoretical interest.

In 1969, Kenneth Keniston, who was a professor of psychiatry at Harvard at the time, published what remains one of the best books of this period—*Young Radicals: Notes on Committed Youth.* While his study focused on a small number of young people during what had been labeled the Vietnam summer of 1967, his conclusions shed light on an entire generation. Keniston describes the two poles of the counterculture that I have identified as mystics and militants as "hippies and radicals": "radicals systematically attempt to reform and change their society, whereas hippies turn their backs on society in their effort to find meaning through an intensification of personal experience."[6] As I have suggested, so-called hippies sought to cultivate authentic experience through drugs as well as experimentation with spiritual traditions as different as Hinduism, Buddhism, Zen, and Native American religions.

Even though the three religions of the book—Judaism, Christianity, and Islam—have important mystical traditions, they were of little interest to the youth culture. In contrast to these latter-day mystics, the New Left was more politically engaged. While many on the left had become disillusioned with traditional Marxism when it degenerated into Stalinism, the so-called New Left was infatuated by the writings of Marx and Mao and generally supported left-wing liberation movements throughout the world. Different ideologies and tactics in the civil rights and antiwar movements were expressed in groups ranging from the Student Non-Violent Coordinating Committee and Congress for Racial Equality to the Students for a Democratic Society and the Weathermen. Important disagreements notwithstanding, most young people on the left agreed on three basic principles:

1. Decisions in America are ultimately determined by the military-industrial complex and are designed to extend economic imperialism by opposing left-wing governments.
2. Traditional liberalism has failed in foreign policy and has proven ineffective in helping the poor.
3. There is a need to develop new social institutions, which should be local and decentralized.[7]

Though passionately concerned about social, political, and economic injustice, the pervasive suspicion of centralized authority and hierarchical power made it impossible for the New Left to become an effectively coordinated movement.

The differences between so-called hippies and radicals should not obscure their noteworthy similarities. A year before Robert Venturi and Denise Scott Brown conducted their famous seminar on Las Vegas, which eventually led to the publication of the book that defined a new postmodern style in architecture (*Learning from Las Vegas*), Keniston argued that what all members of the youth counterculture shared was a new "postmodern style":

> In emphasizing "style" rather than ideology, objectives, positions, traits, I mean to suggest that the similarities in post-modern youth are to be found in the *way* they approach the world, rather than in actual behavior, formal beliefs, or goals. A focus on process rather than on program is perhaps the prime characteristic of the post-modern style, reflecting a world where flux and change are more apparent than direction, purpose, or future. . . . In such a revolutionary world,

where ideologies come and go and radical change is the rule, a style, a *way* of doing things, becomes more tenable and more important than any fixed goals, ideologies, programs, institutions or psychological traits.[8]

In the decades since Keniston wrote these prescient words, the style he identifies has transformed the very fabric of life.

Similar stylistic changes and political critiques were developing at the same time on campuses in Europe and Latin America. New telecommunications technologies created a worldwide web, which led to the spontaneous emergence of the first global revolution. In this tectonic shift, there is a closer relationship between the medium and the message than is initially evident. Countercultural youth, we have seen, resisted centralized authority and sought to cultivate local organizations and decentralized networks of relation. While the New Left remained open to state intervention in social and economic processes, those who sought authentic individual experience tended to be libertarians, who were suspicious of all government intervention and regulation. Since many tended to associate technology with the military-industrial complex, the youth culture was often technophobic. By the early 1970s, however, new technologies brought a change in attitudes. Some of the young people who were dropping acid around Haight-Ashbury were also gathering in nearby garages to form the Homebrew Computer Club, where the personal computer was born. For reformers who thought that the way to change the world was first to change consciousness, the personal computer (PC) revolution created the possibility of a psychosocial revolution. Stewart Brand, one-time member of Ken Kesey's Merry Pranksters (whose band was the Grateful Dead), founder of *Whole Earth Catalogue*, and author of *The Media Lab: Inventing the Future at MIT*, makes this telling point clearly and concisely: "This generation swallowed computers whole, just like dope."[9] PCs promised a world that was simultaneously decentralized and connected, which is precisely what acid-heads were searching for. Revolutions, however, rarely turn out the way those who instigate them intend. Just as Rodchenko and his fellow constructivists never could have imagined Warhol's Factory and consumer culture, so hippies and geeks and the kids in San Francisco garages never anticipated worldwide webs and the global networks of today's finance-entertainment complex.

The decade of the sixties was as confusing as it was energizing; where others saw threats, I saw opportunities. While news media were preoccupied with the death of God and the secular city, studying Hegel and Kierkegaard in 1967-68 enabled me to discern a *religious* revival in the midst of what others believed to be the collapse of religion and morality in nihilistic relativism. The most important lesson I learned in the sixties was the opposite of the conclusion neoconservatives drew: the mortal danger we face, I decided, is not relativism but absolutism. As will become clear in the final chapter, I am a committed relativist or, perhaps more accurately, relationalist, who firmly believes that the future depends on displacing religious foundationalism and exclusive moralism with a religion of life and an ethics without absolutes.

What I did not realize in the sixties—and surely I was not alone in this—was that there was another side to the religious revival that was occurring around me. Rather than being drawn to the counterculture, many people in this country and elsewhere reached the same conclusion as Ratzinger when he was confronted by rebellious students who resisted his authority. In the past several decades, the religious right has achieved remarkable political power through a concerted campaign against what they regard as the moral decay that began in the sixties. Indeed, the New Religious Right is, in large measure, a counter-counterculture. What is most remarkable about this turn of events is the unlikely alliances that have been forged. The neofoundational and neoconservative movements are made up of not only traditional conservatives but also erstwhile members of the left who became disenchanted with the strategies and tactics of the sixties and took a sharp turn to the right.

The career of William Bennett is representative of former leftists who have been reborn as neoconservatives and have assumed extremely powerful positions in government and the media. While an undergraduate philosophy major at Williams College, where I taught for more than three decades, Bennett was involved in radical leftist politics. After graduating in 1965, he pursued a doctorate in philosophy at the University of Texas, where the ultraconservative John Silber was his adviser for a thesis on Kant. When Bennett left Texas, his leftist days were a distant memory, and he quickly became an influential member of the Reagan and Bush administration, initially as the head of the National Humanities Center (1976–81), then chairman of the National Endowment for the Humanities (1981–85), secretary of education (1985–89), and finally the first drug czar (1989). By the time George W. Bush was elected, Bennett had transformed himself into an influential political commentator and archdefender of the New Religious Right. Through a series of books, television appearances, and radio talk shows, he created his own bully pulpit from which he preached to the country about moral virtue and politics. In the wake of September 11, he wrote a book entitled *Why We Fight: Moral Clarity and the War on Terrorism*, in which he argues: "It took George W. Bush, a 'cowboy' president like Ronald Reagan, to revive the language of good and evil. Like Reagan before him, the president did so with precision and justification." Having converted to Catholicism, Bennett echoed Ratzinger by insisting that nothing less than the return to moral absolutes can prepare the country to deal with the crises that lie ahead. When Bush declared to nations around the world, "Either you are with us or against us," Bennett explains, "the war we were being invited to join was a war over ultimate and uncompromising purposes, a war to the finish. Like World War II, like our war with Soviet communism, this is a war about good and evil." Bennett claims that Bush's war on terrorism is actually an extension of the culture wars of the sixties. Maintaining that the legacy of the 1960s was a moral relativism that inevitably leads to anti-Americanism, he traces the moral decline of America to "the adversary culture" of the 1960s, of which he had been such a vocal member. By the late 1990s, Bennett was preaching that moral decline had spread from college campuses to society as a whole: "I am not just talking about the politics of a radical or revolutionary fringe. As contemporary historians have well documented, the ideas and opinions promulgated by the 1960s New Left and counter culture were echoed, in however diluted a form, throughout the institutions of the liberal mainstream, particular the universities and the media." Even more disturbing for the emerging moral majority is the way in which "the relativist ethos of the cultural Left" trickled down to "educators on the primary- and secondary-school levels."[10] The only way out of this moral morass and the political paralysis it brings, Bennett concludes, is a return to religious and moral absolutes and educational, political, and economic fundamentals.

As we will see in what follows, this conclusion, which, unfortunately, is widely shared, is seriously flawed and deeply troubling. In a world where everyone is increasingly interconnected, religious foundationalism and moral absolutism threaten to bring about the very disaster their adherents claim to be trying to avoid. To respond effectively to the exclusionist ideologies rending the world today, it is necessary first to develop a better understanding of how and why the unholy alliance of neofoundational religion, neoconservative politics, and neoliberal economics developed in the late twentieth century and then to provide an alternative religious schema for life in the twenty-first century.

SECURING THE BASE

From June 24 to June 26, 2005, Billy Graham returned to New York City for what was billed as his last crusade. Standing in a long line of religious revivalists, Graham had been conducting crusades since 1949. Although he developed a considerable following in the 1940s through his popular radio program *Hour of Decision*, he did not rise to national prominence until his remarkable ninety-seven-day crusade in Madison Square Garden in 1957. One of my most vivid memories of childhood is listening to Billy Graham and eventually watching him on television with my grandfather Mark Cooper. While many things changed dramatically in the years between Graham's New York crusades, the religious climate in 2005 was in many ways more consistent with his vision than it had been in 1957. Graham has an uncanny ability to weave together religious, political, and business interests in a message whose appeal has proven to be surprisingly enduring. From the earliest days of his ministry, he pitched Evangelical Protestantism as the only viable alternative to "godless Communism." Two days before Graham launched his 1949 revival in Los Angeles, President Truman announced that the Russians had successfully tested an atomic bomb and already had "weapons of mass destruction." This alarming news, which immediately transformed the geopolitical landscape, provided Graham with a point of entry for his message and gave him access to presidents and political leaders throughout the world for more than five decades. He effectively translated the cold war into religious language to create a theology of history that still governs political theory and policy. Preaching in Los Angeles in 1949, Graham declared: "Western culture and its fruits had its foundation in the Bible, the Word of God, and in the revivals of the Seventeenth and Eighteenth Centuries. Communism, on the other hand, has decided against God, against Christ, against the Bible, and against all religion. Communism is not only an economic interpretation of life—communism is a religion that is inspired, directed, and motivated by the Devil himself who has declared against the almighty God."[11]

In 1952, Graham led a five-week crusade in Washington, D.C., which culminated with a rally that drew forty thousand to the steps of the Capitol. In his informative book *With God on Our Side*, sociologist William Martin points out that even though President Truman declined to grant Graham an audience, one-third of all senators and one-fourth of all House members requested special seats at the crusade. With growing political power and the ability to sway approximately sixteen million voters, Graham encouraged Eisenhower to run for president. After beating Truman, Ike "became the first president ever to lead a prayer as part of his own inauguration and followed this with being baptized in the White House. Graham voiced his approval by telling his radio audience that, 'I have been deeply impressed by [the President's] sincerity, humility and tremendous grasp of world affairs. I also sense a dependence upon God. He told me on [two] occasions that the hope of building a better America lay in a spiritual revival.' Graham concluded that the election of Eisenhower was a signal that 'God is giving us a respite, a new chance.'"[12] From Graham's point of view, God has obviously given America many new chances since the election of Eisenhower. Graham's political clout has always been enhanced by his connections with powerful business leaders. The organizing committee for the 1957 crusade included Henry Luce, head of the Time-Life empire, George Champion, president of the Chase Manhattan Bank, Howard Isham, vice president and treasurer of U.S. Steel, and William Randolph Hearst Jr., the publishing tycoon. Graham's mix of conservative Protestantism and anticommunism was just the kind of business-friendly message that financial titans found congenial to their own interests.

Though Graham continued to preach the Word, many people were not buying what he was selling during the Age of Aquarius. However, the social upheavals of the sixties, as well as domestic and international political developments, prepared the way for the unexpected revival of conservative Protestantism in the following decades. In 1976, the country celebrated its bicentennial by electing its first born-again president— Jimmy Carter. As the world began to realize just how serious Carter was about his religious commitments, analysts and commentators turned to Billy Graham to explain what was emerging in their midst. In a nationally televised crusade service in May 1976, Graham answered the question on everybody's lips: "What does it mean to be 'born again'?" He cited the biblical origin of the phrase, in the third chapter of the Gospel according to John, where Jesus informs Nicodemus: "except a man be born again, he cannot see the Kingdom of God."[13] Ever since Luther's privatization of religion, the born-again experience has played an important role in Protestantism. During the tumultuous sixties, when everything once deemed real seemed to be slipping away and the world appeared to be on the edge of chaos, many people sought security and authenticity through a *personal* relationship to Jesus Christ. Though the technologies for spreading the Word changed over the years, the message of Graham and his fellow evangelists has remained constant—for more than five decades, he ended every sermon by asking people to let Christ enter their lives and inviting them to approach the altar to receive God's blessing. For the Evangelical Christian, what is most important is his or her *individual* decision in response to the forgiveness offered by the *transcendent personal* God made present in the person of Jesus Christ.

As this message has become attractive to more and more people over the past four decades, what has occurred can only be described as the Fourth Great Awakening. This spiritual renewal is surprisingly consistent with the revivals of the eighteenth and nineteenth centuries. In contrast to earlier revivals, however, the current awakening is not limited to the United States or to Protestantism but is a *global* phenomenon occurring in many different countries and in virtually all established religious traditions. The media constantly bombard us with news of the explosive growth of what is labeled "the Muslim world," but the fact is that Christianity is the fastest-growing religion in the world today. As Philip Jenkins points out in his highly instructive book *The Next Christendom: The Coming of Global Christianity,* "Over the past five centuries or so, the story of Christianity has been inextricably bound up with that of Europe and European-derived civilizations overseas, above all in North America. Until recently, the overwhelming majority of Christians have lived in White nations, allowing theorists to speak smugly, arrogantly, of 'European Christian' civilizations." But this situation has been changing for almost a century; indeed, "the center of gravity in the Christian world has shifted inexorably southward, to Africa, Asia and Latin America."[14] By 2050, there will be three Christians for every two Muslims and 34 percent of the entire world population will be Christian. Since many of the countries where Christianity is spreading most rapidly have the highest birth rates, the explosive growth shows no signs of subsiding. The sects that are increasing most quickly throughout the world are those that are thriving in the United States—Evangelicalism and Pentecostalism. In this country, the most recent religious revival has occurred in groups that previously have been marginalized—Fundamentalists, Evangelicals, and Pentecostals—rather than mainline churches.

It is important to realize that these contemporary forms of belief and practice do not represent a reversion to premodern forms of life but are distinctly *postmodern* phenomena. Though their social and cultural contexts vary considerably, members of these denominations and sects practice forms of religiosity designed to avoid uncertainty and insecurity by absolutizing, reifying, and fetishizing culturally specific forms of belief and practice. Committed to the exclusionary principle of either/or, these groups establish their identity as much by what they oppose as what they embrace. In promoting their counter-counterculture, neofoundationalists are

Antimodernists
Antisecularists
Anticommunists
Antisocialists
Antihumanists
Antiliberals
Antiscience
Antirelativists
Antifeminists
Antigays
Antielitists

It is, of course, necessary to draw certain distinctions among different groups. On the most basic level, Fundamentalists are preoccupied with scriptural inerrancy, Evangelicals are concerned with the personal relation between the individual believer and God, and Pentecostals emphasize the gifts of the Spirit like visions and speaking in tongues. These differences notwithstanding, all three groups agree on the most important basic principles. First and foremost, as radical monotheists, they believe in a transcendent personal God, who is omniscient, omnipotent, and omnipresent. This God establishes the absolute principles of truth and universal codes of conduct, which provide the secure base upon which a meaningful life can be built. For neofoundationalists, securing the base is a religious necessity as well as a political strategy.[15] These different groups also share a theology of history that conforms to the trinitarian structure I have traced back to the Middle Ages. Mired in sin and caught in a world of darkness, believers create images of an ideal past from which they believe they have fallen and project a perfect future toward which they are supposed to be moving. The present age, which is characterized by a struggle between good and evil, will end when Christ returns to separate believers from nonbelievers and establish a kingdom, which will not be of this world. Variations of this general scheme ranging from apocalypticism and millenarianism to dominion theology and dispensationalism characterize the particular theological positions of different denominations and sects. I will consider these alternative theological perspectives in more detail below. Before proceeding, it is important to stress that, while I cannot develop a cross-cultural analysis in this context, the defining characteristics of neofoundationalism are not limited to Protestantism or even Christianity but can, with certain modifications, be found in different religious traditions throughout the world.[16]

The "culture wars" that have grown out of religion have shown remarkable thematic consistency as far back as the founding of the country. To understand the power of the New Religious Right, it is necessary to trace its emergence from earlier reform movements. I have already considered the different attitudes toward religion expressed in the Declaration of Independence and the Declaration of the Rights of Man and of the Citizen. In contrast to the French, who refer only to a Supreme Being in a perfunctory way and ground authority in the general will of the people, Americans invoke the providential Creator God as the basis of authority and foundation of human rights. There were, however, important differences among the signers of the Declaration of Independence on the question of religion. While Jefferson, Franklin, and John Adams had spent considerable time in France and were quite sympathetic to naturalistic deism, other representatives remained deeply committed to the principles of Protestant orthodoxy. During colonial days, Calvinist New England proved to be more politically conservative than Anglican Virginia. In 1779, Jefferson proposed a bill guaranteeing complete legal equality for citizens of all religions in Virginia, as well as those who professed no religion at all. This was part of the first effort to legislate complete separation of church and state at a time when the Episcopal Church, which by then had won its independence from the Church of England, was the established religion of the State of Virginia. Seven years after Jefferson's original proposal, the Virginia General Assembly finally passed the Act for Establishing Religious Freedom, which became the prototype for the disestablishment clause of the Constitution.[17] In the years leading up to the ratification of the Constitution, many politicians and clergymen became increasingly wary of the social impact of French atheism and materialism. In her study of freethinkers in America, Susan Jacoby cites a passage from a prominent clergyman of the day that has a disturbingly contemporary ring: "Infidelity has lately grown condescending: bred in the speculations of a daring philosophy, immured at first in the cloisters of the learned, and afterwards nursed in the lap of voluptuousness and of courts; having at length reached its full maturity, it boldly ventures to challenge the suffrages of the people, solicits the acquaintance of peasants and mechanics, and seeks to draw the whole nation to its standard." In the early part of the nineteenth century, this kind of moralistic fervor grew as the Second Great Awakening spread from New England to the Deep South.[18]

By the early twentieth century, circumstances had changed more than

theology. The nineteenth century saw the disappearance of agrarian society and the rapid modernization, industrialization, and urbanization
of America. As early as the 1840s, poverty and famine in Europe led to a
flood of Irish and German Catholic immigrants into northern cities. A
second wave of immigrants from Ireland and Italy (largely Roman Catholic) and eastern Europe (mostly Jewish) followed between 1890 and 1910,
leading to what John Davidson Hunter has labeled "the disestablishment
of American Protestantism." Problems associated with industrialization
and urbanization, ranging from crime and alcoholism to prostitution
and the breakdown of the traditional family structure, became associated with these immigrants. To many whose world had been rocked by
these changes, life did not seem to be getting better, and the Social Gospel movement's message of moral progress rang empty. Instead of more
change, people longed for stability. Between 1910 and 1915 oilmen Lyman
and Milton Steward financed a series of works published by the Moody
Bible Institute entitled *The Fundamentals: A Testimony to the Truth*, which
the Presbyterian Church quickly affirmed as the cornerstone of true
faith. By the time the World's Christian Fundamentals Association was
founded in Philadelphia nine years later, Fundamentalism had become
a formidable force in American religion and politics. In its earliest version, Fundamentalism rejected all forms of "Romanism, ritualism and
rationalism" as well as theological liberalism and modernism. Recalling
debates sparked by Strauss's *Life of Jesus*, Fundamentalists argued that
traditional Christianity is incompatible with so-called higher criticism
as well as other forms of rationalistic modern thought. "The keystone,"
Martin explains, "was and is the inerrancy of Scripture, meaning not
only that the Bible is the sole and infallible rule of faith and practice,
but also that it is scientifically and historically reliable. Thus, evolution
could not be true, miracles really did happen just as the Bible describes
them, and on Judgment Day all who have ever lived will be assigned for
eternity to heaven or hell, both of which really do exist. Any attempt
to interpret these or other features of Scripture as myths or allegories
strikes at the very root of Christian faith and must be resisted with every
fiber of one's being."[19] In addition to a belief in scriptural inerrancy and
an apocalyptic vision of history, Fundamentalists shared with Evangelicals and Pentecostals the conviction that a personal relationship with
Jesus Christ is necessary for salvation.

During the early decades of the twentieth century, some tenets of
American Fundamentalism resembled aspects of European neoorthodoxy. Most important, both movements rejected the Enlightenment
faith in reason and humanistic belief in progress. Faced with the devasta-

tion modernity brought in its wake, Fundamentalists and neoorthodoxy called for a return to the two most basic principles of the Reformed tradition, which, they agreed, are God's transcendence and human sinfulness. Where they continued to differ most clearly was in their interpretation of the Word of God. Whereas American Fundamentalists extend the tradition of Protestant scholasticism by restricting God's Word to the purportedly literal words of scripture, neoorthodoxy, especially in the work of a theologian like Barth, remains committed to the omnipotent will of God and thus places no limits on where or how his Word can be revealed. For Barth, Fundamentalism's biblical literalism is another form of idolatry; for Fundamentalists, Barth's freedom of the Word leaves no norm with which to distinguish true from false "revelations."

From colonial times to the present, Fundamentalists have not only promulgated their gospel by the printed word but also promoted religious rallies and crusades, which prefigure twentieth-century mass media and entertainment. During World War I, one of the most popular evangelists was former professional baseball player Billy Sunday. Setting a pattern that Graham and many other preachers would follow, Sunday combined virulent anticommunism with a spirited defense of capitalism to create a religious nationalism that was well suited to the era. When he went so far as to attack the popular Social Gospel movement as "godless social service nonsense," wealthy businessmen like Rockefeller, Morgan, Carnegie, Wanamaker, McCormick, Armour, Swift, and Marshall Field rushed to offer him financial support.[20] Sunday was not the first to profit from the backing of the business establishment. When Charles Finney arrived in New York from England in 1825, a group of businessmen and bankers known as the Association of Gentlemen persuaded him to join their cause. This "pious power elite" was convinced that spiritual renewal would bring a kingdom to earth that would be profitable in more than spiritual ways. Finney told them what they wanted to hear by reassuring them that "the millennium may come in this country in three years."[21]

The outbreak of World War I and the 1917 Bolshevik Revolution provided Fundamentalists with an extraordinary opportunity to spread their message. These developments, they argued, were symptomatic of the illness and evil that unbelief breeds. Pointing to a direct link between modernism and communism, Sunday and his followers

> declared that Satan himself was directing the German war effort, and hinted strongly that it was part of the same process that had begun with the development of biblical criticism in German universities.

Modernism, they asserted, had turned Germany into a godless nation, and would do the same thing to America. The combination of prewar nativism, war-heightened patriotism, the rise of communism, and the rash of strikes, bombings, and advocacy of radical causes after the war helped produce the Red Scare, an atmosphere of aggressive suspicion that saw communists as responsible for many of the nation's troubles (particularly associated with labor) and hell-bent on gaining control of all American institutions.[22]

During the latter half of the nineteenth century and early part of the twentieth century, three additional "cultural issues" preoccupied Fundamentalists: birth control, temperance, and evolution. For many devout believers, sexual promiscuity and alcoholism were ills brought on by modernization and urbanization and thus were associated with newly arriving immigrants. As early as the 1870s, a variety of birth control devices were readily available, and in 1917 the National Birth Control League was established. In England, Annie Besant, who later became the head of the Theosophical Society, was put on trial for selling a booklet on contraception. When the promotion of birth control became more widely available in the United States, Anthony Comstock, founder of the New York Society for the Suppression of Vice, led a crusade asking Congress to pass a law prohibiting the sale and distribution of birth control devices through the mail across state lines. Though the effort to curb the use of birth control met some resistance, what little organized political activity there was proved ineffective. For many women, the alcoholism of their husbands was a more urgent issue than birth control. Large families, combined with excessive drinking, created conflicts and financial difficulties, which often led to the physical abuse of women. To address these personal and social problems, courageous women founded the Woman's Christian Temperance Union in 1874 and the Anti-Saloon League in 1895. As these organizations gained momentum, pastors began supporting their causes from their pulpits, and the political strength of the groups quickly grew. In 1919, Congress passed the Eighteenth Amendment to the Constitution, which prohibited the "manufacture, sale or transportation of intoxicating liquors," only to have the act repealed by the Twenty-first Amendment in 1933.

When Prohibition briefly became the law of the land, reformers turned their attention to the issue of evolution. As I have noted, what makes evolution so important for Fundamentalists is that it calls into question the literal truth of the Bible. If the account of creation is fiction rather than fact, they asked, how can the rest of the biblical narrative be trusted? Former secretary of state and presidential candidate William Jennings Bryan went so far as to declare that "all the ills from which America suffers can be traced back to the teaching of evolution. It would be better to destroy every other book ever written, and save just the first three verses of Genesis."[23] Then, as now, opponents of evolution made the public schools the center of their campaign by attempting to prohibit the teaching of the theory. Today's textbook wars can be traced back to the 1920s, when Texas and Oklahoma formally banned the use of all books that discussed the theory of evolution. The infamous 1925 Scopes trial in Dayton, Tennessee, pitted the Fundamentalist Bryan against Clarence Darrow, an urbane northerner originally trained as a Unitarian minister, and proved to be a complex turning point in the history of Fundamentalism. Though the victory of the opponents of evolution seemed decisive at the time, supporters of the theory actually won by losing. Since the judge and many members of the jury did not conceal their opposition to the teaching of evolution, the outcome of the trial was never in doubt. But when Darrow's portrayal of Scopes's critics as ignorant and backward spread around the world through H. L. Mencken's vivid accounts of the trial, the image of Fundamentalism suffered seemingly irreparable damage.[24] A few days after the trial ended, Bryan died unexpectedly, and the Fundamentalist movement was forced into a retreat, which was not reversed until the latter half of the twentieth century.

The similarities in the careers of leading Fundamentalists and Evangelicals from Billy Sunday to Billy Graham should not obscure differences of opinion about the relationship between religious commitment and political activity. In his study of contemporary Islam, entitled "Fundamentalist Impact on Education and Media," Majid Tehranian develops a helpful taxonomy, which can be used to distinguish different positions within and among Protestant Fundamentalism, Evangelicalism, and Pentecostalism (table 13).[25] As with any typology, the lines separating these positions are not hard-and-fast but overlap considerably. Furthermore, the strategies and tactics of different groups frequently change from time to time and situation to situation. While all four types can be found among today's neofoundationalists, the most influential groups are, predictably, the conservative and reformist.

After the end of World War II, the emergence of a national liberal political agenda, consumer culture, and the cold war combined to create conditions favorable to a widespread return of Fundamentalism and

Table 13. Religious Commitment and Political Engagement

STRATEGIES	AIMS	TACTICS
Conservative	Conserve tradition	Reactionary: alliance with state
Separatist	Avoid contamination	Withdrawal: underground activities
Reformist	Reform society	Accommodationist: electoral politics
Revolutionary	Overhaul society	Militant: propaganda, agitation, terror, violence

Source: Adapted from Majid Tehranian, "Fundamentalist Impact on Education and Media," in *Fundamentalisms and Society: Reclaiming the Sciences, the Family, and Education,* ed. Martin E. Marty and R. Scott Appleby (Chicago: University of Chicago Press, 1993), 323.

Evangelicalism. Though Billy Graham wielded considerable political influence in the early 1950s, most conservative Christians were reluctant to become actively involved in politics until the early 1970s. Three factors in the political, social, and cultural developments of the 1960s were decisive in changing this aversion to politics: (1) the expansion of government power and the growth of social welfare programs; (2) what was perceived as an increasingly active federal judiciary; and (3) the revolution in values brought about by the counterculture. As Robert Wuthnow and Matthew Lawson point out, during the period following World War II, there was an unprecedented increase in federal spending for national defense, public education, and entitlement programs. What began with Roosevelt's New Deal culminated in Johnson's New Society. By the sixties, social welfare programs and civil rights initiatives came together in a broad range of policy initiatives that religious and political conservatives found very troubling. With the rapid expansion of the federal government, there was an inevitable growth in regulations governing many aspects of life. In the polarized climate created by the cold war, many conservatives argued that these political and economic initiatives were heading the country down the road to socialism, which eventually would lead to communism. Such fears seemed to be confirmed by the actions of the federal judiciary, especially during the era of the Warren Court (1953–69). In the 1950s, the growing Soviet threat led to the resurgence of anticommunism and, correspondingly, a marked rise in nationalism and patriotism. With Joseph McCarthy fanning the flames of a second Red Scare, Congress passed legislation to insert "under God" into the pledge of allegiance; a year later a bill approving the inscription of "In God We Trust" on all currency and coins was approved. Less than a decade later, the country seemed to reverse direction when the Supreme Court banned school prayer (1963). Writing for the majority in two critical cases, Justice Black stated that it was "no part of the business of government to compose official prayers." The following year, the Court ruled that Bible reading in schools is unconstitutional. As one of the most outspoken critics of these decisions, Graham declared that the ruling was "a most dangerous trend" and signaled "another step toward secularism in the United States."[26] For many conservatives, these decisions represented a further move to the left that had begun with *Brown v. Board of Education of Topeka* in 1954. One Alabama legislator declared that the justices had "put Negroes in the schools and now they've driven God out."[27]

When the decade of the sixties opened with the election of the first Catholic president, the concerns of right-wing Fundamentalists and Evangelical Protestants deepened. Matters were made worse when conservative values seemed to collapse under the pressure of the counterculture's three-part agenda of civil rights, opposition to the war in Vietnam, and sexual liberation. Throughout the sixties, most Fundamentalists and Evangelicals remained ardent segregationists. "They attacked the twentieth-century civil rights movement as their spiritual ancestors had attacked the nineteenth-century abolitionists and feminist movements. What they saw was what their predecessors had seen—not a struggle for justice but a conspiracy of atheism, political radicalism and sexual libertinism."[28] It is important to note that variations of these views were held not only by rank-and-file segregationists but also by Evangelical leaders like Billy Graham, Jerry Falwell, Pat Robinson, and Bob Jones. Support of the civil rights movement often went hand in hand with support of the antiwar movement, thereby creating further suspicions among religious conservatives. As ardent anticommunists, the New Religious Right interpreted opposition to the war as support for communism and thus saw the "conspiracy of atheism" and "political radicalism" at work in the antiwar movement. Although the New Left was considerably more critical of communism than the previous generation, the New Religious Right believed that opposition to the war in Vietnam was tantamount to support for the Soviet Union and Mao's China. From this point of view, the antiwar movement reflected the erosion of political institutions that signaled national decline. At the same time that the political situation was unraveling, personal morality appeared to be collapsing; the New Religious Right saw in the sexual revolution the demise of the traditional family structure upon which society supposedly rests. For Fundamentalists and Evangelicals, four dates mark pivotal developments:

1960 Federal Drug Administration approval of the sale of Enovid as a birth control pill

1969 Stonewall—the beginning of gay militancy

1972 Congressional passage of the Equal Rights Amendment

1973 *Roe v. Wade* decision legalizing abortion

Each of these events was anathema to conservatives: the pill promotes sexual promiscuity, homosexuality is a crime, the ERA undercuts the "proper" role for women, and abortion is murder. While religious conservatives were seriously concerned about all of these issues, the legalization of abortion proved to be the tipping point in the emergence of the New Religious Right as a major political force. One of the primary factors in this development was a change in alliances among religious groups that previously had been suspicious of each other.

From the middle of the eighteenth century to the early 1970s, Protestant Fundamentalism and Evangelicalism had been largely anti-Catholic. During the 1960s, however, social and cultural changes brought about a realignment among religious groups that transformed the political landscape. Protestants from different denominations as well as Catholics realized that their agreement on social issues outweighed their disagreement on theological issues. Alan Wolfe, director of the Boisi Center for Religion and American Public Life at Boston University, points out, "the theological differences between conservative Catholics and Protestants that created five hundred years of conflict and violence have been superseded by political agreement. They are simply not interested in citing theology so long as they agree on abortion."[29] This new consensus grew out of an agreement about what has come to be known as "moral values" and "cultural issues." Richard Land, who is president of the Southern Baptist Convention's Ethics and Liberty Commission and has twice been appointed by President George W. Bush to the United States Commission on International Religious Freedom, speaks for many conservative Protestants when he declares: "I've got more in common with Pope John Paul II than I do with Jimmy Carter or Bill Clinton." "The real religious divide in the United States," Hanna Rosin points out, "isn't between the churched and the unchurched. It's between different kinds of believers."[30] With this realignment, doctrinal and theological differences *between* and *among* denominations become less important than differences *within* particular traditions. Rather than Presbyterian/Baptist, Protestant/Catholic, or Christian/Jew, the decisive fault line is now orthodox/progressive, rejectionist/accommodationist, and exclusivist/inclusivist. In addition to redrawing the religious and, by extension, the political map, the New Religious Right has hijacked the values issue. The term "cultural values" has become a code for a very limited set of ideological issues favored by conservatives. These values, which are ardently promoted, have more to do with the past than the future. Religious and political conservatives remain obsessed with the very same issues they have been arguing about for two hundred years: family values, reproductive rights, evolution, and religion in the schools. Within this schema, the draw of the past outweighs the call of the future. As change accelerates, an idealized past that never existed becomes more attractive than an uncertain future that cannot be avoided.

From the time of Luther's inward turn, the distinction between the public and the private both formed the basis of religious freedom and set limits upon religious expression. Within the bounds of the American Constitution, all individuals are free to believe or not believe as they choose but are not allowed to impose their beliefs on others. The distinction between interior faith and exterior expression led to the eventual separation of church and state. The Constitution effectively ratifies Luther's privatization and deregulation of religion: the public sphere may be regulated for the good of everyone but the private sphere must remain unregulated. The New Religious Right, however, attempts to reverse this long-standing tradition: while opposing government regulation of political institutions and the economy, they support the regulation of important private decisions. As government regulation shifts from the public to the private sphere, people are free to choose the schools their children attend or how to invest their retirement funds but are not free to terminate an unwanted pregnancy, end unbearable suffering, or conduct research that might lead to the cure of some of the most devastating diseases. In this inverted world, moral values become immoral and the right to life for some is a death sentence for others.[31]

Though individuals and groups in the New Religious Right agree on most value issues, important differences in emphasis often distinguish their positions. The greatest consensus is on the question of abortion. Regardless of denominational affiliation, the right to life is regarded as an absolute value that cannot be violated for any reason. There is less agreement about the question of evolution. Since Catholics are not as preoccupied with biblical inerrancy as Fundamentalists and Evangelicals, they have traditionally not been as concerned about teaching evolution. Indeed, under Pope John Paul II, there was considerably more openness to scientific investigation than there had been in the past. During the early months of his papacy, however, Pope Benedict XVI staked out a position on evolution that is virtually indistinguishable from that of Protestant Fundamentalism. On the issue of the government role in education, there has been little disagreement among members of the New Religious Right for the past four decades. Indeed, what was regarded as government interference in private education in the early 1970s played a major role in forging alliances among different religious groups. Church-related education was, of course, a long-established tradition among both Catholics and Protestants. But after the Supreme Court's 1963 desegregation decision, many new all-white schools opened in the South. At the same time, the conviction that public education was becoming increasingly secular led others to establish private religious schools or to educate their children at home. From the 1970s to the present day, the Christian school and homeschooling movements have been the fastest-growing sector of private education. As the number of children being educated outside public school systems has grown, resistance to federal regulation of education has increased and become more vocal. It is rarely noted, however, that the issue of education exposes inconsistencies and contradictions in the New Religious Right's political agenda. Though conservatives vehemently oppose government "interference" in private education, they strongly support federally funded school choice. Whether by vouchers or some other payment scheme, the expenditure of tax money for private education involves precisely the kind of government support for social welfare programs that conservatives claim they oppose.

The growing political power of the New Religious Right would not have been possible without the emergence of a new generation of religious leaders. Among the many figures who played major roles in the 1970s and 1980s, two in particular stand out: Jerry Falwell and Pat Robertson. What makes the careers of these two pastors so instructive is not only their extraordinary influence but also the fact that they represent alternative positions in the New Religious Right that are strictly parallel to the two poles of the counterculture we have considered. While agreeing on basic theological principles and sharing an appreciation for the importance of media and technology for spreading the Word of God, there are nonetheless subtle but important differences in the positions of Falwell and Robertson.³² Quentin Schultze points out that "in many respects, Robertson and Falwell represent two very different strands of conservative American Protestantism. Falwell's staunchly fundamentalist roots in independent Baptist religion are a far cry from Robertson's more ecumenical roots in the charismatic movement. Each of these university founders comes to higher education with his own religio-cultural baggage. Robertson's brand of conservative Protestantism is generally more open to cross-denominational association and to nonbiblical authority, including reason and personal guidance from the Holy Spirit."³³

In 1956, Falwell became the first pastor of the new Thomas Road Baptist Church in Lynchburg, Virginia. In the following years, a combination of political finesse and media savvy enabled him to build one of the most powerful religious organizations and media empires in the country. A committed segregationist, Falwell founded the Lynchburg Christian Academy (1967) as a private school for whites only. By the early 1970s, however, he had adapted to the times; the academy revised its admissions policy to admit African Americans and the church started an outreach program to minority communities. The school quickly expanded and became Liberty University, which currently has 8,000 on-campus and 15,000 online students. During the early years of their ministries, the most important difference between Falwell and Robertson concerned their positions on the relation between religion and politics. In a manner similar to the young people in the sixties who believed that social change was impossible without authentic experience, Falwell insisted on the primacy of the personal relation to God and the relative unimportance of politics. "Our only purpose on earth," he claimed, "is to know Christ and to make him known. Believing the Bible as I do, I would find it impossible to stop preaching the pure saving Gospel of Jesus Christ and begin doing anything else—including the fighting of communism or participating in the civil rights reform. . . . Preachers are not called to be politicians, but to be soul winners."³⁴ In this, as in other matters, it did not take Falwell long to change his mind; when he cofounded the Moral Majority with Timothy LaHaye, he used his media empire to develop a formidable political machine. LaHaye was instrumental in founding the Council for National Policy, which Craig Unger describes as "a low-profile but powerful coalition of billionaire industrialists, fundamentalist preachers and right-wing tacticians. . . . Though the membership is secret, the rolls have reportedly included Falwell and Pat Robertson; top right-wing political strategists Richard Viguerie, Ralph Reed and Paul Weyrich; Republican senators Jesse Helms and Lauch Faircloth (both of North Carolina), Don Nickles (Oklahoma), and Trent Lott (Mississippi);

and [erstwhile] Republican representatives Dick Armey and Tom Delay (both of Texas)."[35] Commenting on his shift in attitude about political involvement, Falwell recalled: "When we announced that Moral Majority was a political organization, not a religious one, that we welcomed Jews and Catholics and Protestants and Mormons and even nonreligious people who shared our views of family and abortion, strong national defense, and Israel, a great deal of opposition erupted inside our ranks."[36] But within a very short time, resistance gave way to enthusiastic support, and the Moral Majority began to exercise enormous political influence from the local to the national level.

Though Robertson briefly shared some of Falwell's misgivings about mixing religion and politics, he quickly realized that the only way to implement his religious agenda was through organized political action. He established his Freedom Council to develop a grassroots network devoted to advancing Evangelical interests and promoting conservative causes. Explaining his strategy, Robertson writes: "There are 175,000 political precincts in America. My goal was to have ten trained activists in each precinct. I was playing for the long haul, and I knew the answer was to move into the precincts, get to know the people and understand their needs and desires, and to build an organization that would be effective for local school-board races, city council races, legislative races, Congressional races, and ultimately the presidency."[37] By effectively using his radio and television programs to disseminate his ideas and raise money, Robertson laid the groundwork for his 1988 presidential bid. During that campaign, Robertson and Jack Kemp, whose first campaign manager was LaHaye, joined forces in a bid to block Vice President George H. W. Bush in the 1988 Michigan primary. Though they were not successful, their tactical alliance sent a clear signal about the growing political power of conservative Protestantism. Robertson came in first or second in Hawaii, Nevada, Alaska, Minnesota, and South Dakota but was not able to overcome his loss in New Hampshire. His campaign taught religious conservatives an important lesson: it is not necessary to win political office to have a significant influence on the outcome of elections.

LaHaye's experience with Falwell proved decisive for his later career. When Jimmy Carter, a self-proclaimed born-again Christian, declared his candidacy for the presidency, he initially enjoyed widespread support among religious conservatives as a result of his decision to make the restoration of the integrity of the family a cornerstone of his campaign. Indeed, Carter went so far as to declare: "There can be no more urgent priority for the next administration than to see that any decision our government makes is designed to honor and support and strengthen the American family."[38] After the election, however, Evangelicals began to wonder whether Carter was their kind of a conservative. While disillusioned by Carter's failure to cut taxes and curtail welfare, the issue that led to a split with the New Religious Right was his support of the Equal Rights Amendment. After promising to strengthen the family, Carter backed a policy that, in the eyes of many religious conservatives, violated the relation between men and women that God had ordained and thereby weakened the family. With support declining among the Evangelicals who had been crucial for his election, Carter met with a group that included Falwell and LaHaye as well as Oral Roberts and Jim Bakker. When they pressed him on his position on the ERA, Carter's response was not what his interrogators wanted to hear. Martin reports LaHaye's account of his exchange with the president. LaHaye asked Carter "why he as a Christian and pro-family man, as he protested to be, was in favor of the Equal Rights Amendment in view of the fact that it would be so harmful to the family, and he gave some off-the-wall answer that the Equal Rights Amendment was good for the family. Well, I knew when he said that that he was out to lunch. We had a man in the White House who professed to be a Christian, but didn't understand how un-Christian his administration was." Returning to his hotel after the meeting, LaHaye recalled, "I stood there and I prayed this prayer: 'God, we have got to get this man out of the White House and get someone in here who will be aggressive about bringing back traditional moral values."[39] It is no exaggeration to claim that, at that moment, Ronald Reagan effectively became the next president of the United States.

Although Reagan was not nearly as religious as Carter, his so-called moral values and political ideology were much more in keeping with the beliefs of the New Religious Right. In a 1976 interview during the presidential campaign, Reagan claimed to have had a born-again experience, which brought him to realize "a hunger in this land for a spiritual revival; a return to a belief in moral absolutes—the same morals upon which the nation was founded."[40] When coming from Reagan, such statements always seemed to express political expediency more than religious conviction. He and his backers understood the implications of the Fourth Great Awakening before most other politicians, commentators, and scholars. Reagan arrived on the national scene during a speech he gave supporting Barry Goldwater at the 1964 Republican National Convention. Looking back on his work with Goldwater, political operative Morton Blackwell reported almost three decades later that he had advised his fellow conservatives: "If you can identify some segment of the population which is not active and can be activated, or some segment that is miscast in their current party affiliation and can be switched over to your side, you're going to change things dramatically."[41] Reagan and his team realized that the segment they needed to target was the emerging New Religious Right. With all the skill of an accomplished actor, Reagan increasingly invoked religious language to deliver his political message. Confessing faith in divine providence as well as "the divine origin" of scripture, he proceeded to declare: "The Bible contains an answer to just about everything and every problem that confronts us, and I wonder sometimes why we don't recognize that one Book could solve a lot of problems for us." By making religion an instrument for promoting his policies, Reagan quietly began eroding the long-established separation of church and state, which was the one principle of the founders that he and his devout followers chose to ignore. His support for school prayer, creationism, and the right to life were only the most obvious examples of his propensity to moralize politics in what he cast as the nation's struggle for redemption. In crafting his foreign and defense policies, Reagan appropriated the Fundamentalist and Evangelical imagery of an apocalyptic struggle between good and evil to transform politics and economics into a religious campaign. The more fervent he became, the more actively the New Religious Right supported him. Jerry Falwell once went so far as to declare that President Reagan and Vice President Bush were "God's instruments in rebuilding America."[42]

Reagan's "religious" turn set the direction for the future of politics in the United States for decades to come. It is important to pause to consider just how much the role of religion in American life changed during the latter half of the twentieth century. In 1960, John Kennedy had to travel to Houston to reassure Fundamentalists and Evangelicals, who were nervous about the prospect of a Catholic in the White House, that he believed "in an America where the separation of church and state is absolute—where no Catholic prelate would tell the President (should he be Catholic) how to act, and no Protestant minister would tell his parishioners for whom to vote—where no church or church school is granted any public funds or public preference—and where no man is denied public office merely because his religion differs from the President who might appoint him or the people who might elect him."[43] By 2004, this situation had changed completely: Cardinal Josef Ratzinger, with the obvious support of Pope John Paul II, intervened in the American presidential campaign *against* the Roman Catholic John Kerry and in support of the Evangelical Protestant George W. Bush. Ratzinger wrote a letter to American bishops instructing them to deny communion to any Catholic candidate who refused to criminalize abortion. Underscoring his point, the future pope wrote that "a Catholic politician consistently campaigning and voting for permissive abortion and euthanasia laws" was "guilty of formal cooperation with evil and so unworthy to present himself for Holy Communion." In a highly informative and provocative article, "Bush, Benedict, and the Fate of the Republic," Jack Miles makes a plausible case that Ratzinger's intervention tipped the election in Bush's favor. Ratzinger's letter, Miles argues,

> created a large and public question about John Kerry's status as a Roman Catholic. The result was a shift of only six percent, presumably the most conservative six percent, within the Catholic portion of the American electorate. (Recall that we are speaking of six percent of only the Catholic fifth of the general electorate.) Yet this small shift was enough to turn the election in three closely contested states. "Without this shift," political analyst Sidney Blumenthal recently wrote, "Kerry would have had a popular majority of a million votes. Three states—Ohio, Iowa and New Mexico—moved into Bush's column on the votes of the Catholic 'faithful.'" Arguably, then, Ratzinger won the election for Bush.[44]

The difference between the 1960 and 2004 presidential elections shows both how much and how little things have changed.

The New Religious Right sees the hand of God in the conservatives' rise to power during the past several decades. Commenting on the re-election of George W. Bush, Paul Weyrich, who coined the term *Moral Majority* and was the first director of Joseph Coors's Heritage Foundation, confidently declared: "God is indeed a Republican. He must be. His hand helped reelect a president, with a popular mandate." Echoing Billy Graham's reaction to Eisenhower's election, Bob Jones, founder and president of Bob Jones University, who played a decisive role in the 2004 election, read an open letter to Bush in his university's chapel: "in your reelection, God has graciously granted America—though she doesn't deserve it—a reprieve from the agenda of paganism. You have been given a mandate. . . . Don't equivocate. Put your agenda on the front burner and let it boil. . . . Honor the Lord and He will honor you."[45] In these pronouncements, Evangelicals apply the traditional Trinitarian theology of history to current events. Having fallen from perfection and become mired in darkness and evil as a result of human error, the world is rushing toward a heavenly kingdom, which will be ushered in by God's apocalyptic intervention. In contemporary neofoundationalism, the two most popular versions of this ancient story are dominion theology and dispensationalism.

In terms of the typology of religion and politics I have presented, dominion theology, also known as Christian reconstructionism, is the more extreme alternative. While not necessarily supporting the use of violence or terrorism, dominionists call for revolutionary change. Citing Genesis 1:28, they promote a radical Christianization of the entire world. Martin points out that one influential reconstructionist goes so far as to claim that Christians "must realize that pluralism is a myth. God and His law must rule all nations. . . . At no point in Scripture do we read that God teaches, supports, or condones pluralism. Clearly our founding fathers had no intention of supporting pluralism for they saw that the Bible tolerates no such view." The politically well-connected James Dobson, founder and leader of Focus on the Family, is the most prominent representative of dominion theology. Though this theological vision is extreme, many items on his political agenda are familiar: the deregulation of business and education; lower taxes; the elimination of welfare, the "death tax," and social security; the abolition of public schools and establishment of nationwide homeschooling; and the reinforcement of the death penalty, which, in a page borrowed from some of their Islamist counterparts, Dobson and his followers insist should be delivered by stoning.[46] What makes dominion theology distinctive and extreme is its call for establishing a theocracy in the United States.

Dispensationalism is apparently less radical but perhaps more pernicious. This theological schema, which lies deep in the American grain, has recently surfaced in Evangelicals ranging from Graham, Falwell, and Robertson to Hal Lindsey and Timothy LaHaye. After John Nelson Darby brought dispensational theology to the United States from England in the early nineteenth century, it spread quickly through the ministry of Dwight Moody and the efficient distribution network created by the Moody Bible Institute. During the latter half of the twentieth century the center of this fast-growing movement shifted to the Dallas Theological Seminary. While apocalyptic visions have long played an important role in the history of Christianity, the preoccupation with the end of history is the distinguishing feature of dispensational theology. Rejecting any hint of divine immanence and all forms of human progress, dispensationalists view history as a story of decline from which the elect must be redeemed by God's apocalyptic intervention. According to this religious schema, we are now living through the Last Days, or End Times, which lead to the Rapture, when Christ returns to take members of the True

Church to heaven. The period known as the Tribulation culminates in the battle of Armageddon, when Christ and his Christian soldiers defeat the infidels. Though God alone is supposed to know the time and place of Christ's return, dispensationalists have never been hesitant to interpret current events in apocalyptic terms.

In recent years, the two most influential dispensationalists have been Lindsey and LaHaye. Though LaHaye has been active in politics for more than thirty years, his real power lies in his writings and the supporting media empire he has created. There are more than seventy million copies of his immensely popular Left Behind novels in print. Indeed, LaHaye has sold more books than any living author except J. K. Rowling, who is the author of the Harry Potter series. He has tapped into the surge of interest in dispensationalism created by Lindsey's popular 1970 novel and accompanying video *The Late Great Planet Earth*, which was followed a decade later by his equally influential *The 1980s: Countdown to Armageddon*. While Lindsey recites the familiar litany of war, famine, earthquakes, and false messiahs, his diagnosis of developments portending the End is closely tied to his account of actual historical events. The three most decisive signs of the times, he claims, are the movement toward "One-World Religion," reflected in contemporary ecumenism, "One-World Government," evident in the growing influence of the United Nations, and "One-World Currency," which began with the introduction of the euro and is facilitated by the emergence of global financial networks.[47] The groundwork for the impending catastrophic struggle was laid in the 1970s, but the final battle between good and evil, Lindsey predicts, will not occur until the 1980s. The players in this apocalyptic war will be the United States and the Soviet Union, and the site of the decisive showdown will be Afghanistan. According to Lindsey's prophecy, the most obvious sign of the coming of the Messiah is Russia's emergence as a dominant world power. With disturbing prescience, he identifies three interrelated crises: the power of oil, the power of Islam, and the power of Russia. In Lindsey's reading of world events, Russia will use the conquest of Afghanistan as a springboard for the overthrow of Iran, which will give it dominance in the Persian Gulf and control over world oil supplies. This situation is made all the more precarious by the growth of Soviet military power and the relative decline in America's military and moral strength. Since he regards communism as a religion, Lindsey sees the coming conflict as a religious war. The loss of faith in Christian values and in the free-enterprise system makes America vulnerable to external threats. The only solution, Lindsey concludes, is the restoration of

Christian values and military strength: since "the Bible supports build-ing a strong military force," it is "time to use superior technology to cre-ate the world's strongest military power. Only this will stop the Soviet Union's rush to war."[48]

Lindsey's prophecy, written during the 1980 presidential campaign, reads like a position paper for Reagan's defense policy and Star Wars initiative. What most united Reagan and the religious right was a Man-ichaean view of the world in which the powers of good and evil are locked in a life-and-death struggle. The defining image of the Reagan presidency was, of course, "the evil empire," which effectively combined apocalyptic Christianity with George Lucas's *Star Wars* to create a script as simple as black and white. Reagan first introduced the term *evil empire* in a 1983 speech to the National Association of Evangelicals. The USSR, he warned, is "the focus of evil in the modern world."[49] While challeng-ing Gorbachev to tear down the Berlin Wall, Reagan proposed building a wall as high as the heavens. Members of the New Religious Right sup-ported his Strategic Defense Initiative (i.e., Star Wars) by forming the Religious Coalition for a Moral Defense Policy, which quickly became a well-oiled lobbying machine with considerable influence on Capitol Hill and in the Pentagon.

Technology might provide the answers to some problems, but dis-pensationalists feared it also harbored other troubling possibilities. With surprising accuracy, in 1969 Lindsey confidently predicted devel-opments that would change the world in the next two decades: "Do you believe it will be possible for people to be controlled economically? In our computerized society, where we are all 'numbered' from birth to death, it seems completely plausible that some day in the near future the numbers racket will consolidate and we will have just one number for all our business, money, and credit transactions. Leading members of the business community are now planning that all money matters will be handled electronically."[50] What Lindsey foresees is what I have elsewhere described as "network culture."[51] Remarkably, he was one of the first to recognize not only the religious significance of information, communi-cations, and networking technologies but also the ways in which they would transform the world by changing the global socioeconomic in-frastructure.[52] It was left for LaHaye to develop and popularize the far-reaching implications of Lindsey's insights.

In the Left Behind novels, the period leading up to the end of the world is presided over by the sinister counterpart of the Christian Trin-ity: Satan, False Prophet, and Antichrist. In his series of twelve novels and supporting CDs, DVDs, videos, and video games, LaHaye tells the tale of the Antichrist's creation of a totalitarian system that realizes Lindsey's worst fears about the global unification of religion, government, and money. Borrowing an image from the biblical book of Revelation, LaHaye labels this global network "the Beast system." The image of the Beast, which is popular among apocalyptic writers, is drawn from Revelation 15:18:

> It was allowed to give breath to the image of the beast, so that it could speak, and could cause all who would not worship the image to be put to death. Moreover, it caused everyone, great and small, rich and poor, slave and free to be branded with a mark on his right hand or forehead, and no one was allowed to buy or sell unless he bore this beast's mark, either name or number. (Here is the key; and anyone who has intelligence may work out the number of the beast. The number represents a man's name, and the numerical value of its letters is six hundred and sixty-six.)

Through the deft deployment of the most sophisticated technologies, the Antichrist weaves a web of deceit that enables him to exercise control over the masses by persuasion rather than force. Between Lindsey's initial prophecy and LaHaye's dispensationalist novels, both the world and technology changed. The collapse of the Soviet Union revealed the weakness of centralized systems of control and the strength of decentralized, distributed networks operating in financial markets and of the technologies that make them possible. "Despite an initial penchant for totalitarian rule," Glenn Shuck explains, "Antichrist quickly realizes that decentralization makes for more efficient leadership. LaHaye and Jenkins [his coauthor] differ from their forebears in their implicit awareness of network imperatives. . . . Decentralized systems, in which power is distributed throughout flexible networks, prove more responsive, adaptive and less vulnerable to internal failure or external attack."[53]

As I have suggested, the end of the cold war marked the collapse of a bipolar world in which the opposition between good and evil is readily identifiable. LaHaye's interpretation of network culture as the Beast System captures the pervasive anxiety created by the emergence of worldwide webs in which power is exercised invisibly, national sovereignty is compromised, money circulates at the speed of light, and individual autonomy all but disappears. As the network becomes more complex, uncertainty increases. The Antichrist decentralizes his system, but not all nodes are equally important. In the most recent Left Behind novels,

LaHaye shifts the privileged node in the global network from New York to New Babylon. Babylon, of course, was the capital of the ancient territory of Mesopotamia, which is now occupied by Iraq.

The more dominionist and dispensationalist literature one reads, the more difficult it becomes to know whether prophecy is reflecting or determining historical developments. In one of its guises, religion, we have seen, provides schemata that give people a sense of meaning and purpose. For politicians seeking to interpret the world for themselves and others, simplistic religious schemata seem to provide a way to understand a world that is on the edge of chaos. Though the "evil other" changes from communism to so-called radical Islam, the structure of the struggle as well as the narrative of events remains the same. As long ago as 1985, Frances FitzGerald discerned the growing political impact of the dispensationalist vision of history. Commenting on the division of the world among the United States, the Soviet Union, and the Third World, she writes:

> Where this map came from and why it so appeals to Americans in spite of all we know to the contrary are perhaps key questions of American foreign policy. The first question is easily answered, for there is a well-marked trail in American intellectual history leading to the prototype. In the eighteen-eighties and nineties, those Protestant theologians who took their stand on Biblical inerrancy read the Books of Daniel and Revelation as a detailed set of prophecies for the events leading up to the return of Christ and the beginning of his thousand-year reign on earth. According to these prophecies, the Beast and the Antichrist would appear and gather the heathen nations together and assemble a huge army; there would be a period of Tribulations, during which the faith of Christians would be tested, and then a world war between the heathen hordes and Christ's army of saints, culminating in the Battle of Armageddon. The theologians identified Russia as the Biblical land called Ros, where the Beast would appear, and America as the country that would provide the armies of the saints, since America alone contained the saving remnant of Bible-believing Christians.[54]

In the years since these words were written, the explicit and implicit influence of the New Religious Right has grown exponentially. Susan Harding reports that "President George Bush frequently consulted dispensationalist preacher Billy Graham during the Persian Gulf Crisis, including the day he ordered the bombing of Baghdad and started the war."[55] Less than a month before the start of the Gulf War, John Walvoord, former president of the dispensationalist Dallas Theological Seminary, published *Armageddon, Oil and the Middle East Crisis*. Zondervan Publishing House, which is also Lindsey's publisher, quickly sold 600,000 copies, and Billy Graham purchased another 300,000 copies and distributed them free.[56] Evangelical publications, radio programs, and televangelists proclaimed the Gulf War to be "a step toward Armageddon." When their predictions did not come true, these self-proclaimed prophets followed standard operating procedures and recalibrated their timetable. A decade later, George W. Bush, who credits Billy Graham with enabling him to establish a personal relationship with his savior Jesus Christ, extended his father's "new world order" by recasting Reagan's "evil empire" as "the axis of evil." His second inaugural address is as much a religious sermon as a political speech:

> America has need of idealism and courage because we have essential work at home, the unfinished work of American freedom. In a world moving toward liberty, we are determined to show the meaning and promise of liberty. . . .
>
> And now we will extend this vision by reforming great institutions to serve the needs of our time. To give every American a stake in the promise and future of our country, we will bring the highest standards to our schools and build an ownership society. . . . By making every citizen an agent of his or her own destiny, we will give our fellow Americans greater freedom from want and fear and make our society more prosperous and just and equal.
>
> In America's ideal of freedom, the public interest depends on the private character, on integrity and tolerance toward others, and the rule of conscience in our own lives. Self-government relies, in the end, on the government of the self. The edifice of character is built in families, supported by communities with standards and sustained in our national life by the truths of Sinai, the Sermon on the Mount, the words of the Koran and the varied faiths of our people.

While such occasions always invite excessive language, it is a serious mistake to consider this vision a matter of rhetoric rather than substance. Far from hermeneutical supplements to the real world, interpretive religious schemata actually determine the structure of reality itself. For those who understand the theology of history that guides Bush's domestic and foreign policies, his perfunctory nod to the Koran and other faiths rings hollow. In a complex interconnected world, the simplistic dualism that informs dispensationalism harbors disaster, which for true believers is the price of redemption.

MARKETING THE NEW AGE

When you click on www.timlahaye.com, you are greeted by a voice reading 1 Thessalonians 4:16–17:

> Because at the word of command, at the sound of the archangel's voice and God's trumpet-call, the Lord himself will descend from heaven; first the Christian dead will rise, then we who are left alive shall join them, caught up in the clouds to meet the Lord in the air.

The audio is accompanied by a sophisticated animation depicting the Rapture. Though LaHaye recognizes the dangers of the new world order, he freely uses the Beast System to spread his message about the temptations of network culture and to proclaim the urgent need to turn to Jesus Christ. In *The Race for the 21st Century*, he comments on his use of information and communications technologies in his ministry and political activity: "Having established my first network (the American Coalition for Traditional Values, which set up 435 congressional district pastor-chairmen for the 1984 election), I was fascinated by this futuristic concept."[57] In a more recent article in, of all places, *Vanity Fair*, LaHaye boasts: "Now we have media like we've never had before—alternative media, the Internet and Fox News."[58] Elaborating the growing importance of media, he makes a passing reference to certain similarities between his reading of new technologies and the analyses of popular futurists like Alvin and Heidi Toffler. This brief remark is considerably more suggestive than LaHaye and his followers realize.

During the late 1960s and 1970s, the Tofflers' account of the information revolution was extremely influential and especially popular among erstwhile members of the counterculture. Although the reaction to what many regarded as the decadence of the sixties played an important role in the rise of the New Religious Right, I have argued that there are unexpected similarities between Evangelicals and Pentecostals, on the one hand, and, on the other, members of the counterculture who were persuaded that what the world needed most was transformative personal experience. Furthermore, both conservative Evangelicals and countercultural hippies share a commitment to the privatization, deregulation, and decentralization of all systems and networks. I have also noted the resemblance between the values of the counterculture and the organizational logic of PCs connected in distributed networks. The interrelation of religion, the counterculture, and information technologies lies at the heart of the Tofflers' analysis. LaHaye agrees with many of the Tofflers' insights but profoundly disagrees with their assessment of the developments they consider. While LaHaye regards network culture as a sure sign of the looming apocalypse, the Tofflers see it as the sign of the dawn of an era of plenty and riches that promises to bring personal and social fulfillment. The Tofflers' alternative reading of the recent past and approaching future leads to a different understanding of the religious significance and political stakes of media and technology.

Echoing ancient theologies of history in his 1980 book *The Third Wave*, Alvin Toffler divides human history into three eras: agricultural (8000 BCE–1750 CE), industrial (1750–1955), and a new age, which has yet to be named (1955–present). He is unsure what to name this new age but has no doubt about the pervasive changes it brings: "A new civilization is emerging in our lives, and blind men everywhere are trying to suppress it. This new civilization brings with it new family styles; changed ways of working, loving, and living; a new economy; new political conflicts; and beyond all this an altered consciousness as well."[59] A decade and a half later, the Tofflers were still uncertain what to name the third age but were even more convinced of its revolutionary significance. When they published a condensed version of their argument, entitled *Creating a New Civilization: The Politics of the Third Wave*, in 1995, the Speaker of the U.S. House of Representatives, Newt Gingrich, wrote the foreword. It is worth noting that the Tofflers' book was published by Turner Publications, which was a subsidiary of the Turner Broadcasting System, owned and operated by Ted Turner. Having created CNN in the same year that the *Third Wave* was published, Turner was one of the first to understand the implications of network culture. Gingrich, who is from the home state of CNN, had worked with the Tofflers ever since he read Alvin Toffler's influential book *Future Shock* in 1970. In the few brief pages immodestly entitled "A Citizen's Guide to the 21st Century," Gingrich assumes the prophetic voice that became one of his trademarks: "The Tofflers correctly understand that the development and distribution of information has now become the central productivity and power activity of the human race. From world financial markets to worldwide, twenty-four-hour-a-day distribution of news via CNN to the breakthroughs of the biological revolution and their impact on health and agriculture production—on virtually every front we see the information revolution changing the fabric, pace and substance of our lives."[60] As the Contract with America soon would make clear, the Tofflers' analysis of the new age in which we are supposed to be living became the game plan for Gingrich's political program.

In a remarkable anticipation of the role Samuel Huntington's theory of the clash of civilizations would play in political debate at the end of the decade, the Tofflers argue that people are misinterpreting the radical changes that are occurring: "The *wave theory of conflict* tells us that the main conflict we face is not between Islam and the West or 'the rest against the West,' as recently suggested by Samuel Huntington. Nor is America in decline, as Paul Kennedy declares. Nor are we, in Francis Fukuyama's phrase, facing the 'end of history.' The deepest economic and strategic change of all is the coming division of the world into three distinct, differing, and potentially clashing civilizations that cannot be mapped using the conventional definitions."[61] With agriculture society quickly fading, the most important crisis facing the twenty-first century is the conflict between waning industrial society and emerging information society. The Tofflers describe this shift in terms of the movement from massified to de-massified societies, or, in terms I have been using, from centralized to decentralized societies:

> The Second Wave created mass societies that reflected and required mass production. In the Third Wave, brain-based economies, mass production (which could almost be considered the defining mark of industrial society) is already an outmoded form. De-massified production—short runs of highly customized products—is the new cutting edge of manufacture. Mass marketing gives way to market segmentation and "particle marketing," paralleling the change in production. Old industrial-style behemoths collapse of their own mass and face destruction. Labor unions in the mass manufacturing sector shrink. The mass media are de-massified in parallel with production, and giant TV networks shrivel as new channels proliferate. The family system, too, becomes de-massified: the nuclear family, once the modern standard, becomes a minority form while single-parent households, remarried couples, childless families and live-alones proliferate.
>
> The entire structure of society, therefore, changes as the homogeneity of Second Wave society is replaced by the heterogeneity of Third Wave civilization. Massification gives way to de-massification.[62]

While stressing that de-massification will change *every* aspect of life, the Tofflers place special emphasis on economics and politics. Information and network technologies transform the very infrastructure of the global economy. As we have seen, new technologies create the need for and possibility of new financial products, which, in turn, change investment strategies and restructure world financial markets. When the world is wired, walls fall and borders become permeable. Suggesting an apocalyptic vision consistent with Evangelicals and a fascination with altered states of consciousness worthy of aging hippies, the Tofflers write:

> As economies are transformed by the Third Wave, they are compelled to surrender part of their sovereignty and to accept increasing economic and cultural intrusions from one another. Thus, while poets and intellectuals of economically backward regions write national anthems, poets and intellectuals of the Third Wave states sing the virtues of a "borderless" world and "planetary consciousness." The resulting collisions, reflecting the sharply differing needs of two radically different civilizations, could provoke some of the worst bloodshed in the years to come.[63]

The Rapture, it seems, can be worldly as well as otherworldly.

The Tofflers map the oppositions between the Second and Third Waves onto international and domestic politics. They redraw the cold war opposition between the Soviet Union and the United States in terms of massified and de-massified economies and political systems. While communism remains stuck in the past of the Second Wave, with state regulation through centralized command-and-control structures, American democratic capitalism grows out of a commitment to privatization, deregulation, and decentralization. Since centralized systems cannot manage a decentralized world, the collapse of the Soviet Union, the Tofflers and Gingrich confidently predict, is inevitable. On the domestic front, the distinction between centralization and decentralization marks the difference between the Democratic and Republican Parties:

> The difference between the parties, however, is that while the Second Wave "nostalgia pushers" in the Democratic Party are concentrated in its core constituencies, their counterparts in the Republican Party tend to be found on its frenetic fringe. This leaves room for the center of the party, if it is inclusive and open to change, to seize the future—lock, stock and barrel. This is the message that Newt Gingrich, the Republican Speaker of the House of Representatives, has been trying, but so far with only limited success, to deliver to his own party. If Gingrich succeeds and the Democrats remain chained to their pre-computer ideology, they could, for good or for ill, be trampled in the political dust.[64]

From this point of view, liberal Democrats are still committed to the vestiges of socialism and industrialism representative of the Second Wave, and conservative Republicans seek to ride the crest of the Third Wave by ushering in the market-state. One of the centerpieces of this new age is the transformation of the U.S. military. "The new Army doctrine," Gingrich explains, "led to a more flexible, fast-paced, decentralized, information-rich system which assessed the battlefield, focused resources and utilized well-trained but very decentralized leadership to overwhelm an industrial-era opponent."[65] These reforms began under Bush I and were continued under Bush II. Gingrich appropriates the Tofflers' analysis to anticipate former Secretary of Defense Donald Rumsfeld's ill-fated effort to refashion the military by cutting its size, increasing the use of technology, and creating a mobile structure that resembles the operational logic of distributed networks. The extension of the Gulf War to the War with Iraq demonstrates the problems with this policy. With commanders on the ground clamoring for more troops, Rumsfeld's refusal to reconsider his assumptions testifies to the depth of his ideological commitments.

The emergence of Gingrich Republicans in the 1980s and 1990s reflected a very important demographic shift for both politics and religion. In his richly informative book *Selling God: American Religion in the Marketplace of Culture*, R. Laurence Moore points out:

> The United States never developed religiously based political parties, just as it never developed class-based political parties. Nonetheless, religious affiliation was part of the equation determining how people distinguished their political allies from their political enemies. From the Civil War until Richard Nixon, most northern white Protestants voted for the Republican party, leaving white southern Protestants, black Protestants (after 1932), Catholics, and Jews to form an unstable and normally unsuccessful electoral base for the Democratic party. Theological differences had little to do with the political differentiation. What mattered was the general cultural outlook of religious groups, as well as their place in the social hierarchy.[66]

By the 1980s, this situation was changing dramatically—party lines were shifting and, more important, Evangelicals were expanding their demographic base. The traditional line between upper-class mainline Protestants and lower-class Evangelicals, Pentecostals, and Fundamentalists began to erode as a growing number of middle- and even upper-class people were drawn to conservative Protestantism. In the spring of 2005, the *New York Times* ran a remarkable series of articles on class in America. One of the most interesting reports was entitled "On a Christian Mission to the Top: Evangelicals Set Their Sights on the Ivy League." Commenting on the growing power and influence of Evangelical Christians, Laurie Goodstein and David Kirkpatrick write:

> What has changed is the class status of evangelicals—Protestants who emphasize the authority of the Bible, the importance of a "born-again" conversion experience and spreading the faith. In 1929, the theologian H. Richard Niebuhr described born-again Christianity as the "religion of the disinherited." But over the last 40 years, evangelicals have pulled steadily closer in income and education to mainline Protestants in the historically affluent establishment of denominations. In the process they have overturned the old social pecking order in which "Episcopalian," for example, was a code word for upper class, and "fundamentalist" or "evangelical" shorthand for lower. Evangelicals are now increasingly likely to be college graduates and in the top income brackets. Evangelical C.E.O.'s pray together on monthly conference calls, evangelical investment bankers study the Bible over lunch on Wall Street, and deep-pocketed evangelical donors gather at golf courses for conferences restricted to those who can give more than $200,000 annually to Christian causes.[67]

The Republican Party was quick to realize the enormous political significance of this change. As the class status of Evangelicals shifts, the geography of the political landscape literally changes. The New Religious Right is a largely rural and exurban phenomenon—its center of gravity tilts away from the coasts to the South and Southwest and from cities to the country and suburbs. The most important index of this change is the explosion of megachurches and their rapidly expanding media networks.

On Billy Graham's slick Web site (www.billygraham.org), there is a statement of the articles of faith espoused by members of his Evangelistic Association. The list concludes with the claim that members believe "in using every modern means of communication available to us to spread the Gospel of Jesus Christ throughout the world." Ever since Luther's recognition of the importance of print, Protestants have understood the role of media and communications technology in their religious mission. Though somewhat counterintuitive, the most media savvy Protestants are conservatives rather than liberals. Committed to spreading the Word, Fundamentalists and Evangelicals have always used every technological means at their disposal. From the Reformation to the early twentieth century, the most effective technology remained print. In this country, the origin of modern mass culture and mass media can be traced directly to eighteenth- and nineteenth-century Protestantism. The crusades of televangelists like Billy Graham, Jimmy Swaggart, Jim and Tammy Faye Bakker, Rick Warren, Ted Haggard, Joel Osteen, and countless others are latter-day versions of revivals that accompanied the earlier Great Awakenings. Appearances to the contrary notwithstanding, these revivals were among the earliest forms of mass entertainment. Deploying theatrical techniques developed in carnivals, circuses, and traveling road shows, preachers learned to pitch their message like carnies on the midway. It is instructive to note that these revivals became the prototype for political rallies, whose founding coincided with the early Great Awakenings. During the nineteenth century, the use of print technology to spread the Word took new forms. David Morgan goes so far as to credit "the evangelical Christians of the American Tract and Bible Societies [with] the invention of mass media in America."[68] One of the most important innovations in the nineteenth century was the development of richly visual literature and teaching materials for children. Throughout history it has always been iconoclasts who have really appreciated the power of images. Since no one understood this better than nineteenth-century Evangelical Protestants, they were the first to produce attractive texts with rich images that were very popular with both children and adults. More appealing texts created new markets for printed materials. Moore points out, "The technology and distribution networks that made possible the creation of larger and larger reading audiences stimulated alert entrepreneurs who concluded that personal contact was neither necessary nor even particularly useful in efforts to affect people's behavior. The trail opened by this discovery led eventually to Madison Avenue, but before that it led to the formation of modern politics."[69]

Though print remained popular well into the twentieth century, the emergence of radio created new opportunities for entrepreneurial Evangelists to hawk their spiritual wares. The first regular radio program was broadcast on KDKA in Pittsburgh in 1920. Two months later, this station started broadcasting weekly church services, and within four years there were 600 radio stations in the country, 63 of which were owned by churches.[70] The Moody Bible Institute was one of the most enthusiastic radio marketers of religion. By the 1930s, its programs were syndicated on 187 stations nationwide. In 1922, the head of the Bible Institute of Los Angeles, Charles Fuller, launched KJS to broadcast his *Old-Fashioned Revival Hour*. A canny businessman, Fuller initiated a practice many others would imitate when he used contributions solicited on the radio to establish Fuller Theological Seminary in Pasadena.[71] While Protestants were more aggressive in their use of radio, Catholics were not completely absent from the airways. As early as the 1920s, Charles Coughlin and Fulton Sheen created popular programs. Coughlin's rabid anticommunism and overheated rhetoric on social issues has earned him the title "father of hate radio."[72] Sheen, who developed a successful television show in the 1950s, was more moderate and attracted a more mainstream audience.

Billy Graham's radio program *Hour of Decision* laid the groundwork and provided financial resources for his television ministry. Graham was not, however, the first to recognize the importance of TV for preaching. As early as 1953, Rex Humbard began televising his sermons from Akron, Ohio, and three years later Oral Roberts started what would become one of the most successful TV ministries in history.[73] Pat Robertson took telievangelism to another level in 1960, when he, along with Jim and Tammy Faye Bakker, bought a bankrupt UHF station and started the Christian Broadcast Network. Before their spectacular fall from grace, the Bakkers split from Robertson and created their own TV station (Praise the Lord Network—PTL) and founded Heritage Christian theme park, which was something like a Great Escape for Christians. Throughout the 1970s, Robertson continued to expand his media empire by establishing the for-profit CBN, Inc., later named the Family Channel, on which he broadcast his daily talk show *The 700 Club*. Dedicated to "spreading Christian values," CBN played a vital role in Robertson's presidential campaign. Following the lead of Fuller, Robertson opened Regent University and Evangelical School in 1978. As the demographics of Evangelicals changed, the university expanded its mission to include the liberal arts and graduate schools of law, business, communications, education, and psychological counseling. Jerry Falwell and Bob Jones followed the same course by using radio and television to preach the Word and raise money, which they used to fund K–12 schools as well as universities. Falwell confidently predicted that his media empire would turn a profit of $400 million in 2006. While Robertson, Falwell, and Jones represent different positions on the spectrum of the New Religious Right, they are united in their insistence that new technologies are effective means to spread the Word and should never become ends in themselves. Those who have come after them have tended to change the message to fit the media.

Other Protestant pitchmen have been quick to realize the growing importance of media. In a recent *Los Angles Times* article entitled "God's Call Comes by Cellphone," Stephanie Simon reports, "Nearly 60% of Protestant churches have websites now, up from 35% in 2000. More than half use email blasts to communicate with their congregation and 12% let the faithful tithe online." Some uses of the Internet have become quite inventive, to say the least. In Granger, Indiana, an Evangelical church created remarkable billboards with a picture of a man's and a woman's feet sticking out from under the sheets of a bed. Under the image a Web site was listed: www.mylamesexlife.com. When you click on the site, there is hip music and a slick series of images of a man and a woman with questions floating across them.

> Is your sex life a bore? A chore?
> Feeling like you want more?
> It's supposed to be fun, right?
> After all, sex isn't supposed to leave you guilty or frustrated
>   or empty.
> So why is everyone else having fun?
> Is there anyone who will give you straight answers?
> Do you have an open mind?
> No hype, no pulling punches, no condemnation.

At the end of the video loop, viewers are taken to the Web site of the Granger Community Church with the banner: "PURE SEX: We're not afraid to talk about it." "In the spring of 2006, Granger Community Church finished a five-week series called PureSex. . . . Talking topics like 'The Greatest Sex You'll Ever have,' 'The Language of Lust,' 'Straight Talk for Men and Women,' 'What Happens in Vegas WON'T Stay in Vegas,' and 'Porn: What's the Big Deal?' have allowed for lots of interesting conversations for Granger's guests and the community." When you click on the hot button "Pure Sex Series Graphics," you are taken to a page where you can pay $130 to download a package that "includes the graphic elements Granger Community Church used to promote the popular Pure-Sex weekend message series." Simon reports that "Pastor Mark Beeson credits the campaign with boosting attendance 70% the week he gave a sermon entitled 'The Greatest Sex You'll Ever Have.'"[74] Six weeks after the series ended, weekly church attendance still topped six thousand, up from five thousand before the ad campaign.

Other tactics are less extreme but no less creative. With many parishioners too busy to attend church, pastors are taking the message to the people through Webcasts, podcasts, and cellphones. Christopher Chisholm, described as a "TV-executive-turned-digital-evangelist," recently launched "FaithMobile, a service that will send a daily Bible verse to your cellphone for $5.99 a month." Chisholm also "offers Christian-themed computer wallpaper (a crucifix glinting in the sun, a hand resting on a Bible) and video reminders to stay on the straight and narrow."[75] With these developments, not only does high become low, but the sublime becomes ridiculous in a parody of the Word becoming Flesh.

While religious entrepreneurs use multiple media to spread their message, the media have become obsessed with religion. On February 7, 2005, the cover story of *Time* magazine was "The 25 Most Influential Evangelicals in America." Directly below the title were two questions: "What does Bush owe them?" and "Do the Democrats Need More Religion?" The first person on the list was Rick Warren, pastor of the 80,000-member Saddleback Church in the stronghold of American conservatism—Orange County, California. As if to signal the passing of the Evangelical torch to a new generation of Evangelists, *Time* dubs Warren "America's New People's Pastor." With a photograph of "Pastor Rick" purposively gazing heavenward, the article begins:

> These are heady times for Rick Warren. His book *The Purpose Driven Life*, which says that the meaning of life comes through following God's purposes, has sold more than 20 million copies over the past two years and is the best-selling hardback in U.S. history. When he took the podium to pray on the final night of Billy Graham's Los Angeles crusade at the Rose Bowl in November, the 82,000 congregants cheered as if he had scored the winning touchdown. And on the eve of the presidential Inauguration, Warren . . . delivered the Invocation at the gala celebration. Later he met with 15 Senators, from both parties, who sought his advice and heard his plan to enlist Saddleback's global network of more than 40,000 churches in tackling such issues as poverty, disease and ignorance. And when 600 senior pastors were asked to name the people they thought had the greatest influence on church affairs in the country, Warren's name came in second only to Billy Graham's.

Warren's Web site boasts that in the past seven years he has started thirty-four "daughter churches," and 350,000 pastors from 160 countries have attended his Purpose-Driven church seminars.[76] The promotional material accompanying his book makes his marketing strategy clear: "Calling him a 'spiritual entrepreneur,' *Forbes* magazine said, 'If Warren's ministry was a business it would be compared to Dell, Google, or Starbucks in impact.'" Warren's extraordinary popularity is a result of his ability to tap into people's deep need for meaning and purpose during a period of rapid social change. For millions of his followers, the promise of a purpose-driven life holds out the prospect of the kind of real or authentic experience they believe can provide the foundation of a meaningful existence.

Warren is aware that he comes perilously close to a form of pop psychology or spirituality that he and his fellow Evangelicals vehemently claim they reject. In the first chapter of his book, he declares: "This is not a self-help book. It is not about finding the right career, achieving your dreams, or planning your life. It is not about how to cram more activities into an overloaded schedule. Actually, it will teach you how to do *less* in life—by focusing on what matters most. It is about becoming what *God* created you to become."[77] The more one reads, however, the clearer it becomes that Warren protests too much—a self-help book is precisely what he has written. The gospel he preaches is Christianity-Lite, which more closely resembles the feel-good messages of New Agers than the demanding challenges of earlier Evangelicals. In an unwitting parody of Jesus' sojourn in the desert and Saint Ignatius's *Spiritual Exercises,* Warren offers his readers forty daily lessons. While claiming to be Protestant, nothing could be farther from Luther's divided subject than Warren's congenial religion of healthy-mindedness. His message reaches comic proportions when he reassures readers, worried about their body image, *"God wants you to enjoy using the shape he has given you."*[78] You can eat all you want and still enter the kingdom of God. In the facile idiom of the sixties' "I'm OK—you're OK," every vestige of doubt and uncertainty disappears in the calm self-assurance of a faith that is as simple as the person who preaches it.

Warren is not alone in promoting a reassuring gospel in uncertain times. In his book *Dog Training, Fly Fishing and Sharing Christ in the 21st Century,* Ted Haggard, founder and former pastor of the 11,000-member New Life Church in Colorado Springs, described by Jeff Sharlet as "America's most powerful megachurch," summarizes goals that guide his ministry: "I want my finances in order, my kids trained, and my wife to love life. I want good friends who are a delight to provide protection for my family and me should life become difficult some day. I want a church I can stay in for years. I don't want surprises, scandals, or secrets from my church leaders. I want stability, and at the same time, steady, forward movement. I want the church to help me live well, not exhaust me with endless 'worthwhile' projects."[79] "Worthwhile projects" is a euphemism for social welfare programs for the poor and underprivileged, and "living well" means enjoying the benefits that capitalism is supposed to bestow.

For Haggard, free-market capitalism is not merely a strategy for market-ing religion but constitutes the central content of his purportedly reli-gious message. Evangelical Christians, who are "pro–free markets" and "pro–private property," he maintains, seek "to harness free-market capi-talism in [their] ministry."[80] Sounding a theme that is by now familiar, Haggard argues:

> This is the primary lesson of the twentieth century. At its core, the twentieth century was a global struggle over central government with command economies or government by and for the people with free markets. Freely elected government with free markets won, hands down, and people all around the world are better off for it.
>
> We are wise to understand clearly why free markets create wealth, provide what people want and need, and allow people to find their maximum productions. When we understand the value that God places on people, and when we allow them to create and become in-novative, their products and services far outreach the things we could produce from our offices by ourselves. The fact of the matter is that free-market systems will help us all build much stronger ministries within our churches.

Haggard has been deeply influenced by *New York Times* columnist Thomas Friedman's *The Lexus and the Olive Tree: Understanding Globaliza-tion*. Having become convinced of the superiority of distributed bottom-up networks to centralized top-down systems, Haggard applies the prin-ciple of free markets to church organization and government. He allows parishioners to self-organize in small groups, which are not controlled by any central authority. "In a free-market arrangement, the church gov-ernment sets up systems so that people can establish whatever ministry they think others might be interested in. If lots of people attend and it meets their needs, others are free to start similar ministries. The market creates more and more so the supply meets the demand. If, however, the idea doesn't appeal to people, then those who are going to offer that min-istry choose another ministry that will more effectively meet the needs of people, and both the people and the one offering the ministry are more productive for the kingdom of God."[81] Here the precepts of Chris-tian charity are displaced by the market principle of the survival of the fittest.

It is important to note that the New Life Church's geographical loca-tion is central to its mission. Colorado Springs has become the Evangeli-cal capital of America. With the Air Force Academy nearby and secret military installations in the surrounding mountains, God and country become inseparable for Haggard's Christian soldiers. Colorado Springs is also the home of James Dobson's powerful organization Focus on the Family, whose media empire claims to reach 220 million people. Though not always as visible as Dobson, Haggard exercises considerable political influence. As president of the National Evangelical Association, he represents 30 million conservatives from 45,000 churches. *Time* magazine, which also included Haggard among the twenty-five most influential Evangelicals in the country, reports, "Every Monday he participates in the West Wing conference call with evangelical leaders." The purpose of these calls is to keep the pressure on the White House to enact the conservative agenda on issues ranging from abortion and the marriage amendment to tax reduction, aid to religious schools and, most important, judicial appointments.

Sunday services at the New Life Church draw tens of thousands of worshipers. Like many other megachurches, Haggard uses glitzy architecture for marketing purposes. In 1994, the church opened a massive World Prayer Center, equipped with state-of-the-art computers and telecommunications systems. The church's Web site describes this "spiritual NORAD" as "the hub for this worldwide real-time prayer network that will change lives and change history forever." The main sanctuary, named "the Tent" to recall its revivalist roots, is designed to accommodate church services that approximate rock concerts. The central stage is equipped with huge speakers, multiple projectors, six massive video screens, and even fog machines. As image becomes reality, "Pastor Ted" seems to materialize magically out of thin air, and the show begins with a promotional video about the founding and development of the church. Jeff Sharlet describes the multimedia experience:

> The light pods dilated and blasted the sanctuary with red. Worship Pastor Ross roared: "*Let the King of Glory enter in!*" Ushers rushed through the crowds throwing out rainbow glow strings. Watching the screens, we moved in slow motion through prairie grass. A voiceover announced, "The heart of God, beating in our hearts." Then the music and video quickened as the camera rose to meet the new sanctuary. Images spliced and jumped over one another: thousands of New Lifers holding candles, and dozens skydiving, and Pastor Ted, Bible in hand, blond head thrust forward above the Good Book, smiling, finger shaking, singing, more smiling. . . . The lights came up. Pastor Ted [is] now before us in the flesh.[82]

After an entrance hardly reminiscent of a lowly man riding a donkey, Haggard proceeds to preach his sermon with PalmPilot in hand. Though this is a hard show to top, in the competitive world of market capitalism, newcomers must up the ante or perish.

Joel Osteen, pastor of Houston's Lakewood Church and the leading televangelist today, is the most unapologetic pitchman for pop psychology passing as Pentecostal Christianity. With weekend services attracting over 30,000, the church decided to purchase the 16,000-seat Compaq Center, erstwhile home of the Houston Rockets, for $90 million. With weekend services now drawing 120,000 worshipers, Osteen foresees a market that knows virtually no bounds. When asked about his remarkable success in a *Business Week* interview, he replied without hesitation, "The No. 1 thing that brings them in is our TV."[83] With weekly broadcasts on national cable networks like USA Network, ABC Family, Discovery, Black Entertainment Television, Trinity Broadcasting, and Daystar Television Network as well as CNBC Europe, Vision Canada, CNBC Australia, and Middle East Television, Osteen's programs reach over seven million people every week. Forbes.com reports that Lakewood is the nation's fastest-growing church.

When Osteen took over his father's church after his death in 1999, he had never preached a sermon and had no seminary training. A member of the Pentecostal tradition, he claimed his authority came directly from the Holy Spirit, and thus he did not need education, formal training, or previous experience. Though his father had developed a successful ministry and broadcast his Sunday services on a local cable channel, it quickly became clear that the son's ambitions were considerably grander. One of Osteen's first decisions was to buy airtime on one of the four top networks in the twenty-five largest TV markets throughout the country. The results were immediate—his audience grew quickly and within a very short time the church had its own International Broadcast and Production Studio, whose responsibilities include preparing materials for worldwide release. After attracting people to the church through television, Osteen keeps them coming back by offering a broad range of entertainment opportunities. For example, church members and potential recruits can use the new Compaq Center's ice rink and basketball court. The new facility is also used for sporting events and concerts as well as conventions, business workshops, and personal-growth seminars. Osteen's multifaceted operation is fast becoming the most effective deployment of the finance-entertainment complex for marketing religion that has yet been developed. Indeed, it is not too much to suggest that

Lakewood is to the new millennium what Vegas was to the 1980s. While Vegas put the virtualization of the economy on display, Lakewood reveals the economy of redemption to be nothing more than a vacuous play of images. What started as the anxious effort to recover the real turns into a frivolous re-covery of the real.

Osteen's success is not only the result of the media he uses; his message also sells well. He translates Haggard's promotion of free markets into the language of pop psychology and self-help to create his "prosperity gospel." The motto of Osteen's ministry is "Discover the Champion in You." Sounding more like Tony Robbins than Jonathan Edwards, Osteen confidently proclaims, "It is God's will for you to live in prosperity and not poverty." This message is not, of course, new. "Beginning early in the nineteenth century," Moore points out, "religious leaders contributed to a process that made the organization of spiritual affairs in America congruent with an individualistic market-driven economy. Some of the results were intentional, leading some people to say in retrospect that ministers had struck a deal with wealthy capitalists. Alarmed at their shrinking significance, they agreed to preach a gospel of wealth in return for protection and financial assistance."[84] Though Osteen knows nothing about his evangelical precursors, he does know his market. In a promotional video for the Compaq project on the church's Web site, he summarizes the vision behind his ministry:

> We're all about building people up. We're all about helping people reach their full potential. We don't push some kind of religion . . . all we push is joy and peace and victory through Jesus Christ. . . . Our message every single week is through faith in God you can live an overcoming life of victory. . . . I believe that's the message this generation needs to hear. We've heard a lot about the judgment of God and what we can't do and what's going to keep us out of heaven. But it's time people started hearing about the goodness of God, about a God that loves them. A God that believes in them. A God that wants to help them. That's our message here at Lakewood.[85]

Needless to say, this is not exactly what Dietrich Bonhoeffer had in mind when he proclaimed "religionless Christianity." Nor is this vision shared by dominionists like Dobson or dispensationalists like LaHaye. While Fundamentalists and Evangelicals see the world sunk in sin and corruption and rushing toward destruction, which will bring a kingdom not of this world, the charismatic Pentecostal Osteen preaches a realized eschatology in which the kingdom is present here and now. This is the message of his best-selling book, *Your Best Life Now: Seven Steps to Living at Your Full Potential*. In a reversal as astonishing as it is suggestive, Osteen effectively updates Nietzsche's claim, "'Bliss' is not something promised: it is here if you live and act in such and such a way."[86] Osteen's bliss, however, is hardly Nietzsche's "gay wisdom"—rather, it is nothing more than a good family, a good job, and, above all, financial success. Once again outward change presupposes inward transformation. "The first step to living to your full potential," Osteen explains, "is to enlarge your vision. To live your best life, now, you must start looking through eyes of faith, seeing yourself rising to new levels. See your business taking off. See your marriage restored. See your family prospering. See your dreams coming to pass. You must conceive and believe it is possible if you ever hope to experience it."[87] Like a champion athlete going through visualization exercises before the main event, Osteen encourages his followers to imagine the life they *want* to live. In this religious schema, seeing is being: if you can only see yourself as happy, successful, and wealthy, that is what you will become. By preaching this gospel, Osteen has drifted about as far from his purported Protestant ancestors as possible. Worldly success is no longer a sign of election for a heavenly kingdom but is the full realization of the kingdom on earth here and now. Committed to living what he preaches, Osteen recently signed a contract for his next book with Free Press, an imprint of Simon and Schuster, that brings him up to $13 million, $3 million more than President Clinton received for his autobiography.

The appeal of Osteen's message is obvious. Since the early 1980s, financial capitalism has generated unprecedented wealth for a very small percentage of the population. At the same time, ever-expanding media networks have created a growing awareness of and desire for material well-being among people from all social classes. While the ideologues of ownership society preach a gospel of opportunity rather than entitlement, Osteen reassures people that they too can enjoy prosperity if they will simply take control of their lives by looking at things differently. But Osteen also offers people something else—a sense of security, certainty, and authenticity that comes from participation in a worldwide network of like-minded believers. Deploying Third Wave technologies for a Second Wave agenda, Osteen and his fellow Evangelists use distributed networks to allow people to become One in Christ. In Osteen's media empire, the bite has disappeared from LaHaye's Beast.

Looking back over the last half century, it becomes clear that the search for the real becomes an obsession the moment it disappears. So-

cial, political, and economic changes brought by the emergence of network culture have created a pervasive longing for authenticity and security, which, in turn, has led to the rise of neofoundationalism in many
religious traditions. During the last half of the twentieth century, the
New Religious Right in the United States has been dominated by Protestants and Catholics committed to turning back what they perceive to
be the rising tide of secularism. But opposites, we have repeatedly discovered, are never merely opposite; rather, they are codependent and,
when pushed to extremes, reverse themselves—religiosity finally becomes indistinguishable from secularism, transcendence collapses into
immanence, and dualism dissolves in monism. In Osteen's realized eschatology, the oppositional ideology of Fundamentalists and Evangelicals disappears in a gospel of prosperity that is indistinguishable from
the secular gospel of wealth. While Osteen claims to eschew politics, his
message is precisely what promoters of the market-state want to hear.
The free market is divinely ordained and predestined to prevail. Moreover, personal religious struggles, like military campaigns designed to
defeat the powers of evil in the world, require no sacrifice. The solution
to both outward and inward struggles is the same: "Go shopping!"

BASE CLOSURES

The history of theology in the West, we have discovered, is the story of
the repeated "altarnation" between monisms in which the real is immanent, that is, in some way *present* here and now, and dualisms in which
the real is transcendent, that is, *absent* or, more precisely, present elsewhere. Appearances to the contrary notwithstanding, these theological
alternatives are not simply opposites but are dialectically related in such
a way that, when either is pushed to its limit, it negates itself and turns
into the other. In the course of the twentieth century, the immanence
of liberalism gives way to the transcendence of neoorthodoxy, which, in
turn, is negated by the death of God theology. For many religious conservatives, the death of God was symptomatic of the relativism and nihilism of the sixties. The recent emergence of neofoundationalism represents the effort to reverse this perceived decline by reasserting religious
and moral absolutes in a world that seems to be drifting toward chaos.
Then, through an unexpected reversal, the dialectical interplay between
immanence and transcendence is reenacted within the New Religious
Right. While Fundamentalists, Evangelicals, and Pentecostals promote
oppositional ideologies in which the impending apocalypse is eagerly

awaited, what can best be described as New Age Evangelicals and Pente-costals fill the megachurches of exurbia by preaching gospels of wealth and self-help that take all the protest out of Protestantism. Though claiming devotion to a transcendent God, the message of these masters of media and markets, who promote satisfaction here and now, is indis-tinguishable from the realized eschatology of the death of God.

Recent history suggests that neither monistic nor dualistic schemata are adequate for life in the increasingly complex world of the twenty-first century. Both these alternatives are in different ways nihilistic. Du-alism presupposes an otherworldliness that tends to devalue life in this world, and monism—however it is disguised—is so committed to the world as it is that every possibility of critical reflection and transforma-tive practice disappears. As connectivity continues to spread, history is fast approaching a tipping point that portends a major phase shift. If this transition is to be negotiated imaginatively and creatively, new ways of thinking and acting must be figured. The task of thinking at the end of modernism and postmodernism is to develop schemata that are *nei-ther* monistic (both/and) *nor* dualistic (either/or) but figure something different—something other, which remains so near that it is infinitely distant.

The resources for figuring this unthought theological or, more pre-cisely, a/theological "altarnative" between theism and atheism can be found in critical trajectories launched in France during the late 1960s. French poststructuralism might seem to have little relevance for contem-porary neofoundationalism. As we have discovered, however, through-out the modern period, theory and theology have always been more closely related than most critics realize. Indeed, theory is implicitly theological or a/theological, and theology and a/theology are inescap-ably theoretical. To understand the implications of the interrelation of theology and theory, it is necessary to complete the map I have gradually been developing throughout this book (fig. 19). The struggle between foundationalism and neofoundationalism is not limited to theology and philosophy but has been at the heart of most important critical debates in the arts and humanities for the past half century. During the 1960s, poststructuralism emerged as a response to the foundationalism inher-ent in structuralism. The relevance of the controversy between structur-alists and poststructuralists for the emergence of neofoundationalism in recent decades can be clarified by returning to the definition of religion I proposed in the first chapter. Religion, I argued, is an emergent complex adaptive network of symbols, myths, and rituals that, on the one hand,

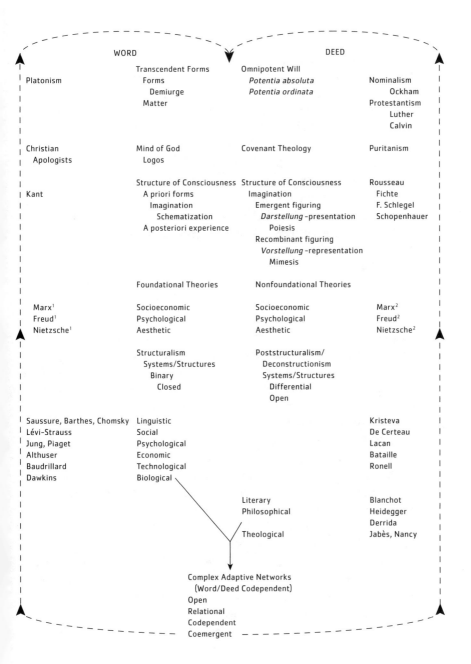

Figure 19. Theological Genealogy of Modernism, Postmodernism, and Complex Adaptive Networks

figure schemata of feeling, thinking, and acting in ways that lend life meaning and purpose and, on the other, disrupt, dislocate, and disfigure every stabilizing structure. There are, then, two interrelated aspects of religion: one structures and stabilizes, and the other destructures and destabilizes. Structuralism, like neofoundationalism, gives priority to the former moment, and poststructuralism privileges the latter. When placed within the context of the history of theology and philosophy, structuralism appears to be a latter-day version of the theology of the Word, and poststructuralism the latest version of the theology of the Deed. The intersection of Word and Deed in the mid-1960s transformed the critical landscape in ways that both reflected the approaching end of the cold war and anticipated the emergence of network culture at the end of the millennium.

In the fall of 1966—only a few months after *Time* had asked, "Is God Dead?"—a symposium entitled "The Languages of Criticism and the Science of Man" was held at the Johns Hopkins Humanities Center. Five years later, the proceedings of the conference were published in *The Structuralist Controversy*. The list of participants reads like a who's who of critical theory during the past five decades: René Girard, Georges Poulet, Tzvetan Todorov, Roland Barthes, Jean-Pierre Vernant, Jacques Lacan, and Jacques Derrida. This conference and the accompanying book introduced both structuralism and poststructuralism to America. In the following years, these abstract and often-arcane discussions spilled beyond the walls of the university to fuel culture wars that still continue.

French philosophy in the sixties, like Protestant theology during the first half of the century, represented an extension of the debate between Hegel and Kierkegaard. The importance of Hegel for French thought can be attributed to the influence of Alexandre Kojève's seminars on Hegel (1933–39), which later were published under the title *Introduction to the Reading of Hegel*.[88] Many of the people who became the leading figures in French culture during the middle decades of the century heard and were profoundly influenced by these seminars: Jacques Lacan, Georges Bataille, Jean-Paul Sartre, Maurice Merleau-Ponty, Raymond Queneau, and Raymond Aron. Kojève's nuanced interpretation of Hegel drew on the writings of Marx and Heidegger to suggest productive tensions in his philosophy. The participants in the seminar who became so influential did not, however, appreciate the subtlety of Kojève's analysis and tended to read the system simplistically as a totalizing structure that repressed individuals by negating differences. In fashioning a critique of this aspect of Hegelianism, existentialists returned to Kierkegaard's analysis of the radically free individual, who is isolated from others and completely responsible for his or her decisions. As the social and political implications of this radical individualism became clear, many critics concluded that the cure was worse than the disease. Structuralism arose as a response to and critique of the notion of individual subjectivity that ultimately grew out of Luther's nominalistic theology. If truth is subjectivity, critics argued, individuals are wrapped in solipsism, and communication, community, as well as responsible social action, become impossible. In an essay entitled "The Word of Nietzsche," Heidegger summarized what many saw as the pernicious implications of modern subjectivity: "man has risen up into the I-ness of the *ego cogito*. Through this uprising, all that is, is transformed into an object. That which is, as the objective, is swallowed up into the immanence of subjectivity. The horizon no longer emits light of itself. It is now nothing but the point-of-view posited in the value-positing of the will to power."[89] With the availability of nuclear technology as well as other weapons of mass destruction, Heidegger concludes, the exercise of the unfettered will to power is of more than philosophical interest.

Though rarely noted, other emerging technologies were also quietly shaping postwar philosophical discourse. It is no accident that structuralism emerged at the precise moment new information machines and global media networks were being developed and deployed. These technologies implied a different understanding of the human-machine interface. Instead of individuals creating systems that were subject to their control, systems, it seemed, were creating individuals by situating them in networks and structures that regulate all exchange. Far from a center of action, the subject appears to be a function of the system or structure it constitutes. When understood in this way, structuralism is the philosophical reflection of a seismic technosocial shift. By arguing that systems constitute individuals more than individuals create systems, however, structuralists commit the opposite error of existentialism: whereas existentialism privileges the individual over the system, structuralists privilege the system over the individual. For the new generation that arrived on the world stage during the Paris uprisings in 1968, structuralism seemed every bit as totalizing as Hegelianism had seemed to the existentialists several decades earlier. The challenge poststructuralists faced was to articulate a nonoppositional difference that would subvert hegemonic systems—cultural, social, political, psychological, and economic—that they believed had become so destructive. In developing their responses, the critics of structuralism discovered an invaluable resource in what at the time appeared to many to be a most unlikely place—Hegel's speculative philosophy.

While it is difficult to overestimate the importance of Kojève's *Introduction to the Reading of Hegel*, no less important, though rarely acknowledged, is the work of Jean Hyppolite. Hyppolite's *Genesis and Structure of Hegel's Phenomenology of Spirit* (1946) remains the best commentary on Hegel's masterwork. Hyppolite, who taught an influential seminar entitled Hegel and Modern Thought that many who became France's leading philosophers and critics followed religiously, participated in the Hopkins symposium but did not live to see the publication of the proceedings. Remarkably, Hyppolite and Kojève, like Barth, both died in 1968. Hyppolite's influence on *les soixante dix-huitards* was not always obvious but is everywhere present. Though best known for his study of the *Phenomenology*, his little-read book *Logic and Existence: An Essay on the Logic of Hegel* (1952) is more important for the structuralist controversy. This patient analysis of the relation between the *Science of Logic* and the *Phenomenology* creates the possibility of reading Hegel against the grain in a way that opens the space for the intervention of Hyppolite's most important student—Jacques Derrida. Hyppolite demonstrates that when pushed to its logical conclusion, Hegel's system, far from thoroughly consistent and totally comprehensive, subverts itself:

> Here perhaps we get to the decisive point of Hegelianism, to the torsion of thought through which we are able to think conceptually the unthinkable, to what makes Hegel simultaneously the greatest irrationalist and the greatest rationalist who has ever existed. We cannot emerge from the Logos, but the Logos emerges from itself by remaining itself; since it is the indivisible self, the Absolute, it thinks the non-thought. It thinks sense in its relation to non-sense, to the opaque being of nature. It reflects this opacity into its contradiction. It raises thought, which would be only thought, over itself by obliging it to contradict itself; it turns this contradiction into the speculative means by which to reflect the Absolute itself.[90]

In attempting to comprehend everything, Hegel inadvertently approaches the unthinkable limit that reason presupposes yet cannot apprehend. The two sides of Hegelianism—the logical and the a-logical—correspond to structuralism and poststructuralism respectively. At the Hopkins conference Barthes represents the structuralist perspective and Derrida the poststructuralist point of view.

Structuralism is the neofoundationalism of contemporary theory. As such, it represents an inverted Platonism in which eternal Forms descend from the heavens to become the universal infrastructures that ground all reality. When fully comprehended, these forms constitute an all-inclusive system, which, if decoded, serves as the functional equivalent of the divine Word or Logos. Barthes follows other structuralists by appropriating linguist theories—especially those of Saussure, Beneviste, and Jakobson—to develop his comprehensive analysis of culture:

> We see culture more and more as a general system of symbols, governed by the same operations. There is unity in this symbolic field: culture, in all its aspects, is a language. Therefore it is possible today to anticipate the creation of a single, unified science of culture, which will depend on diverse disciplines, all devoted to analyzing, on different levels of description, culture as language. Of course, semio-criticism will be only part of this science, rather of this discourse on culture. I feel authorized by this unity of the human symbolic field to work on a postulate, which I shall call a postulate of *homology*: the structure of the sentence, the object of linguistics, is found again, homologically, in the structure of works. Discourse is not simply an adding together of sentences: it is, itself, one great sentence.[91]

As the foregoing chart (fig. 19) of theology and theory indicates, this "greater sentence" can be translated into different languages: literary, social, psychological, technological, biological, and, of course, theological. Though the terms differ, the metaphysical structure of interpretation remains the same: cultural artifacts are understood by reducing superficial differences to underlying identities constituted by universal codes. We have already encountered other versions of this dream of total transparency in the theories of Marx, Freud, and Nietzsche. Structuralists, however, forget the lessons their precursors eventually were forced to learn: transparency is impossible because foundations can never be secure. There is always an elusive remainder that slips away in the very effort to grasp it. This excess is the "non-sense" that Hegel, *malgré lui*, confesses forever remains obscure.[92]

Derrida makes precisely this point in the opening lines of his contribution to the symposium: "Perhaps something has occurred in the history of the concept of structure that could be called an 'event,' if this loaded word did not entail a meaning which it is precisely the function of structural—or structuralist—thought to reduce or to suspect. But let me use the term 'event' anyway, employing it with caution as if in quotation marks. In this sense, this event will have the exterior form of a *rupture* and a *redoubling*."[93] The distinction between structure and event is isomorphic with the difference between the eternal Word and the temporal Deed. There is a complex relation between structure (Word) and event (Deed). Whereas structure is the condition of the possibility of presence and hence of representation, event is the condition of the possibility of structure. According to Derrida, structures are not eternal or permanent but are *emergent*. The eventuality of structure entails a strange temporality that dislocates every present and disrupts all presence. As the condition of the possibility of structures, which, in turn, are the condition of the possibility of presence, the originary event is never present but is always already past. Since this past is not a past present, it can never be re-presented. The event of emergence is indistinguishable from the originary will that is antecedent to and a condition of the possibility of the Word in voluntaristic theologies. Every structure, Derrida argues, emerges through events that can be neither anticipated nor controlled. This eventual emergency is the incomprehensible excess that decenters structures by repeatedly displacing originary presence. Derrida goes so far as to argue that "the notion of a structure lacking any center represents the unthinkable itself."[94] From this point of view, nonhierarchical, decentered, and distributed networks are the unthinkable condition of the possibility and impossibility of all thought. When one attempts to think this unthinkable thought, the ground begins to disappear beneath one's feet, thereby creating a panic, which results in the effort to re-cover the opening of space and time where the event of emergence occurs. By struggling to secure the ground at the precise moment it slips away, structuralists, in a manner not unlike representatives of the New Religious Right, seek to provide security and certainty in a world of the frenzied flux and flow of signs. "The concept of centered structure," Derrida argues, "is in fact the concept of a play based on a fundamental ground, a play constituted on the basis of a fundamental immobility and a reassuring certitude, which itself is beyond the reach of play. And on the basis of this certitude anxiety can be mastered, for anxiety is invariably the result of a certain mode of being implicated in the game, of a being caught by the game, of being as it were at stake in the game from the outset."[95] Such strategies, however, inevitably fail; the repressed never goes away and always returns to create openings in bases that seemed to be closed. System and excess are not opposites but are codependent: there can no more be a structure apart from the supplementary excess that disrupts it than there can be an event of disruption without the stabilizing structures it dislocates. This excess is never present as such but emerges by withdrawing at the precise moment the system or structure seems to achieve closure. Recovery is always a re-covering and, therefore, inevitably remains incomplete. In this way, closure dis-closes without re-vealing the openness of every foundational base.

Though he invokes a seemingly endless series of terms to suggest what cannot be represented, Derrida's privileged "category" for the un-thinkable condition of the possibility and impossibility of systems and structures is his well-known neologism *différance*. In his most important essay, published in the fateful year 1968, he comes as close as ever to de-fining this deliberately elusive term: "What is written as *différance*, then, will be the playing movement that 'produces'—by means of something that is not simply an activity—these differences, these effects of differ-ence. This does not mean that the *différance* that produces differences is somehow before them, in a simple and unmodified—in-different—present. *Différance* is the non-full, non-simple, structured and differen-tiating origin of difference. Thus, the name 'origin' no longer suits it."[96] In explicating what he describes as "the non-concept *différance*," Derrida draws on analyses we have previously considered: Freud's interpreta-tion of the irreducibility of the unconscious that haunts all conscious-ness, Heidegger's account of the unrepresentability of presencing that is presupposed in every representation, and Nietzsche's reading of the groundless play of signs that subverts all foundations once deemed se-cure. The most interesting and least likely precursor Derrida identifies, however, is Hegel. Far from dismissing Hegelian philosophy as the cul-mination of Western logocentrism, he discerns a seminal caesura in the midst of Hegel's logic, which creates what Hyppolite had described as the "torsion of thought through which we are able to think conceptu-ally the unthinkable." At a pivotal point in his argument, Derrida cites a suggestive passage from the Jena *Logic* in which Hegel analyzes what he describes as *absolute differente Beiziehung*:

> The infinite, in its simplicity, is, as a moment opposed to the equal-to-itself, the negative, and in its moments, although it is (itself) presented to and in itself the Totality, (it is) what excludes in general, the point or limit; but in its own (action of) negating, it is related immediately to the other and negates itself by itself. The limit or moment of the pres-ent (*der Gegen-wart*), the absolute "this" of time, or the now, is of an absolutely negative simplicity, which absolutely excludes from itself all multiplicity, and, by virtue of this, is absolutely determined; it is not whole or a *quantum* which would be extended in itself (and) which, in itself, would also have an undetermined moment, a diversity which, as indifferent (*gleichgultig*) or exterior in itself, would be related to an other (*auf ein anderes bezöge*), but in this relation absolutely different from the simple (*sondern es ist absolute differente Beziehung*).[97]

Commenting on this complicated passage, Derrida notes that the French translator, Alexandre Kroyé, proposes to render *differente Beziehung* as "different Relation." Tweaking Kroyé's translation, Derrida suggests that "differentiating relation" is more accurate. Neither Kroyé nor Derrida, however, comments on Hegel's qualification of the differentiating relation as absolute. This oversight is very important because Hegel's *absolute differente Beziehung* anticipates Kierkegaard's characterization of God as "the absolutely different [*absolute Forskjellighed*]" or "infinitely and qualitatively different."[98] Absolute difference is a difference, a more radical difference, than the difference that is the opposite of identity or the same. As such, it can be interpreted as the nonoppositional difference that is the condition of the possibility of all differences and every identity. Through what Derrida describes as an "infinitesimal and radical displacement," Kierkegaard and Hegel intersect in a differentiating relation that is translated "*différance*." This displacement creates an alternative space for the imagination. By reading Hegel's notion of constitutive relationality through Kierkegaard's account of absolute difference, it becomes possible to refigure Derridean *différance* in a way that makes it possible to figure a complex schema that is neither monistic nor dualistic. This unthought third can provide a critique of and response to the religious and political neofoundationalism that threatens to sunder our world.

From Derrida's poststructuralist perspective, every structure or system is formed by binary or dialectical opposites. These oppositions, however, presuppose a "differentiating relation" that "resists opposition." In a manner reminiscent of Heidegger's presencing, which reveals itself by hiding, *différance* "exposes itself" as what "cannot be exposed."

> What am I to do in order to speak of the *a* of *différance*? It goes without saying that it cannot be *exposed*. One can expose only that which at a certain moment can become *present*, manifest, that which can be shown, presented as something present, a being-present in its truth, in the truth of a present or the presence of the present. Now if *différance* is (and I also cross out the "is") what makes possible the presentation of the being-present, it is never presented as such. It is never offered to the present. Or to anyone. Reserving itself, not exposing itself, in regular fashion it exceeds the order of truth at a certain precise point, but without dissimulating itself as something, as a mysterious being, in the occult of a nonknowledge or in a hole with indeterminable borders (for example, in a topology of castration). In every exposition it would be exposed to disappearing as disappearance. It would risk appearing: disappearing.[99]

As the condition of the possibility and impossibility of presence and absence, *différance* is neither present nor absent, neither here nor there, neither immanent nor transcendent. Whatever is or is not is constituted by the ceaseless altarnation of opposites. This play, which is always an interplay, disrupts structures that seem secure and thereby portends a future that remains inescapably uncertain. To play without security is to give up the dream of the foundational presence that has become the nightmare of our time.

> Play is the disruption of presence. The presence of an element is always a signifying and substantive reference inscribed in a system of differences and the movement of a chain. Play is always play of absence and presence, but if it is to be thought radically, play must be conceived before the alternative of presence and absence. Being must be conceived as presence or absence on the basis of the possibility of play and not the other way around. ... Turned towards the lost or impossible presence of the absent origin, this structuralist thematic of broken immediacy is therefore the saddened, *negative*, nostalgic, guilty Rousseauistic side of the thinking of play whose other side would be the Nietzschean *affirmation*, that is the joyous affirmation of the play of the world of signs without fault, without truth, without origin, which is offered to active interpretation. *This affirmation then determines the noncenter otherwise than as loss of the center.* And it plays without security.[100]

Such Nietzschean play is not the Dionysianism of a realized eschatology— nor does it signal that the end is forever deferred. Since this play has no aim other than itself, it is simultaneously complete and incomplete, or in different terms, the interplay of differences is complete in its incompletion.

It should be clear that Derridean play is directly related to one aspect of the operation of the imagination. The imagination, I have argued, involves the interplay of figuring and disfiguring in which there are two moments—one constructive, the other deconstructive (fig. 20). The imagination is the activity through which the figures that pattern the data of experience emerge, are modified, and dissolve. Insofar as every figure presupposes the process of figuring, it includes as a condition of its own possibility something that cannot be figured. In a manner reminiscent of the torsion of thought through which we are able to think the unthinkable conceptually, figures "include" but do not incorporate something that can be neither represented nor comprehended. Figures, therefore, are always disfigured *as if* from within. This disfiguring is the

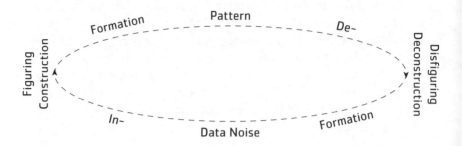

Figure 20. Imagination and Deconstruction

deconstructive activity through which figures are breached by an "interior" exteriority that leaves them open for further emergence.

It is important to recall that the two sides of the imagination are expressed in the two moments of religion. Constructive figuring provides the forms and norms that render life meaningful and purposeful. Once articulated, however, these figures and patterns tend to become fixed and resist change by being absolutized in various types of religiosity. Eventually, ideas and norms that fail to adapt to changing circumstances are displaced by competing schemata that allow people to function more effectively. Deconstructive disfiguring makes change not only possible but also necessary by disrupting and dislocating fixed schemata. Although inseparable from a certain destruction, this moment of disruption is the condition of creative emergence. The activity of the imagination, I have insisted, is objective as well as subjective. Just as information is distributed in cultural, social, and natural systems and networks, so the imagination is at work wherever noise is effectively patterned. The imagination, in other words, emerges objectively in natural, social, and cultural processes that are not necessarily conscious or self-conscious.

There can no more be deconstruction without construction than there can be figuring without disfiguring. The codependence of figuring and disfiguring shows why neither structuralism nor poststructuralism (i.e., deconstruction) taken by itself is adequate. To see why this is necessary and how it is possible to move beyond the opposition between structuralism and poststructuralism, it is helpful to return to figure 19, which plots the relation between theologies and theories of word and deed. As a latter-day version of Platonism (Word), structuralism identifies the foundational forms of nature, society, and culture. Always preoccupied with synchronic, rather than diachronic, relations, structuralists are uninterested in and unable to explain historical development. Foundational codes, they believe, are universal and as such unchanging. The task of interpretation is to reduce difference (superstructure) to identity (infrastructure). For poststructuralists, this strategy is philosophically misguided and politically dangerous. They argue that inasmuch as structuralists insist that differences are epiphenomenal, they present a repressive hermeneutic that reflects and promotes the very hegemonic political systems that have wrought havoc throughout the twentieth century. Moreover, structuralism's claim that foundational structures are universal and hence ahistorical makes any fundamental change impossible. The very structure of structuralists' arguments, however, poses problems for their critics. Since the metastructure that grounds all structures is binary opposition, direct disagreement only confirms the structuralists' position: to oppose, in other words, is to confirm. Just as Kierkegaard had to attack Hegel's comprehensive dialectical system indirectly, so poststructuralists have to criticize structuralists indirectly by exposing lacunae in structures and closures that appear to be complete and, therefore, closed. Insofar as structures emerge, they are necessarily temporal and this originary temporality exposes their intractable openness. As we have seen, however, the event of emergence is never present but is always already past. The origin, therefore, is forever missing; this lack renders return impossible and destines everyone to an erring that knows no end.

By exposing the openness of structures and setting them in motion, poststructuralism provides a necessary corrective to structuralism. But deconstruction is so preoccupied with the task of criticism that it cannot provide the constructive gesture so desperately needed to respond to today's raging neofoundationalism. Every system and structure, poststructuralists argue, totalizes by repressing differences and excluding otherness. The challenge, they conclude, is to resist hegemonic repression by repeatedly cultivating differences and soliciting otherness. In a manner reminiscent of existentialism, this strategy ends by committing the opposite error of structuralism: poststructuralism privileges difference to such an extent that any commonality or unity becomes effectively impossible. At this point, the philosophy of difference turns into a politics of identity in which all common ground disappears and differential *différance* becomes the oppositional difference it is designed to subvert. To overcome this impasse, it is necessary to acknowledge that two of the most important assumptions of poststructuralism are wrong: first, not all systems and structures totalize; and second, decentered structures do not represent the unthinkable itself. What poststructuralists cannot imagine is a nontotalizing structure that nonetheless acts as a whole. But this is precisely what complex adaptive networks do. As I have argued, decentralized, distributed, and deregulated networks have an identifiable structure that is isomorphic across media and have a discernible operational logic, which, though different from binary and dialectical systems, can nonetheless be clearly conceived and precisely articulated. Through the multiple nonlinear actions of related agents, complex adaptive networks act as a whole in a way that promotes unity without necessarily becoming repressive. In these relational webs, codependent individuals emerge and coevolve through processes of punctuated equilibrium in which disruptive change issues in creative transformation. What structuralists view as fixed forms are actually emergent figures that provide the ever-changing parameters of constraint within which individual identities and differences are constantly formed and reformed. Inasmuch as they determine the structure and govern the operation of natural, social, cultural, and technological systems as well as the interrelations among them, complex adaptive networks disclose the nonlogocentric logos of contemporary network culture.

A fully elaborated theory of complex adaptive networks makes it possible to develop the complex religious schema I described in the first chapter. The relation among dualistic, monistic, and complex schemata is simultaneously linear and nonlinear. On the one hand, there is a progressive ontogenetic and phylogenic movement from monism through dualism to complexity. In this logico-historical progression, complex adaptive systems are neither fully deployed nor conceptually grasped until the coemergence of network society and postmodern art and philosophy. Complexity, however, is not the synthesis of the two previous moments; to the contrary, the complex schema bends back on itself to form the margin of difference that is constitutive of monism and dualism. In this way, the third schema is both the result and the presupposition, which is not to say foundation, of the first and second stages of the coevolutionary process. The neither/nor of complexity simultaneously makes possible and renders incomplete the both/and of monism and the either/or of dualism. The complexity of this neither/nor harbors the theoretical resources and practical principles for negotiating the conflicts of the twenty-first century.

Far from linear, temporality is the complex interplay of an after that is before and a before that is after. In the play of time, the past that was never present eternally returns as the future that never arrives to disrupt the present that never is. Always already disturbed as if from within, the present is *virtual*. Never present as such, the gift of the present is present by that which arrives by not arriving. The proximity of this spectral, which is not to say speculative, arriving withdrawal renders all reality virtual. The virtual is not simply the possible but is the fluid *matrix* in which all possibility and actuality arise and pass away. Always betwixt and between, virtual reality is neither here and now nor elsewhere and beyond, neither immanent nor transcendent. To the contrary, the virtual is something like an immanent transcendence, which is inside as an outside that can never be incorporated. This interior exterior and exterior interior is the source of the endless disruption that interrupts all forms of religiosity by keeping complex systems open and making them subject to endless transformation.

In religious schemata West and East, God or the divine traditionally has been interpreted in terms of either being or nothing. Like presence and absence, however, being and nothing are mirror images of each other, which are finally identical. If what once was named being is irreducibly temporal, the present is never present and God, who is being-itself, does not exist. This does not mean, however, that everything becomes nothing; to the contrary, absolute nothingness is no more real than absolute being. All reality is virtual, and virtual reality emerges and withdraws in complex adaptive processes that are infinite. At this point—in this point—God and the imagination become one in the bacchanalian revel of a world that is a work of art.

> The evanescent itself must . . . be regarded as the essential, not as something fixed, cut off from the True, and left lying who knows where outside it, any more than the True is to be regarded as something on the other side, positive and dead. Appearance is the arising and passing away that does not itself arise and pass away, but is "in itself" and constitutes the actuality of the movement of the life of truth. The True is thus the Bacchanalian revel in which no member is sober; and yet because each member collapses as soon as he drops out, the revel is just as much transparent and simple repose.[101]

What Stevens describes as the "permanence composed of impermanence" in which everything arises and passes away is the Infinite, and this Infinite is life itself. The Infinite comes by not coming after God. "We keep coming back and coming back / To the real."[102] Monism and dualism are both theologies of death: in the former, individual differences collapse in the entropic totality where Eros becomes Thanatos; in the latter, oppositional differences negate themselves by destroying each other. To overcome this destructive nihilism, it is necessary to cultivate emergent creativity in complex adaptive networks that figure, disfigure, and refigure what once was believed to be the substance of things seen and unseen. Always after God, the endless restlessness of the Infinite is the eternal pulse of life.

Religion without God

REFIGURING LIFE

In 1836, just five years after Hegel's death, Emerson anonymously published an essay entitled simply "Nature." Though this short work concisely summarized the most important ideas that shaped transcendentalism, it was not well received and was not reissued until 1847. As prose seamlessly slips into poetry, Emerson crafts one of the most enduring images in all American literature. "In the woods, we return to reason and faith. There I feel that nothing can befall me in life—no disgrace, no calamity (leaving me my eyes), which nature cannot repair. Standing on the bare ground—my head bathed by the blithe air and uplifted into infinite space—all mean egoism vanishes. I become a transparent eyeball; I am nothing; I see all; the currents of the Universal Being circulate through me; I am part or parcel of God."[1] In these brief lines, Emerson imagines the world that Wallace Stevens described over a century later: "Nothing is itself taken alone. Things are because of interrelations or interactions."[2] In this vision of the world, *to be is to be related* or, in a more contemporary idiom I have already invoked, *to be is to be connected.* Nature, Emerson suggests, is a global network of networks through which the currents that sustain life constantly circulate. In a manner reminiscent of Adam Smith's interpretation of the market, all parts work together for the good of the whole, which, in turn, nourishes the parts from which it emerges. "Nature, in its ministry to man, is not only the material, but is also the process and the result. All the parts incessantly work into each other's hands for the profit of man. The wind sows the seed; the sun evaporates the sea; the wind blows the vapor to the field; the ice, on the other side of the planet, condenses rain on this; the rain feeds the plant; the plant feeds the animal; and thus the endless circulations of divine charity nourish man."[3]

The fluxes and flows of the natural world form and follow dynamic patterns of interdependence that operate according to principles that would not be adequately defined until the twentieth century. Freely admitting that his vision is thoroughly idealistic, Emerson insists: "The mind is part of the nature of things; the world is a divine dream, from which we may presently awake to the glories of the day. Idealism is a hypothesis to account for nature by other principles than those of carpentry and chemistry." Carpentry and chemistry are mechanical but the world is a living organism. Matter and mind, body and spirit, the finite and the infinite, are not opposites, because life in all its complexity is the embodiment or, more precisely, the incarnation of the divine mind. Far from merely subjective, the activity of the mind is the "substance" of the world. In the discourse of the universe, "Words are the finite organs of the infinite mind."[4] This understanding of the relation between art and life is what inspired the texts my mother most loved to teach. In the margin of Emerson's "Nature," she had written: "I became a transparent eyeball. I am nothing. I see all. I become part of God. This universal being is the only reality."

As I have noted, Emerson imported his vision from the German romantics and idealists by way of English romanticism. From the standpoints of Anglo-American positivism and analytic philosophy as well as Continental existentialism and poststructuralism, romanticism and idealism repeatedly have been dismissed as philosophically mistaken and politically suspect. The failure to appreciate the continuing importance of these closely related traditions has led critics to overlook the rich resources they provide for contemporary reflection. In addition to making important contributions to the arts and humanities, nineteenth-century romanticists and idealists anticipated some of the most interesting and promising ideas that are shaping *scientific* inquiry today. In the following pages, I will attempt to show how the philosophical, theological, and aesthetic trajectories we have been following lead to an understanding of life as an emergent complex adaptive network in which natural, social, cultural, and technological systems interrelate to form the infinite fabric of life. The interplay of art and life figures and disfigures the divine milieu in which everything arises and passes away.

The critical issue once again turns on Kant's interpretation of inner teleology. As we have seen, in the Third Critique this notion constitutes the structural principle of both the work of art and the living organism. In contrast to machines, in which parts are externally related, in the organism and in the work of art parts and whole are reciprocally related in such a way that neither can be apart from the other. "An organized being [*organisiertes Wesen*] is, therefore, not a mere machine. For a machine has solely *motive* power [bewegende *Kraft*], whereas an organized being possesses inherent *formative* power [*in sich* bildende *Kraft*], and such, moreover, as it can impart to the material devoid of it—material that it organizes. This, therefore, is a self-reproducing formative power [*sich fortpflanzende bildende Kraft*], which cannot be explained by the capacity of movement alone, that is to say, by mechanism." The self-reproducing formative (*bildende*) power is the natural embodiment of the formative or figurative power of the imagination (*Ein-bildungs-kraft*). The distinction between machines as externally moved and organisms as self-moving proved decisive not only for later philosophy and art but also for the natural sciences. Kant identified the *principle of self-organization* that scientists have shown is constitutive of living organisms. While both works of art and organisms embody the principle of inner teleology, only living organisms are *self*-organizing:

> We do not say half enough of nature and her capacity in organized products when we speak of this capacity as being the *analogue of art*. For what is here present to our minds is an artist—a rational being—working from without. But nature, on the contrary, organizes itself, and does so in each species of its organized products—following in a single pattern certainly, as to general features, but nevertheless admitting deviations calculated to secure self-preservation under particular circumstances. We might perhaps come nearer to the description of this impenetrable property if we were to call it an *analogue of life*.[5]

In this remarkable passage, Kant makes several closely related points whose significance will become clear in what follows. First, in living organisms order is internally *emergent* rather than externally imposed. Second, the relation between parts and whole is thoroughly *interactive*—the whole simultaneously emerges from the interplay of parts and acts back on these parts to constitute their differential identities. Third, the whole is an integrative *relational structure*—it is, in other words, the interplay of parts. Fourth, while the whole provides a certain stability, it is not a fixed form but a *dynamic pattern* that changes constantly. And finally, this relational structure provides the *parameters of constraint* within which parts continue to develop. Since the whole is refigured as parts change, whole and part are *codependent and coevolve*.

The far-reaching implications of Kant's seminal insight are only now being realized. Theoretical biologist Stuart Kauffman was one of the first to recognize the relevance of Kant's work for debates in contemporary biology:

> Immanuel Kant, writing more than two centuries ago, saw organisms as wholes. The whole existed by means of the parts; the parts existed both because of and in order to sustain the whole. This holism has been stripped of a natural role in biology, replaced with the image of the genome as the central directing agency that commands the molecular dance. Yet an autocatalytic set of molecules is perhaps the simplest image one can have of Kant's holism. Catalytic closure ensures that the whole exists by means of the parts, and that they are present both because of and in order to sustain the whole. Autocatalytic sets exhibit the emergent property of holism. If life began with collectively autocatalytic sets, they deserve awed respect, for the flowering of the biosphere rests on the creative power they unleashed on the globe— awed respect and wonder, but not mysticism.[6]

The leap from Kant to contemporary biology was not, of course, direct but was mediated inter alia by nineteenth-century romanticism and idealism. Kant was more interested in art than biology, and it is not clear whether he realized the important implications of his own insight. Hegel, however, was quick to grasp the importance of Kant's discovery of self-organizing systems. In his *Science of Logic*, he writes: "One of Kant's great services to philosophy consists in the distinction he has made between relative, or *external*, and *internal* purposiveness; in the latter he has opened up the Notion of life, the Idea, and by so doing has done *positively* for philosophy what the *Critique of Reason* did but imperfectly, equivocally, and only *negatively*, namely raised it above the determinations of reflection and the relative world of metaphysics."[7] Here, as elsewhere, the strictures Kant places on epistemology prevent him from recognizing the ontological significance of his insights. In Kant's critical philosophy, the self-relational structure of inner teleology remains subjective— it is a heuristic device that is useful for organizing experience but does not necessarily tell us anything about the objective world. For Hegel, by contrast, the notion of self-organization is embodied in the social and natural world and as such is nothing less than the relational structure that forms the Logos of life. Hegel's most concise definition of life discloses its inherent complexity:

Its [i.e., Life's] sphere is completely determined in the following moments. *Essence* is infinity as the sublation [*Aufgehobensein*] of all distinctions, the pure movement of axial rotation [*die reine achsendrehende Bewegung*], its self-repose being an absolutely restless infinity [*absolut unruhiger Unendlichkeit*]; independence itself, in which the differences of the movement are resolved, the simple essence of time which, in this equality with itself, has the stable shape [*Gestalt*] of space. The differences, however, are just as much present as *differences* in the simple universal medium; for this universal flux [*Flüssigkeit*] has its negative nature only in being the sublation of them; but it cannot sublate the different moments if they do not have an enduring existence [*Bestehen*]. It is the very flux as a self-identical independence that is itself an *enduring existence* in which, therefore, they are present as distinct members and parts existing on their own account. *Being* no longer has the significance of *abstract* being, nor has their pure essentiality the significance of *abstract* universality; on the contrary, their being is precisely the simple fluid substance of pure movement within itself. The *difference*, however, *qua* difference, of these members with respect to one another consists in general in no other *determinateness* than that of the moments of infinity or of the pure movement itself.[8]

The intricate structure of life that Hegel articulates in this tangled passage is isomorphic with the self-reflexive structure he identifies in both the Trinity and self-consciousness. There is no life apart from living beings, and there can be no living beings apart from life. As the embodiment or incarnation of Spirit, life is not merely the sum of individual organisms but is the organic structure of interrelationship in and through which living beings emerge and pass away. As a "universal fluid medium," "life is a *process*" that is autotelic.[9] The purpose of the process, in other words, is nothing other than the process itself. Since life creates *itself* in producing everything that lives, this vital process is self-renewing and thus infinite. For Hegel as for Kant, this autotelic structure in-forms both the living organism and the work of art. The work of art, we have seen, must be understood as both product (i.e., art object) and process (i.e., production of objects). When understood expansively, the work of art is *poiesis*—the activity of creative emergence through which patterns, forms, and schemata are figured, disfigured, and refigured. Since organizational figures and the figurative processes through which they emerge are not merely subjective, life is the objective embodiment of art. Just as art creates itself in creating individual works, so life produces itself in producing particular living beings. Translated into terms of contemporary theoretical biology, art and life are *autopoietic*.

In his provocative book *How the Leopard Changed Its Spots: The Evolution of Complexity*, Brian Goodwin, professor of biology at the Open University in England, points out that an organism "is a functional *and* a structural unity in which the parts exist for *and by means of* one another in the expression of a particular nature. This means that the parts of an organism—leaves, roots, flowers, limbs, eyes, heart, brain—are not made independently and assembled, as in a machine, but arise as a result of interactions within the developing organism." As we will see, Goodwin develops a critique of the geneocentrism of much contemporary biology by appropriating the theory of complex adaptive systems to reinterpret the dynamics of morphogenesis. Goodwin, like Kauffman, traces the closely related notions of self-organization and autopoiesis to Kant: "Kant knew nothing about these dynamic processes, but he did correctly describe the emergence of parts in an organism as the result of internal interactions instead of the assembly of preexisting parts, as in a mechanism or a machine. So organisms are not molecular machines. They are functional and structural unities resulting from a self-organizing, self-generating dynamic."[10] The minimum conditions of an organism include self-organization, self-maintenance, and reproduction (sexual or asexual) or regeneration.

Humberto Maturana and Francisco Varela coined the term *autopoiesis* to describe the processes of active self-generation and self-maintenance. Underscoring the importance of the principle of self-organization in biology, they argue: "living systems are machines that cannot be shown by pointing to their components. Rather, one must show their organization in a manner such that the way in which all their peculiar properties arise becomes obvious." When so understood, autopoiesis subverts the opposition between machines and organisms that Kant and Hegel posited by establishing a synthesis in which one complements the other. Organisms are self-organizing systems that presuppose the effective operation of molecular machines. "An *autopoietic machine is organized (defined as a unity) as a network of processes of production (transformation and destruction) of components that produces the components, which: (i) through their interactions and transformations continuously regenerate and realize the network of processes (relations) that produced them; and (ii) constitute it (the machine) as a concrete unity in the space in which they (the components) exist by specifying the topological domain of its relation as such a network.*" The self-reflexivity of such autopoietic "machines" is isomorphic with the self-reflexivity of Kant's self-organizing being as well as with Hegel's self-developing whole.[11] Maturana and Varela offer what is in effect a gloss on Hegel's account of the dialectical relation between parts and whole when they argue that "an autopoietic machine continuously generates and specifies its own organization through its operation as a system of production of its own components, and does this in an endless turnover of components under conditions of continuous perturbations and compensation of perturbations."[12] As Maturana and Varela suggest, the relationality of autopoietic machines conforms to the structure of networks whose operational logic I will consider in more detail below.

The constitutive interrelation of parts and whole in autopoietic machines harbors an apparent aporia: If neither parts nor whole can function independently, then how can organic structures originate? Parts cannot gradually assemble themselves to form the whole, because the whole is the condition of the possibility of the operation of the parts. Since parts and whole are codependent, it would seem they must emerge simultaneously. The only plausible explanation for the emergence of autopoietic systems is the process of "bootstrapping" or, in more precise terms, an autocatalytic process in which molecules are involved in interactions necessary for their own formation. Any such reaction is clearly nonlinear and subject to the dynamics of positive feedback in which there can be discontinuous phase shifts. In his account of what he calls "the networks of life," Kauffman describes the process of autocatalysis:

> At its heart, a living organism is a system of chemicals that has a capacity to catalyze its own reproduction. Catalysts such as enzymes speed up chemical reactions that might otherwise occur, but only extremely slowly. What I call a collectively autocatalytic system is one in which the molecules speed up the very reactions by which they themselves are formed: A makes B; B makes C; C makes A again. Now imagine a whole network of these self-producing loops. Given a supply of food molecules, the network will be able constantly to re-create itself. Like the metabolic networks that inhabit every living cell, it will be alive. What I aim to show is that if a sufficiently diverse mix of molecules accumulates somewhere, the chance that an autocatalytic system—a self-maintaining and self-reproducing metabolism—will spring up becomes a near certainty. If so, the emergence of life may have been much easier than we have supposed.

To illustrate his point, Kauffman offers the example of a simple autocatalytic set in which two dimer molecules (i.e., two molecules that act together as a unit)—and BA—catalyze their own formation from two simple molecules, A and B. "Since AB and BA catalyze the very reactions

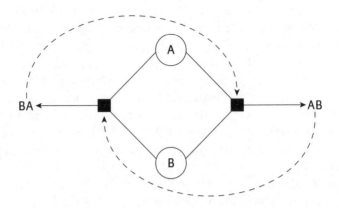

Figure 21. Simple Autocatalytic Set (Stuart Kauffman, *At Home in the Universe: The Search for the Laws of Self-Organization and Complexity* [New York: Oxford University Press, 1995], 49)

that join As and Bs to make the dimers, the network is autocatalytic" (fig. 21).[13] For life to originate, the chemicals in the "prebiotic soup" must be sufficiently dense and diverse. With sufficient time, the interplay of molecules approaches the condition of self-organized criticality or, in more popular terms, the tipping point, where more becomes different. As complexity and interactivity increase, molecules, cells, and organisms self-organize, and new organizational patterns emerge. This process requires no external agency but is completely autotelic; inasmuch as life makes itself, it is autopoietic. As will become apparent in what follows, whether the systems are biological, social, political, economic, or cultural, the dynamics of emergent creativity are everywhere the same.

In their analysis of autopoietic machines, one of the most important refinements Maturana and Varela introduce to previous interpretations of organic structure is the use of the language of networks—autopoietic systems, they argue, are networks or, more precisely, networks of networks:

> Autopoietic machines are unities whose organization is defined by a particular network of processes (relations) of production of components, the autopoietic network, not by the components themselves or their static relations. Since the relations of production of components are given as processes, if the processes stop, the relations of production vanish; as a result for a machine to be autopoietic, its defining relations of production must be continuously regenerated by com-

ponents which they produce. Furthermore, the network of processes which constitute an autopoetic machine is a unitary system in the space of the components that it produces and which generate the network through their interactions.[14]

The structure and function of these networks conform to the structure and operational logic of complex adaptive systems as I described them in the first chapter. As a network of networks, autopoietic systems are fractal—from the micro- to the macrolevel, life is an emergent self-organizing process. "An autopoietic entity," Lynn Margulis and Dorion Sagan explain, "metabolizes continuously; it perpetuates itself through chemical activity, the movement of molecules. Autopoiesis entails energy expenditure and the making of messes. Autopoiesis, indeed, is detectable by that incessant life chemistry and energy flow which is metabolism. Only cells, organisms made of cells, and biospheres made of organisms are autopoietic and can metabolize."[15]

The transfer of energy points to an important feature of organisms that is easily obscured by the notion of autopoiesis: living organisms are open, rather than closed, systems. Though autopoietic systems appear to be circular and, therefore, closed, we have discovered that self-referential structures always include as a condition of their possibility something they cannot completely incorporate. This excess or unassimilable remainder traces an opening that makes it possible for the system or network to continue to evolve. Living organisms take in energy from the world around them and release heat into the environment through their metabolic processes. This heat increases entropy, which has been thought to contribute to the ultimate heat death of the universe. While individual organisms are necessarily open, the universe seems to be a closed system. Every closed system, Norbert Wiener explains, inevitably moves toward the entropic state of equilibrium: "As entropy increases, the universe, and all closed systems in the universe, tend to deteriorate and lose their distinctiveness, to move from the least to the most probable state, from a state of organization and differentiation in which distinctions and forms exist, to a state of chaos and sameness."[16] The term "negentropy," which was coined by Erwin Schrödinger in his seminal book *What Is Life?*, is negative entropy. Whereas entropy represents the absence of differences constitutive of organizational structure, negentropy designates the opposite state, which occurs when differentiated structures, systems, and networks emerge in the midst of disorder. Ilya Prigogine and Isabelle Stengers label the islands of negentropy that emerge in the midst of entropy "dissipative structures." This term can be confusing and must be understood precisely. Since entropy refers to a state of homogeneity, increasing entropy would seem to dissipate the differences upon which organization, as well as order, depends. Dissipative structures dissipate this dissipation in a process that approximates a dialectical negation of negation of order. When understood in this way, double negation is a condition of the possibility of emergent order without which life is impossible.[17]

The relationship between entropy and negentropy suggests that living organisms can be understood as information-processing machines. In classical information theory, the interplay between information and noise is interpreted in terms of the relation between negentropy and entropy respectively. "Just as entropy is the measure of disorganization," Wiener argues, "the information carried by a set of messages is a measure of organization. In fact, it is possible to interpret the information carried by a message as essentially the negative of entropy, and the negative logarithm of its probability." If, however, there are extrinsic sources of energy, the progressive realization of entropy is not inevitable. Wiener continues: "But while the universe as a whole, if indeed there is a whole universe, tends to run down, there are local enclaves whose direction seems opposed to that of the universe at large and in which there is a limited and temporary tendency for organization to increase. Life finds its home in these enclaves."[18] Wiener's qualifications are important—complete certainty about the laws of thermodynamics presupposes a knowledge of the whole universe that is inaccessible to human beings. This uncertainty creates the possibility that counterentropic tendencies are at work in the cosmos and has led an increasing number of scientists to doubt the inevitable heat death of the universe. Living organisms are nonequilibrium systems that resist entropic drift through processes of self-organization and as such are negentropic. Whereas entropy represents the loss of differences constitutive of organizational structure, negentropy designates the temporary reversal of the process, which occurs when differentiated structures emerge in the midst of disorder. The question that remains is whether negentropy affects the teleological trajectory of entropy.

In his suggestive book *The Life of the Cosmos,* professor of physics Lee Smolin raises questions about the applicability of the second law of thermodynamics to the cosmos as a whole:

Two ideas from nineteenth-century science may have particularly shaped expectations of early twentieth-century cosmologists. The first is the mistaken idea that the universe must necessarily evolve to a "heat death," after which it would be devoid of life or structure. A second reason for the prejudice that the universe is unstructured on large scales might be that this idea is a vestige of the old Newtonian cosmology based on absolute space. Absolute space is supposed to be absolutely uniform and, while it is invisible, in any cosmology based on it there is a tendency to assume that the matter is more or less distributed uniformly, mirroring the uniformity of absolute space.

Rather than extending the Newtonian model of intrinsically stable systems to the universe as a whole, Smolin appropriates the interpretation of evolution as a complex adaptive system developed in the biological sciences to explain the emergence of the laws of physics and the structure of the cosmos. From this perspective, natural laws are not fixed and eternal but evolve according to the principle of natural selection. "To construct the formal analogy," Smolin argues, "we begin by taking the genes to be analogous to the parameters [of the laws of physics]. The collection of all possible sequences of DNA is then something like the space of parameters." The formal representation of natural selection applies equally well to both biology and cosmology. I will consider the dynamics of the evolutionary process in more detail below; in this context, it is important to understand the similarities between physical and biological systems. "If this theory is right," Smolin concludes,

the universe shares certain features with biological systems. In both cases there is a large collection of distinguishable individuals, the properties of each of which are specified by a set of parameters. In both cases, the configurations that would be realized for most values of these parameters are very uninteresting. In both cases one has the development of the structures that are stable over time scales that are very long compared to the fundamental time scales of the elementary dynamical processes. In both cases what needs to be explained is why the parameters that are actually realized fall into these small sets that give us an interesting, highly structured world. And, if the theory I have proposed is right, the explanation in both cases is found in the statistics behind the principles of natural selection.[19]

The cosmos, then, does not necessarily tend toward equilibrium in which all differences disappear; it is possible that the universe, like biological organisms, is structured at every level and develops most creatively in conditions far from equilibrium.

While there are multiple ways in which organisms function as information-processing machines, I will concentrate on two in this context: the first and more obvious is the genetic code, and the second is the emergence of order from chaos or information from noise through the operation of schemata that function as complex adaptive networks. The metaphors used to describe genetic processes are insistently linguistic. In the simplest terms possible, the genome is "the book of life" whose alphabet consists of a four-letter code. The genetic information necessary to create an organism consists of sequences of bases arranged in a specific order in DNA's double helix. The four-letter code in the base pairs (adenine [A], guanine [G], cytosine [C], thymine [T]) of DNA are grouped in three-letter codons that determine the amino acids necessary for the production of the protein molecules. David Depew and Bruce Weber describe this process in terms of transcription technology once used in computers:

> The making of amino acids is accomplished through the intermediary of single-stranded messenger RNA (mRNA), a nucleic acid closely related to DNA. mRNA carries the *transcribed* message from the "master tape" of DNA, as if it were a cassette, to a readout or decoder device called the "ribosome," which in turn translates the nucleotide code into a polypeptide chain of amino acids with the aid of soluble transfer RNA (tRNA) molecules, which recognize codon triplets and carry, through a covalent chemical bond, specific amino acids. When series of amino acids are strung together, the resulting "polypeptide" folds up in regular ways to produce the globular or fibrous entities called proteins.[20]

Proteins are critical for the creation and survival of cells. In addition to forming the structural components of cells, proteins serve as enzymes necessary for catalyzing chemical reactions required by all living organisms. Deciphering the enormous complexity of the structure and function of proteins is at least as important as the determination of the genome for understanding the intricacies of life. Rather than the key that unlocks the book of life, decoding the genome is only the first step in a long—perhaps endless—*interpretation* of living organisms.

The details about genetic processes need not detain us here. There are, however, two important points that deserve further consideration: first, what Francis Crick called the "central dogma" of the genetic revolution and, second, the structuralist tendencies of genetic biology. Proteins cannot copy themselves directly but can only be reproduced by the specific nucleic acids that correspond to them. Nor can a protein sequence be translated into a nucleic acid sequence. The transfer of information is always from nucleic acid to protein. This insight constitutes Crick's central dogma. "A consequence of this central dogma," Nobel laureate Christian de Duve explains, "is that an acquired modification of a protein cannot be transmitted to offspring, because the information cannot be transferred to the gene coding for that protein."[21] The unidirectionality of information transfer constitutes the molecular argument against Lamarckianism, that is, the view that acquired traits can be inherited.

The discovery that the genetic code is essentially universal and that information flows one way has led many to conclude that the genome is something like a fixed program that is analogous to a universal language. When understood in this way, genetic biology represents what is in effect an alternative version of philosophical and linguistic structuralism. There are, however, different versions of biological structuralism, which derive from different theories of language. While Brian Goodwin and Gerry Webster explore the relationship between nineteenth-century rational morphology and the theories of Lévi-Strauss, Piaget, and Chomsky, Atuhiro Sibatani appropriates Saussurian linguistics to interpret genetic processes. Summarizing the conclusions of his suggestive article, "How to Structuralise Biology?" Sibatani writes: "I sought to apply structuralism in biology by identifying, by analogy, the infinitely variable act of protein synthesis in the cell with the *parole* of Saussure. By so doing I related the creative aspect of synthesizing different proteins to the similarly creative aspect of personal discourse, which emerges under the social constraint relevant to any language at any time and place, i.e., the *langue* of Saussure. Then, the biological counterpart of the *langue* should be the genetic code, or more precisely, the genetic code system."[22] From this point of view, the genotype functions as something like an elemental universal grammar (i.e., language, or *la langue*), and the phenotype operates like particular speech events (*la parole*). The four nucleotide bases are analogous to elements or morphemes that recombine through chemical reactions that approximate syntactic rules of grammar.

The problem with this line of analysis is the same as with every version of structuralism: it is so preoccupied with synchronic structures that it cannot explain diachronic development and, therefore, is unable to account for morphogenesis, the emergence of life, or evolution. In the next section, I will consider how rational morphology and structural biology can be modified to complement the neo-Darwinianism that lies at the heart of contemporary genetic theory. To see why such a modification is not only possible but also required, it is necessary to establish that the genome is neither closed nor fixed but is open and emergent. Biological organisms are not isolated systems but are imbricated in constitutive and transformative networks that both encompass and surpass them. The interrelation of organisms and the environment, for example, can result in evolutionary changes that can affect the genome over time. The environment, in turn, is constantly transformed by cultural, social, economic, and technological influences as well as chemical and biological processes. If all of these factors are taken into consideration, it becomes necessary to shift from models of universal language and fixed programs or templates to figures and schemata that conform to the dynamics of emerging complex adaptive networks.

This conclusion has far-reaching implications. "It has become clear," Depew and Weber explain, "that 'reverse information flow' does in fact occur. Moreover, genomic DNA, once thought to be a static and unchanging 'information store,' turns out to be extremely fluid. Amplifications, deletions, rearrangements, and mutations occur frequently during development and in response to environmental stimuli."[23] This is a critical discovery that harbors a significant shift in the understanding of life. "Since the advent of recombinant DNA research," Mae Wan Ho points out, "molecular geneticists have discovered that the genome is essentially fluid. In other words, genomic DNA is functionally and structurally as flexible and changeable as the rest of the organism."[24] It is important to stress that the structure as well as the function of the genome *can* be modified. Moreover, as Depew and Weber explain, amplifications, deletions, rearrangements, and mutations not only occur for "internal" reasons but are also the result of environmental stimuli.

If the genome resembles a schema that is a complex adaptive network, it can function at the biological level in a way that is strictly parallel to the manner in which symbolic/cognitive networks function at the cultural level. Since complex systems are adaptive, their evolution is coevolutionary. When systems as well as networks adapt to systems and networks that are adapting to them, change is necessarily correlative. Gell-Mann underscores the importance of coadaptation in his analysis of the interrelation between the genotype and the environment in the formation of the phenotype:

> The genotype satisfies the criteria for a schema, encapsulating in highly compressed form the experience of the past and being subject

to variation through mutation. The genotype itself does not usually get tested directly by experience. It controls, to a great extent, the chemistry of the organism, but the ultimate fate of each individual depends also on environmental conditions that are not at all under the control of the genes. The phenotype, in other words, is codetermined by the genotype and by all those external conditions, many of them random. Such an unfolding of schemata, with input from new data, to produce effects in the real world is characteristic of a complex adaptive system.[25]

Gell-Mann's description of the relation between the genotype and the phenotype points to the second way in which organisms can be understood as information-processing machines. The emergence of life, we have discovered, is a negentropic process that delays the drift toward increased entropy. By extending Wiener's information theory, it becomes possible to interpret the polarity between entropy and negentropy in terms of a series of related binaries.

Entropy / Negentropy
Disorganization / Organization
Undifferentiation / Differentiation
Chaos / Order
Noise / Information

Regardless of the media in which they are found, these polarities are not exclusive oppositions but are codependent and coevolve: each depends on the other and neither can be apart from the other.

To understand additional ways in which organisms function as information-processing machines, it is helpful to return to the notion of "dissipative structures." In contrast to closed systems, which tend toward equilibrium, open systems emerge far from equilibrium and create eddies in which entropy is *dissipated* through complex processes of self-organization:

The remarkable feature is that when we move from equilibrium to far-from-equilibrium conditions, we move away from the repetitive and the universal to the specific and the unique. Indeed, the laws of equilibrium are universal. Matter near equilibrium behaves in a "repetitive" way. On the other hand, far from equilibrium there appears to be a variety of mechanisms corresponding to the possibility of occurrence of various types of dissipative structures. For example, far

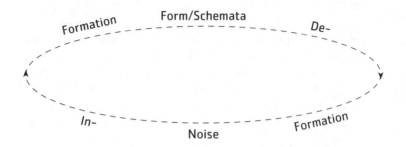

Figure 22. Noise In-Formation

from equilibrium we may witness the appearance of chemical clocks, chemical reactions which behave in a coherent, rhythmical fashion. We may also have processes of self-organization leading to nonhomogeneous structures to nonequilibrium crystals.[26]

In dissipative structures, disorder does not merely destroy order, structure, and organization but it is also a condition of their formation and transformation. As we have seen, momentarily resisting entropy, dissipative structures dissipate the dissolution of the differences necessary for organization. Inasmuch as life is negentropic, disorder is actually necessary to its emergence, renewal, and development.

With these insights, let us return to the relation between information and noise. The structure and function of living organisms conform to a pattern that is by now familiar (fig. 22). At every level—cellular, organismic, species, environmental—emergent forms function as schemata that process data circulating in surrounding fluxes and flows to create order out of chaos. Information and noise are not opposites; rather, information is noise in (the process of) formation; there can be neither form nor formation, figure nor figuration, without the noise from which it emerges and to which it returns. When information is understood as process rather than product, the line separating it from noise is difficult to determine with certainty. Noise is not absolute but is relative to the system it disrupts and reconfigures, and conversely, information is not fixed and stable but is always being figured and refigured in relation to noise. Life is lived on the edge between order and chaos, difference and indifference, negentropy and entropy. This margin between figuring and disfiguring is the site or, more precisely, nonsite of emergent creativity.

EMERGENT CREATIVITY

While evolution has always posed theological questions, it has traditionally been more vexing for Protestants than Catholics. As we have seen,
if evolution is scientific fact rather than speculative theory, the biblical
story of creation is wrong and scriptural inerrancy, which is so important for many Protestants, is called into question. Furthermore, if the
cosmos were a self-organizing system, the recourse to the classical teleological argument for its existence or its contemporary reformulation
in the theory of so-called intelligent design would become unnecessary.
Order would not be imposed from without but would emerge within interacting systems and networks whose structure and operation can be
deciphered through rational inquiry and empirical investigation.[27]

The controversy between theology and evolution has changed remarkably little since Darwin advanced his theory in 1859. While a student at
Cambridge University, Darwin studied with the leading defender of the
teleological argument at the time—William Paley. By the time he set sail
in 1831, Darwin had committed Paley's influential book *Natural Theology, or Evidences of the Existence and Attributes of the Deity Collected from
the Appearance of Nature* (1802) to memory and fully expected to become
a country pastor when he returned to England. But what he saw during
his sojourn not only changed his mind but also transformed modern science and, by extension, modern society and culture. Though few, if any,
people realized it at the time, the theory of evolution raised issues that
ran much deeper than the viability of the teleological argument for the
existence of God. The debate between Darwin and his critics extends the
controversy between nominalism and realism from theology and philosophy to natural science. Figure 23 suggests the theological and philosophical genealogy of different interpretations of evolution and points
in the direction of a reformulation of the theory that I will develop in the
following pages.

The intellectual climate in which Darwin began to develop his theory
was dominated by the arguments of creationists like Paley as well as rational morphologists like Étienne Geoffroy Saint-Hilaire and Georges
Cuvier. Disputes between uniformitarians and catastrophists about
recent geological discoveries further complicated debates about evolution.[28] One of the most influential lines of analysis grew out of an alliance
between creationists and morphologists. Geoffroy Saint-Hilaire formulated the "Principle of Connections," according to which "certain patterns of relationship between structural elements in organisms remained

	WORD		DEED

WORD   DEED

Rational Morphology   Darwinism and Neo-Darwinism

Realism   Nominalism

Essentialist: Form/Structure Antiessentialist: Individual
ontologically prior   ontologically prior to
to individual   Form/Structure

Whole: structure of fixed   Whole: aggregate of
relations and irreducible   and reducible to
to individual parts   individual parts

Constraint internal   Constraint external

Development within but   Development within and between
not between types   types linear, gradual, continuous

Complex, Dynamic Morphogenesis

Neither realist nor nominalist:
Individual and Form/Structure
codependent

Whole and parts reciprocally related:
whole emerges from but cannot be
reduced to parts

Constraint "internal" and "external"
Development: punctuated equilibrium

Figure 23. Complex, Dynamic Morphogenesis

constant even though the elements themselves changed." According to this theory, all tetrapod limbs, for example, are "transformations of a single ground plan of structural elements so that the diversity of forms is logically grounded in a unity of type."[29] The process of development is characterized by a progressive branching from a common origin. Geoffroy Saint-Hilaire's theory sparked heated debates within and beyond the natural sciences. Baron Georges Cuvier formulated an influential alternative by developing a critique of Geoffroy Saint-Hilaire's position in which he rejected the foundation of the Principle of Connections by calling into question the claim that all animal species are transformations of a single "ground plan." To counter Geoffroy Saint-Hilaire's argument, Cuvier attempted to rationalize Aristotle's account of natural organisms by identifying four distinct types, or "embranchments," of animals: vertebrates, mollusks, arthropods (insects), and radiolaria (e.g., sea urchins and hydras).[30] The cornerstone of Cuvier's theory is his insistence that it is impossible for different types to develop from one another or to cross the putative lines separating one type from another. Within this framework, when a species becomes extinct as the result of a natural catastrophe, God must intervene to create a new species. The theological appeal of this position is twofold: first, the creative role of God is preserved in the formation of typical species, and second, since the types remain distinct and cannot develop from one another, the uniqueness of human beings is preserved and their difference from so-called lower animals is secured. Though Cuvier formulated his position by refining Aristotelianism, his conclusions represent what amounts to a latter-day version of Platonism. The different types of animals are in effect Platonic forms or archetypes, each of which is defined by certain inherent characteristics that are gradually revealed over the course of time. There is, however, no constitutive interrelation between or among different types of organisms.

While some investigators used such typologies for taxonomic purposes, rational morphologists considered the different forms to be the ontological ground of each determinate species. In rational morphology, as in philosophical realism, the whole is prior to and a condition of the possibility of the parts. The purpose of morphological analysis is to identify the form or structure that constitutes the essence of the species. The "ground plan" of the species is a structural whole formed of fixed relations that cannot be reduced to the sum of its individual parts. This structure establishes internal constraints on development within the species, but since the different forms remain strictly independent, it prevents any development between and among species. Instead of originating from a common ancestor in an evolutionary tree, each species is created independently of all others.

Darwin overturned every assumption of rational morphology. Stephen Jay Gould explains why the significance of Darwin's account of evolution extends far beyond biology:

> Darwin's revolution should be epitomized as the substitution of variation for essence as the central category of natural reality. (See Mayr, our greatest living evolutionist, *Animal Species and Evolution*, for a stirring defense of the notion that "population thinking," as a replacement for Platonic essentialism, forms the centerpiece of Darwin's revolution.) What can be more discombobulating than a full inversion or "grand flip" in our concept of reality: in Plato's world, variation is accidental, while essences record a higher reality; in Darwin's reversal, we value variation as a defining (and concrete earthly) reality, while averages (our closest operational approach to "essences") become mere abstractions.[31]

This reversal is not, of course, new—it effectively repeats the shift from medieval realism to nominalism, which we have previously considered. Though he never makes his philosophical assumptions explicit, Darwin is consistently antiessentialist: the individual (organism within species as well as trait within organism) is ontologically prior to general forms and structures. The whole is the aggregate of the parts and is, therefore, subject to reductive analysis. Change, which is accidental and incremental, is directed by external circumstances (i.e., independent environmental conditions). Darwin did not borrow these assumptions and principles from the biological sciences of his day but organized his observations of nature according to principles defined by Isaac Newton, Thomas Malthus, and Adam Smith.

The Newtonian model of physical systems serves as the basis of Darwin's interpretation of structure and function of biological systems. Six basic principles inform his analysis: empiricism, individualism, efficient or external causality, equilibrium, continuity, and reductionism. As we have seen, nominalism's voluntaristic theology issued in an empirical epistemology, which was decisive for the rise of modern science. If everything is ultimately grounded in the divine will, knowledge has to be rooted in observation and sense experience. Analysis, therefore, must be inductive rather than deductive. This empirical epistemology leads to an individualistic ontology in which investigation focuses on individual organisms and their particular traits. Darwin scrupulously followed these principles by carefully gathering information about individual animals and plants and from these data built a general theory. Since causes in the Newtonian model are external rather than internal, Darwin had "to find an external force, like Newtonian gravity, rather than an internal drive, that impinged on the developmental and reproductive cycle with sufficient force to drive and shape evolutionary diversity. That force must, moreover, be a *vera causa*, a real cause that can be seen at work this very day." He discovered this cause in the notion of natural selection. As Depew and Weber point out, "in calling the external force that drives evolution 'natural selection,' Darwin extend[ed] the 'artificial selection' of variant organisms by plant and animal breeders, thereby treating the general mechanism they share as a *vera causa*."[32] This argument raises several crucial points. First, unlike the deliberate actions of animal breeders, natural selection occurs by chance; Darwinian evolution is, in Jacques Monad's apt phrase, "chance caught on the wing."[33] Although there are constantly minor mutations in organisms, natural systems, like physical systems, tend toward equilibrium and do not change simply for internal reasons. In this theory, transformation occurs when a particular mutation better equips an organism for survival in an environment that is external to it. The core of Darwin's argument is *random* variation combined with selection by *external* environmental factors. The underlying assumption that change is continuous because it is the result of the gradual accumulation of particular adaptations creates difficulties for the explanation of speciation.

Within Darwin's schema, the Newtonian method of investigation and model of systems were necessary but not sufficient to explain the development of living organisms. The various strands of his theory did not come together until he had two moments of illumination separated by almost two decades. The first came when he was reading Malthus's *On Population*, and the second occurred eighteen years later when he realized the importance of Adam Smith's account of the division of labor in *The Wealth of Nations*. Darwin's mature theory of evolution results from the synthesis of his field observations with the population studies of Malthus and the economic theory of Smith. While the influence of Darwin's account of evolution on economic theory from Marxism to contemporary neoliberalism is widely acknowledged, few people realize the extent to which Darwin's theory itself is based on population studies and economic speculation. As Darwin understood it, Malthus's claim that population increases geometrically and the food supply only arithmetically demonstrates that organisms are always subject to *external* pressures. The limitation of resources creates competition among both individuals within a species and among different species. What Darwin needed to complete his theory was Smith's account of the division of labor among different individuals. Survival in a ruthlessly competitive world depends upon the ability of individuals and species to adapt to niches where they can profit from their labors. Populations, like industries and companies, must diversify and specialize to remain competitive. Fitness is not a matter of relative strength but is the ability to adapt and fit into an available niche in the competitive landscape. When understood in this way, Darwin's natural selection is the biological version of Smith's invisible hand, which, we have discovered, is the doctrine of divine providence rewritten as economic theory. Evolution, in other words, is the immanentization of providence.

When fully developed, rational morphology and Darwinism represent binary opposites that are both insufficient when taken by themselves. Like every form of structuralism, rational, or structural, morphology makes the mistake of assuming that the forms that are the foundations of organisms are fixed and independent of each other. Given these assumptions, evolution is, in fact, impossible: there can be no variations within individual species and no development of different species from each other. Darwinism, by contrast, presupposes a notion of individualism in which organisms are externally related to each other as well as to the environment. This understanding of individuality gives priority to isolation over relation and privileges competition over cooperation as the driving force of development. Change is accidental and is subject to no internal or structural constraints.

To develop a more adequate account of the process of evolution, it is necessary to synthesize rational morphology and Darwinism by rethinking the structural foundations of living organisms through the notion of complex adaptive systems to create a theory of dynamic morphogenesis that can account for creative emergence. As we have discovered, complex systems are emergent and self-organizing. Kauffman goes so far as to argue that "self-organization may be the *precondition* of evolvability itself. Only those systems that are able to organize themselves spontaneously may be able to evolve further."[34] According to this line of analysis, natural selection alone cannot account for evolution. This does not mean, however, that it is necessary to invoke external causes as explanatory principles; to the contrary, self-organizing structures provide flexible parameters of constraint within which selection can occur. These structures are constituted and function like schemata in complex social and cultural networks—they are not fixed but emerge through the interrelations of their elements or components as well as the interactions with other schemata. In a richly suggestive chapter entitled "Living Form in the Making," Goodwin writes:

> Similar patterns of activity can arise in systems that differ greatly from one another in their composition and in the nature of their parts. It does not seem to matter much whether we are dealing with chemical reactions, aggregating slime mold amoebas, heart cells, neurons, or ants in a colony. They all show similar types of dynamic activity— rhythms, waves that propagate in concentric circles, spirals that annihilate when they collide, and chaotic behavior. The important properties of these complex systems are found less in what they are made of than in the way the parts are related to one another and the dynamic organization of the whole—their relational order.

In contrast to the isolated forms of rational morphology and the atomistic individualism of Darwinism, complex, dynamic morphogenesis involves a relational notion of differential identity. It is important to stress once again that structures from micro- to macroscopic levels are isomorphic. At the micro level, "what counts in the production of spatial patterns is not the nature of the molecules and other components involved, such as cells, but the way these interact with one another in time (their kinetics) and in space (their relational order—how the state of one region depends on the state of neighboring regions). These two properties together define a field, the behavior of a dynamic system that is extended in space—which describes most real systems." The interplay between whole and part in these relational structures is nonlinear. On the one hand, the form or figure emerges from but cannot be reduced to the parts, and on the other hand, the whole constitutes the parts without which the whole itself cannot exist. The emergence of constitutive figures is not programmed in advance but is spontaneous and, therefore, genuinely creative.

> This is the emphasis on self-organization, the capacity of these fields to generate pattern spontaneously without any specific instructions telling them what to do, as in a genetic program. These systems produce something out of nothing. Now, we can see precisely what is meant by "nothing" in this context. There is no plan, no blueprint, no instructions about the pattern that emerges. What exists in the field is

a set of relationships among the components of the system such that the dynamically stable state into which it goes naturally—what mathematicians call the generic (typical) state of the field—has spatial and temporal pattern.

In this way, emergent self-organizing forms and figures generate what Stephen Jay Gould labels "morphospace," which "is the space of possible morphologies for species organized according to certain principles."[35] Figures within this topological space are not infinite but are formed and transformed by their relational dynamics. Specific forms in morphospace function like attractors in dynamical systems: they are points of stability upon which different trajectories tend to converge.

So understood, evolution is not simply an arbitrary process in which all things are possible. Once development starts down a certain path, alternatives are necessarily limited. Selection and self-organization are complementary: emergent self-organizing structures create networks of constraint within which natural selection can occur. Since form functions as a schema, the relation between organism and mutation can be interpreted in terms of the interplay between information and noise. Just as noise disrupts stable patterns to provide the opportunity for the creative reconfiguration of organizing schemata, so mutations make it possible for organisms to change in ways that enable them to interact more effectively with other organisms as well as the overall environment. Mutations, in other words, are creative disfigurings that allow new figures to emerge.

Within dynamic morphogenetic fields, everything is codependent, and therefore, all evolution is coevolution. Inasmuch as complex systems are open rather than closed, they are necessarily adaptive. In the case of living systems, organisms must constantly adjust to each other as well as to their environment (fig. 24). In a manner strictly parallel to the complex symbolic networks we considered in chapter 1, organic morphogenesis occurs within webs of synchronic and diachronic relations. Organisms (O) are constituted by their relations to other organisms in space at a given time (O_A^2, O_B^2, O_C^2) as well as to developmental changes that occur over time (T^1, T^2, T^3). Since organisms and environment are inseparably interrelated, the environment forms a fitness landscape (FL) that carves out niches to which organisms must adapt. These landscapes are not fixed or static but are constantly changing in relation to other fitness landscapes (FL_X^2, FL_Y^2, FL_Z^2) as well as in relation to the transformations of the particular organisms that make them up. These fitness landscapes are correlative to and limited by each other and, therefore, are

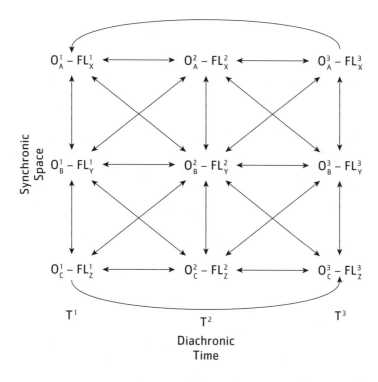

Figure 24. Coevolution of Organisms and Fitness Landscapes

not completely random. Comparing living organic fitness landscapes to artificial fitness landscapes produced by highly compressed computer programs, Kauffman writes:

> Once we understand the nature of these random landscapes and evolution on them, we will better appreciate what it is about organisms that is different, how their landscapes are nonrandom, and how that nonrandomness is critical to the evolutionary assembly of complex organisms. We will find reasons to believe that it is not natural selection alone that shapes the biosphere. Evolution requires landscapes that are not random. The deepest source of such landscapes may be the kind of principles of self-organization that we seek. Here is one part of the marriage of self-organization and selection.[36]

The environment, in other words, is itself a relational network in which fitness landscapes emerge through a self-organizing process $(FL_X^1 \mid FL_Y^1 \mid$

CHAPTER SEVEN / 338

$FL_z^1 - FL_x^2 \mid FL_y^2 \mid FL_z^2 - FL_x^3 \mid FL_y^3 \mid FL_z^3$). This network, in turn, forms the parameters for the emergence of the self-organization of self-organizing systems in relation to their self-organizing fitness landscapes ($O_B^2 - FL_y^2 \mid O_A^2 - FL_x^2 \mid O_C^2 - FL_z^2 - O_B^1 - FL_y^1 \mid O_A^1 - FL_x^1 \mid O_C^1 - FL_z^1 - O_B^3 - FL_y^3 \mid O_A^3 - FL_x^3 \mid O_C^3 - FL_z^3$). Within these networks, everything is in motion and change is constant. Pockets of stability form, transform, and dissolve in dynamic flows of energy, matter, and information whose vectors resemble patterns emerging and vanishing in fleeting clouds and rushing whirlpools.

In contrast to Darwin's account of evolution in terms of a Hobbesian war of all against all, coevolution necessarily involves cooperation as much as competition. This cooperation occurs within and among organisms as well as between organisms and their environments. The relations among codependent systems are necessarily symbiotic. The terms *symbiosis* and *symbiogenesis* were coined by the Russian botanist Konstantin Merezhkovsky in 1909 to describe the relationship between two organisms that may be but is not necessarily beneficial to both. The most prominent contemporary proponent of the theory of symbiosis is Lynn Margulis. Though her ideas were initially resisted because of the problems they posed for traditional Darwinism and suspicions about their New Age flavor, recent research has confirmed some of the most important aspects of symbiosis that Margulis was the first to identify. Borrowing a term coined by Arthur Koestler, Margulis maintains that life is "an emergent holarchy arisen from the self-induced synergy of combination, interfacing, and recombination." Emergent holarchies are structured and function like emergent self-organizing systems. Margulis identifies two types of symbiosis: the first is *between* different organisms, and the second, which she labels *endosymbiosis*, is *within* organisms. Symbiosis, she explains, "refers to an ecological and physical relationship between two kinds of organisms that is far more intimate than most associations." The second type of symbiosis is more interesting but more controversial: "Organisms form many kinds of symbioses, but the most awe-inspiring is the exceedingly close association known as endosymbiosis. This is a relationship in which one being—microbe or larger—lives not just near (nor even permanently on) another, but inside it. In endosymbiosis, organic beings merge. Endosymbiosis is like a long-lasting sexual encounter except that the participants are members of different species. Indeed, some endosymbiotic linkages have become permanent."[37] When endosymbiotic linkages become permanent, new systems and organisms can emerge.

The insight that forms the foundation of all of Margulis's work grew out of her early research in cell biology. In 1970, she published a highly controversial work with the forbidding title *Origin of Eukaryotic Cells: Evidence and Research Implications for a Theory of the Origin and Evolution of Microbial, Plant and Animal Cells on the Precambrian Earth*. Though the argument is long and the evidence complicated, Margulis's conclusion is straightforward: mitochondria[38] and chloroplasts,[39] she claims, have evolved symbiotically: "Genetic similarities that cross kingdoms are the biological equivalent of ancient 'fingerprints,' proving that photosynthetic organelles did not evolve gradually by a buildup of mutations in the DNA of plant and algal progenitors, but suddenly, when digestion-resistant bacteria took up residence in larger cells."[40] In other words, mitochondrial DNA provides evidence that different organisms with distinct DNA unite to form a single eukaryotic cell. This discovery poses serious difficulties for standard Darwinian and neo-Darwinian theory. First, if symbiogenesis produces new cells, then evolution is not simply a function of chance mutation and the survival of the fittest. The privileging of competition over cooperation appears to be more of a philosophical predilection or ideological prejudice than a scientific conclusion.[41] Second, if symbiogenesis produces new individuals, everything is not programmed in the genome. Reductive analysis, therefore, will never disclose all the secrets of life. Finally, if symbioants can form new organisms, evolution is not simply a gradual and continual process but is punctuated by disruptive events that create unexpected gaps in the narrative of life's history. Margulis extrapolates her insights from the cellular to the global and even the planetary level. From 1977 to 1980, she was the chair of the National Academy of Science's Space Science Board Committee on Planetary Biology and Chemical Evolution. In this capacity, one of her primary responsibilities was to develop research strategies for NASA. In all of her work, Margulis repeatedly comes to the same conclusion: "Life on earth is a holarchy, a nested fractal network of interdependent beings." Since life is a relational network, "independence," she insists, "is a political, not a scientific, term."[42]

The discontinuities that symbiogenesis introduces are critical to the evolutionary process. Inasmuch as complex adaptive networks are self-organizing, the event of emergence is the moment of creativity without which novelty and innovation are impossible. The dynamics of emergence, however, must be understood precisely. In contrast to the intrinsically stable systems of the Newtonian universe, living systems, I have argued, drift toward the edge of chaos. Creative emergence occurs along the margin of neither/nor: neither too much nor too little order, neither too much nor too little disorder. In the past several decades, the exponential increase in the power and speed of computers has combined with much more sophisticated software to create new areas of research known as artificial life and digital biology. If biological organisms are in important ways information-processing systems, then it ought to be possible to simulate life and evolution digitally. While still in its infancy, this new field has already yielded some important insights. During the early 1980s, John Holland, professor of computer science, electrical engineering, and psychology at the University of Michigan, Chris Langton, his student, and Stephen Wolfram, physicist and creator of Mathematica, made an important discovery while experimenting with cellular automata.[43] Cellular automata are computer programs in which each cell or unit has a set of instructions telling it how to respond to the actions of surrounding cells. The patterns generated by interacting automata are often remarkably lifelike. Holland and his colleagues discovered that cellular automata can be classified according to four typical patterns of behavior: (1) rigid structures that do not change; (2) oscillating patterns that change periodically; (3) chaotic activity that exhibits no stability; and (4) patterns that are neither too structured nor too disordered, which emerge, develop, divide, and recombine in endlessly complex ways. Langton quickly realized that the fourth category of automata is the most interesting. Though the principles governing the behavior of this intermediate domain remained obscure, he suspected activity in this region would be characterized by "a phase transition between highly ordered and highly disordered dynamics, analogous to the phase transition between the solid and the fluid states of matter."[44] As Langton studied the dynamics of this phase transition in more detail, he discovered that the four patterns of behavior fall into a regular three-step sequence: an ordered regime, a chaotic regime, and a transitional regime. Kauffman summarizes Langton's conclusions: "Just between, just near the phase transition, just at the edge of chaos, the most complex behavior can occur—orderly enough to insure stability, yet full of flexibility and surprise. Indeed, this is what we mean by complexity."[45] The patterns identified in these computer simulations correspond to operations in living organisms. From the level of the cell to the species, morphogenesis is impossible apart from the nonlinear dynamics of emergence. Goodwin observes the phase transition that Langton describes in digital organisms in his study of the giant unicellular algae known as *Dasycladeles*:

> The distinctive quality of morphogenetic dynamics in living organisms appears to be shape generated within and by a moving bound-

ary, the dynamics changing the shape while the changing shape feeds back into the dynamics, stabilizing the modes that generate the form and creating conditions for the next bifurcation. Ordered complexity, therefore, emerges through a self-stabilizing cascade of symmetry-breaking bifurcations that have an intrinsically hierarchical property, finer spatial detail emerging within already established structure, as whorls arise from tips and fine branching occurs in growing laterals. These hierarchical cascades of bifurcations are a characteristic feature of morphogenesis in all species.[46]

Complex dynamic forms fold back on themselves to shape the processes from which they emerge. While the details of morphogenesis vary from organism to organism, every pattern is punctuated by moments of emergence.

The data collected from experiments with digital life and living organisms indicate that the emergence follows a common pattern across different systems and in multiple media. In his definitive study *Emergence: From Chaos to Order*, Holland summarizes the basic principles of emergence:

1. *Emergence occurs in systems that are generated.* These systems are composed of copies of a relatively small number of components that obey simple laws. . . .
2. *The whole is more than the sum of the parts in these generated systems.* The interactions between the parts are nonlinear, so the overall behavior *cannot* be obtained by summing the behaviors of the isolated components. . . .
3. *Emergent phenomena in generated systems are, typically, persistent patterns with changing components.* Emergent phenomena recall the standing wave that forms in front of a rock in a fast-moving stream, where the water particles are constantly changing though the pattern persists. . . . Organisms are also persistent patterns; they turn over *all* their constituent atoms in something less than a two-year span, and a large fraction of their constituents turn over in a matter of weeks. . . .
4. *The context in which a persistent emergent pattern is embedded determines its function.* Because of the nonlinear interactions, a kind of aura is imposed by the context. . . .
5. *Interactions between persistent patterns add constraints and checks that provide increasing "competence" as the number of such patterns increases.* . . . The sophistication of response, interactions, and hence the possible

sophistication of response, rises extremely rapidly (factorially) with the number of interactions.

6. *Persistent patterns often satisfy macrolaws.* When a macrolaw can be formulated, the behavior of the whole pattern can be described without recourse to microlaws (generators and constraints) that determine the behavior of its components. . . .

7. *Differential persistence is a typical consequence of the laws that generate emergent phenomena.* . . . The patterns that are likely to take a significant role early in the generation process are those that persist through many kinds of interaction. Then, many possible combinations are sampled, increasing the likelihood that some more complex persistent pattern will be discovered. These generalist patterns can also provide a niche for specialist patterns that have a more restricted range of interaction.[47]

In addition to these aspects of emergence, several other features of the process must be emphasized in this context. The relation between emergence and pattern conforms to the relation between event and structure through which schemata are figured. Emergence, in other words, is the presencing that is the condition of the possibility of the presence of every organism. While the pattern or the schema is lawful, it does not seem to be possible to determine a law for the event of emergence itself. This is a very important point because it means that emergence is always in some way aleatory. The aleatory event disturbs, disrupts, and dislocates patterns to create different figures that constitute new organisms. In this way, the event of emergence is the moment of creativity, which is never possible apart from a certain destruction.

This interpretation of emergence has important implications for our understanding of evolution. In contrast to Darwin's view of evolution as a continuous linear process in which effects are proportionate to their causes, in nonlinear complex adaptive networks, effects can be disproportionate to their causes and, therefore, development is not always continuous but is characterized by punctuated equilibrium. In punctuated equilibrium, periods of relative stability are interrupted by phase shifts that occur from what Goodwin describes as "a cascade of symmetry-breaking bifurcations." The breakdown of symmetry and, correlatively, equilibrium creates instability, which eventually self-organizes to form new patterns. This account of evolution helps to explain, among many other things, the speciation events that prove so difficult to account for in classical Darwinian and neo-Darwinian theory.

The theory of punctuated equilibrium makes it clear that morphogenesis is a complex dynamic process that simultaneously incorporates and transforms important principles formulated in rational morphology as well as traditional Darwinism (fig. 23). Since the patterns, forms, and figures that constitute life are coemergent and thus codependent, they necessarily coevolve. Coevolution, however, is not limited to biological organisms. Living systems, I argued in chapter 1, are always embedded in complex social, cultural, and technological milieux that comprise multiple networks. All of these networks as well as their interrelations are, in different ways, information-processing systems, which, when fully deployed, are global: everything—absolutely everything—is entwined, enmeshed, interrelated, interconnected. Within these coevolving networks, different systems codetermine each other. Cultural systems, for example, condition natural systems as much as natural systems influence cultural systems. Religious attitudes shape values, which issue in political and economic policies that literally transform the fabric of life. These changes, in turn, provide the parameters of constraint for human activity. Far from a simple biological force, life is a complex global network of natural, social, economic, political, and cultural relations (fig. 25). To sustain life it is necessary to cultivate all of these relations. As connections proliferate and relations multiply, the network of life becomes increasingly complex. This complexity produces instabilities that are the condition of the infinite restlessness of life itself.

This understanding of life brings us back to our point of departure without precisely having come full circle. Art and religion meet in life. Art, I have argued, is a creative process that involves the figuring and disfiguring of schemata that shape experience and pattern the world. This process is staged through the imagination, which is not limited to the activity of the creative subject but also includes the creative emergence through which the objective world comes into being. In Schlegel's terms: "No poetry, no reality."[48] The structures of the work of art and the biological organism, as Kant insisted, are isomorphic: each is an autotelic, self-organizing system. Since the event of emergence is aleatory, these structures are open rather than closed and, thus, are necessarily codependent. Just as the work of art is both product and process, so life is simultaneously embodied in particular organisms and is the process in and through which particular living beings are created and destroyed. "It is life," Stevens explains, "that we are trying to get at in poetry." To understand life, it must be grasped as a work of art. "Art, broadly, is the form of life or the sound or color of life. Considered as form (in the ab-

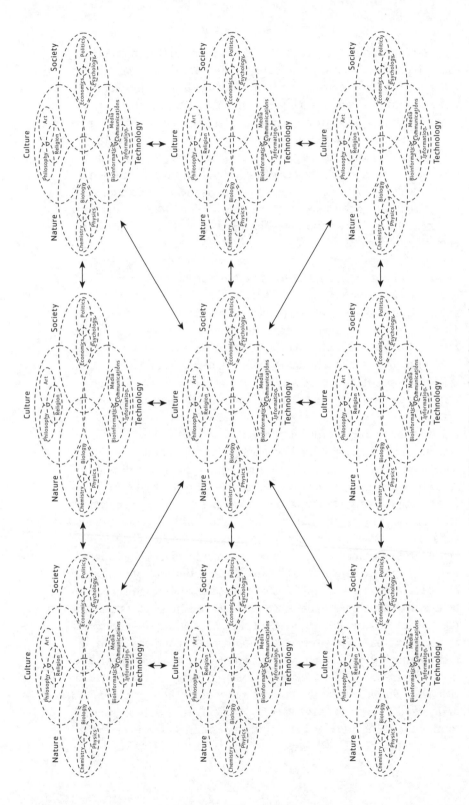

Figure 25. Coevolution of Global Networks

stract) it is often indistinguishable from life itself." But Stevens does not stop with the integration of art and life. Just as Hegel had argued that art, religion, and philosophy are *three* versions of *one* truth, so Stevens insists that poetry refigures religion: "After one has abandoned a belief in god, poetry is that essence which takes its place as life's redemption."[49] After God—art; after art—life. Three-in-one—One-in-three.

But how is *after* to be understood? On the one hand, to come after is to be subsequent to what previously has been, and on the other hand, to be after is to be in pursuit of what lies ahead. Betwixt and between past and future, after is never present as such but is the approaching withdrawal and withdrawing approach that allow presence to be present. Neither here nor there, neither present nor absent, after is the trace of that which gives and takes being. God is not the ground of being that forms the foundation of all beings but the figure constructed to hide the originary abyss from which everything emerges and to which all returns. While this abyss is no thing, it is not nothing—neither being nor nonbeing, it is the anticipatory wake of the unfigurable that disfigures every figure as if from within. Far from simply destructive, disfiguring is the condition of the possibility of creative emergence. Even when expected, emergence is surprising—without surprise, there is no novelty; without novelty, there is no creativity; without creativity, there is no life. To live within the confines of the expected, which seems to provide stability, security, and certainty, is to be dead even when alive; to be exposed to the unexpected is to be open to the chance of life—and of death. This opening is the space-time of the desire that does not seek satisfaction but cultivates the dissatisfaction that issues in endless restlessness. Satisfaction is entropic—it is the equilibrium that brings everything to a halt; dissatisfaction is negentropic—it is the disequilibrium that keeps everything in motion. Restlessness need not always lead to the melancholy of unhappy consciousness that wallows in interminable mourning but can engender the vitality that in-forms creativity. The dissatisfaction with satisfaction and satisfaction with dissatisfaction mark the end of the end that brings everything to a close. What the apocalyptic imagination in all of its guises regards as life eternal is eternal death. Eternal life is the endless restlessness of a creative process that is the Infinite.

The Infinite is not God but is always after the God who is after it. Neither simply immanent nor transcendent, after comes before to allow every god to be god. Regardless of how powerful they appear, gods are always finite. Their finitude is their determinate being that sets them over against other gods as well as the world and human beings. Though such gods are often declared infinite, their purported infinity is finite. The oppositions between and among gods or their functional equivalents ground the logic of either/or that is constitutive of all dualisms. When this oppositional logic is extended from theological speculation to practical activity, it becomes not only destructive but self-destructive: by defending self through the negation of the other, one destroys the other without whom one cannot be oneself. This conflict cannot be overcome by a monism that reduces differences to an original identity in which everything and everyone becomes one, because the erasure of differences is every bit as destructive as their violent clash. The true Infinite is neither dualistic nor monistic but is the creative interplay in which identity and difference are codependent and coevolve. As such, the Infinite is an emergent self-organizing network of networks that extends from the natural and social to the technological and cultural dimensions of life.

The structure of the Infinite is fractal—it is isomorphic at every level and across all media. Moreover, its operational logic is always triadic, or trinitarian: creativity emerges at the edge of chaos between alternative states of order that tend to drift toward disorder. Disorder is the noise without which the new cannot be heard. Far from unique, human creativity is but a moment in this infinite process. Thus, "every poem," as Stevens avers, "is a poem within a poem." If art is *poiesis*, the world is a work of art. "The theory of poetry is [therefore] the theory of life."⁵⁰ Just as the work of art is its own purpose, so the end of life is life itself. In human beings, this creative process becomes aware of itself. But this awareness is always incomplete and hence must forever be refigured. Since emergence is aleatory, life is always surprising: plans are frustrated, schemata shattered—who would want it otherwise? Moreover, the infinite process in which human life is entwined and enmeshed "knows" things finite beings can never know. Since the whole emerges from but cannot be reduced to the sum of its parts, and since the activity of imagination is not limited to the "subjective" deeds of human agents but is also the "objective" production of things in the world, there is something like mind or the Logos at work within this process. Neither external nor transcendent, this mind or Logos emerges through the self organization of the autopoietic process of life. Never fixed or stable, this is a nonlogocentric Logos that is figured, disfigured, and refigured through the dynamic morphogenesis of the constitutive networks from which it emerges and, in turn, shapes. The activity of mind does not presuppose self-consciousness but involves information processes that are *distributed* throughout natural, social, cultural, and technological networks. The buzz of noise is the murmur of life emerging. Though this murmur can never be figured, there is no art-iculation apart from its echo.

The Infinite, then, has two codependent rhythms: finitizing the infinite and infinitizing the finite. As such, the Infinite is neither above nor below, neither behind nor beyond, the finite but is the divine milieu in which everything is relative because all is related. The two rhythms of the Infinite correspond to the two moments of religion. The finitizing of the infinite figures the schemata that lend life meaning and purpose. These forms function as screens or filters that bring order to chaos by creating a world that provides temporary stability. The more effective schemata are, however, the more rigid they become until security breeds a certainty that turns destructive. Religion degenerates into religiosity when the finite as such is absolutized by constructing foundations that are purported to be unshakable. Fixed structures, however, cannot adapt to changing circumstances. Excessive order, paradoxically, drifts toward chaos, which unexpectedly creates the conditions for the creative emergence of new patterns of order. The infinitizing of the finite disrupts, dislocates, and disfigures every stabilizing structure, thereby keeping (the) all in play. Rather than fixed forms, emergent schemata that effectively order experience and shape the world are complex dynamic networks that are subtly shifting pockets of stability in the midst of fluxes and flows whose end is nothing other than themselves. Since emergence is aleatory, change is episodic and evolution is discontinuous. Gaps in time as well as space mark the edge of the abyss that is the groundless ground of everything that is and is not. Life is lived along this unfigurable edge.

CHAPTER EIGHT

Ethics without Absolutes

GUIDE FOR THE PERPLEXED

A sense of crisis pervades the world today. As old figures and patterns break down, people realize that we are at a tipping point, but they cannot yet discern the contours of the so-called new world order. This unease is not merely the result of the anxiety that typically accompanies a new millennium. Rather, there is a growing awareness that the very structures constituting the world are changing ever faster, and thus reality itself is being transformed in unexpected ways. Such moments of transition tend to provoke feelings of insecurity and uncertainty. In our day, as in Luther's time, the ground is slipping from beneath our feet, and people are seeking a secure foundation that once again can provide meaning and purpose in their lives. With the present unsettling and the future uncertain, many of the perplexed turn to the past for guidance. If the changes now occurring are, indeed, radical, this strategy is doomed to failure. Old maps cannot provide adequate guidance for new territories.

The simultaneous end of the cold war and emergence of network culture have thoroughly transformed the landscape we must navigate. With increasing connectivity creating more intense uncertainty and greater instability, people sense that things are spinning out of control and search for simplicity, certainty, and stability. Confronted by a world they cannot comprehend, many who count themselves among the faithful declare that America is reaping what it sowed in the 1960s. In a refrain that has become as common as it is influential, current personal and social problems are attributed to a "crisis of values" that began during that "decadent decade" of the sixties, when standards supposedly broke down and everything was permitted. As we have seen, within this schema, the problem is relativism and the solution appears to be absolutism. We must, the argument—if it is an argument—goes, return to time-tested truths and basic or fundamental values. When this program is put into action, however, its limitations become glaringly obvious to all but the truest of believers. Morality is reduced to the questions of God, guns, and gays and the evil empire is replaced by the axis of evil, which it is our mission to dominate or destroy. This simplistic agenda is nothing less than irresponsible in today's complex and rapidly changing world.

There is, in fact, a crisis of values, but it is caused by the militant moralists who are leading the crusade to return to a past that never existed. Contemporary moralism and the religiosity supporting it issue in programs and policies that are actually dangerous to life on earth. Far from the solution to present woes, the commitment to absolutism in all of its guises is one of the most urgent problems that must be addressed. Every version of absolutism rests upon the dualistic logic of either/or: either God or Satan, right or wrong, left or right, black or white, blue or red. . . . For true believers armed with certainty, history becomes a struggle between the forces of light and darkness or good and evil. When fully deployed, the logic of either/or leads to closed systems in which negotiation is impossible and compromise is unacceptable. The situation becomes perilous when equally self-certain and uncompromising systems with significant power and access to sophisticated technologies encounter each other. According to what I have described as the oppositional logic of self-identity, each side in the conflict attempts to secure itself by negating the other. What neither side realizes is that such struggles are always self-defeating—to negate the other without whom one cannot be what one is, is to negate oneself. Nothing is more dangerous today than the growing devotion to dualistic either/or ideologies in a neither/nor world. If disaster is to be avoided, there must be a radical transvaluation of values that both reflects global complexity and promotes an ethic of life.

In the foregoing chapters, I have begun to spin the threads of a response to this pressing dilemma; now I must weave them together in a way that makes the practical implications of this analysis explicit. While my comments will focus primarily on the role of the New Religious Right in the United States, the argument needs to be extended to other religious traditions and political situations. The rise of neofoundational religion in this country during the last half century, I have argued, has been inseparable from the emergence of neoconservative politics and neoliberal economics. These interrelated developments have their roots in the Reformation. By privatizing, deregulating, and decentralizing the relation between God and the individual subject, Luther prepared the way for political and economic transformations that continue to shape our world. Neofoundationalism, neoconservatism, and neoliberalism all presuppose an understanding of the human subject that is traceable to Luther. It is, however, important to stress that each in its own way simplifies what it appropriates. While emphasizing the importance of choice and individual responsibility, they all overlook the complexities of subjectivity that lend Luther's analysis its richness and abiding significance. When not directly contradicting the tradition they claim to follow, neofoundationalists tend to promote a version of Luther-Lite crafted to be more palatable than demanding. The most significant characteristics of the notion of subject that have become so important in religion and politics today presuppose the dualistic logic of absolutism represented by the stark alternative of either/or. Within this schema, each individual stands alone and must decide for himself or herself. The influence of other people and the impact of social institutions are secondary and in no way mitigate individual responsibility. From this point of view, autonomy is freedom *from* relationship rather than the freedom *in* relationships. The individual is independent of others, and the social totality is nothing more than the sum of its constituent members. If isolated individuality is privileged in this way, participation in sociopolitical organizations poses a threat to the purported authenticity of the individual.

When this schema is appropriated and adapted to today's world, the proliferation of choices comes to be regarded as an unquestioned good—the more choices, the better. As choice becomes an end in itself, however, it tends to be trivialized. No longer existentially fraught, subjectivity is reduced to style, and choice degenerates into a consumerism that defines individuals by what they own. When fully developed, this notion of the subject becomes one of the cornerstones of the market-state or, in more fashionable political terms, "ownership society." In contrast to the nation-state, which promises to protect territorial, economic, and cultural integrity while at the same time providing entitlements and public goods and services, the market-state, I have argued, is designed to expand opportunities for individuals by creating more choices and by making individuals responsible for their own decisions. The second cornerstone of the market-state is market fundamentalism, which privileges competition over cooperation. For true believers in economic providence, the market always knows what is best, and therefore, "external" intervention by human beings whose knowledge is necessarily limited can only interfere with the smooth operation of the well-oiled economic machine. This theology of the market leads directly to policies of privatization, decentralization, and deregulation. What previously had been social obligations (e.g., education, health care, and retirement) now become individual responsibilities. As we will see in more detail below, one of the areas in which this agenda is being pursued with a vengeance is environmental deregulation. Businesses and government officials beholden to them have formed an alliance to oppose legislation designed to protect the environment upon which life itself depends in order to safeguard short-term economic profits. Bobbitt's account of the importance of this shift bears repeating in this content: "The basic ethos of the Entrepreneurial Model is libertarian: the conviction that it is the role of society to set individuals free to make their own decisions. This ethos counsels minimal state intervention in the economy as well as in the private lives of its citizens. Privatized health care, housing, pensions, and education as well as low taxes and low welfare benefits all characterize such states."[1] To maximize choice, neoconservatives and neoliberals argue, it is necessary to create a competitive environment by privatizing services and deregulating markets. As school vouchers and IRAs proliferate, the social safety net unravels and individuals are thrown back on their own resources.

It is important to stress that the neoconservatives' agenda of deregulation represents an inversion of pivotal Protestant principles in whose name it is often promoted. For Luther, as for many of today's politicians and economists, privatization and deregulation go hand in hand. Luther's understanding of the relation between self and God establishes a clear distinction between the public and private domains. The private sphere, he argues, should remain free from any regulation or outside intervention. As a result of human sin, however, the maintenance of civic order requires the regulation of the public sphere. Neofoundationalists and neoconservatives reverse this policy by attempting to deregulate the public and regulate the private sphere. While proclaiming the gospel of individual choice and personal responsibility when privatizing social services and deregulating markets as well as the environment, they readily intervene in private affairs by attempting to legislate morality and impose religious beliefs. Nowhere is this more evident than in the so-called culture of life.

The New Religious Right, I have argued, formed in the 1970s when

Protestants and Catholics decided that the social issues uniting them were more important than the doctrinal issues separating them. Although the Supreme Court decision banning school prayer, which had been prompted by the self-proclaimed atheist Madalyn O'Hair in 1963, contributed to forging a consensus among conservative Christians, the Court's legalization of abortion a decade later had a catalytic effect that first thrust religious conservatives onto the national political stage. The banner under which opponents of *Roe v. Wade* rally is the now familiar slogan "Right to Life." As the strength of this movement has grown, "right to life" has expanded into what has been dubbed the culture of life, whose goals are considerably more ambitious. The most vocal opponents of abortion tend to be absolutists for whom nothing is gray and everything is black and white: either life or death. The same absolutistic principle informs the insistence that life begins at the moment of conception. This dualistic logic of either/or, however, can never comprehend the inexhaustible complexity of life. Even at the most rudimentary level, there is a liminal condition in which the egg has been successfully fertilized but is not yet a human being. While claiming to champion life, opponents of abortion give little attention and virtually no support to family planning, sex education, and contraception, which would reduce unwanted pregnancies. In addition to this, socially regressive economic policies discourage government support for health services for impoverished families.

Though not all foes of abortion are religiously motivated, the politics of abortion has become inextricably entangled with the New Religious Right. These religious conservatives insist that life is not merely a natural force but is, more importantly, a gift from the transcendent Creator God, and as such must be protected regardless of the cost or consequences. As they defend their position, however, it becomes clear that they actually do reduce the infinite complexities of life to a simple biological force. Consider, for example, the impact of the abortion debate on the vitally important issue of stem cell research. As is well known, many informed scientists think stem cells can be reprogrammed in ways that will create the possibility of improved treatment, if not actual cures, for debilitating and deadly diseases like diabetes, Alzheimer's disease, and Parkinson's disease. One of the most pressing problems for this research is securing enough stem cells with which to work. The most readily available supply of stem cells is unused human eggs that were originally harvested for in vitro fertilization. Members of the right-to-life movement, who believe that life begins at conception, oppose the use of these eggs for stem cell research. To "destroy" these eggs, they argue, would be to commit murder. In response to the growing political power of the New Religious Right, President George W. Bush and a majority of the Congress have placed significant restrictions on the use of these eggs. Of the sixty preexisting stem cell lines for which the president has permitted federal funding, only ten are usable and many of these have abnormal chromosomes. Moreover, all of these lines were cultivated with mouse cells and, therefore, cannot be used for treating human patients. As a result of these strictures, much research that holds the promise of relief and perhaps even the cure for many devastating diseases has been severely limited if not completely shut down. Opponents of abortion are not wrong when they insist that stem cell research is a right-to-life issue, but their perspective is partial because their understanding of life is simplistic. By what definition of life is such a "moral" agenda enacted? Whose right to life is being defended and whose is being denied? What about the right to life of people whose lives might be saved by stem cell research? What is moral and what is immoral in such research? The issues *are not* black or white. By protecting "life" not yet human, moral crusaders condemn countless people to prolonged suffering and early death.

The end of life has become as important a religious, moral, and political battleground as the beginning of life. In both cases, technological developments are creating new possibilities that pose difficult questions. With some respected scientists arguing that in the very near future technology will make it possible for human beings to live forever, it is clear that these problems are only going to become more vexing.[2] Those who defend the right to life often deny the right to death. Since life is an absolute good, they believe it should be defended at all costs and extended by every available means. Within this schema, death is not a "natural" part of life but is an enemy that must be defeated. The gospel of choice ends with a woman's right to choose whether or not to terminate an unwanted pregnancy and a suffering patient's right to choose whether or not to continue his or her life. The absurdity of some of the central claims of the so-called culture of life became undeniably apparent in the 2005 case of Terri Schiavo. Though most doctors familiar with the case agreed that Ms. Schiavo had been in a persistent vegetative state for years and would never recover, her parents nonetheless wanted to continue to do whatever was necessary to extend her life indefinitely. When her condition deteriorated and her husband concluded that there was no prospect for any improvement, he decided to discontinue life support. The conflict between Ms. Schiavo's parents and husband eventually reached the halls of Congress and the office of the president. Politicians who had devoted their entire careers to an agenda of getting government out of the lives of people by rolling back regulations caved into pressure from the New Religious Right and passed legislation to prevent the withdrawal of life support. The practical effect of this law was to mandate the reinsertion of the feeding tube. In the media circus surrounding this case, misguided moralists and shamelessly opportunistic politicians declared that they were prolonging life when they were really prolonging death. Cases like this show that the so-called culture of life is really a culture of death. The death this culture harbors is not, however, limited to isolated individuals but threatens the entire planet.[3]

To counter the culture of death, it is necessary to develop a global ethic of life that can guide individual decisions and inform social policy from the local to the international level. To accomplish this ambitious goal, it is not enough to criticize and oppose positions deemed problematic, for, as Kierkegaard once observed, to do the opposite is also a form of imitation. What is required is a thoroughgoing reframing of the issues by articulating a new vision of the world that not only helps us understand our place in it but also provides guiding principles for negotiating conflicts that often seem nonnegotiable. I have, of course, been developing such an alternative schema from the outset. Now it is necessary to spell out its practical implications.

As a point of departure, it is helpful to translate Kant's well-known aphorism about theoretical reason into practical terms: theory without practice is empty; practice without theory is blind. Theory and practice, in other words, are inextricably interrelated and, therefore, mutually conditioning. Theories or interpretive schemata always have practical consequences, and human activities transform the frameworks that inform them. In terms developed in chapter 1, schemata process data in such a way that information, knowledge, and meaning are woven together to create patterns for thought and action, which, in turn, bring about revisions and adaptations in the schemata. And yet, throughout the history of Western philosophy and theology, there has been a consistent tendency to maintain a sharp distinction between theory and practice or thinking and acting. Theoretical reason is supposed to define what *is*, and practical reason is supposed to define what *ought* to be. Theory, in other words, is descriptive and hence ontological, and practice is prescriptive or axiological. Here as elsewhere, distinctions tend to become oppositions; when this occurs, *is* and *ought* enter into conflict. If what is, is not what ought to be, moral activity (i.e., the realization of the ought) requires the negation of the world as we know it (i.e., what is). Rather than creative or productive, such nay-saying, as Nietzsche argues so persuasively, is profoundly nihilistic. This has never been clearer than in the shrill voices of many of today's self-proclaimed moralists. For the apocalyptic imagination, the best way to hasten the arrival of the next world is by working for the destruction of this world. As neofoundationalism spreads across the globe, the threat of violence and massive destruction grows. To overcome this nihilism that advertises itself as moral or even religious, it is necessary to return to the function of schemata as I described it in chapter 1.

For a system—be it natural, social, or cultural—to survive and function effectively, it must first be able to identify patterns in its environment accurately and then respond in ways that maximize its adaptability. Schemata operate both theoretically and practically by screening data to detect, form, and reform patterns that simultaneously describe entities and predict as well as prescribe events in the world. If the descriptive and predictive models of the environment are inadequate or inaccurate, activity is ineffective, and the viability of the schema as well as those using it decreases. The environment or fitness landscape, we have seen, is not fixed but constantly changes as a result of prescribed activities as well as the interactions with other schemata. Far from opposed, description and prescription are joined in nonlinear feedback loops that render thinking and acting codependent. The codependence of schematic description (i.e., is) and prescription (i.e., ought) points toward the unending interplay between ontology and axiology (fig. 26). On the one hand, what is implies what ought to be, and on the other hand, the realization of what ought to be transforms what is. It is important to stress that this relation between ontology and axiology does not imply compliance with static structures but entails engagement with emergent processes that are constantly undergoing transformation. For action to be effective in this milieu, there must be a congruence, which is not to say a perfect identity, between the map and the territory.

The question, then, becomes: What is the *ought* that *is* harbors? If, as I have argued, life is a complex adaptive network in which everything is codependent and coevolves, then absolutism must give way to relationalism. Within the infinite web of life, nothing is absolute because everything is related. *Absolute*, which derives from the Latin *absolutus* (*ab-*, "away from," plus *solvere*, "to loose"), means, among other things: "perfect in quality or nature, complete; not mixed, pure, unadulterated; not limited by restrictions or exceptions, unconditional; not limited by constitutional provisions or other restraints; unrelated to and independent of anything else; not to be doubted or questioned, certain."[4] Such

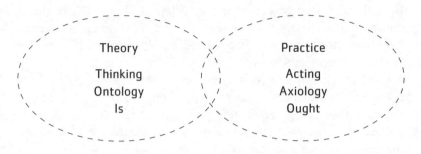

Figure 26. Theory and Practice

disconnectedness or unrelatedness, however, is self-negating: in the very effort to secure its independence from everything else, that which is deemed absolute establishes its necessary relation to other(s). The absolute, in other words, is relative, and relativity is absolute. Such relativity does not involve a subjectivism that leads to nihilistic solipsism but entails a relationalism that draws everything and everybody out of isolation and into a condition of creative codependence. Far from a simple biological force, life is impossible apart from the ceaseless interaction of mutually conditioning networks of social, cultural, and technological factors. There can be no orientation within these networks without different schemata—religious and otherwise—that provide alternative norms for conduct. In the particular schema I have been elaborating, self and other, part and whole, local and global, are mutually constitutive and, therefore, must emerge and develop together. This interplay of differences does not issue in a closed whole or complete totality; to the contrary, systems and structures that appear to be complete are always rent as if from within and, thus, are open and constantly in the process of becoming. In human beings, the emergent self-organization of this whole process becomes self-aware, and its direction is, accordingly, influenced by deliberate activity informed by schematic norms. Relationalism provides the contours within which an ethic of global life adequate for emerging network culture can be articulated.

With these insights in mind, four governing principles should guide the perplexed as they struggle to formulate the policies and programs in emerging network culture.

1. *Embrace complexity.*

While increasing complexity can be overwhelming, it tends to enrich life by fostering creative differences. Those who find complexity threatening seek to avoid the strange and protect the familiar by keeping everything the same. However, inasmuch as identity and difference, oneness and manyness, unity and plurality, are not exclusive opposites but are codependent, the production of differences in complex networks need not lead to conflict. Greater diversity can strengthen life and make natural, social, cultural, and technological systems more robust, thereby increasing their viability. Conversely, the reduction of heterogeneity to homogeneity renders systems more fragile and vulnerable. For those who appreciate the value of complexity, subtlety and nuance become important virtues. All too often in a world dominated by the exclusive logic of either/or, the insistence that things are neither simply this way nor that way is often labeled indecisive muddleheadedness, which must be rejected in the name of the clarity that decisive action is supposed to require. But clarity is not necessarily a virtue, and decisiveness can be destructive in a complex world where things are not always clear.

2. *Promote cooperation as much as competition.*

From the molecular to the human level, life, we have discovered, involves cooperation as much as competition. The combination of a simplified understanding of autonomous individuality with Darwin's evolutionary theory and Smith's political economy has led to a privileging of competition over cooperation in all realms of life. Different versions of such "muscular" schemata both presuppose and promote the dualistic logic of either/or, which, when pushed to extremes, degenerates into destructive conflict. While competition is necessary for any healthy organism, organization, or system, it is fatal if it is not tempered by cooperation. As interdependence increases, it becomes all the more important to foster strategies of cooperation.

3. *Accept volatility.*

Though the volatility and insecurity accompanying greater complexity can become destructive, they are also necessary conditions of creativity. Creativity emerges *between* too much and too little order. On the one hand, security breeds stasis, which tends to repress the infinite restlessness of life, and on the other hand, life becomes impossible when order completely dissolves. Since creative emergence occurs in conditions far from equilibrium, the volatility and instability it engenders provide opportunities that do not have to be threatening. Since genuinely creative actions and events inevitably destabilize systems and structures, some deconstruction is a necessary moment in every constructive process.

4. *Cultivate uncertainty.*

Certainty is the symptom of death; uncertainty, the pulse of life. Death is, of course, possible before the end of life; living death occurs when possibilities seem exhausted because the future is nothing more than repetition of the past. This condition is despair (Latin *desperare: de-*, "reversal," plus *sperare*, "to hope")—to suffer despair is to be without hope. Hope is the fleeting trace of the inexhaustible openness of the systems and structures without which life is impossible. Apart from uncertainty, there is no future, and without a future, there is no hope. The nourishment of uncertainty serves as a therapeutic corrective to every truth that claims to be absolute. Inasmuch as uncertainty marks the elusive horizon of life, the future is threatened less by doubters than by true believers who insist that their way is the only way. Since knowledge inevitably includes as a condition of its own possibility that which remains incomprehensible, it is always incomplete. The acknowledgment of this incompletion issues in the learned ignorance that keeps us open to the unexpected, which is the gift of the future.

When taken together these four principles suggest that the only adequate ethics in emerging network culture is *an ethics without absolutes.* The guiding tenets of relationalism call into question what I have identified as the most important principles shaping much personal morality and public policy today.

1. *Dualism.*

Relationalism displaces the either/or of absolutism with a neither/nor that subverts clear oppositions. The recognition of complexity does not necessarily lead to indecisiveness but can foster deliberate decisions that are sensitive to their unavoidable limitations as well as the possibility of their unforeseeable ramifications.

2. *Foundationalism.*

There seems to be no underlying ground or foundation that can secure the meaning and purpose of life. More precisely, the groundless ground from which all emerges and to which all returns (without having come full circle) approaches by withdrawing in a way that faults every foundation that seems secure. The absence of ground issues in the endless restlessness of life, in which everything is in motion and (the) all is in flux.

3. *Proliferating choices.*

Though free decision is formative of subjectivity, choice is not an end in itself. The proliferation of choices is of no consequence if their content is trivial or even destructive. *What* one chooses is as important as *that* one chooses. Moreover, in an interconnected world, the limitation of choice is sometimes a common good and as such can be an ethical imperative. In contemporary society, the ideology of choice promotes a consumerism that threatens to spin out of control. In this situation, limiting alternatives by establishing reasonable parameters of constraint can actually promote creativity.

4. *Regulation and deregulation.*

Luther had it right: deregulate the private and, where necessary, regulate the public. The neoconservative and neoliberal ideology of deregulation rests upon a misguided market fundamentalism that entails a mistaken anthropology. Like the transcendent God, the market is believed to be omniscient, omnipotent, and omnipresent, and inasmuch as human beings have limited knowledge, their interventions are inevitably counterproductive. If the market knows what is best, the most prudent policy is to let it run by itself. This line of analysis presupposes an external relation between individual agents and the economic system as a whole that is simply wrong. Networks and subjects are integrally, rather than externally, related. Consequently, human action is the self-determination of the system itself, instead of an external intervention in an ostensibly autonomous structure. Within the nonlinear loops of complex adaptive networks, competing schemata provide regulation at every level. As the network of networks becomes self-aware in human consciousness and self-consciousness, regulation becomes deliberate and must be guided by carefully chosen norms. The question, then, is not whether or not to regulate but what principles should guide regulation. Since knowledge is necessarily limited and effects can be disproportionate to their causes, all regulatory and deregulatory decisions must be made with extreme caution. If, as I have argued, the trajectory of the coevolutionary process is toward increasing connectedness, it will become more and more urgent to develop an ethics without absolutes that can support and enrich the infinite complexity of life.

FLUID DYNAMICS

The foregoing analysis is admittedly abstract; in an effort to lend greater specificity to these general principles, I will conclude by considering a particular ethical issue—water. While not usually included in discussion of ethics, I select this example for five primary reasons. First, water plays an important role in almost every religious tradition; second, water will, I believe, be one of the most pressing *global* problems of the twenty-first century; third, water not only poses very difficult ethical questions but also raises complicated scientific, technological, political, and economic issues; fourth, water cannot be understood apart from the complex nonlinear systems through which it circulates; and fifth, water effectively figures the interplay of stabilization and destabilization in the infinite complexity of life. Though oil and water do not mix, the problems associated with them are inseparably interrelated. Indeed, in the coming century, water will become even more valuable than oil. In his timely book *When the Rivers Run Dry: Water—the Defining Crisis of the Twenty-first Century*, Fred Pearce writes:

> The Nile in Egypt, the Yellow River in China, the Indus in Pakistan, the Colorado and Rio Grande in the United States—all are reported to be trickling into the sand, sometimes hundreds of miles from the sea. Individually, these were interesting stories. Taken together, they seemed to me to be something more. Some kind of Cataclysm was striking the world's rivers. . . .
>
> Israel is draining the Jordan River into pipes before it reaches the country that bears its name. There has been drought on the Ganges because India has sucked up the holy river's entire dry-season flow. The great Oxus, the Nile of Central Asia, was diverted into the desert, leaving the Aral Sea to dry out. This was a real shocker; the shoreline shown on most maps of what was once the world's fourth largest inland sea was hundreds of miles distant from the reality. Even the chalk streams of my childhood were disappearing.
>
> The wells have been drying up, too. Half a century of pumping on the Great Plains of the United States has removed water that will take two thousand years of rain to replace. In India, farmers whose fathers lifted water from wells with a bucket now sink boreholes more than half a mile into the rocks—and still they find no water.[5]

While there are substitutes for oil, there are no substitutes for water. This crisis will, therefore, quickly become a matter of life and death, which, if not managed effectively, threatens to create global conflicts.

Water, of course, can be both creative and destructive—life can be sustained only if there is *neither* too little *nor* too much water. The ambiguity of water lends it a symbolic richness that has long provided resources for the human imagination. Eliade underscores common features of water symbolism across different traditions:

> To state the case in brief, water symbolizes the whole of potentiality; it is the *fons et origo*, the source of all possible existence. . . . The prin-

ciple of what is formless and potential, basis of every cosmic manifestation, container of all seeds, water symbolizes the primal substance from which all forms come and to which they will return either by their own regression or in a cataclysm. . . . In cosmogony, in myth, ritual and iconography, water fills the same function in whatever type of cultural pattern we find it; it *precedes* all forms and *upholds* all creation. Immersion in water symbolizes a return to the pre-formal, a total regeneration, a new birth, for immersion means a dissolution of forms, reintegration into the formlessness of pre-existence; and emerging from water is a repetition of the act of creation in which form was first expressed. Every contact with water implies regeneration: first, because dissolution is succeeded by a "new birth", and then because immersion fertilizes, increases the potential of life and of creation. In initiation and funeral rites it assures rebirth after death. Because it incorporates in itself all potentiality, water becomes a symbol of life ("living water").[6]

Within this interpretive framework, the symbolic value of water is best understood in terms of a series of binary opposites we have encountered in other contexts: Formlessness/Form, Potentiality/Actuality, Chaos/Cosmos. We have already discovered that the creation myths in the ancient Babylonian narrative *Enuma elish* and the book of Genesis in the Hebrew Bible conform to the pattern Eliade identifies. The struggle between Tiamat, who appears as a marine monster, and Marduk, who is a warrior, represents the cosmogonic process in terms of the emergence of order from chaos. By slaying Tiamat, Marduk establishes social as well as natural order and secures the celestial and terrestrial hierarchies necessary for its preservation. In Genesis, Babylonian polytheism gives way to Hebraic monotheism, but vestiges of the earlier myth remain. In the opening chapters of Genesis, there are two creation myths: in the first, form emerges from formlessness when God's creative word passes over the dark waters, and in the second, the Babylonian water monster survives as the serpent, who, by tempting Eve, introduces disorder into the harmony of Eden. These myths capture the ambiguity of water by suggesting that it represents not only the divine creative power necessary for life but also destructive force, which sometimes brings death.

The same ambiguity runs throughout the New Testament, where water usually is associated with ritual cleansing. The most salient use of water is in the rite of baptism. Just as the original creation involved the emergence of order from chaos, so the believer is re-created or born again by having his or her sins washed away through the ritual immersion in and emergence from water. This pattern is evident in John 3:3–7, one of the foundational texts for born-again members of the New Religious Right: "Jesus answered, 'In truth, in very truth I tell you, unless a man has been born over again he cannot see the kingdom of God.' 'But how is it possible,' said Nicodemus, 'for a man to be born when he is old? Can he enter his mother's womb a second time and be born?' Jesus answered, 'In truth I tell you, no one can enter the kingdom of God without being born from water and spirit.'" Throughout the Gospel according to John, water or, more precisely, "living water" is closely associated with the spirit that brings eternal life. When a Samaritan woman refuses Jesus' request for a drink, he responds:

> "If only you knew what God gives, and who it is that is asking you for a drink, you would have asked him and he would have given you living water." "Sir," the woman said, "you have no bucket and this well is deep. How can you give me 'living water'? Are you a greater man than Jacob our ancestor, who gave us the well, and drank from it himself, he and his sons, and his cattle too?" Jesus said, "Everyone who drinks this water will be thirsty again, but whoever drinks the water that I shall give him will never suffer thirst any more. The water that I shall give him will be an inner spring always welling up with eternal life." (John 4:10–14)

Not all images of water in the New Testament, however, represent life and renewal. In the harrowing visions that conclude the Revelation of John, water harbors a second death rather than a second birth: "Then Death and Hades were flung into the lake of fire. This lake of fire is the second death; and into it were flung any whose names were not to be found in the roll of the living" (Revelation 20:14–15). Water, then, is neither simply creative nor destructive and thus can be exclusively associated with neither life nor death. As we will see, the ambiguous neither/nor of water implies an alternative reading of its significance.

While water has not played as significant a role in philosophy, it is possible to argue that philosophy actually started with a meditation on water. The history of philosophy began with Thales (c. 620–546 BCE), who founded the Milesian school of natural philosophy. Though none of his writings has survived, Aristotle reports in *The Metaphysics* that Thales believed that the *archē* (i.e., the originary foundation) of all things is water. Ever polymorphous, water forms the "substance" of everything. In the course of the history of philosophy, this foundational principle has been reinterpreted materially, spiritually, and conceptually. Hegel argues that by identifying water as "the absolute essence of everything," Thales makes water "God over [or, perhaps, under] all." Within Hegel's speculative history of philosophy, this interpretation of water is a material representation of what eventually is conceptually comprehended as the Idea that is the substance of all reality. "This universal stands in direct relationship to the particular and to the existence of the world as manifested. . . . All particular existence is transient, that is, it loses the form of particular and again becomes the universal, water. The simple proposition of Thales, therefore, is philosophy, because in it water, though sensuous, is not looked at in its particularity as opposed to other natural things, but as thought in which everything is resolved and comprehended."[7]

In retrospect, Hegel recognizes Thales' account of water as a prototype of his own interpretation of spirit. He notes, however, two important differences between Thales' metaphysics of water and his own fluid dynamics of spirit. First, and most obvious, Hegel translates the materiality of Thales' sensuous representation into the ideality of the philosophical concept; and second, whereas for Thales water is formless and, therefore, dissolves differences, the Hegelian Idea is a complex unity that preserves differential identity. These disagreements notwithstanding, it is possible to detect lingering traces of Thales' archaic principle in Hegel's account of life. "Life in the universal fluid medium, a passive separating out of the shapes becomes, just by so doing, a movement of those shapes or becomes Life as a *process*. The simple universal fluid medium is the *in-itself*, and the difference of the shapes is the *other*. But this *fluid medium* [emphasis added] itself becomes the *other* through this difference; for now it is *for the difference* which exists in and for itself, and consequently it is the ceaseless movement by which this passive medium is consumed: Life as a *living thing*."[8] Substance . . . Subject . . . Spirit . . . Water . . . Life . . . Circulation. The structure and fluid dynamics of this "universal medium" become explicit in the complex adaptive networks we have been exploring.

To understand the currents circulating through these webs, it is helpful to recall the intersecting networks that form the fabric of life (see fig. 25). Issues related to water involve every aspect of this complex network of networks. Religious beliefs, philosophical assumptions, and artistic visions entail values that shape political and economic policies, which, in turn, promote the development of technologies that transform the natural environment and condition cultural evolution. As a result of the nonlinearity of complex networks, these influences are always multidirectional. To address the impending global water crisis responsibly, it is, therefore, necessary to take into account natural, social, cultural, and technological issues.[9]

The two most obvious problems related to water are quantity and quality. With increasing frequency throughout the world, there seems to be either too little or too much water. Droughts and floods are, of course, interrelated—conditions that bring too much water to one area can result in too little water in other areas. Many scientists are now convinced that the hot ocean waters that contributed to the large number and excessive violence of Atlantic storms in 2005 played an important role in the drought that plagued the Amazon rainforest, which is usually one of the wettest places on earth.[10] According to Robert Engelman and Pamela LeRoy of Population Action International, though conditions are constantly changing, there is "no more fresh water on the planet today than there was 2,000 years ago when the earth's human population was three percent its current size of 5.5 billion people."[11] Current estimates are that by 2015 three billion people will live in countries with inadequate water supplies. The problem is most acute in Asia, which has approximately 60 percent of the world's population but only 36 percent of the world's renewable freshwater. Declining water supplies have a direct impact on food production and thus contribute to world hunger. It takes one thousand cubic meters of water to grow one ton of grain. Sandra Postel and Aaron Wolf point out that "groundwater depletion alone places 10 to 20 percent of grain production in both China and India at risk. Water tables are falling steadily in North China, which yields more than half of China's wheat and nearly one third of its corn, as well as in northwest India's Punjab, another major breadbasket." These changes will inevitably lead to a global reallocation of agriculture resources. To make matters worse, the problem is not limited to developing countries. Agriculture throughout the American West depends on extensive irrigation. A recent study conducted by the Scripps Oceanographic Institute concluded that in the "best-case scenario for future climate change" (i.e., small temperature increases) the water available in the Greater Los Angeles area would be reduced by 50 percent as early as 2050.[12]

Water use worldwide quadrupled between 1940 and 1990. While half of this increase was the result of rising consumption, population growth accounted for the other half.[13] When the population increases, people expand into new areas where water supplies aboveground (i.e., streams, rivers, lakes, oceans, and reservoirs) and belowground (i.e., aquifers) are often limited. As demand increases and supplies decrease, there is

more competition for limited water resources and questions of ownership and access become urgent at the local, national, and international
level: Is water public or private property? Who owns water and who can
control its flow? Who must pay for the development of water delivery
and treatment facilities? The answers to such questions are not always
clear, because many of the laws regulating water use are antiquated
and need to be thoroughly revised. In the American West, for example,
overdevelopment is pitting rural and urban, as well as agriculture and
industrial, interests against each other. In most western states, agriculture claims about 80 percent of scant water resources at prices far below
market value. While declining water supplies have not yet led to privatization programs in this country, the situation is different in developing
countries.[14] Under pressure from the U.S. government, the International
Monetary Fund and the World Bank are making much-needed loans contingent upon initiatives that place the control of water in the hands of
private corporations. As long as such neoliberal economic policies go
unchallenged, it is likely that corporations soon will attempt to extend
their efforts to privatize access to water in this country.

Shifts in political power and climate change inevitably will create
pressure to change long-standing laws and agreements at every level of
government. Indeed, conflicts are already breaking out in this country.
There is now considerable evidence to suggest that the twentieth century was unusually wet in the American West and, therefore, that the
enormous westward expansion took place under anomalous conditions.
If precipitation declines, demands on limited water resources will increase and conflicts will become more intense. With water tables already
dropping precipitously in many places, there is no doubt that the chief
factor limiting further development will be the availability of water.
In other parts of the world with little or no water, ambitious desalini-
zation projects raise questions about ownership of ocean water. Some
Middle Eastern countries are turning oil into water by using their new-
found wealth to build fanciful cities and oases in the desert. Creating
ski slopes in the Arabian Desert makes as much sense as creating water
follies in the Nevada desert. The environmental impact of desalination
is currently minimal, but it is difficult to predict what might happen if
a significant portion of the world population became dependent on the
oceans for their water. New technologies and the changing geopolitical
situation will make it necessary to enact new international regulatory
agreements and enforcement procedures for water use. In the absence of
such developments, the oil wars of the twentieth century are likely to be-

come the water wars of the twenty-first century. Former United Nations Secretary General Kofi Annan has already predicted that "fierce competition for fresh water may become a source of conflict and wars in the future." A recent report of the U.S. National Intelligence Council lends credibility to this warning when it concludes that the likelihood of interstate conflict will increase during the next fifteen years "as countries press against the limits of available water."[15]

The problem of the quality of water is at least as critical as its supply. The water supply of 1.2 billion people is so polluted that it poses significant health risks. According to the Millennium Ecosystem Assessment (2001–5), entitled *Ecosystems and Human Well-Being: Wetlands and Water,* "inadequate water and sanitation result in 1.7 million deaths annually. In poor countries, water-related diseases like malaria and diarrhea are leading causes of death."[16] In addition to obvious culprits like sewage and industrial pollution, the deforestation that accompanies population growth also contributes significantly to the degradation of surface water. As erosion increases, topsoil collects in streams and rivers vital to the water supply. In recent years, human activities have increased sediment flows in rivers by approximately 20 percent. Groundwater is as susceptible to contamination as surface water. While surface pollutants from home, factory, and mines leach into underground water and make it unfit for human consumption, some of the most destructive contaminants are by-products of agricultural practices. New technologies and farming methods developed to meet the food demands of a growing population have damaged the environment in unexpected ways. "Improved" plows pulverize the soil so finely that topsoil is swept away at an alarming rate, thereby exacerbating the problem of erosion. By some estimates, the production of one bushel of corn results in the loss of six bushels of topsoil. With this kind of soil depletion, erosion can become so bad that the process of desertification begins. Another intersection of oil and water creates conditions that are at least as damaging as such erosion. To minimize labor and maximize crop yields, corporate farms use massive amounts of pesticides and fertilizers, most of which derive from petrochemicals. To raise one acre of hay requires two hundred pounds of fertilizer. A significant portion of these pesticides and fertilizers finds its way into surface and groundwater. The complex interplay among different systems compounds the problems that most need solution: technologies developed to meet the growing demand for food destroy the soil and contaminate the water necessary for successful farming as well as the support of life. Many of these fertilizers are rich in nitrogen, phosphorous, and sulfur, which have a significant impact on freshwater and coastal ecosystems, which play an important role in both global water cycles and global weather patterns. Fertilizer runoff nourishes some plant life but compromises or destroys other flora and fauna. The complexity of these interrelated systems makes it difficult to predict the far-reaching effects of such pollutants:

> There is *established but incomplete* evidence that the changes being made are increasing the likelihood of nonlinear and potentially abrupt changes in ecosystems, with important consequences for human well-being. These nonlinear changes can be large in magnitude and diffi-cult, expensive or impossible to reverse. For example, once a threshold of nutrient loading is crossed, changes in freshwater and coastal eco-systems can be abrupt and extensive, creating harmful algal blooms (including blooms of toxic species) and sometimes leading to the formation of oxygen-depleted zones killing all animal life. Capabili-ties for predicting some nonlinear changes are improving, but on the whole scientists cannot predict the thresholds at which change will be encountered. The increased likelihood of these nonlinear changes stems from the loss of biodiversity and growing pressures from multi-ple direct drivers of ecosystem change. The loss of species and genetic diversity decreases the resilience of ecosystems.[17]

The marginal area between land and sea is particularly susceptible to such disruption. As we will see below, fragile and increasingly endan-gered wetlands play a critical role in climate regulation.

Water, I have stressed, not only is creative but also can be destruc-tive—too much water can pose as many difficulties as too little. When its full force is unleashed, nothing can resist water's power. In recent years, weather extremes have been more common. From the American West to Africa, major areas are suffering prolonged droughts that strain people as well as the land. In other regions of the world, the number of hurricanes and typhoons has remained relatively constant worldwide, but their violence has been increasing and their geographic distribu-tion changing. Though scientists remain divided on the importance of global warming for climate change, a growing number of climatologists maintain that there is mounting evidence that these developments are the result of global warming.[18] In the wake of Hurricane Katrina, leading meteorologist and hurricane specialist Kerry Emanuel recalled: "I pre-dicted years ago that if you warmed the tropical oceans by a degree Cen-tigrade, you should see something on the order of a five percent increase in the wind speed during hurricanes. We've seen a larger increase, more like ten percent, for an ocean temperature increase of only one-half degree Centigrade."[19] Since hurricanes draw their energy from ocean surface currents, a rise in water temperature increases the energy available for storms. Emanuel reports that in August 2005 Katrina gathered its enormous force when it passed over a deep layer of water in the Gulf of Mexico that had risen to an unbelievable 90° Fahrenheit.[20] Such developments make it highly likely that hurricanes and typhoons will become even more destructive in the future.

Nothing shows the practical implications of the dynamics of complex adaptive networks more clearly than climate changes associated with global warming. Nonlinear feedback loops within, between, and among natural, social, cultural, and technological systems create a coevolutionary process in which development is neither gradual nor continuous. In previous chapters, I have argued that various cultural forces are conspiring to bring us close to a tipping point; now I must add that natural systems are also approaching a condition of self-organized criticality. Moreover, these two processes are inextricably interrelated: cultural values issue in political and economic policies that destabilize natural systems, thereby provoking "corrective" measures that often exacerbate the problems they are supposed to solve.

In an address to the American Geophysical Union in December 2005, James Hansen, professor of earth, atmospheric, and planetary sciences at MIT, delivered a dire warning:

> The earth's climate is nearing, but has not passed, a tipping point beyond which it will be impossible to avoid climate change with far-reaching undesirable consequences. These include not only the loss of the Arctic as we know it, with all that this implies for wildlife and indigenous peoples, but losses on a much vaster scale due to rising seas.
>
> Ocean levels will increase slowly at first, as losses at the fringes of Greenland and Antarctica due to accelerating ice streams are nearly balanced by increased snowfall and ice sheet thickening in the ice sheet interiors.
>
> But Greenland and West Antarctica ice is softened and lubricated by meltwater, and as buttressing ice shelves disappear because of a warming ocean, the balance will tip toward the rapid disintegration of ice sheets.
>
> The earth's history suggests that with warming of two or three degrees, the new sea level will include not only most of the ice from Greenland and West Antarctica, but a portion of East Antarctica, rais-

ing the sea level by twenty-five meters, or eighty feet. . . . This grim
scenario can be halted if the growth of greenhouse gas emission is
slowed in the first quarter of this century.[21]

There is now a widespread consensus among scientists that global
warming is occurring and that human activity (or "anthropogenetic interference") is contributing significantly to this process. Indeed, 2005
was the hottest year on record. While natural processes play a role in
global warming, the increase in greenhouse gases—especially methane
(CH_4) and carbon dioxide (CO_2)—is largely responsible for accelerating
this process. The single most important factor in this increase is, of
course, the burning of fossil fuels. Last year global emissions reached
7 billion tons, of which 20 percent, or 1.6 billion metric tons of carbon,
came from the United States. Since CO_2 takes about one hundred years to
break down, its growing accumulation in the atmosphere poses a long-
term problem. "For every added increment of carbon dioxide," Elizabeth
Kolbert explains, "the earth will experience a temperature rise, which
represents what is called the equilibrium warming. If current trends
continue, atmospheric CO_2 will reach five hundred parts per million—
nearly double pre-industrial levels—around the middle of the century.
It is believed that the last time CO_2 concentrations were that high was
during the period known as the Eocene, some fifty million years ago. In
the Eocene, crocodiles roamed Colorado and sea levels were nearly three
hundred feet higher than they are today."[22] Projections like this lend undeniable urgency to Hansen's warning.

Hansen's concern is widely shared by many members of the scientific
community. Indeed, the more informed the scientist, the more alarmed
he or she tends to be. This concern does not, however, extend to the general public. Bill McKibben, author of the much-discussed book *The End
of Nature* (1989), recently observed: "Climate change somehow seems unable to emerge on the world stage for what it really is: the single biggest
challenge facing the planet, the equal in every way to the nuclear threat
that transfixed us during the past half-century and a threat we haven't
even begun to deal with."[23] Some of the responsibility for the lack of
public awareness rests with scientists, who are not always successful
in translating their knowledge into laymen's terms. Another contributing factor is the understandable tendency of people to want to avoid
such difficult issues when there seems to be little immediate evidence
for a rapidly deteriorating situation. But the most important and pernicious cause of the growing gap between scientific knowledge and public
awareness is the concerted effort of politicians and corporations to dis-

credit the reliability of science by engaging in calculated disinformation campaigns. The enormous financial resources of special-interest groups make it very difficult for scientists and public-interest groups to counter deceptive arguments and specious claims. Even more disturbing than such actions by private citizens and companies are the efforts of government officials from the president on down to advance their political and economic agendas by casting doubt on reliable scientific research and accepted scientific conclusions.[24] The Bush administration has actually gone so far as to censor some government scientists who have attempted to bring the issue of global warming to the attention of the general public.[25] In response to such irresponsible actions, every effort must be made to expose these programs for what they are and to correct the misunderstandings they continue to convey.

Ground Zero for global warming is the Arctic. The disproportionate effect global warming has on the Arctic can be seen in its impact on permafrost, sea ice, and glaciers.[26] In each case, the interplay of complex networks creates positive feedback loops that accelerate the warming process, thereby moving global systems closer to the condition of self-organized criticality. The term *permafrost* designates ground that has remained frozen for at least two years. The depth of permafrost can vary from a few feet to a mile. Most of today's permafrost dates back to the last glacial period 120,000 years ago. In recent years, holes known as thermokarsts have begun to open in permafrost throughout Alaska. In many places, according to Kolbert, scientists have discovered that the permafrost is less than one degree below freezing, and elsewhere melting has already begun. As the ground literally disappears from beneath one's feet, the infrastructure breaks down and buildings as well as roads collapse. But there is another even more devastating effect of melting permafrost. The outermost layer of permafrost thaws in the summer and thus can support plant life and even small trees. Arctic life cycles, however, differ from those in more temperate zones. Due to low temperatures, plants and trees do not completely decompose when they die. As this organic material settles and freezes over the centuries, permafrost becomes a storage receptacle for vast amounts of carbon. When it melts, permafrost releases CO_2 and CH_4 into the atmosphere. In some parts of Alaska, this melting has already led to a 60 percent increase in atmospheric methane. This release of CH_4 and CO_2 results in higher temperatures, which then increases the rate of melting, thereby discharging yet more greenhouse gases.[27]

The effects of this process are not, of course, limited to permafrost. The vast sheets of sea ice covering the Arctic region play a critical role in global climate patterns. There are two kinds of sea ice—seasonal, which melts each year, and perennial, which does not. In 1979, perennial sea ice covered an area roughly equal to the size of the United States; by 2005, it had decreased by an area equal to the size of New York, Georgia, and Texas.[28] The depth of the sea ice has been decreasing at a similar rate. Throughout the 1990s, the Greenland ice sheet shrank by twelve cubic miles each year, and according to current projections, perennial sea ice will completely disappear by 2080. The effects of this development will be overwhelming because sea ice is critical to stabilizing global temperatures. Its expansive white surface reflects sunlight and heat back into the atmosphere. As this reflecting surface decreases, the dark absorptive surface of water increases; with the absorption of more heat by the water, more ice melts and another positive feedback loop is created.

The effects of these interrelated processes on global climate networks can be seen most dramatically in what is happening to glaciers. The majority of the world's glaciers have been melting since the 1960s. In Glacier National Park, for example, there were 150 glaciers in the 1800s; today there are only 35, and computer models predict that by 2030 there will be none. Though deglaciation did not begin in Iceland until the 1990s, it is now progressing so rapidly that scientists calculate that by the end of the next century Iceland will have no ice. The effects of glacial meltdown are somewhat more complex than the melting of permafrost and sea ice. The first and most obvious result will be rising sea levels with all the related problems. If the entire Greenland ice sheet alone melted, the level of seas throughout the world would rise by twenty-three feet. But the more serious problems created by melting glaciers are even more complex. Glaciers are made of freshwater, which differs in density from saltwater. When glaciers melt, they change the mix of freshwater and saltwater in oceans, and this leads to a shift in both water and air currents. Kolbert offers a concise account of this extraordinarily complex process, which deserves to be quoted at length:

> "When you freeze sea ice, the salt is pushed out of the pores, so that the salty water drains," [Konrad] Steffen [professor of geography at the University of Colorado and head of the Swiss Camp in the Arctic] explained to me. . . . "And salty water's actually heavier, so it starts to sink." Meanwhile, owing both to evaporation and to heat loss, water

from the tropics becomes denser as it drifts toward the Arctic, so that near Greenland a tremendous volume of seawater is constantly sinking toward the ocean floor. As a result of this process, still more warm water is drawn from the tropics toward the poles, setting up what is often referred to as a "conveyor belt" that moves heat around the globe.

"This is the energy engine for the world climate," Steffan went on. "And it has one source: the water that sinks down. And if you just turn the knob here a little bit . . . we can expect significant temperature changes based on the redistribution of energy." One way to turn the knob is to heat the oceans, which is already happening. Another way is to pour more freshwater into the polar seas. This is also occurring. Not only is runoff from coastal Greenland increasing; the volume of river discharge into the Arctic Ocean has been rising. Oceanographers monitoring the North Atlantic have documented that in recent decades its waters have become significantly less salty. A total shutdown of the thermohaline circulation is considered extremely unlikely in the coming century. But, if the Greenland ice sheet started to disintegrate, the possibility of such a shutdown could not be ruled out.[29]

Such a shutdown would, of course, be catastrophic. But even if this worst-case scenario does not occur in the near future, deglaciation is already having an important impact on the global climate. Shifting ocean currents change atmospheric conditions and alter wind currents, which, in turn, influence the weather patterns that determine location and amount of precipitation.

These changes also have disastrous effects on coastal and inland wetlands. I have already considered the damage being done to wetlands by various pollutants. The effects of global warming are exacerbating this already-deteriorating situation. Coastal as well as inland wetlands play four crucial roles in maintaining the quality, availability, and circulation of water as well as regulating global climate change. First, wetlands serve as a natural barrier that protects coastlines during storms. They are particularly effective in limiting or preventing the contamination of freshwater by the influx of saltwater. As sea levels rise and storms become more violent, these protective barriers will be damaged or destroyed. Second, wetlands act as filters to detoxify water passing through them. "Metals and many organic compounds may be absorbed to the sediments (that is, accumulated on their surface) in the wetlands. The relatively slow passage of water through wetlands provides time for pathogens to lose their viability or be consumed by other organisms in the ecosystem."[30] Without wetlands to serve this function, pollutants would circulate freely and spread contamination much more widely. Third, wetlands, like permafrost, capture and store significant amounts of carbon, thereby decreasing greenhouse gases. Inland water systems and boreal peatlands sometimes associated with them are especially important CO_2 sinks. "Although covering only 3–4% of the world's land area, peatlands arc estimated to hold 540 gigatons of carbon, representing about 1.5% of the total estimated carbon storage and about 25–30% of that contained in terrestrial vegetation and soils."[31] The destruction of these ecosystems not only results in the release of stored gases but also eliminates a primary resource for their sequestration. Finally, inland and coastal wetlands are important habitats for a wide variety of plant and animal life. As wetlands shrink or disappear, biodiversity is further compromised. For example, approximately one-third of the world's amphibian species (1,856) face extinction, and of these 964 species depend on freshwater supplied by wetlands.[32] Though extinction rates vary, there are similar patterns in many plants and animals, ranging from fish and reptiles to birds and water mammals. While it is impossible to calculate the effects of such wide-scale extinction with accuracy, there is no doubt that as biodiversity decreases, the fragility of ecosystems increases.

The interactive systems that regulate global climate conform to the structure and operational logic of complex adaptive systems. Networks of networks are joined in nonlinear feedback loops in which positive feedback can lead to accelerating changes that eventually result in an abrupt phase shift. Change, therefore, is not necessarily continuous and at critical junctures can be caused by seemingly insignificant events. Just as one cannot know which additional grain will cause an avalanche in a sand pile, so it is impossible to be sure which incremental increase in temperature will precipitate a seismic shift in the global climate. It is, however, undeniable that if temperatures continue to rise, there will be an abrupt change and a disaster will occur—it is definitely not a question of *whether* but of *when* this will happen. Even as our knowledge about climate change becomes more sophisticated, we continue to destroy the very conditions that make life possible. This is neither science fiction nor Hollywood hyperbole but the sober assessment of responsible scientists.

And yet, astonishingly, little is being done to address these problems. A tepid beginning was made at the United Nations "Earth Summit" held in Rio de Janeiro in 1992. The purpose of the meeting was to discuss the

U.N. Framework Convention on Climate Change, whose objective was "the stabilization of greenhouse gas concentrations in the atmosphere that would prevent dangerous anthropogenic interference with the climate system."[33] Though 160 countries ratified a treaty agreeing to reduce greenhouse gases to 1990 levels, by 1995 emissions were still rising. The 1997 Kyoto conference was called to strengthen the original agreement by making commitments mandatory rather than voluntary and establishing different standards for industrial and nonindustrial countries. The United States, however, undercut the negotiations by refusing to accept the agreement. The Senate passed a resolution 95-0 warning the Clinton administration not to accept the Kyoto accord. This vote makes unmistakably clear the utter irresponsibility of both political parties on what is surely the most critical issue of our time. In recent years, the situation has become even worse. Although George W. Bush committed to reduce CO_2 emissions in the 2000 election, he has failed to carry through on his promise and has actually enacted policies that have exacerbated the problem. In late 2001, Bush went so far as to reject a report of his own Environmental Protection Agency that concluded that "continuing growth in greenhouse gas emissions is likely to lead to annual average warming over the United States that could be as much as several degrees Celsius (roughly 3 to 9 degrees Fahrenheit) during the 21st century."[34] At every point, the policies of the Bush administration have been guided by two fundamental principles: first, the aversion to regulation, which grows out of faith in the market; and second, the privileging of economic concerns over all other factors. In a comment explaining his reasons for withdrawing from the Kyoto Protocol, Bush leaves no doubt about his position: "I will explain as clearly as I can, today and every other chance I get, that we will not do anything that harms our economy. . . . That's my priority. I'm worried about the economy."[35] The market, however, does not always know what is best. What profit a country if it saves its economy but loses life itself?

As the networks nourishing life become more interconnected, they become less stable and secure. Though disruption and dislocation can be creative, if carried to extremes they can become destructive. Many of the policies and programs now being pursued in this country and elsewhere have put us on a suicidal course. Once again it becomes clear that what is promoted as a culture of life harbors a culture of death that might actually lead to planetary extinction. Again, this is not an exaggeration but a fact—indeed, extinction is already occurring. A recent article published in *Nature* entitled "Widespread Amphibian Extinctions from Epidemic

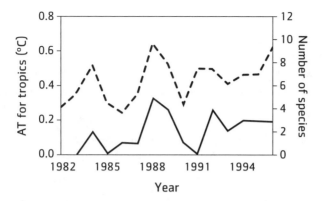

Figure 27. Signatures of Global Warming in *Atelopus*
Extinctions (J. Alan Pounds et al., "Widespread Amphibian
Extinctions from Epidemic Disease Driven by Global
Warming," *Nature* 439 [January 12, 2006]: 164). AT stands
for air temperature; the solid line represents the number of
species observed for the last time, and the dotted line charts
the air temperature for the preceding year.

Disease Driven by Global Warming" provides startling evidence for the
direct correlation between the increase in global temperature and the
extinction of species. This analysis is based on the investigation of harlequin frogs (*Atelopus*) in Costa Rica's Monteverde cloud forest. Figure 27
makes the point with disturbing clarity.

It is important to note that the correlative rise in global temperatures
and species extinction involves the interplay of several of the factors we
have been considering. In the area the scientists studied, deforestation
enhanced the sensitivity of the local environment to warming caused by,
among other things, increasing greenhouse gases. Changes in air and
water temperature led to more water vapor and, correlatively, thicker
and prolonged cloud cover, which created conditions favorable to the
survival, growth, and reproduction of chytrids, a fungus fatal to harlequin frogs. The investigators draw these factors together in summarizing their conclusions:

> We establish that global climate change is already causing the extinc-
> tion of species. Taking our results and recent findings that tie the
> same losses to disease, we conclude that climate-driven epidemics

are an immediate threat to biodiversity. Our study sheds light on the amphibian-decline mystery by showing that large-scale warming is a key factor. It also points to a chain of events whereby this warming may accelerate disease development by translating into local or microscale temperature shifts—increases and decreases—favorable to *Batrachochytrium*. The case illustrates how greenhouse warming and the resultant intensification of the hydrological cycle, together with aerosol pollution, may affect life on earth. Influencing patterns of formation, these agents alter thermal, light and moisture environments of many organisms, changing ecological interactions and threatening species survival.[36]

It would be a profound mistake to overlook the far-reaching implications of these developments. What is occurring in the remote cloud forests of Costa Rica exposes the increasing fragility of the infinitely complex network of life upon which human beings depend. Unless extensive corrective actions are undertaken quickly on a global scale, the fate of the harlequin frog might well prefigure the fate of life on earth.

The process of global warming, I have stressed, cannot be reversed but can only be slowed down. This will not occur without an extraordinary international commitment that will require nothing less than a transvaluation of values. Since life is a global web in which everything is (k)notted, nurturing it requires the acceptance of schemata that disclose and support our complex interconnections rather than ideologies that reinforce divisive oppositions. The radical changes necessary to keep the future open will be impossible without a major redistribution of wealth and reallocation of resources between and among industrial, industrializing, and nonindustrial nations. Cooperation, in other words, must complement competition if we are to create the new global institutions necessary to regulate the natural, social, cultural, and technological currents that make life on this planet possible. Within these fluxes and flows, nothing is absolute because everything is related. It seems that the only alternative to impending disaster and the death it will bring is the willingness to commit to an ethics without absolutes that promotes global life. Though the obstacles appear overwhelming, the task is urgent—life itself hangs in the balance. To affirm possibility while confessing impossibility, I have insisted, requires risking a faith that embraces uncertainty and insecurity as conditions of creative emergence. If faith is not strong enough to rise to the challenge of affirming life in the face of impending death, nothing else matters.

Religiosity and morality, Nietzsche taught us, can be nihilistic. For many of today's neofoundationalists from different religious traditions, life in this world is not intrinsically valuable but has meaning and purpose only insofar as it prepares the way for the glory of eternal life yet to come. In the apocalyptic imagination, the kingdom of God cannot arrive until this world passes away.[37] If, however, the divine is neither an underlying One, which dissolves differences, nor a transcendent Other, which divides more than unites, but is incarnate in the eternal restlessness of becoming, then life in this world is infinitely valuable. The figure of this infinite life is water—not water that represents chaos and disorder, which must be destroyed for the cosmos and order to be created, but water whose fluid dynamics figure the virtuality in and through which everything is figured, disfigured, and refigured.

> That the glass would melt in heat,
> That the water would freeze in the cold,
> Shows that this object is merely a state,
> One of many, between two poles.[38]

Merely a state, one of many, between two poles. There is nothing else—there is nowhere else. Neither One nor the Other. To err in the wake of the virtual is to be after God—forever after God.

NOTES

CHAPTER ONE / THEORIZING RELIGION

1. "Toward a Hidden God," *Time* 87, no. 14 (April 8, 1966): 82.

2. Quoted in Anne C. Loveland, *American Evangelicals and the U.S. Military, 1945–1993* (Baton Rouge: Louisiana State University Press, 1997), 211.

3. For a consideration of these developments, see my *The Moment of Complexity: Emerging Network Culture* (Chicago: University of Chicago Press, 2001); and *Confidence Games: Money and Markets in a World without Redemption* (Chicago: University of Chicago Press, 2004).

4. Wallace Stevens, "An Ordinary Evening in New Haven," in *The Collected Poems of Wallace Stevens* (New York: Knopf, 1981), 489.

5. Jonathan Z. Smith, "Religion, Religions, Religious," in *Critical Terms for Religious Studies*, ed. Mark C. Taylor (Chicago: University of Chicago Press, 1998), 269.

6. Ibid., 276.

7. For a very helpful elaboration of these developments, see Tomoko Masuzawa, *The Invention of World Religions; or, How European Universalism Was Preserved in the Language of Religious Pluralism* (Chicago: University of Chicago Press, 2005).

8. Mircea Eliade, *The Sacred and the Profane*, trans. Willard Trask (New York: Harper and Row, 1957), 16.

9. Ibid., 17.

10. Ibid., 9.

11. As will become clear in later chapters, poststructuralism and deconstruction are closely related but not identical. Poststructuralism refers to the generalized critique of forms of essentialism that range from New Criticism to phenomenology and different versions of structuralism. Critics as different as Michel Foucault, Gilles Deleuze, Jacques Lacan, and Julia Kristeva can be de-

scribed as poststructuralist. Deconstruction, by contrast, refers specifically to the critical strategy devised by Jacques Derrida and elaborated by his many followers. In later chapters, I develop a theological genealogy of poststructuralism and deconstruction.

12. Murray Gell-Mann, "Complexity and Complex Adaptive Systems," in *The Evolution of Human Languages*, ed. John A. Hawkins and Murray Gell-Mann (New York: Addison-Wesley, 1992), 10.

13. Ibid., 23–24.

14. I will consider the importance of creation myths in more detail in chapter 4.

15. Quotations from the Bible are from *The New English Bible, with the Apocrypha* (New York: Oxford University Press, 1970).

16. Claude Shannon and Warren Weaver, *The Mathematical Theory of Communication* (Urbana: University of Illinois Press, 1949), 99.

17. Gregory Bateson, *Steps to an Ecology of Mind* (New York: Ballantine Books, 1972), 453.

18. I have borrowed this distinction from Clifford Geertz's classic essay "Religion as a Cultural System." See Clifford Geertz, *The Interpretation of Cultures: Selected Essays* (New York: Basic Books, 1973). The argument in this chapter attempts to overcome the inadequacies and shortcomings of Geertz's influential analysis.

19. In the diagrams throughout the book, I have used ellipses instead of circles to indicate that these processes are open rather than closed. This openness creates the possibility of interaction between and among systems and networks. The broken lines of the ellipses suggest the interactivity necessary for codependence and coevolution.

20. *The American Heritage Dictionary of the English Language* (New York: Houghton Mifflin, 1970), s.v.

21. I will examine historical examples of these arguments in chapter 4.

22. Though the past always conditions the present and influences the way in which the future is imagined, it is not fixed. To the contrary, the past is repeatedly refigured in light of the present and the anticipated future.

23. Per Bak, *How Nature Works: The Science of Self-Organized Criticality* (New York: Springer-Verlag, 1996), 1–2.

24. In chapter 3, I will consider the theory of the imagination that Kant developed in his critical philosophy and that the Jena romantics extended to elaborate their interpretation of the world as a work of art. I have discussed the relationship between figuring and disfiguring in my *Disfiguring: Art, Architecture, Religion* (Chicago: University of Chicago Press, 1992).

25. Since being is relational and, therefore, selfhood is always intersubjective, I include psychology under the more encompassing category of society.

26. William James, *The Varieties of Religious Experience: A Study in Human Nature* (New York: New American Library, 1958), 42. My account of James's position is drawn from lectures 4–8. Charles Taylor has recently invoked James in *Va-*

rieties of Religion Today (Cambridge: Harvard University Press, 2002). Taylor is particularly interested in what he describes as "expressive individualism," which, he argues, has given rise to a "culture of authenticity." This form of religiosity is supposed to reinforce the neoconservative politics and neoliberal economics of global capital. This argument raises issues I will consider in chapters 5–6. For the moment, it is sufficient to note that Taylor's argument suffers from two serious limitations: first, he has an inadequate understanding of the Western religious and theological tradition, and second, he simply does not comprehend the complexities of finance capitalism.

27. I will return to Emerson at several points in later chapters. While not completely wrong, James's reading of Emerson is one-sided. If Emerson is read through Hegel, his religious vision appears to be considerably more complex.

28. Paul Tillich, "Two Types of Philosophy of Religion," in *Theology of Culture*, ed. Robert Kimball (New York: Oxford University Press, 1964), 10. Quotations in the following paragraphs are from this essay.

29. The difference between the redeemed and condemned in the dualistic type is not the same as the distinction between the enlightened and the unenlightened in the monistic type. While the former distinction is ontological, the latter is epistemological. In contrast to the condemned, who is separated from God or the real by a gap that he or she cannot bridge, the unenlightened is united with God or the real even though he or she does not yet realize it.

30. I have borrowed the term *relationalism* from philosophical and scientific arguments about the nature of space and time. In his "Scholium on Absolute Space and Time," Newton argues that "space and time are endowed with various structures rich enough to support an absolute, or nonrelational, conception of motion." Though Leibniz vehemently contested this claim, Newton's position has remained remarkably influential. Recently, however, a heated debate about absolute space and time has broken out among philosophers and physicists. In his book *World Enough and Space-Time: Absolute versus Relational Theories of Space and Time,* John Earman explains that some physicists propose replacing Newton's absolutism with what they describe as relationalism. For relationalists, "All motion is the relative motion of bodies, and consequently, space-time does not have, and cannot have, structures that support absolute qualities of motion" (John Earman, *World Enough and Space-Time: Absolute versus Relational Theories of Space and Time* [Cambridge: MIT Press, 1989], 12). See also Lawrence Sklar, *Philosophy and Spacetime Physics* (Berkeley and Los Angeles: University of California Press, 1985); Gordon Belot, *Rehabilitating Relationalism*, at www.google.com/search? hl=en&q=rehabilitating+relationalism. The details of this argument need not detain us here. Suffice it to note that inasmuch as recent cultural controversies have made any sophisticated understanding of the notions of "relativism" and "relativity" virtually impossible, I will use the term *relationalism*

to develop a critique of religious, philosophical, and political absolutism in later chapters. At this point, it is important to stress that relationalism does not entail the solipsistic subjectivity often associated with relativism. To the contrary, relationalism draws every subject out of itself and into constitutive relations with other subjects as well as the surrounding world. Moreover, relationalism does not lead to an attitude in which, as critics never tire of charging, "anything goes" but issues in practices, policies, and procedures guided by norms constructed within patterns of constraint that provide the conditions for creative action.

31. That is to say, every subject is a node in a complex web of relations, which constitute its identity as differential.

CHAPTER TWO / THE PROTESTANT REVOLUTION

1. Patrick Collinson, *The Reformation: A History* (New York: Modern Library, 2004), 6–7.
2. To avoid confusion it is important to distinguish *modernity* from *modernism* and *modernization*. While *modernity* designates a historical period, *modernism* refers to cultural developments usually but not exclusively associated with the arts and literature. *Modernization*, by contrast, is the social, political, and economic process through which societies have developed during the past two centuries. I will consider issues related to modernism in chapter 3 and the importance of modernization in chapter 4.
3. Martin Heidegger, *The Question concerning Technology and Other Essays*, trans. William Lovitt (New York: Harper and Row, 1977), 107.
4. Ibid., 132, 77.
5. Hegel's account of "Absolute Freedom and Terror" in *Phenomenology* anticipates Nietzsche's notion of the will to power:

> Before the universal can perform a deed it must concentrate itself into the One of individuality and put at the head an individual self-consciousness; for the universal will is only an *actual* will in a self, which is a One. But thereby all other individuals are excluded from the entirety of this deed and have only a limited share in it, so that the deed would not be a deed of the *actual universal* self-consciousness. Universal freedom, therefore, can produce neither a positive work nor a deed; there is left for it only *negative* action; it is merely the *fury* of destruction. (*Phenomenology of Spirit*, trans. A. V. Miller [New York: Oxford University Press, 1977], 359)

6. Francis Oakley, *The Medieval Experience* (New York: Scribner's, 1974), 1.
7. Paul Tillich, *A History of Christian Thought*, ed. Carl Braaten (New York: Harper and Row, 1968), 178. My account of Joachim's position is drawn from Tillich's work. In chapter 4, I will examine the implications of the Christian doctrine of the Trinity.
8. Ibid., 178–79.

9. William James, *Varieties of Religious Experience: A Study in Human Nature* (New York: New American Library, 1958), 196–97.

10. The best study of Luther's personality is still Erik Erikson's *Young Man Luther: A Study in Psychoanalysis and History* (New York: Norton, 1958).

11. Paul Tillich, *The Courage to Be* (New Haven, CT: Yale University Press, 1952), 58–59.

12. Oakley, *Medieval Experience*, 104.

13. Ibid., 4.

14. Thomas Aquinas, *Introduction to St. Thomas Aquinas*, ed. A. C. Pegis (New York: Random House, 1948), 193, 215.

15. Ibid., 292.

16. Joan Acocella, "The End of the World: Interpreting the Plague," *New Yorker*, March 21, 2005, 82. The following details about the plague are drawn from this article.

17. Saint Francis was every bit as opposed to the abuse of the poor by the rich as any Protestant, but he did not believe it necessary to deny the authority of the pope. Rhetorically, the Protestant Reformers made much of the luxurious lives of the Catholic clergy, but they chose not to stop at moral reform. They also wanted devolution of church authority from the pope to the individual believer. In short order, this became the national authority of nationally established Protestant churches, which, in practice, often tended to restrain religious individualism.

18. There is now some dispute about whether Melanchthon's account of this event is historically accurate. Some historians argue that it is more likely that Luther conformed to the practice of submitting the theses for debate to Albert of Mainz as well as to friends and colleagues at other universities.

19. Quoted in Diarmaid MacCullough, *The Reformation: A History* (New York: Viking, 2003), 123.

20. Reinhold Niebuhr's famous Serenity Prayer is known today in Germany as Das Gelassenheitsgebet.

21. Pierre Alféri, *Guillaume d'Ockham: Le singulier* (Paris: Éditions de Minuit, 1989), 458–59. Alféri is the maiden name of Pierre Derrida's mother, Marguerite. His analysis makes it perfectly clear that there is a direct line from Ockham's nominalism to Jacques Derrida's deconstruction. Thus, in writing about Ockham, the son is actually writing about the father. I will consider the implications of this trajectory in detail in chapter 4.

22. As these remarks suggest, aspects of Ockham's argument prefigure the third religious schema I described in the last chapter. I will explore the importance of this perspective in later chapters.

23. Giorgio Agamben attempts to draw a line from Paul through Luther to Hegel by pointing out that Luther translates *katargēsis* as *aufheben*:

> Luther uses *Aufheben*—the very word that harbors the double meaning of abolishing and conserving (*aufbewahren* and *aufhören lassen*) used

by Hegel as a foundation for his dialectic! A closer look at Luther's vocabulary shows that he is aware of the verb's double meaning, which before him occurs infrequently. This means that in all likelihood the term acquires its particular facets through the translation of the Pauline letters, leaving Hegel to pick it up and develop it. It is because of the word's having been used by Luther to convey the antinomial gesture in Paul's *katargesis* in Romans 3:31 . . . that the German verb then took on this double meaning, which was a "delight" for "speculative thought." (*The Time That Remains: A Commentary on the Letter to the Romans*, trans. Patricia Dailey [Stanford, CA: Stanford University Press, 2005], 99).

But here as elsewhere, Agamben's argument is at best misleading. His analysis of Luther's text is simply mistaken. In the first place, it is not the noun form *katargēsis* but a first-person plural verb form, *katargoumen*, that occurs in this passage. Second and more fatal to Agamben's argument, *katargoumen* occurs in the previous question Paul poses: "Does this mean that we are using faith to undermine the law?" Thus, when Luther translates *katargoumen* as "*heben . . . auf,*" or, more specifically, "*Heben wir denn das Gesetz auf durch den Glauben?*" he is using *heben . . . auf* to mean "undermine." The verb that Luther uses for "place on a firmer footing" is *richten . . . auf.* Continuing the quotation, we find "*Das sei ferne. Sondern wir richten das Gesetz auf.*" Luther seems to understand *aufheben* to mean "get rid of" or "take away." This use of the term does not include the preservation of what is negated, which is the key to Hegel's understanding of *aufheben.* Hegel, as we will see, is deeply indebted to Luther, but this is not the essential point of contact between them.

24. Quoted in introduction to *Luther: Lectures on Romans*, trans. W. Pauck (Philadelphia: Westminster Press, 1961), xxxviii.

25. Martin Luther, "A Commentary on St. Paul's Epistle to the Galatians," in *Martin Luther: Selections from His Writings*, ed. John Dillenberger (New York: Doubleday, 1961), 101.

26. Ibid., 130.

27. It should be evident that Luther's God shares much with Yahweh in the Hebrew Bible. As will become clear in the next chapter, Puritan theology, which grew out of Calvin's extension of Luther's theological insights, draws on the Old Testament to develop a covenant theology, which was crucial for the founding of the United States.

28. G. W. F. Hegel, *The Philosophy of History*, trans. J. Sibree (New York: Dover, 1956), 416.

29. See chapter 3 for a definition of this neologism.

30. These quotations from Luther's works are in Norman O. Brown, *Life against Death: The Psychoanalytic Meaning of History* (New York: Random House, 1959), 226, 221, 228.

31. Luther, "Ninety-five Theses," in *Martin Luther*, ed. Dillenberger, 493.

32. It is, of course, possible to argue that in their very corruption and decadence, many medieval Catholics were in fact incipiently secular.

33. Ibid., 447.

34. Ibid., xxxiii.

35. As we will see in chapter 4, this opposition between the public and the private is a condition of modern secularity.

36. http://www.thecaveonline.com/APEH/reformdocument.html#anchor revolt.

37. John Calvin, *Institutes of the Christian Religion*, ed. John McNeill (Philadelphia: Westminster Press, 1967), 1:35.

38. Alister McGrath, *A Life of John Calvin: A Study in the Shaping of Western Culture* (Malden, MA: Basil Blackwell, 1990), 250. This fine book has been my primary reference for the details of life in France during Calvin's time.

39. Ibid., 176.

40. William Bousma, *John Calvin: A Sixteenth-Century Portrait* (New York: Oxford University Press, 1988), 230–31.

41. I will consider the importance of Luther's translation of the Bible in the next section.

42. McGrath, *Life of John Calvin*, 135, 133.

43. Ibid., 134.

44. John Calvin, *Institutes of the Christian Religion*, trans. Ford L. Battles (Philadelphia: Westminster Press, 1960), 1:197.

45. Ibid., 199, 201, 208.

46. Myron Gilmore, *The World of Humanism, 1453–1517* (New York: W. Langer, 1952), 186.

47. Arthur Geoffrey Dickens, *Reformation and Society in Sixteenth-Century Europe* (New York: Cambridge University Press, 1968), 51. This work is cited in Elizabeth Eisenstein's two-volume study *The Printing Press as an Agent of Change: Communications and Cultural Transformations in Early-Modern Europe* (New York: Cambridge University Press, 1979). Eisenstein's monumental work is the best account of the impact of printing on the early modern period. I have drawn on her work in developing the following analysis of the relationship among printing, literacy, and the Reformation.

48. Eisenstein, *Printing Press*, 1:51.

49. Mark Edwards, *Printing, Propaganda, and Martin Luther* (Berkeley and Los Angeles: University of California Press, 1994), 39.

50. Eisenstein, *Printing Press*, 1:344, 347.

51. Ibid., 304.

52. Jack Miles, "Translation, Lingualism, and the Bible," lecture delivered at the Claremont Graduate School, February 3, 1997.

53. Eventually the British monarchy decided to allow a vernacular edition of the Bible but insisted that it had to be a single, imposed, royally sanctioned version: the King James Version, also known as the "Authorized Version."

54. For a helpful consideration of the relation between Protestantism and literacy in America, see David Nord, *Faith in Reading: Religious Publishing and the Birth of Mass Media in America* (New York: Oxford University Press, 2004).
55. Rudolf Hirsch, *Printing, Selling, and Reading, 1450–1550* (Wiesbaden: Harrassowitz, 1967), 90. Quoted in Eisenstein, *Printing Press*, 1:347.
56. Eisenstein, *Printing Press*, 1:117–18.
57. Collinson, *Reformation*, 43.
58. Samuel Edgerton, *The Renaissance Rediscovery of Linear Perspective* (New York: Basic Books, 1975), 56.
59. Ibid., 164.
60. Eisenstein, *Printing Press*, 1:88.

CHAPTER THREE | SUBJECTIVITY AND MODERNITY

1. Friedrich Schlegel, *Philosophical Fragments*, trans. Peter Firchow (Minneapolis: University of Minnesota Press, 1991), 48.
2. M. H. Abrams, *Natural Supernaturalism: Tradition and Revolution in Romantic Literature* (New York: W. W. Norton, 1971), 334.
3. Karl Marx, *The Marx-Engels Reader*, ed. Robert Tucker (New York: W. W. Norton, 1972), 60, 61.
4. Mark Noll, *America's God: From Jonathan Edwards to Abraham Lincoln* (New York: Oxford University Press, 2002), 10.
5. Perry Miller, *The New England Mind: From Colony to Province* (Cambridge, MA: Harvard University Press, 1953), 13.
6. Saul K. Padover, ed., *The Complete Jefferson* (New York: Duell, Sloan, and Pearce, 1943), 414.
7. http://usinfo.state.gov/usa/infousa/facts/democrat/2.htm.
8. Miller, *New England Mind*, 21.
9. http://www.mtholyoke.edu/acad/intrel/winthrop.htm.
10. Miller, *New England Mind*, 22.
11. Noll, *America's God*, 56.
12. Just as Luther became alarmed when the social underclass rebelled in the name of Christian liberty, so some of the Founding Fathers were concerned about the anti-authoritarian implications of "utopian individualism." For this reason, they resisted direct democracy and insisted on a strong central executive.
13. Ibid., 381.
14. As we will see below, there is another less often noted strand in Calvinism that values aesthetic experience and eventually contributes to the interpretation of the world as a work of art.
15. http://www.law.indiana.edu/uslawdocs/declaration.html.
16. Quoted in Steven Shapin, *The Scientific Revolution* (Chicago: University of Chicago Press, 1996), 34.
17. Alexander Pope, "Epitaph. Intended for Sir Isaac Newton, in Westminster Abbey."

18. Ernst Cassirer, *Philosophy of Enlightenment*, trans. Fritz Koelln and James Pettegrove (Princeton: Princeton University Press, 1951), 6–7.

19. Voltaire, *Traité métaphysique*, chaps. 3 and 5. Quoted by Cassirer, *Philosophy of Enlightenment*, 12.

20. I will return to this issue in the next chapter.

21. Quoted in Francis Oakley, "Christian Theology and the Newtonian Science: The Rise of the Concept of the Laws of Nature," in *Creation: The Impact of an Idea*, ed. D. O'Connor and F. Oakley (New York: Charles Scribner's Sons, 1969), 60.

22. Ibid., 309.

23. William Paley, *Natural Theology* (New York: Sheldon and Co., n.d.), 6.

24. Locke, *An Essay concerning Human Understanding*, ed. A. C. Fraser (Oxford: Clarendon Press, 1894), 2:308.

25. Ibid., 413.

26. Ibid., 416.

27. Ibid., 438.

28. John Toland, "Christianity Not Mysterious," in *Religious Thought of the Eighteenth Century*, ed. J. M. Creed and J. S. Boys-Smith (Cambridge, UK: University Press, 1939), 20.

29. Ibid., 19.

30. Matthew Tindal, "Christianity as Old as Creation," in *Religious Thought of the Eighteenth Century*, ed. Creed and Boys-Smith, 36.

31. It is important to note that the Roman Catholic Church was not overthrown in Britain by the Protestant revolution but by the Act of Supremacy, which established the Church of England as an autocephalous church with Henry VIII as its effective pope. Catholicism was criminalized and all church property expropriated. The collapse of the Catholic Church in England seemed to fuel conflicts among Protestant sects and between these sects and the established Anglican Church. The lesson the American founders drew from these ongoing conflicts was that the state should support no form of religion; the lesson the French revolutionaries drew from it was that the state should repress religion.

32. Quoted in Lucien Goldmann, *The Philosophy of the Enlightenment*, trans. Henry Maas (Cambridge, MA: MIT Press, 1973), 68.

33. The fate of the Catholic Church in France was finally settled when Napoleon signed the Concordat with Pius VII (1801), by which he was allowed to fire all the bishops of France and hire new ones, in effect, creating a kind of state Catholicism on the model of the newly emerging state Protestantisms, and by which the church was given charge, once again, of the primary and secondary schools of France. As for the religion of Reason, it ultimately proved to be a failure, and that bore on Napoleon's decision not to continue fighting a war against the church that he could not win. The rationalists did not really need the religion of Reason, and the Catholics rejected it and continued a rearguard resistance. Napoleon's concordat with the pope was part of his plan to save the revolution from itself.

34. Quotations from the Declaration of the Rights of Man and of the Citizen are from http://www.constitution.org/fr/fr_drm.htm.

35. Jean-Jacques Rousseau, *The Social Contract: Essays by Locke, Hume and Rousseau*, ed. Ernst Baker (Oxford: Oxford University Press, 1962), 206.

36. It is important to distinguish the different fates of the Lutheran and the Reformed traditions in Europe. While Lutheranism became dominant in northern Germany, Scandinavia, and pockets of eastern Europe, Calvinism became dominant in Switzerland, Holland, Scotland, and England. Elsewhere, Catholicism remained dominant.

37. F. W. J. Schelling, quoted in Dieter Henrich, *Aesthetic Judgment and the Moral Image of the World: Studies in Kant* (Stanford, CA: Stanford University Press, 1992), 87.

38. Marx, "Contribution to the Critique of Hegel's *Philosophy of Right*," in *Writings of the Young Marx on Philosophy and Society*, ed. Lloyd D. Easton and Kurt H. Guddat (Garden City, NY: Doubleday Anchor, 1967), 59.

39. Kant, "What Is Enlightenment?" in *On History*, trans. Lewis White Beck, Robert E. Anchor, and Emil L. Fackenheim (Indianapolis: Bobbs-Merrill, 1963), 3.

40. Kant, *Critique of Practical Reason*, trans. Lewis White Beck (Indianapolis: Bobbs-Merrill, 1956), 3.

41. Julien Offray de La Mettrie, *Man a Machine*, in *Les Philosophes: The Philosophers of the Enlightenment and Modern Democracy*, ed. N. L. Torrey (New York: Capricorn Books, 1960), 173.

42. David Hume, *A Treatise of Human Nature*, ed. T. H. Green and T. H. Grose (London: Longmans, Green and Cox, 1886), 1:390–91.

43. David Hume, *Dialogues concerning Natural Religion*, ed. H. D. Aiken (New York: Hafner, 1966), 23.

44. Though eighteenth-century critics of Hume did not do so, it is possible to argue that his analysis of the subjectivity of causality leaves open the possibility that human actions are free. Given Hume's epistemology, however, there is no way to mount a rational argument for human freedom.

45. Hume and representatives of the French Enlightenment like d'Holbach, Étienne Bennot de Condillac, and Adrien Helvétius anticipated some of the most important criticism of religion developed in the nineteenth century. In chapter 4, I will consider the relationship between theology and different theories of religion.

46. Immanuel Kant, *Critique of Pure Reason*, trans. Norman Kemp Smith (New York: St. Martin's Press, 1965), 144.

47. Ibid., 181.

48. I will consider further implications of Kant's account of the imagination below.

49. Kant, *Critique of Practical Reason*, 30, 31, 39.

50. Dieter Henrich, *Between Kant and Hegel: Lectures on German Idealism*, ed. David

Pacini (Cambridge, MA: Harvard University Press, 2003), 19. Henrich proceeds to explain the significance of Kant's argument:

This insight into the interconnection between concepts of the mind and images of the world is the origin of the modern methods of historical interpretation. Fichte was the first to bring the world *Weltanschauung* (image of the world) to philosophical prominence; it captured the theoretical correlation he was developing in his own work. Similarly, employed methodologically, this correlation between mind and world image is the foundation of Hegel's *Phenomenology*: because all stages of the development of the mind are simultaneously stages of the development of the conception of the world, we cannot talk about either one apart from the other. (20)

I was fortunate enough to hear Henrich's lectures when he first delivered them at Harvard in 1972. I also took a seminar with Henrich on Hegel's *Science of Logic*. The lectures and the seminar decisively shaped my interpretation of Hegel and have influenced my thinking for more than three decades.

51. Kant, *Critique of Practical Reason*, 4.

52. Ibid., 33–34.

53. Ibid., 114, 133, 118.

54. Immanuel Kant, *Critique of Judgment*, trans. James Meredith (New York: Oxford University Press, 1973), part 2, 21.

55. Henrich, *Between Kant and Hegel*, 287.

56. Jean-Luc Nancy, *The Experience of Freedom*, trans. Bridget McDonald (Stanford, CA: Stanford University Press, 1993), 54.

57. Kant, *Critique of Pure Reason*, 314.

58. Rodolphe Gasché, "Ideality in Fragmentation," foreword to Schlegel, *Philosophical Fragments*, trans. Firchow, xix–xx.

59. Martin Heidegger, *Hegel's Concept of Experience*, trans. Kenley Dove (New York: Harper and Row, 1970), 48–49.

60. Martin Heidegger, *Schelling's Treatise on the Essence of Human Freedom*, trans. Joan Stambaugh (Athens, OH: Ohio University Press), 162.

61. Kant, *Critique of Judgment*, part 2, 86.

62. Nancy, *Experience of Freedom*, 13.

63. Martin Heidegger, *Kant and the Problem of Metaphysics*, trans. Richard Taft (Bloomington: Indiana University Press, 1997), 118.

64. G. W. F. Hegel, *The Logic of Hegel*, trans. William Wallace (New York: Oxford University Press, 1968), 162.

65. G. W. F. Hegel, *Hegel's Philosophy of Mind*, trans. William Wallace (New York: Oxford University Press, 1971), 3.

66. Heidegger, *Kant and the Problem of Metaphysics*, 112.

67. Maurice Blanchot, *The Space of Literature*, trans. Ann Smock (Lincoln: University of Nebraska Press, 1982), 30–31. I will consider further implications of this insight for art in the next chapter.

68. F. W. J. Schelling, *Ideas for a Philosophy of Nature*, trans. Errol Harris and Peter Heath (New York: Cambridge University Press, 1988), 174–75.

69. See below for a definition.

70. Søren Kierkegaard, *The Sickness unto Death*, trans. Howard Hong and Edna Hong (Princeton: Princeton University Press, 1980), 13.

71. Maurice Blanchot, *Thomas the Obscure*, trans. R. Lamberton (New York: David Lewis, 1973), 107–8.

72. Friedrich Nietzsche, *The Birth of Tragedy*, trans. Francis Golffing (New York: Doubleday, 1956), 74–75.

73. Wallace Stevens, *Opus Posthumous*, ed. Samuel French Morse (New York: Random House, 1957), 178.

74. Friedrich Nietzsche, *Will to Power*, trans. Walter Kaufmann (New York: Random House, 1968), 36.

75. Nietzsche, *Birth of Tragedy*, 9, 22, 65, 56.

76. Ibid., 42. I will consider the issue of self-reflexivity in artistic creation below.

77. Kant, *Critique of Judgment*, part 1, 90.

78. Jean-Luc Nancy, "The Sublime Offering," in *Of the Sublime: Presence in Question*, trans. Jeffrey Librett (Albany: State University of New York Press, 1993), 38.

79. Schlegel, *Philosophical Fragments*, 70.

80. This is a revised version of Ernst Behler and Roman Struc's formulation in their introduction to Friedrich Schlegel's *Dialogue on Poetry and Literary Aphorisms* (University Park: Pennsylvania State University Press, 1969), 15.

81. Stevens, *Opus Posthumous*, 174; *Collected Poems*, 486.

82. Kant, *Critique of Judgment*, part 1, 168.

83. Maurice Blanchot, *The Infinite Conversation*, trans. Susan Hanson (Minneapolis: University of Minnesota Press, 1993), 354.

84. Quoted by Blanchot in ibid., 356.

85. Quoted by Henrich in *Between Kant and Hegel*, 227.

86. I will develop the further implications of this interpretation of altarity in later chapters.

87. Schlegel, *Philosophical Fragments*, 96, 55.

88. Samuel Taylor Coleridge, *Biographia Literaria*, ed. J. Shawcross (New York: Oxford University Press, 1967), 1:202.

89. Jacques Derrida, "Economimesis," *Diacritics*, June 1981, 9.

90. Schlegel, *Philosophical Fragments*, 48.

CHAPTER FOUR / RELIGIOUS SECULARITY

1. Susan Jacoby, *Freethinkers: A History of American Secularism* (New York: Metropolitan Books, 2004), 1.

2. According to traditional accounts of American religious history, the first three Great Awakenings ran from the 1730s to the 1740s, from the 1820s to the 1830s, and from the 1880s to the 1900s.

3. In the *Oxford English Dictionary*, the first definition offered is "Of clergy: living 'in the world' and not in monastic seclusion, as distinguished from 'regular' and 'religious.'"

4. Peter Berger, *The Sacred Canopy: Elements of a Sociological Theory of Religion* (New York: Doubleday, 1969), 107.

5. If carefully formulated, typological analysis can facilitate the comparative interpretation of religion without necessarily inscribing an essentialism that erases or suppresses historical variations. By considering alternative interpretations of common issues, the similarities and differences between and among different traditions can be clearly formulated.

6. I will consider the second and third moments in chapter 5 and the fourth moment in chapter 6. In chapter 7, I will explore the possibility of developing the notion of immanent transcendence to develop an account of the divine as the infinite life of creative emergence.

7. Henri Frankfort et al., *Before Philosophy: The Intellectual Adventure of Ancient Man* (New York: Penguin, 1966), 237.

8. Mircea Eliade, *The Sacred and the Profane*, trans. Willard Trask (New York: Harper Torchbooks, 1959), 130. I will return to the issue of water symbolism in chapter 8.

9. In developing the following account of the *Enuma elish*, I have followed Eric Voegelin, *Order and History*, vol. 1, *Israel and Revelation* (Columbia: University of Missouri Press, 2001), 82–84; and Tikva Frymer-Kensky, "Enuma Elish," in *The Encyclopedia of Religion*, ed. Mircea Eliade (New York: Macmillan, 1987), 5:124–27.

10. Nietzsche uses the image of the sea and the horizon in the infamous passage where he declares the death of God. See *The Gay Science*, trans. Walter Kaufmann (New York: Random House, 1974), 181.

11. Voegelin, *Order and History*, 82.

12. In the first chapter of Genesis, God's creative word goes out over "the surface of the waters." The water that is already there prior to God's creative act is a vestige of the ancient myths we have been considering. As such, it represents the chaos that the divine word orders.

13. Frankfort, *Before Philosophy*, 245.

14. As we will see below, some of the most influential Christian theologians of the nineteenth and twentieth centuries were committed to a God who is as radically transcendent as Yahweh.

15. Origen, *On First Principles*, ed. G. W. Butterworth (New York: Harper and Row, 1966), 16, 26.

16. Ibid., 33–34.

17. Arius, "The Letter of Arius to Eusebius of Nicomedia," in *Christology of the Later Fathers*, ed. Edward Hardy (Philadelphia: Westminster Press, 1954), 330.

18. Athanasius, "Against the Arians," in *Readings in the History of Christian Thought*, ed. Robert Ferm (New York: Holt, Rinehart and Winston), 148.

19. Nicene Creed, in *Christology of the Later Fathers*, 338.
20. Athanasius, "On the Incarnation of the Word," in *Christology of the Later Fathers*, 107–8.
21. See *Christology of the Later Fathers*, 124–25.
22. Nestorius, "The First Letter of Nestorius to Celestine," in *Christology of the Later Fathers*, 348.
23. *Christology of the Later Fathers*, 373.
24. *American Heritage Dictionary*, s.vv.
25. Leonard Hodgson, *The Doctrine of the Trinity* (London: Nisbet and Co., 1943), 90–91. In developing his argument, Hodgson was strongly influenced by John Laird's interpretation of the tripartite structure of the self. See John Laird, *Problems of the Self* (London: Macmillan, 1917).
26. Søren Kierkegaard, *Philosophical Fragments*, trans. David Swenson (Princeton: Princeton University Press, 1971), 47, 76.
27. In his extensive study *Nicaea and Its Legacy: An Approach to Fourth-Century Trinitarian Theology* (New York: Oxford University Press, 2004), Lewis Ayres develops a detailed history of historical developments surrounding the fourth- and fifth-century Christological and Trinitarian controversies. While Ayres is informative on many particular theological issues, his analysis suffers from important philosophical limitations. Two points must be emphasized in this context: the first concerns one of the principal claims he develops throughout the book and the second involves his account of Hegel.

    In his introduction, Ayres writes: "Throughout the book I will argue that we should avoid thinking of these controversies as focusing on the status of Christ as 'divine' or 'not divine.' They focus, first, on debates about the generation of the Word or Son from the Father. Second, the controversies involve debates about the 'grammar' of human speech about the divine" (3). While the emphasis on the complexities of grammar is, as we have seen, important, Ayres's criticism of analyses of "the status of Christ as 'divine' or 'not divine'" is misleading. Our consideration of the contrasting strands in Origen's theology has made it clear that the question of the generation of the Word or Son from the Father is nothing other than the question of the divine or nondivine status of the Son.

    This point is closely related to problems Ayres encounters in his discussion of Hegel's view of the Trinity and the influence it has exercised on later thinkers. Summarizing his misgivings about Hegel's position, Ayres writes:

    > Because Spirit operates both as the name for a Trinitarian person and as a controlling concept for his system as a whole, Hegel can clearly present the realization of the Spirit as a distinct moment beyond the Son's. Even if we must, in Hegel's case, bear in mind the sophistication with which he deploys the concept of God in Godself, his separation of the roles of Son and Spirit and his lack of interest in the notion of the Body of Christ in favor of the Spirit-filled community take up themes

from previous Protestant tradition and reinforce the direction of its arguments. (406)

As will become clear in what follows, this is a serious misunderstanding of Hegel's position that fails to recognize the radical notion of Incarnation that informs his entire speculative philosophy. In addition to an inadequate grasp of Hegelian philosophy, Ayres's argument suffers from a failure to work out the historical, social, and cultural implications of the doctrines of the Incarnation and the Trinity.

28. Hegel, *Phenomenology of Spirit*, 9–10.

29. Hegel, *Philosophy of History*, 319.

30. The notion of unhappy consciousness, which provides the key to the *Phenomenology of Spirit*, lies at the heart of the entire Hegelian system. Indeed, it is not too much to insist that Hegel's overriding preoccupation is to find a way of overcoming unhappy consciousness.

31. Hegel, *Phenomenology of Spirit*, 131.

32. Ibid., 133–34.

33. Luther often cites 1 Corinthians 7:20 to support his doctrine of vocation. His interpretation of this text varies in different contexts. This is the verse he used as the basis of his rejection of the Peasants' Revolt in his infamous treatise "Against the Robbing and Murdering Hordes of Peasants."

34. Gustav Wingren, *The Christian's Calling: Luther on Vocation*, trans. Carl Rasmussen (London: Oliver and Boyd, 1957), 4–5.

35. Luther, "Exposition of Psalm 147," quoted in Wingren, *Christian's Calling*, 137–38.

36. Hegel, *Philosophy of History*, 422.

37. Augustine, *On the Trinity*, in *The Basic Writings of Saint Augustine*, trans. Whitney Oates (New York: Random House, 1948), 2:792.

38. G. W. F. Hegel, *Philosophy of Religion*, trans. E. B. Speirs and J. Burdon Sanderson (New York: Humanities Press, 1968), 3:99–100.

39. G. W. F. Hegel, *Lectures on the Philosophy of Religion*, ed. Peter C. Hodgson, trans. R. F. Brown (Berkeley and Los Angeles: University of California Press, 1985), 3:78.

40. Hegel, *Phenomenology of Spirit*, 14.

41. Hegel, *Philosophy of Religion*, 3:18.

42. Hegel, *Lectures on the Philosophy of Religion*, 3:219. In terms of the ancient Christological debates, this formulation leaves Hegel open to the charge of Sabellianism or Patripassionism. Hegel would dismiss this charge by responding that it reveals the shortcomings of any theological perspective that presupposes divine immutability. Within Hegel's scheme, the divine, or the Absolute, is the *process* of its own becoming. As such, it is thoroughly historical and temporal and, therefore, undergoes *constant* change. In chapter 7, I will argue that this process is eternal. Transcendence—whatever its guise—can never be completely negated; immanentization always engen-

ders transcendentalization, which, in turn, is sublated without being completely obliterated.

43. In chapter 7, I will extend this line of analysis to develop an interpretation of God as notion of infinite life.

44. Hegel, *Phenomenology of Spirit*, 10.

45. I have already made repeated use of the figure of the ellipse in developing the theory of religion presented in chapter 1. This figure will return in the analysis of poststructural theory in chapter 6.

46. Stevens, "An Ordinary Evening in New Haven," in *Collected Poems*, 476.

47. Paul Ricoeur, *Freud and Philosophy: An Essay on Interpretation*, trans. Denis Savage (New Haven, CT: Yale University Press, 1970), 32–36.

48. Franklin Baumer, *Religion and the Rise of Skepticism* (New York: Harcourt Brace, 1960), 118–19.

49. Frank Moore Cross, "The History of Israelite Religion: A Secular or Theological Subject?" *Biblical Archaeology Review*, May/June 2005, 43.

50. This is not to imply, of course, that earlier thinkers had not considered the question of the origin of religion. Although philosophes like d'Holbach and d'Alembert wrote critical works on this subject, the most important consideration of the origin of religion prior to the nineteenth century was David Hume's *The Natural History of Religion* (1757).

51. Marx, *Marx-Engles Reader*, 4.

52. Peter Berger, *Sacred Canopy*, 4.

53. Marx, *Marx-Engles Reader*, 523.

54. Ibid., 60, 61.

55. Ibid., 473n.

56. Sigmund Freud, *The Interpretation of Dreams*, trans. James Strachey (New York: Avon Books, 1965), 311–12.

57. Sigmund Freud, *Civilization and Its Discontents*, trans. James Strachey (New York: Norton, 1961), 17.

58. Ibid., 15, 19.

59. Sigmund Freud, *Beyond the Pleasure Principle*, trans. James Strachey (New York: Norton, 1961), 30.

60. Ibid., 32.

61. Sigmund Freud, *Totem and Taboo*, trans. James Strachey (New York: Norton, 1950), 154–55.

62. Ibid., 161.

63. I have indicated these alternative readings with superscripts. Marx[1], Freud[1], and Nietzsche[1] represent foundational or structuralist readings of cultural phenomena (Word), and Marx[2], Freud[2], and Nietzsche[2] represent nonfoundational or poststructuralist readings (Deed). I will explore the implications of these two trajectories in later chapters.

64. Nietzsche, *Birth of Tragedy*, 9.

65. Friedrich Nietzsche, *The Will to Power*, trans. Walter Kaufmann (New York:

Random House, 1967). Nietzsche did not intend the aphorisms collected in this book to be published in their present form. The book was edited by his sister Elisabeth Förster-Nietzsche, who eventually married a member of the National Socialist Party. This publication history partially accounts for the problematic legacy of the book.

66. Ibid., 98, 99, 101.
67. Friedrich Nietzsche, "The Twilight of the Idols," in *The Portable Nietzsche* (New York: Penguin, 1980), 501, 562.
68. Hegel, *Phenomenology of Spirit*, 27.
69. Nietzsche, "Twilight of the Idols," 548.
70. Karl Marx, *Grundrisse: Foundations of the Critique of Political Economy (Rough Draft)*, trans. Martin Nicholas (New York: Penguin Books, 1973), 230–31.
71. Freud, *Interpretation of Dreams*, 143n.

CHAPTER FIVE / ECLIPSE OF THE REAL

1. Directly below the article on Barth's death was an article on the death of Thomas Merton.
2. Friedrich Schleiermacher, *Speeches on Religion*, trans. Richard Crouter (New York: Cambridge University Press, 1988), 112–13.
3. Friedrich Schleiermacher, *Speeches on Religion*, trans. John Oman (New York: Harper Torchbooks, 1958), 88.
4. Schleiermacher, *Speeches on Religion*, trans. Crouter, 139. Translation modified.
5. Adolf von Harnack, *What Is Christianity?* trans. Thomas Saunders (New York: Harper and Row, 1957), 20, 51.
6. Walter Rauschenbusch, *A Theology for the Social Gospel* (New York: Abingdon, 1954), 142–43.
7. *New York Times*, December 11, 1968. Two of Barth's teachers who signed the manifesto were Harnack and Wilhelm Herrmann.
8. Karl Barth, *The Epistle to the Romans*, trans. Edwyn Hoskyns (New York: Oxford University Press, 1968), 10.
9. Ibid., 110, 99.
10. Ibid., 97–98.
11. Ibid., 39, 28.
12. The major difference between Hegel's *Early Theological Writings* and his mature system concerns the question of identity and difference. Whereas in the former the difference is lost when unity is recovered, in the latter identity is differential, and difference, therefore, not only is preserved but is also constitutive of identity as such.
13. G. W. F. Hegel, *Early Theological Writings*, trans. T. M. Knox (Philadelphia: University of Pennsylvania Press, 1971), 271.
14. Søren Kierkegaard, *Fear and Trembling*, trans. Howard Hong and Edna Hong (Princeton: Princeton University Press, 1983), 55.

15. Ibid., 39.
16. Though Altizer remains the most important death of God theologian, other notable members of the group were William Hamilton, Gabriel Vahanian, and Paul Van Buren.
17. Nietzsche, "The Anti-Christ," in *The Portable Nietzsche*, ed. Walter Kaufmann (New York: Penguin, 1968), 585.
18. Thomas J. J. Altizer, *The Gospel of Christian Atheism* (Philadelphia: Westminster, 1966), 16–17.
19. Ibid., 63, 43–44.
20. Ibid., 46.
21. Thomas J. J. Altizer, *History as Apocalypse* (Albany: State University of New York Press, 1985), 254.
22. Thomas J. J. Altizer, *The Self-Embodiment of God* (New York: Harper and Row, 1977), 82.
23. Thomas J. J. Altizer, *Total Presence: The Language of Jesus and the Language of Today* (New York: Seabury, 1980), 102.
24. Altizer, *History as Apocalypse*, 254.
25. Andy Warhol, *The Philosophy of Andy Warhol (From A to B and Back)* (New York: Harcourt Brace, 1977), 91.
26. Wassily Kandinsky, *Concerning the Spiritual in Art*, trans. M. T. H. Sadler (New York: Dover Publications, 1977), 10.
27. Wassily Kandinsky and Franz Marc, *The Blaue Reiter Almanac*, ed. Klaus Lankheit (New York: Viking Press, 1974), 250.
28. Marit Werenskiold, "Kandinsky's Moscow," *Art in America* 77 (March 1989): 98.
29. Kandinsky, *Concerning the Spiritual in Art*, 14, 32.
30. Harold Osborne, ed., *The Oxford Companion to Twentieth-Century Art* (New York: Oxford University Press, 1987), 284.
31. Walter Gropius, "Address to the Students of the Staatliche Bauhaus, Held on the Occasion of the Yearly Exhibition of Student Work in July 1919," in *The Bauhaus*, ed. Hans M. Wingler (Cambridge, MA: MIT Press, 1986), 36.
32. Walter Gropius, "Program of the Staatliche Bauhaus in Weimar," in *Bauhaus*, 31.
33. Walter Gropius, *The New Architecture and the Bauhaus*, trans. P. Morton Shad (Cambridge, MA: MIT Press, 1989), 29.
34. Osborne, *Twentieth-Century Art*, 125.
35. Quoted in Camilla Gray, *The Russian Experiment in Art, 1863–1922* (New York: Henry Abrams, 1962), 249.
36. Christian Lodder, *Russian Constructivism* (New Haven, CT: Yale University Press, 1987), 1.
37. Hubertus Gassner, "The Constructivists: Modernism on the Way to Modernization," in *The Great Utopia: The Russian and Soviet Avant-Garde, 1915–1922* (New York: Solomon R. Guggenheim Foundation, 1922), 299.

38. Quoted in Mary Portas, *Windows: The Art of Retail Display* (New York: Thames and Hudson, 1999), 14. The marketing strategies of museums during the last several decades have made Warhol's prediction even more prescient.

39. There is, of course, a direct line from nineteenth-century arcades to today's shopping malls.

40. Walter Benjamin, *The Arcades Project*, trans. Howard Eiland and Devin Mc-Laughlin (Cambridge, MA: Harvard University Press, 1999), 37.

41. Quoted in William Leach, *Land of Desire: Merchants, Power, and the Rise of a New American Culture* (New York: Random House, 1993), 60.

42. As we will see below, the introduction of information and network technologies transforms mass production into mass customization. This change in the manufacturing process has a significant impact on culture.

43. Benjamin, *Arcades Project*, 34.

44. Warhol, *Philosophy of Andy Warhol*, 229, 92, 134.

45. Ibid., 77.

46. Guy Debord, *Society of the Spectacle* (Detroit: Black and Red, 1977), nos. 20, 21.

47. There is, however, always another way to interpret Warhol's art. His relentless sense of irony makes it unclear whether he is embracing or criticizing consumerism. It is precisely this ambiguity that lends Warhol's art its lasting significance and sets it above the work of simpleminded epigons like Jeff Koons.

48. Warhol, *Philosophy of Andy Warhol*, 100–101, 149, 178.

49. Frank Stella, quoted in David Galenson, "Questions to Stella and Judd," in *Minimal Art: A Critical Anthology*, ed. Gregory Battcock (Berkeley and Los Angeles: University of California Press, 1969), 136.

50. Stevens, *Collected Poems*, 485.

51. Jean Baudrillard, *Simulations*, trans. Paul Foss, Paul Patton, and Philip Beitchman (New York: Semiotext[e], 1983), 2. In a surprisingly prescient anticipation of reality TV, Baudrillard analyzes what he describes as an "American TV-*verité* experiment on the Loud family in 1971." Like MTV's *Real World* and the shows it spawned more than a decade later, producers placed cameras in a family home for seven months of uninterrupted shooting. Baudrillard writes: "In this 'truth' experiment, it is neither a question of secrecy nor perversion, but a kind of thrill of the real, or of an aesthetics of the hyperreal, a thrill of vertiginous and phony exactitude, a thrill of alienation and of magnification, of distortion of scale, of excessive transparency all at the same time" (49–50).

52. Ibid., 1, 12. Baudrillard regularly cites unattributed quotations, many of which are his own creations. In some instances these are supposed to have come from other written sources, but in many cases he claims to be reporting things other people have said.

53. Jean Baudrillard, *Symbolic Exchange and Death*, trans. Iain Grant (London: Sage Publications, 1993), 6–7.

54. Though this phrase is usually associated with Smith, he actually borrowed it from Bernard Mandeville's *Fable of the Bees; or, Private Vices, Publick Virtues* (1714), which greatly influenced his work.

55. Adam Smith, *The Wealth of Nations*, ed. Edwin Cannan (New York: Modern Library, 2000), 3.

56. Ibid., 5–6.

57. Berger, *Sacred Canopy*, 151–52.

58. Quoted in Thomas Bass, *The Predictors: How a Band of Maverick Physicists Used Chaos Theory to Trade Their Way to a Fortune on Wall Street* (New York: Henry Holt, 1999), 9.

59. Martin Shubik, *The Theory of Money* (Cambridge, MA: MIT Press, 199), 1:142.

60. Gregory Bateson, *Steps to an Ecology of Mind* (New York: Ballantine, 1972), 453.

61. Marx, *Marx-Engles Reader*, 476.

62. For an important analysis of the far-reaching significance of the increase of debt in recent decades, see Kevin Phillips, *American Theocracy: The Peril and Politics of Religion, Oil, and Borrowed Money in the 21st Century* (New York: Viking, 2006). Although Phillips's treatment of oil and debt is better than his account of recent developments in religion, he is one of the few to have made an effort to unravel the tangled relations among religion, politics, and economics.

63. F. A. Hayek, *The Fatal Conceit: The Errors of Socialism*, ed. W. W. Bartley (Chicago: University of Chicago Press, 1988), 86, 146–47.

64. There is an interesting parallel between the relationship between Catholicism and Protestantism, on the one hand, and communism/socialism and democracy/capitalism, on the other. In the former the individual exists by virtue of participation in the group, and in the latter the social whole emerges from the association of independent individuals.

65. Francis Fukuyama, "The End of History?" *National Interest*, Summer 1989, 3.

66. To his credit, Fukuyama has acknowledged that he was mistaken. This admission should not, however, obscure the enormous influence his book had on the rise of neoconservatism during the 1990s and the first decade of the twenty-first century. See Francis Fukuyama, *America at the Crossroads: Democracy, Power, and the Neoconservative Legacy* (New Haven, CT: Yale University Press, 2006).

67. Philip Bobbitt, *The Shield of Achilles: War, Peace, and the Course of Human History* (New York: Knopf, 2002), 215. My account of the relationship between the nation-state and the market-state follows Bobbitt's analysis.

68. Ibid., 667.

69. Ibid., 222.

70. Ibid., 670–71.

CHAPTER SIX / RECOVERING THE REAL

1. David van Biema, "The Turning Point," *Time*, May 2, 2005, 38. I have drawn the details about Ratzinger's life from this informative article as well as other news reports at the time of his election as pope.

2. Joseph Ratzinger, "*Dominus Iesus*: On the Unicity and Salvific Universality of Jesus Christ and the Church," at www.vatican.va/roman_curia/congregations/cfaith/documents/rc.

3. Mark Kurlansky, *1968: The Year That Rocked the World* (New York: Ballantine Books, 2004), xvii.

4. Theodore Roszak, *The Making of a Counter Culture: Reflections on the Technocratic Society and Its Youthful Opposition* (New York: Doubleday, 1969), 3. For another very helpful account of the different political currents in the 1960s, see Mark Hamilton Lytle, *America's Uncivil Wars: The Sixties Era from Elvis to the Fall of Richard Nixon* (New York: Oxford University Press, 2006).

5. Vance Packard, *The Status Seekers: An Exploration of Class Behavior in America and the Hidden Barriers That Affect You, Your Community, Your Future* (New York: David McKay, 1959), 198.

6. Kenneth Keniston, *Young Radicals: Notes on Committed Youth* (New York: Harcourt Brace, 1969), 274–75.

7. Ibid., 16–17.

8. Ibid., 275.

9. Quoted in Theodore Roszak, *The Cult of Information: The Folklore of Computers and the True Art of Thinking* (New York: Pantheon, 1986), 150. Two recent books present detailed accounts of the relations between the counterculture and the rise of information society and digital culture: Fred Turner, *From Counterculture to Cyberculture: Stewart Brand, the Whole Earth Network, and the Rise of Digital Utopianism* (Chicago: University of Chicago Press, 2006); and John Markoff, *What the Dormouse Said: How the Sixties Counterculture Shaped the Personal Computer Industry* (New York: Viking, 2005).

10. William Bennett, *Why We Fight: Moral Clarity and the War on Terrorism* (New York: Doubleday, 2002), 45, 138, 139, 68.

11. Quoted in William Martin, *With God on Our Side: The Rise of the Religious Right in America* (New York: Broadway Books, 1996), 20. Martin's book is the best available account of the rise of the religious right. I have drawn on his insightful analysis in developing my argument in this section.

12. Ibid., 32–33.

13. Ibid., 149–50.

14. Philip Jenkins, *The Next Christendom: The Coming of Global Christianity* (New York: Oxford University Press, 2002), 1–2. The following statistics are from Jenkins's book.

15. The metaphor of the base has recently become important in Islam. *Al-Qaʿida* means "the base," "foundation" but also "the support," "principle," "rule," "formulated method," "manner," "mode," "model," and "pattern." The noun

is derived from a verb, which means "to take a seat," "to abide," "to lie in wait for," "to waylay," and "to abstain."

16. Ellis Goldberg develops a careful comparison between Calvinism and the Sunni version of Islam. He identifies four basic principles of Protestantism:

> 1. The claims about a single and all-powerful God made by believers.
>
> 2. The recognition of the danger that there exist loyalties antagonistic to God.
>
> 3. The nature of education, socialization, and authority required to interpret scripture and determine what actions validly fulfill divine claims.
>
> 4. The relation of revealed scripture to received interpretations of it.

He proceeds to argue that "it is possible to examine a set of religious concepts in Sunni Islam that at least make it possible to examine a correspondence with Puritanism."

> 1. *Jihad* (the nature of the activity to which true believers are called).
>
> 2. *Taghut* (the existence of competing claims over the behavior of believers).
>
> 3. *Ijma'* (a relationship between scripture and received interpretations of it).
>
> 4. The role of the ʿulama (the nature of socialization and education required for interpreting scripture).

See Ellis Goldberg, "Smashing Idols and the State: The Protestant and Egyptian Sunni Radicalism," *Comparative Studies in Society and History* 33, no. 1 (January 1991): 8, 11.

17. Susan Jacoby, *Freethinkers: A History of American Secularism* (New York: Metropolitan Books, 2004), 19.

18. Ibid., 56–57.

19. Martin, *With God on Our Side*, 11.

20. Ibid., 10.

21. Ibid., 4–5.

22. Ibid., 11.

23. Ibid., 13.

24. Ibid., 13–15.

25. Majid Tehranian, "Fundamentalist Impact on Education and Media," in *Fundamentalisms and Society: Reclaiming the Sciences, the Family, and Education*, ed. Martin E. Marty and R. Scott Appleby (Chicago: University of Chicago Press, 1993), 323. He uses these categories to characterize contemporary religious movements in different countries: Wahhabi (Saudi Arabia), Takfir-wa-Hijra (Egypt), Haredi Jews (Israel), Moral Majority (USA), and the Hizbullah (Iran, Lebanon).

26. Jacoby, *Freethinkers*, 321.

27. Ibid.

28. Ibid., 326.

29. Quoted in Hanna Rosin, "Beyond Belief," *Atlantic Monthly*, January–February 2005, 119.

30. Ibid.

31. In the next chapter, I will develop an expanded interpretation of life that leads to very different ethical conclusions.

32. In the next section, I will consider the use of media and technology to promote religion during the past half century.

33. Quentin Schultze, "The Two Faces of Fundamentalist Higher Education," in *Fundamentalisms and Society*, ed. Marty and Appleby, 520.

34. Martin, *With God on Our Side*, 69–70.

35. Craig Unger, "American Rapture, *Vanity Fair*, December 2005, 217.

36. Martin, *With God on Our Side*, 204.

37. Ibid., 259.

38. Ibid., 155.

39. Ibid., 189.

40. Quoted in Anne C. Loveland, *American Evangelicals and the U.S. Military, 1945–1993* (Baton Rouge: Louisiana State University Press, 1996), 211.

41. Quoted in Martin, *With God on Our Side*, 191.

42. This and the previous quotations are from Loveland, *American Evangelicals*, 211.

43. Quoted in Jacoby, *Freethinkers*, 316.

44. Jack Miles, "Bush, Benedict, and the Fate of the Republic," *Los Angeles Times*, April 27, 2005. The quotation from Ratzinger's letter is from this article.

45. Quoted in Rosin, "Beyond Belief," 120.

46. Martin, *With God on Our Side*, 353–54.

47. The best analysis of Lindsey and LaHaye is Glenn Shuck's *The Marks of the Beast: The Left Behind Novels and the Struggle for Evangelical Identity* (New York: New York University Press, 2005). In developing my understanding of the growing importance of Evangelicalism, I have been guided not only by Shuck's informative book but by many conversations with him.

48. Hal Lindsey, *The 1980s: Countdown to Armageddon* (New York: Bantam Books, 1981), 149, 154.

49. Quoted in Loveland, *American Evangelicals*, 165–66.

50. Hal Lindsey, *The Late Great Planet Earth* (Grand Rapids, MI: Zondervan, 1970), 113.

51. Mark C. Taylor, *The Moment of Complexity: Emerging Network Culture* (Chicago: University of Chicago Press, 2001). Glenn Shuck first brought this connection to my attention. He analyzes the relation between my understanding of network culture and the interpretations of Lindsey and LaHaye in his *Marks of the Beast* (see especially chap. 3).

52. Mark C. Taylor, *Confidence Games: Money and Markets in a World without Redemption* (Chicago: University of Chicago Press, 2004).

53. Shuck, *Marks of the Beast*, 102.

54. Frances FitzGerald, "Reflections: The American Millennium," *New Yorker*, November 11, 1985, 105.

55. Susan Harding, "Imagining the Last Days: The Politics of Apocalyptic Lan-

guage," in *Accounting for Fundamentalisms: The Dynamic Character of Movements*, ed. Martin E. Marty and R. Scott Appleby (Chicago: University of Chicago Press, 1994), 72.

56. Ibid.

57. Timothy LaHaye, *The Race for the 21st Century* (Nashville, TN: Thomas Nelson, 1986), 46.

58. Craig Unger, "American Rapture," 200.

59. Alvin Toffler, *The Third Wave* (New York: Bantam Books, 1980), 9.

60. Newt Gingrich, "A Citizen's Guide to the 21st Century," foreword to *Creating a New Civilization: The Politics of the Third Wave*, by Alvin Toffler and Heidi Toffler (Atlanta: Turner Publishing, 1995), 14–15.

61. Toffler and Toffler, *Creating a New Civilization*, 27.

62. Ibid., 31–32.

63. Ibid., 33.

64. Ibid., 78–79.

65. Ibid., 15.

66. R. Laurence Moore, *Selling God: American Religion in the Marketplace of Culture* (New York: Oxford University Press, 1994), 70.

67. Laurie Goodstein and David Kirkpatrick, "On a Christian Mission to the Top: Evangelicals Set Their Sights on the Ivy League," *New York Times*, May 22, 2005.

68. David Morgan, "Protestant Visual Practice and American Mass Culture," in *Practicing Religion in the Age of Media*, ed. Stewart Hoover and Lynn Schofield Clark (New York: Columbia University Press, 2002), 40.

69. Moore, *Selling God*, 76.

70. Ibid., 231–32.

71. Schultze, "Two Faces of Fundamentalist Higher Education," 490.

72. Jacoby, *Freethinkers*, 276.

73. Moore, *Selling God*, 247.

74. Stephanie Simon, "God's Call Comes by Cellphone," *Los Angles Times*, May 16, 2006.

75. Ibid.

76. It is no accident that Billy Graham uses a .org URL and the new generation of Evangelists use .com URLs.

77. Rick Warren, *The Purpose Driven Life: What Am I on Earth For?* (Grand Rapids, MI: Zondervan, 2002), 19.

78. Ibid., 253.

79. Ted Haggard, *Dog Training, Fly Fishing and Sharing Christ in the 21st Century* (Nashville, TN: Thomas Nelson, 2002), 8–9. Though Haggard might not want surprises, scandals, or secrets from his church, he does not seem to have any problem with secret conduct that is both surprising and scandalous for his church. On November 1, 2006, Mike Jones, a former male prostitute in Denver, claimed that Haggard had been a monthly customer for several years and

had regularly purchased methamphetamines. While Pastor Ted, as he was known to his followers, wrote a letter to his congregation asking for forgiveness, church officials relieved him of his duties several days after learning about the scandal. With his fall from grace, Haggard takes his place in a long line of prominent Evangelical ministers extending from Elmer Gentry to Jim Bakker who have succumbed to "the sins of the flesh." Haggard regularly boasted about his access to the Bush White House. News of his liaison broke just a few days before the 2006 midterm elections and further eroded the political power of the New Religious Right.

80. Quoted in Jeff Sharlet, "Soldiers of Christ," *Harper's Magazine*, May 2005, 47.

81. Haggard, *Dog Training*, 82–84.

82. Sharlet, "Soldiers of Christ," 45.

83. "Meet the Prosperity Preacher," at www.businessweek.com. I have drawn the following details about the operations of Lakewood Church from this article.

84. Moore, *Selling God*, 119.

85. Quoted in Jackie Alnor, "Joel Osteen: The Prosperity Gospel's Coverboy," at www.cultlink.com/ar/osteen.htm.

86. Nietzsche, *Will to Power*, 99.

87. Joel Osteen, *Your Best Life Now*, at www.amazon.com/gp/reader.

88. One of the ironies of recent intellectual history is that the editor of the American edition of Kojève's lectures was Allan Bloom, many of whose students are leading neoconservatives who have shaped government policy and public opinion for three decades. Bloom's book *The Closing of the American Mind*, which became the bible of the political and cultural conservatives, blames many of the French intellectuals who were inspired by Kojève's seminars for promoting the relativism and nihilism that have led to the decline of the West. See Alexandre Kojève, *Introduction to the Reading of Hegel*, ed. Allan Bloom (New York: Basic Books, 1969).

89. Martin Heidegger, *The Question concerning Technology and Other Essays*, trans. William Lovitt (New York: Harper Torchbooks, 1977), 107.

90. Jean Hyppolite, *Logic and Existence*, trans. Leonard Lawlor and Amit Sen (Albany: State University of New York Press, 1997), 102.

91. Roland Barthes, "To Write: Intransitive Verb?" in *The Structuralist Controversy: The Languages of Criticism and the Science of Man*, ed. Richard Macksey and Eugenio Donato (Baltimore, MD: Johns Hopkins University Press, 1971), 136.

92. As the analysis in chapter 3 suggests, Marx, Freud, and Nietzsche can be read as either protostructuralists (indicated on fig. 19 by Marx[1] , Freud[1], and Nietzsche[1]) or proto-poststructuralists (indicated on fig. 19 by Marx[2], Freud[2], and Nietzsche[2]).

93. Jacques Derrida, "Structure, Sign, and Play in the Discourse of the Human Sciences," in *Structuralist Controversy*, ed. Macksey and Donato, 247.

94. Ibid., 248.

95. Jacques Derrida, "Structure, Sign, and Play in the Discourse of the Human Sciences," in *Writing and Difference*, trans. Alan Bass (Chicago: University of Chicago Press, 1978), 279.

96. Ibid.

97. Jacques Derrida, "Différance," in *Margins of Philosophy*, trans. Alan Bass (Chicago: University of Chicago Press, 1982), 13–14.

98. Søren Kierkegaard, *Philosophical Fragments*, trans. D. F. Swenson and H. V. Hong (Princeton: Princeton University Press, 1971), 55.

99. Derrida, "Différance," in *Margins of Philosophy*, 5–6.

100. Derrida, *Writing and Difference*, 292.

101. Hegel, *Phenomenology of Spirit*, 27.

102. Stevens, *Collected Poems*, 472, 471.

CHAPTER SEVEN / RELIGION WITHOUT GOD

1. Ralph Waldo Emerson, "Nature," in *The Selected Writings of Ralph Waldo Emerson*, ed. Brooks Atkinson (New York: Modern Library, 1950), 35.

2. Wallace Stevens, *Opus Posthumous: Poems, Plays, Prose*, ed. Samuel French Morse (New York: Vintage Books, 1982), 163.

3. Emerson, "Nature," 8.

4. Ibid., 35, 25.

5. Kant, *Critique of Judgment*, 22–23.

6. Stuart Kauffman, *At Home in the Universe: The Search for the Laws of Self-Organization and Complexity* (New York: Oxford University Press, 1995), 69. I will discuss autocatalytic sets below.

7. Hegel, *Science of Logic*, 737.

8. Hegel, *Phenomenology of Spirit*, 106–7.

9. Ibid., 107.

10. Brian Goodwin, *How the Leopard Changed Its Spots: The Evolution of Complexity* (New York: Simon and Schuster, 1994), 197.

11. It is important to note that Maturana and Varela's use of the term *machine* differs from Kant's, Hegel's, and Emerson's use of the term. The structure and operation of autopoietic machines conform to the way organisms operate in romantic poetry and idealistic philosophy.

12. Humberto Maturana and Francisco Varela, *Autopoiesis and Cognition: The Realization of the Living* (Boston: D. Reidel, 1980), 78–79.

13. Kauffman, *At Home in the Universe*, 49–50.

14. Maturana and Varela, *Autopoiesis and Cognition*, 79.

15. Lynn Margulis and Dorion Sagan, *What Is Life?* (Berkeley and Los Angeles: University of California Press, 1995), 17–18.

16. Norbert Wiener, *The Human Use of Human Beings* (Boston: Houghton Mifflin, 1950), 12.

17. Ilya Prigogine and Isabelle Stengers, *Order out of Chaos: Man's New Dialogue with Nature* (New York: Bantam Books, 1984), 13.

18. Wiener, *Human Use of Human Beings*, 21.

19. Lee Smolin, *The Life of the Cosmos* (New York: Oxford University Press, 1997), 166, 105.

20. David Depew and Bruce Weber, *Darwinism Evolving: Systems Dynamics and the Genealogy of Natural Selection* (Cambridge, MA: MIT Press, 1995), 346.

21. Christian de Duve, *Life Evolving: Molecules, Mind, and Meaning* (New York: Oxford University Press, 2002), 35.

22. Atuhiro Sibatani, "How to Structuralise Biology?" in *Dynamic Structures in Biology*, ed. Brian Goodwin, Atuhiro Sibatani, and Gerry Webster (Edinburgh: Edinburgh University Press, 1989), 7.

23. Depew and Weber, *Darwinism Evolving*, 396.

24. Mae-Wan Ho, "A Structuralism of Process: Towards a Post-Darwinian Rational Morphology," in *Dynamic Structures in Biology*, ed. Goodwin, Sibatani, and Webster, 32.

25. Gell-Mann, *The Jaguar and the Quark*, 69.

26. Prigogine and Stengers, *Order out of Chaos*, 13.

27. While claiming to reject relativism, the New Religious Right's promotion of intelligent design as a plausible alternative for understanding human life leads to a subjectivism that undercuts scientific inquiry. This tactic is part of a larger strategy to discredit science in ways that are epistemologically disingenuous and politically dangerous. I will return to this issue in the next chapter.

28. Modern geology also created difficulties for biblical literalists. With a more sophisticated understanding of geological processes, it became apparent that the earth is much older than the biblical account suggests. Faced with the choice between geological evidence and scriptural authority, many people then as now chose faith over science.

29. Goodwin, *How the Leopard Changed Its Spots*, 145.

30. Ibid., 145.

31. Stephen Jay Gould, *Full House: The Spread of Excellence from Plato to Darwin* (New York: Harmony Books, 1996), 41.

32. Depew and Weber, *Darwinism Evolving*, 71.

33. Quoted in Kauffman, *At Home in the Universe*, 71.

34. Ibid., 185.

35. Goodwin, *How the Leopard Changed Its Spots*, 77, 51, 51–52, 112.

36. Kauffman, *At Home in the Universe*, 166.

37. Margulis and Sagan, *What Is Life?* 9, 119–29.

38. Mitochondria are "intracellular cell organelles, the sites of ATP synthesis, [which] probably began as oxygen respiring purple bacteria. They were incorporated with others through symbiosis to create new kinds of cells. Today mitochondria persist even in human cells as organelles that use oxygen to perform respiration and generation of chemical energy" (ibid., 260).

39. Chloroplasts are "intercellular structures, or organelles in which photo-

synthesis occurs. They contain chlorophylls that are active in synthesizing starch, protein, and other materials" (ibid., 257).

40. Ibid., 121.

41. Richard Lewontin has presented the most extensive criticism of Darwinism as economic and political ideology. The theory of evolution, he argues, reflects early-nineteenth-century political theory, in which capitalism is regarded as the superior economic system. See Richard Lewontin, *Biology as Ideology: The Doctrine of DNA* (New York: HarperPerennial, 1991).

42. Margulis and Sagan, *What Is Life?* 90, 20.

43. Mathematica is a popular program language that "integrates a numeric and symbolic computational engine, graphics system, programming language, documentation system, and advanced connectivity to other applications." It facilitates complex symbolic calculations and solves differential equations either numerically or symbolically. It also has the capability to create models and simulations for systems as diverse as "galaxy collisions, financial derivatives, complex biological systems, chemical reactions, environmental impact studies, and magnetic fields in particle accelerators" (http://www.wolfram.com).

44. Quoted in Peter Covenery and Roger Highfield, *Frontiers of Complexity: The Search for Order in a Chaotic World* (New York: Fawcett Columbine, 1995), 274.

45. Kauffman, *At Home in the Universe*, 87.

46. Goodwin, *How the Leopard Changed Its Spots*, 111.

47. John Holland, *Emergence: From Chaos to Order* (Reading, MA: Addison Wesley, 1998), 225–28.

48. Schlegel, *Philosophical Fragments*, 70.

49. Stevens, *Opus Posthumous*, 158.

50. Ibid., 174, 178.

CHAPTER EIGHT | ETHICS WITHOUT ABSOLUTES

1. Bobbitt, *Shield of Achilles*, 215.

2. See Ray Kurzweil, *The Singularity Is Near: When Human Beings Transcend Biology* (New York: Viking, 2005). This book complements the argument developed in *The Age of Spiritual Machines: When Computers Exceed Human Intelligence* (New York: Viking, 1999). Many of Kurzweil's arguments seem to be outlandish and it would be easy to dismiss them quickly. But his views are not to be taken lightly—he is a widely respected scientist and inventor whose previous contributions suggest that his ideas deserve consideration. Kurzweil summarizes his argument: "The Singularity will represent the culmination of the merger of our biological thinking with our technology, resulting in a world that is still human but that transcends our biological roots. There will be no distinction, post-Singularity, between human and machine or between physical and virtual reality. If you wonder what will remain unequivocally human in such

a world, it's simply quality: ours is the species that inherently seeks to extend its physical and mental reach beyond current limitations" (9).

3. This phrase was first introduced by Pope John Paul II and appropriated by Pope Benedict XIV as well as by Protestant Fundamentalists and Evangelicals from Pat Robertson to Jerry Falwell. While these religious conservatives associate the culture of death with abortion and euthanasia, I am arguing that the ideology that advertises itself as pro-life is actually pro-death.

4. *American Heritage Dictionary*, s.v.

5. Fred Pearce, *When the Rivers Run Dry: Water—the Defining Crisis of the Twenty-first Century* (Boston: Beacon Press, 2001), x.

6. Mircea Eliade, *Patterns in Comparative Religion*, trans. Rosemary Sheed (New York: World Publishing Co., 1963), 1:188–89.

7. G. W. F. Hegel, *The History of Philosophy*, trans. E. S. Haldane and Frances Simson (New York: Humanities Press, 1968), 175, 179.

8. Hegel, *Phenomenology of Spirit*, 107.

9. The problems related to water are obviously enormously complex; indeed, it is precisely this complexity that makes them so instructive. It will not be possible to probe relevant issues sufficiently in this context. I will focus on issues that are most closely related to the interplay between ontology and axiology that I have been considering in this chapter.

In developing the following account, I have drawn on Elizabeth Kolbert, "The Climate of Man," *New Yorker*, April 25, May 2, and May 9, 2005; "Butterfly Lessons," *New Yorker*, January 9, 2006; Bill McKibben, "The Coming Meltdown," *New York Review of Books*, January 12, 2006; Mark Hertsgaard, *Earth Odyssey: Around the World in Search of Our Environmental Future* (New York: Broadway Books, 1998); and Jared Diamond, *Collapse: How Societies Choose to Fail or Succeed* (New York: Viking, 2005). Kolbert's articles have been collected and published in her *Field Notes from a Catastrophe: Man, Nature, and Climate Change* (New York: Bloomsbury, 2006). Another recent book that is very informative is Tim Flannery, *The Weather Makers: How Man Is Changing the Climate and What It Means to Life on Earth* (New York: Atlantic Monthly Press, 2006).

10. Eugene Linden, "Cloudy with a Chance of Chaos," *Fortune*, January 23, 2006, 136.

11. "Sustaining Water, Easing Scarcity," http://www.population.org/resources/publications/water/water97.pdf.

12. Sandra Postel and Aaron Wolf, "Dehydrating Conflict," www.globalpolicy.org/security/natres/water/2001/2002fpol.htm.

13. Hertsgaard, *Earth Odyssey*, 211.

14. Oilman and corporate raider Boone Pickens thinks the future will be more about water than oil. He is aggressively buying up water rights whenever and wherever they become available in North America. His most ambitious plan is to build a pipeline to transport water from Canada to the United States.

15. Hertsgaard, *Earth Odyssey*, 211.
16. *Ecosystems and Human Well-Being: Wetlands and Water,* a report of the Millennium Ecosystem Assessment (Washington, DC: World Resources Institute, 2005), 3.
17. Ibid., 4.
18. The title of a recent *Wall Street Journal* article suggests that these debates themselves become overheated: "Hurricane Debate Shatters Civility of Weather Science—Worsened by Global Warming? Spats Are So Tempestuous, Sides Are Barely Talking—Charge of 'Brain Fossilization'" (February 2, 2006).
19. Claudia Dreifus, "With Findings on Storms, Centrist Recasts Warming Debate," *New York Times,* January 10, 2006.
20. Linden, "Cloudy with a Chance of Chaos," 136.
21. Quoted in McKibben, "The Coming Meltdown," 18.
22. Elizabeth Kolbert, "The Climate of Man—III," *New Yorker,* May 9, 2005.
23. McKibben, "The Coming Meltdown," 16.
24. The attack on science is not limited to environmental issues but extends to debates about abortion and evolution.
25. Andrew Revkin, "Climate Expert Says NASA Tried to Silence Him," *New York Times,* January 29, 2006.
26. In my discussion of permafrost, sea ice, and glaciers, I have drawn on Kolbert's *Field Notes from a Catastrophe.*
27. See Kolbert, "The Climate of Man—I," *New Yorker,* April 25, 2005.
28. Ibid.
29. Ibid.
30. *Ecosystems and Human Well-Being,* 34.
31. Ibid., 34.
32. Ibid., 28.
33. Quoted in ibid.
34. Quoted in ibid.
35. Quoted in McKibben, "The Coming Meltdown," 18.
36. J. Alan Pounds et al., "Widespread Amphibian Extinctions from Epidemic Disease Driven by Global Warming," *Nature* 439 (January 12, 2006): 165.
37. It is important to note that there is growing disagreement in the Evangelical community about the issue of global warming. In February 2006, a group of influential Evangelicals issued "An Evangelical Call to Action" encouraging Congress and the Bush administration to address the problem of global warming. The statement calls for federal legislation that would reduce carbon dioxide emissions through "cost-effective, market-based mechanisms." This is the first stage they describe as an "Evangelical Climate Initiative." Rev. Richard Cizik, a powerful Washington lobbyist for Christian groups, asks: "Isn't it the task of the Biblical believer to warn society, not just about sin, but about mortal threats to our very being?" Not all Evangelical leaders sup-

port the measure; Ted Haggard declined to sign the statement, and Charles Colson and James Dobson have issued a letter to the National Association of Evangelicals insisting that scientific investigation is inconclusive on the issue of global warming. See Laurie Goodstein, "86 Evangelical Leaders Join to Fight Global Warming," *New York Times*, February 8, 2006; and Karen Breslau and Martha Brant, "God's Green Soldiers," *Newsweek*, February 13, 2006. The issues separating the two camps are not only theological but also political and economic.

38. Stevens, "The Glass of Water," in *Collected Poems*, 197.

INDEX

Page numbers in italics refer to figures and tables.